Alienated Minority

Alienated Minority

The Jews of Medieval Latin Europe

Kenneth R. Stow

Harvard University Press
Cambridge, Massachusetts
London, England

Copyright © 1992 by the President and Fellows of Harvard College
All rights reserved
Printed in the United States of America
Second printing, 1994

First Harvard University Press paperback edition, 1994

Library of Congress Cataloging-in-Publication Data

Stow, Kenneth R.
  Alienated minority: The Jews of medieval Latin Europe / Kenneth R. Stow
    p. cm.
  Includes bibliographical references and index.
  ISBN 0-674-01592-4 (alk. paper) (cloth)
  ISBN 0-674-01593-2 (pbk.)
  1. Jews—History—70-1789. 2. Jews—Europe—History. 3. Judaism—Europe—History.
  4. Jews—Europe—Social conditions. 5. Middle Ages. 6. Europe—Ethnic relations.
  I. Title.
DS124.S79 1992
940'.04924—dc20
91-45067
CIP

Who can find a good woman . . . whose righteousness preserves her husband . . . Her husband's heart trusts in her . . . She does him good, not evil . . . She girds her loins with strength.

Midrash Mishle on Proverbs 31:10–31

Acknowledgments

This book was written over the past four years. Preceding them were many more years of thought during which I presented many of my ideas to students at the University of Haifa, the Jewish Theological Seminary, Yale, and the University of Michigan. An appointment to the Helen and Louis Padnos Visiting Professorship at the University of Michigan allowed me to complete the final draft.

To my students, in particular, and to their insightful comments, I owe a very great debt. I owe no lesser debt to my colleague Menahem Kellner—and especially to my late friend Robert Cohen—who plodded through the text and graciously commented on every suspect comma, period, and obscure usage, not to mention the content itself. Many other colleagues as well, both known and unknown to me, have read the book. They include Anna Foa, who watched the book grow from outline to final draft; Robert Stacey, whose comments on the final chapters were invaluable; David Berger, who pointed out numerous issues and especially the right understanding of a difficult tosafist passage; Maurice Kriegel, who gave unflagging encouragement; and David Ruderman, Ivan Marcus, and William Jordan. I thank them profusely. I also wish to thank Maria Ascher for her editorial care, and Margaretta Fulton, who has shepherded the book throughout all the stages of its growth. Responsibility for the book's content, of course, is mine alone.

To my family goes another kind of thanks. The time and attention they willingly dispensed with and, most of all, their kindness and love can never adequately be repaid.

Contents

Alienated Minority

IRELAND

ENGLAND

•YORK
•LINCOLN

BRISTOL•
NORWICH•
•LONDON AMSTERDAM
CANTERBURY•   Rhine R.

Elbe R.

MAGDEBURG•   •POZNAN
Oder R.

POLAND

HOLY

•AACHEN
•COLOGNE

ROUEN•
PARIS• RHEIMS
Seine R. TRIER
  TROYES SPEYER
  •STRASBOURG
Loire R.

MAINZ• •FRANKFURT A.M.
•WORMS
  •PRAGUE

GERMANY

ROMAN• •REGENSBURG
Danube R.

FRANCE

BASEL•

EMPIRE

HUNGARY

Garonne R.

LYON•

MILAN•
•PAVIA Po R. •VENICE
BOLOGNA•

LEON•
BURGOS•

Ebro R.

TOULOUSE•
NARBONNE•

AVIGNON•
MARSEILLE•

•LUCCA
FLORENCE•

Douro R.

SARAGOSSA•

ITALY

SPAIN

Tagus R.
•TOLEDO

TARRAGONA•
TORTOSA• •BARCELONA

CORSICA

•ROME
CAPUA• •SIPONTO
NAPLES• •BARI
  VENOSA• •BRINDISI
SALERNO•
  ORIA• •OTRANTO

SEVILLE• CORDOVA•
•Guadalquivir R.
•GRANADA

BALEARIC ISLANDS

SARDINIA

•GIBRALTAR
TANGIER•

PALERMO•

SICILY

KAIRWAN•

WESTERN EUROPE
IN THE
MIDDLE AGES

0   200   400 miles

Introduction

This is a book about the Jews of medieval Latin Europe. By Latin Europe I mean much of that region which is today called Western Europe: principally England, France, parts of Germany, and Italy. The Jews of Spain—which admittedly was and is part of Latin Europe—will be mentioned, but only where their history intersects with that of Jews elsewhere. Most often, this history is a distinct one, as is the history of medieval Spain as a whole; it should be, and traditionally has been, treated as such. My references to the Jews of the Muslim East will also be limited. These Jews, who constituted the largest Jewish population during most of the Middle Ages, influenced their counterparts in the West through their philosophical and especially their legal writings. But geographically, politically, socially, and structurally, they lived in a world apart.

My focus on the Latin West was dictated by my desire to trace the development of a series of intellectual concepts and social realities over a continuous period. In my estimation, this period begins with Saint Paul and ends, in the sixteenth century, with Pope Paul IV. Our point of departure, however, is the fifth century, when autonomous Jewish rule in Palestine came to a close, Christian concepts penetrated Roman imperial law, and the papacy, led by Gregory the Great, established enduring principles regarding Jewish-Christian relations. We will proceed chronologically, and sometimes geographically, but this is not intended as a serial history. What we particularly want to know is how Jews coped in medieval Christian society and how medieval Christian society coped with Jews. Where, we will ask, did Jews and Christians share common ideas, perspectives, and practices, and where did the two diverge? Did commonality, especially of religious heritage, promote or discourage coping—or was coping perhaps most successful where divergence prevailed and where Jews and Christians each went their own way?

In many spheres, medieval Christian society was far removed from that of the Jews. Jews did not have a warrior nobility, at least not outside Spain, where possibly some Jews did live by the sword. Jews also did not base their power structures, whether political or intellectual, on the possession of land or on physical strength. As a result, Jews were free to emphasize preexisting nuclear family structures and to deemphasize extended ones, with their concomitant need to manipulate inheritances. In addition, Jews did not have a distinct clergy—certainly not in the sense of the clergy as a class apart—to which a special sanctity was attributed. Nor did they have a clerical perception of society that competed with one produced by a Jewish laity. Whereas all of these were "nots" in Jewish culture, they were essential characteristics of medieval Christian life. On the other hand, like Christians, Jews emphasized the centrality of religious behavior. More important, Jews and Christians agreed that this behavior must always be exegetically justified—that is, by interpreting received texts and applying these interpretations to contemporary events. Exegesis also provided the basis for intellectual and social, as well as religious, action in both spheres; it furnished the instrumentalities of culture, institutions, and myths. Moreover, Jews and Christians were interpreting the same texts. In particular, they both delved into the Hebrew Bible, directly and by way of the Bible's later interpretative elaborations, such as the Christian New Testament or the Jewish Midrash.

Yet Christian and Jewish interpretations of given texts often differed radically. These differences, as we will see, generated the cruxes of the Jewish-Christian medieval condominium. For Jews and Christians differed especially about which one of them the Hebrew Bible's texts designated as God's divinely chosen heir. And out of this intellectual difference arose conceptual, social, and even economic friction. Another consequence was distortion. The exegetically drawn picture that Jews had of Christians, and vice versa, led to an image of the other which more often than not had little to do with the other's reality. Indeed, it was just because of these frictions, distortions, and false images that Jews and Christians failed to live together comfortably. Jews limited their contacts with Christians, and even more with Christianity. Christians, especially as their religious and political institutions matured, first raised—and then acted on—the question of whether the Jews might be incorporated into medieval society or whether, instead, they were an unassimilable minority.

I would like to try to answer at least some of these questions and to do so by studying not only the interactions of Jews and Christians but also the Jews' internal world, the spheres that were intrinsically theirs and theirs alone. For only in this way will we know what it meant to be a medieval Jew. We want to know how Jews governed themselves and what theories of governance they developed. What, moreover, was the connection between these practical matters and intellectual ones—in particular, the study of the Bible and the Talmud? Jews also produced historical, liturgical, and pietistic thought that deserves attention. Their sometimes unique familial ideals, too, will be examined. Jewish internal life, as we will see, was often similar to that of Christians, but invariably it was distinguished by uniquely Jewish elements. It is these elements that sometimes were most responsible for Jewish survival. Biblical exegesis and halachic interpretation, especially, often provided polemical and practical tools without which Jews would have lost self-esteem and been unable to carry out everyday tasks necessary to compete in the larger Christian world.

This book challenges a common view of relations between Christians and Jews in the Middle Ages. It is said that beginning with Louis the Pious (in about 826), Jews were treated well, even as allies of the kings and other Christian rulers. By the eleventh century and even more by the thirteenth, matters had deteriorated. Jews were increasingly and ruthlessly declassed, taxed, and expelled. Doctrines of degradation and ostracism, apparently traceable to ecclesiastical teachings, became downright threatening. They became so in particular as the accusation of deicide (the killing of Christ) spread widely and inflamed passions. This accusation—which perhaps reflects the greater personification of Christ's image in the High Middle Ages—led, in turn, to the view of a scheming Jewish enemy. Such a Jew had to be restrained or even violently removed. Originally this view was confined to the lower classes. Yet kings, too, soon endorsed it, and, urged on directly or indirectly by ecclesiastical officials, they eventually decreed the Jews' expulsion from their kingdoms.

But was there really such a well-defined downward progression? Did the medieval state of the ninth through eleventh centuries really maintain an alliance with the Jews? And just what kind of pressure did ecclesiastical forces exert? Rather than charting a loss of royal support in response to ecclesiastical demands, I will argue that what principally governed Jewish life in the earlier Middle Ages was a firmly defined legal and constitutional status. So long as that status endured, the Jews flourished—although stability and even wealth should not be confused, as they sometimes have been, with political power. In the later Middle Ages, such as at the end of the thirteenth century, glaring instability and a now unique legal status, created expressly for the Jews, led to their being pictured as an impediment to the "common good," an impediment that the kings themselves soon chose to remove.

The Jew's negative functions in society were also presented in spiritualized terms: he was the mythical enemy of the Christian polity. And it was for this reason that he was eventually expelled. Such a conception would seem to reinforce the thesis that ecclesiastical policies were instrumental in determining the Jew's fate. Neverthless, with rare exceptions, these policies were not predicated on a view of the Jews as a social menace. The regnant and continuous opinion held that however stubborn, wrong, or even "ungrateful" the Jew was, he did not seriously threaten the medieval Christian harmony. His errors and sins could be corrected, his temporary disruptions of social equilibrium repaired. Besides, his presence was necessary. As evil and perversity incarnate—which the Jew was considered to be—his presence sustained the balance—a concept central to medieval thought—between belief and disbelief, reward and punishment. Thus, paradoxically, the Church—as an institution, and as opposed to a certain few of its radical clergy—was not the driving force toward drastic measures. The stated goal of ecclesiastical policy toward Jewry was instead to achieve stability; the method consisted of selective if sometimes harsh regulation—a regulation, moreover, that changed little throughout the Middle Ages (as surprising as this claim may initially appear to be). To be sure, this method represents the ecclesiastical ideal, whose realization was forever being impeded by clerical behavior. And the result was severe Jewish trauma. Still, the ideal itself was consistently maintained through at least the middle of the sixteenth century.

I am proposing, then, that it is incorrect to link the Jew's medieval fortunes to a direct transfer of ideas and practices from Church to State. The Church, as an institution and through its doctrines, certainly had a profoundly negative effect on Jewish life. Yet the Jew's ultimate fall was a product of medieval society in its entirety, the unique nature of its secular institutions, and of the mythical Jewish image which that society's members fostered.

In the Middle Ages the Jew belonged to an alienated minority. Yet in his own right, he contributed vibrantly to the shaping of basic medieval social and ideological structures. In that sense, this is a book about the Middle Ages as a whole as much as it is about medieval Jews.

1 A Christianizing Society

Students of medieval Jewish history have frequently assigned the Jews an important role in medieval affairs. Generalists (as historians of the Jews refer to historians who study other topics) might disagree. For decades the latter have written full-length medieval histories in which the Jewish role is a minimal one, and, at first glance, they seem to have been correct. In no medieval kingdom, except Spain, did Jews ever compose more than 1 percent of the population, and in no medieval city did their number ever exceed 1,500. Political, spiritual, and economic exigencies also kept the Jewish population constantly in voluntary or forced motion. The only community of Jews that survived the Middle Ages without dislocation was that of Rome.

In the early Middle Ages, Jews lived mainly on the Mediterranean coast. Many of these Mediterranean communities persisted until the fifteenth century, and some even afterward. Yet as early as the mid-twelfth century, Spanish Jews were forced to desert the Muslim south for the Christian north. The communities of southern Italy were nearly destroyed in the 1290s. New Jewish settlements arose between the eleventh and thirteenth centuries in the heartlands of Germany, France, and England. The locations of these communities are well known, but statistically useful information about size or the sexual distribution of their inhabitants is not; details about age, the crucial data in demographic calculations, are nonexistent. Toward the year 1300, a series of expulsions forced a migration eastward. The Jews were expelled from England in 1290, from France in 1306 (and again in 1322 and 1394), from Spain in 1492, from numerous German cities and territories in the early fifteenth century, and from Sicily and southern Italy by 1541. By 1500, the ma-

Table 1.1. Number of Jews in Europe in 1300 and 1490, in comparision to the size of the general population.*

Country*	1300		1490	
	Jews	General population	Jews	General population
France	100,000	14,000,000	20,000	20,000,000
Empire	100,000	12,000,000	80,000	12,000,000
Italy	50,000	11,000,000	120,000	12,000,000
Spain	150,000	5,500,000	250,000	7,000,000
Portugal	40,000	600,000	80,000	1,000,000
Poland and Lithuania	5,000	500,000	30,000	1,000,000
Hungary	5,000	400,000	20,000	800,000
Total	450,000	44,000,000	600,000	53,800,000

*Salo Baron's admitted population "guesstimates." See *Encyclopaedia Judaica*, 1971: "population." See also Stow, 1986c.

jority of Europe's Jews resided in its central and eastern regions. Demographically speaking, therefore, the medieval Jewish population was a relatively inconspicuous one (see Table 1.1).

In other spheres, the Jewish presence was not inconspicuous. Jews of course contributed significantly to medieval society as participants and through their own rich lives. But more noticeably, because they remained insistently loyal to their Jewish identity, Jews were a source of enormous social anxiety. Their loyalty to Judaism, as medieval people interpreted it, intrinsically challenged Christianity's truth. And to this challenge medieval people reacted by construing a Jewish image that typologically and symbolically was one of injustice personified. Eventually some Christians so inflated this image and its meaning that they accused the Jews of endangering Christian social stability. This was, to be sure, pure myth.[1]

Yet seeking the origins of this myth requires some careful distinctions. It did not derive solely from Christian religious teachings. Political and social forces were equally important. In thirteenth-century France and England, for example, Jews came to represent for both kings and barons, each for their own reasons, the inverse of the right social and political order. Only one element of that order was right belief. In the eleventh-century Rhineland, Jewish social and family structure reflected bourgeois,

1. See Langmuir, 1987; idem, 1990: 154.

or at least protobourgeois, stability. Envy of this stability may have aroused the marginal Crusader bands who slaughtered Rhenish Jews no less than did the cry for a holy war against the enemies of the Cross. And in the sermons of William of Tournai, imagined Jewish sexual perversions proved as disturbing as did creedal diversity. For reasons, therefore, that were as political and social as they were also religious, the Jews became an object onto which medievals transferred their unexplained rage, their frustrations, and, most important, the blame for social inequities. In no small measure, that is, the Jews' fortunes reveal the underlying insecurities and psychological discomforts from which all medieval people suffered. Consequently, to understand the Jews' fate is not a restricted exercise but one that illuminates medieval history as a whole. As for that fate itself, more often than not it was tragic.

Early Christian Thought

Both in shaping the Jews' fate and in generating their mythical image, however, Christian religious teachings were decisive. From the time of the Apostles, these teachings not only created the main lines of that image but also gave it verbal and pictorial expression. Pictorial representations were particularly acute, as may poignantly be learned from the example of the late twelfth-century statues of the two ladies *Ecclesia* and *Synagoga*, which adorn the central portals of Notre Dame Cathedral in Paris. Epitomizing countless other portrayals of these two figures, a triumphant *Ecclesia* opposes a defeated *Synagoga*. Crowned and clear sighted, *Ecclesia* stands erect, sure in her faith and superiority. Carrying a broken spear and shaped in the *S* curve used by medieval sculptors to arouse pity, *Synagoga* is blindfolded (on Notre Dame, the blindfold is a serpent) and clearly inferior. She has lost sight of the truth which Scripture should have taught her. Her way is the wrong one; that of *Ecclesia* is right. Yet, marvelously, the two figures exist side by side in a seemingly perpetual balance. Medieval people entering the cathedral, or seeing the pictorial representations of *Ecclesia* and *Synagoga* adorning bibles and psalters, well understood this portrayal and its underlying concept of perpetual balance. The ideology the statues depict summarizes in one scene dozens of laws, theological tracts, and New Testament discourses on the Jewish place in Christian society. This ideology also varied little over time. About the year 600, the pictorial message transmitted hundreds of years later by the statues *Ecclesia* and *Synagoga* was already being verbally conveyed.[2]

Responding to a complaint made by Jewish residents of papal territories, Pope Gregory the Great (590–603) wrote to the bishops Virgilius of Arles and Theodorus of Marseilles. Many Jews in southern France, he said, "had been brought to the baptismal font more by force than by persuasion." Such baptisms had to cease. Not only did no biblical passage justify forced baptism, but experience taught that forced converts quickly returned to their "vomit." "To lighten the darkness," therefore, Jews must be approached not violently but with sweet words. Gregory clearly was ambivalent. The Jews were stained, he believed, by the sins of their fathers, and they followed the way of darkness (in his *Moralia on Job*, he even associates Jews with the Devil). Yet he would condone neither force nor arbitrary treatment as means of convincing them to abandon their ways. For the time being—in anticipation of the Jews' conversion—Christians must instead establish a condominium with them; Christians must also respect Jewish rights. No wonder that Jews in Rome turned to Gregory for help. Still, Gregory had no question about priorities: the superiority or "honor" of the Church—as canon lawyers would eventually phrase it—must come first. "However," Gregory continued, condemning Fantinus, his papal viceregent in Palermo, for unwarrantedly confiscating Jewish communal buildings and consecrating them as churches, "the Jews are not to be [unjustly] restrained; nor shall injustice be done them." Gregory was defining the same balance between superiority, inferiority, and coexistence that the statues of *Ecclesia* and *Synagoga* would eventually portray.[3]

Yet this balance reflects not only Christian theology but also the interplay between that theology and Roman imperial and legal traditions. Gregory's position is the same as that proposed by the legal Code of the Roman emperor Theodosius, compiled in the year 438. Jewish legal rights, the Code says, must be preserved, but only so long as Jews respect those of Christianity. Medieval Christian teachings on the Jews are thus inherently complex, based on traditions such as those of Roman law, as well as on Christian theology. Yet the theological aspect of these teachings was never submerged. Judaism and its continued existence were accepted,

2. Seiferth, 1970: 111–116.
3. Marcus, J. R., 1965: 111–114.

but as errors that would eventually become extinct. Moreover, extrapolating from these teachings in order to arrive at radical conclusions proved to be neither difficult nor uncommon. Accordingly, any fundamental understanding of the Jewish medieval world requires that Christian teachings on the Jews be studied in great detail.

Paul and the Pauline Tradition

The roots of Christianity lie in Pauline thought. What motivated Paul to give form and content to the beliefs of Jesus' faithful has been discussed in hundreds if not thousands of volumes. However, a general consensus admits that Paul was influenced by three prime factors. The first was the Hellenistic mystery cults that flourished in Paul's day, with their elaborate rituals and belief in a dying and then resurrected deity. Second were Jewish groups, like the Dead Sea Sect—the sect of the Dead Sea Scrolls— with its faith in a mythical Teacher of Righteousness, who would redeem a coterie of initiates in the imminent messianic period. Members of this sect also claimed the distinction of being the True Israel, which was one of Paul's central claims for Christianity. Nevertheless, Paul arrived at this claim principally in response to the third, and most obvious, influence on his thought, namely his own Jewish background. This influence was so great that it has been argued that Pauline Christianity was largely a "transvalued" Judaism. A new Torah, that of Jesus, takes the place of the old, that of Mount Sinai, just as there is a new covenant and a new people.[4]

Intrinsically—although not necessarily intentionally—Pauline Christianity challenges Judaism's continued legitimacy. This may be seen in Paul's (New Testament) Epistle to the Romans, a work that could well be subtitled "The Theology of Salvation through Grace." In the first four chapters, Paul argues that those whom he calls the Righteous will live eternally through their Faith, and, as proof of this claim, he points to the Jews: they live by the Law, the Torah, and this has led to their perdition. For "man is justified by faith quite apart from success in keeping the law" (Rom. 3:28). "Law," in fact, "brings only the consciousness of sin" (Rom. 3:20). This is so, Paul explains in chapters 5–8, because after the fall of Adam, man lives in a state of sin. His case is hopeless, no matter what his deeds; he must be justified and reborn through faith into an everlasting

4. Flusser, 1960; Davies, 1960; Goodenough, 1968.

spiritual state of grace, "to continue at peace with God" (Rom. 5:1) "in eternal life" (5:21).

Jews—still living in the presence of their Jerusalem Temple and on reasonably good terms with the Roman Empire—must have wondered what Paul meant. Individual "justification" and "faith" were terms that had little meaning for them. Salvation was primarily a mass resurrection of the dead in a post-messianic World to Come; it had nothing to do with a personal sense of inner tranquillity. God's sovereignty over His people and His land were givens; the Jew's obligation was not to have faith in God, which was assumed, but to observe the Torah's precepts. God would take care of the rest. Even members of the Dead Sea Sect, who spoke of a divine illumination descending upon the elect, did not eschew the commandments. Nor would they have placed their trust in a freely given "Grace" out of a conviction that man was irreparably condemned. How much the less, therefore, did Jews understand what Paul went on to write in chapters 9–11 of his Epistle, which outline the place of the Jews in the Christian soteriology. In these chapters, Paul explicitly compares the Jew and the believer in Christ. "The true Jew," Paul had already said in chapter 2 (vv. 28–29), "is he who is such inwardly." In chapter 9 (vv. 6–13), he explained: "Not all descendants of Israel (Jacob) are truly Israel, nor, because they are Abraham's offspring, are they all his true children." Rather, the true children are those "born through God's promise," like Isaac, and even more so, like Jacob. Physical descent from Abraham, therefore, was not a requirement for membership in the True Israel. Through their faith, Gentiles could equally, if not more properly, belong.[5]

The uncertainties implied by this conclusion perturbed no one more than Paul himself. "I," he emphasized repeatedly, "am an Israelite myself, of the stock of Abraham, of the tribe of Benjamin" (Rom. 11:2). Thus, he was convinced that "God has not rejected the people which he acknowledged of old as his own" (11:2). Rather, the Jews were like branches of an olive tree that had been "lopped off" so that new ones could be "grafted in" (11:17–21). And if they "do not continue faithless, they will be (re)grafted in." (11:23) Their regrafting was indispensable. Paul could not conceive of a world in which Jews and believers in Jesus would live perpetually side by side. More, in Paul's salvationary scheme, the Jews' "grafting in" meant "nothing less than life from the dead!"

5. Gager, 1983: 193–225; cf. Langmuir, 1990: 37–40.

(11:15). Accordingly, the ultimate justification for Paul's new elect required the assent of the old elect to its beliefs. And if that assent did not come at once, because the Jews currently were "blind to the truth" (11:7), "this partial blindness has come upon Israel only until the Gentiles have been admitted in full strength; when that has happened, the whole of Israel will be saved." Paul's attitude toward the Jews was thus ambivalent, insecure, and dependent. In his own portentous phrasing, "In the spreading of the Gospel, they [the Jews] are treated as God's enemies for your [the Gentiles'] sakes; but God's choice stands, and they are his friends for the sake of the patriarchs" (11:28). Future generations would turn this metaphoric dictum into fact.

The Gospels and the Church Fathers

As for Paul himself, his power resided in more than brilliant thought. He also headed a new religious movement. It was his leadership that pushed this movement toward a Gentile orientation and into proselytism, an activity which Jews themselves were then pursuing with great zeal and success.[6] However, this new movement had roots that were solidly planted in Judaism. Its members saw themselves as Jews, who, unlike Paul, did not reject the Torah and its Commandments. Their uniqueness resided in their conviction that the Messiah had already come. When, therefore, Paul spoke of his movement as Judaism, he was not using terms loosely. Moreover, even in its Pauline dress, Christianity maintained certain distinctively Jewish elements, in particular, the midrashic exegesis of Scripture which is evident throughout the Epistle to the Romans. Nevertheless, Paul's thought was so radical that a purely Pauline Christianity might have chosen to ignore Judaism entirely. The original believers in Jesus ensured that this did not occur. They insisted on identifying Jesus of Nazareth with the Messiah of the root of David, whom Jews had expected for centuries. They also drew no distinctions between an Old and New Israel. The first chapter of the Gospel According to Matthew, which traces Jesus' genealogy, is transparent in this regard.

But had not David's last known descendant, Zerubbabel, disappeared in Persia more than five hundred years earlier? To remove this difficulty, the author of Matthew invented a line of descent. Verses taken from the Book of Ruth (Matt. 1:2–6) traced David's direct ancestry. King lists (vv.

6. Baron, 1952: 1:171–179.

7–11) and verses from Chronicles (vv. 11–13) reached Zerubbabel. This wholly legitimate pedigree was then followed by a fictitious one leading from Zerubbabel to Jesus (vv. 13–16). Yet this fiction did not invalidate Matthew's efforts. For such fictions were a perfectly traditional Jewish exegetical tactic. As late as the ninth century c.e., Jews themselves were inventing genealogies to prove that the Exilarchs, or Heads of the Jews, in Baghdad, descended directly from David through the same Zerubbabel.[7] No less legitimate was Matthew's division (1:17) of world history into three periods of fourteen generations each. Its roots are in Chronicles; and as late as the twelfth century, Maimonides made a similar division in the Introduction to his *Mishneh Torah*.

The Jewishness of early Christianity was ubiquitous. Christians adopted the entire range of scriptural literature, from the Torah through post-canonical apocryphal and even pseudepigraphical texts. Jesus' immediate disciples observed the *mitzvot* (commandments of the Torah). Some, apparently following Jesus' lead, may have been strict legal constructionists. Christians also put great emphasis on table fellowship and the sacred meal, both of which were prime concerns of the Pharisees, the leading Jewish spiritual (and perhaps also political) force of the day. The Sacrifice of the Mass, too, has many similarities to Jewish temple ritual. Friction between the early Christians and other Jewish groups was thus inevitable.[8]

With the addition of Pauline theology, friction turned into confrontation. But this confrontation could not be defused, as Mohammed later did, by calling the Jews the "People of the Book," who, as such, were entitled perpetually to live among Muslims undisturbed. By its very nature, Christianity was forced to challenge Judaism's legitimacy or lose its raison d'être. The challenge was laid before the Jews by Paul himself. In the Acts of the Apostles, Paul is seen preaching in synagogues outside the Land of Israel. At first, he presented himself as a Pharisee, but eventually he turned to his own teachings, preaching that to abandon the Torah was just. This tactic provoked violent reactions. Diaspora Jewry's civil autonomy, like self-rule in Palestine, rested on the Torah as a civil constitution. Paul, in other words, was preaching civil, perhaps even more than religious, sedition.[9] Moreover, upon his return to Jerusalem, Paul took the lead in a discussion critical for the future of the Church.

7. Neubauer, 1895: 1:176–178,179–184, 2:72–76.
8. See Werner, 1959.
9. Goitein, 1964: 46–61; Smith, 1967.

Proselytism, it was decided, would be directed principally at the Gentiles; continued observance of the Commandments would be allowed to the weak. Nevertheless, in his ambivalence toward Judaism, Paul went to the Temple to fulfill sacrificial vows. This act provoked further antagonism and led directly to Paul's arrest by the Roman authorities.

Paul's disassociation from the Jews was followed by that of the Christian sect as a whole, first during the Jewish revolt against Rome, in 66 C.E., and again, seventy years later, during the messianic Bar Cochba revolt. Jewish-Christian antagonism increased as Christian preaching made headway, however slowly, and Jewish proselytizing efforts failed, especially in the second century. About the time of Augustus Caesar at the turn of the Common Era, the number of Jews, including *sebomenoi* (Fearers of the Lord, or Fellow Travelers, who never quite converted), may have grown to encompass up to 10 percent of the Roman Empire as a whole and 20 percent of the Eastern Empire. The revolts of the first and second centuries and subsequent Roman legislation reversed this process. By the year 202, all Jewish proselytizing activities had been outlawed. But so had those of the Christians, who were also being openly persecuted. One result of these troubles was the growth of polemic on both sides.[10]

The Jewish sallies were biting. In various rabbinic texts, most of which were eventually censored by medieval Christian Hebraists, Jesus was pictured as a magician who had dealings with Satan; and Jews were warned not to approach Jesus or his disciples for healing or even to mention his name, lest they lose their place in the World to Come. Alternately, Jesus was described as a bastard, the son of a harlot and a procurer, or a rebel who deserved to be hanged. The Apostles were said to be guilty of capital offenses. The word "Gospel," *evangelion* in Greek, was made the butt of a Hebrew pun: *Aven Gilayon* or *Avon Gilayon,* the blank or sinful page. Christian places of worship were considered less worthy than the temples of idolators. It was also said that the "sectaries" (a circumlocution normally meaning "Christians" by the second or third century) were worse than all other factions and even worse than the pagans (a claim, it is worth noting, that appears with reference to Jews in the canon *peiores* of Gratian's 1140 textbook of canon law, the *Decretum*). And a benediction calling for the destruction of sectaries was introduced into the daily prayers. Jewish Midrash also responded frontally to Pauline teachings, insisting that repentance comes through deeds,

10. See Parkes, 1934; Reuther, 1974; Simon, 1964.

not faith, and denying that God had replaced the Jews with a new people.[11]

Christians responded to these charges in kind. Their missionary frustrations had been too great to allow them to remain silent in the face of Jewish claims. Frustration is certainly the underlying theme of the lengthy *Dialogue of Justin Martyr with Trypho the Jew* (not the rabbi, Tarfon), written about the year 135. The first half of the dialogue is a defense of Christianity based on midrashic exegesis. Expressions like the "Rock of Circumcision," wrote Justin, must be understood not literally, as the Jews understand it, but figuratively. The Rock is God (Hebrew, *tsur*—a not unusual appellation for the deity); hence, as Paul has taught, the proper circumcision is performed by God, on the heart. Justin adduces literally hundreds of such examples.[12] The second half of the dialogue encourages Christians, reassuring them that irrespective of contemporary setbacks, the Church is a ship capable of outsailing any storm (an image that would have a long afterlife). Part of that reassurance, however, took the form of an attack. The rabbis, says Justin, are lustful, carnal men, who commit perverse acts and are the "enemies" of Christianity. Their guile expresses itself in benedictions, like that against the sectaries, and in their "tampering" with biblical texts (a charge that Muslims, beginning with Mohammed, would also make) so as to expunge any reference to Jesus.

Justin's themes are repeated in the writings of Tertullian. Lawyer, preacher, and father of the Latin liturgy, Tertullian, who lived in Carthage around the year 200, typifies the militant, martyr spirit of the persecuted Christian communities of North Africa. Tertullian's millenarian beliefs inflamed his zeal even further. His Jews are not actual people but typological objects playing preassigned Pauline eschatological roles. In a letter purportedly sent to the Roman emperor, Tertullian questioned why the emperor was persecuting loyal Christians rather than the rebellious Jews, the true enemies of the regime. Tertullian's *Adversus Iudaeos,* an internal apologetic written to reinvigorate flagging confidence, carries the typologies even further. As exponents of inverted understanding, the Jews persist in carnal circumcision rather than circumcision of the heart, and they observe the earthly Sabbath instead of awaiting the eternal one at the End of Days.[13]

A need for reassurance surfaces once more in the responses of Origen of Caesarea (ca. 185–250), replying to the sophisticated arguments made

11. Rokeah, 1971 (*Shir ha-shirim rabbah,* 1: 41); Mihaly, 1964 (*Sifre,* Dt. 32: 9).
12. Justin Martyr, 1965.
13. Tertullian, 1971.

against Christianity by spokesmen of late Neoplatonic paganism. In 178, the pagan Celsus had charged Christianity with pursuing Judaism's self-centered cultic and social practices. In fact, Celsus was reviving accusations made in the time of the Maccabees by Egyptian priests like Apion, which the Jewish historian Josephus Flavius had summarily refuted. Specifically, Celsus had claimed that Christians were guilty of blood sacrifices and of transmitting venereal disease. Origen might have limited himself to repeating Josephus' refutations. Instead, he chose to argue that Apion's charges applied only to the ancestors of the contemporary Jews. Like their ancestors, contemporary Jews offered sacrifices to the Devil and dealt in magic. The original Jews, to whom Apion's charges did not apply, lived just lives; their descendants were the Christians.[14]

Origen's skillful manipulations, simultaneously protecting Christianity and condemning Judaism, are especially disconcerting. For Origen spent twenty-five years of his life in Caesarea, on the Palestinian coast. He knew the Jews well, but, even more, he was a student of Hebrew. His *Hexapla*, or six-column translation of the Bible, remains today a classic of biblical scholarship and a necessary tool for current biblical research. Nevertheless, when confronting Jews, Origen retreated into theology, defensive posturing, and typological exegesis. Origen also adopted Tertullian's charges of magic and devil sacrifice. No longer the passive "enemy" of Romans, nor the falsifier of Justin Martyr's *Dialogue*, the Jew has become the actual perpetrator of wrongful acts. What he threatens is the continuity of Christian belief.

This sense of a Jewish threat eventually dominated the writings of the Jews' most vociferous detractors. In this, they had been anticipated by Paul himself. The notion of a Jewish threat is already imminent in Paul's first-century Letter to the Galatians. In Romans, Paul had spoken of the Jews' "blindness" and their merited "retribution," yet he had still viewed "God's enemy," as well as Judaism itself, as an object of charity. In Galatians (chapters 4 and 5), Paul views with anxiety Jewish practices, or perhaps more precisely, Judaizing by Gentile converts.[15] Certain Gentile Christians, Paul warns, were Judaizing. They were planning to circumcise themselves and so were endangering their salvation; for "if you seek to be justified by way of law, your relation with Christ is completely severed" (5:4). "'A little leaven,' remember, 'leavens all the dough'" (5:9).

14. Origen, 1965; *Encyclopaedia Judaica,* 1971: s.v. "Origen"; De Lange, 1976.
15. Gager, 1983: 227.

Contact with Jewish practice, just like contact with idolatry, can be the "leaven" that ruins the dough. Yet to remove the danger of this "leaven," "what does Scripture say? 'Drive out the slave woman [Hagar] and her son [Esau], for the son of the slave shall not share the inheritance with the free woman's [Sarah's] son [Isaac, the symbol of the new Christian True Israel]'" (4:28–30).

It would appear, therefore, that Paul and the subsequent Pauline Christian tradition really posited two distinct approaches toward Judaism, not one, as is usually assumed. The first is the classic doctrine of Romans, balancing disappointment with hope, which became the basis of normative Church policy. The second is a doctrine of anxiety, which, irrespective of Paul's attitude toward Jews and Judaism, radicals soon exploited to censure both. The number of these radicals, the force of their arguments, and the list of practices they censured would grow throughout the Middle Ages. In 1569 and 1593, popes Pius V and Clement VIII cited Jewish crimes against Christians, including black magic, as grounds for expelling Jews from the Papal State. However, before this doctrine became truly threatening, the ideas of Galatians had to be combined with those Paul expressed in I Corinthians. Here, Paul once again warns that "a little leaven leavens all the dough" (5:7). But this time his concern is that Christians avoid not Jews but idolators. Christians should not even "eat with any such person"; they would do better to avoid the threat entirely and "root the evildoer from your community." Expanding on this theme, in I Cor. 10:20, Paul cautions: "You cannot drink the cup of the Lord and the cup of demons." Paul did not mention the Jews in either of these passages, nor did he ever hint that Jews were to be considered idolators. Nevertheless, in typically medieval exegetical style, later churchmen exploited the common presence of the concept of "leaven" in both Galatians and Corinthians to equate (or nearly equate) Judaism with idolatry and demon worship—indeed, sometimes to equate the demonic with the Jews themselves.

The Augustinian Equilibrium

But the equation of Jews and demons did not become universal. Thanks in particular to the writings of Augustinus Aurelius, or Saint Augustine, the man sometimes called the true founder of Western Christian thought, the normative doctrine concerning the Jews was to become that of Paul in Romans. This he achieved by weaving all the strands of Christian thought into one coherent cloth, in which he also successfully meshed the realities of a Roman Empire that even in Augustine's day, the late fourth and early fifth centuries, was still according the Jews numerous legal rights.[16]

Augustine's contribution was to turn Paul's metaphors into programmatic statements. It is not by chance that scholars speak more often of an Augustinian than of a Pauline approach to the Jews. That approach is typified by Augustine's teachings on Jewish witness, which he summed up in his *Adversus Judaeos* and in the *City of God* by citing Psalm 59 (Masoretic text numbering), "Kill them not, lest my people forget" (v. 12). Augustine did not intend this verse to be taken literally, just as he also did not actually consider whether Jews should be treated as criminals who might be violently driven from society, a conclusion that might be inferred from Augustine's likening the Jews, in his *Contra Faustum,* to Cain, forced to wander the earth in memory of his "crime." Thoughts of that kind did not enter Christian theological discourse until the thirteenth century, and even then they remained hypothetical until the end of the fifteenth.[17] Rather, in the *City of God* (18:46), Augustine explained: "He has not slain them—that is, He has not let the knowledge that they are Jews be lost in them." It was God's will that Judaism should endure and not be "slain." As Augustine elaborated on other occasions, should the Jews and, along with them, Judaism cease to exist, then Christians, too, might neglect God's revelation and desert the faith. They might also lose sight of that revelation's venerability, and its consequent verification of Christianity's claims to authenticity. Most important, the Jews' continuity furnished a permanent counter-example to Christianity's virtues. The Jews personified the absence of Grace and its effects—or, as Thomas Aquinas would phrase it in the thirteenth century, the absence of belief. As such, the Jews had an ongoing, integral, and indeed a necessary role in the Christian economy. The citation of Psalms 59:12 was merely a prooftext to signify and summarize this broad concept; and so indeed it was understood throughout the Middle Ages by the many popes who referred to it in their texts.

Not accidentally, Augustine first discussed the role he assigned the Jews in his response to the Manichees. Augustine himself had once belonged to this sect, which taught the total opposition between the realms of the

16. Augustinus, 1965; idem, 1950; Marrou, 1957.
17. Cohen, J., 1986.

spiritual and the physical; these, in turn, were equated with the realms of good and evil. This sense of opposition, of good and of evil, had become a fixed part of Augustine's intellectual baggage, and when he converted to Christianity, it affected his view of Judaism. But Paul, too, had sharply distinguished between the physical and spiritual descendants of Abraham. Augustine thus had little difficulty assimilating his Manichean background to his new Christian faith. Indeed, the basic assumption informing Augustine's teachings on the Jews was the permanence of good and evil—that is, of spiritual good (represented by Christianity) and carnal evil (represented by the Jews). Jewish carnality embodied the opposite of the reformed, spiritually pure society Augustine envisioned as the earthly ideal. Naturally, one hoped for spirituality's ultimate triumph over such carnality, but reality dictated that for the (long enduring) present, the two had to coexist. It was to the fact of this coexistence that the Jews truly bore witness. Augustine said so in his *Adversus Judaeos*. He also knew that in the Epistle to the Romans coexistence between the old carnal Israel and the new spiritual one was a central theme.

The *Adversus Judaeos* reflects Augustine's most mature thinking about the Jews. It was written in 429, only five years after the *City of God*, Augustine's most famous work, which describes the Jews' eventual reconciliation to Christianity at the End of Days in even more apocalyptic terms than those used by Paul in chapter 11 of Romans. The *Adversus Judaeos* may really be a sermon on good and evil. It is cast in the form of an admonition to the Jews, but this was strictly a rhetorical device. The statement in chapter 1, "See then the goodness and the severity of God: his severity towards those who have fallen, but the goodness of God towards thee if thou abidest in his goodness" (actually a verbatim citation of Romans 11:22), embodies Augustine's true agenda.

In the tradition of other *Adversus Judaeos* texts, the first nine chapters in Augustine's tract are heavily laden with prooftexts. Augustine's version, nevertheless, stands out from others of its ilk. The stress on spiritual-carnal opposites, not simply on the opacity of Jewish understanding, runs throughout the tract like the proverbial scarlet thread. In addition, the implications of verses like Genesis 25:23, "The elder shall serve the younger," first used metaphorically by Paul in Romans 9, are fully drawn. The Jews are "Esau"; they must recognize from the Christians' natural increase and success not only that God has instituted a new covenant but that they have become subservient to the Christians, who "have replaced them." What was metaphor has now become reality. Augustine also instilled urgency into the concept of Jewish spiritual blindness. What had been a figure of speech in Romans now justified policy. If you Jews are blind, Augustine wrote, we cannot "now attempt to show you, blind and deaf as you are in your spiritual senses, how these words [which validate Christianity] are to be accepted spiritually." For the same reason, the Jews had limited responsibility; Augustine would not attempt to show them that by imitating the beliefs and practices of their parents they were equally guilty (as he firmly believed) of the murder of Jesus—a charge, it should be noted, which had heretofore rarely been equated with deicide, as it would so commonly be from the time of the Crusades.[18] The Jews simply could not understand their error. As Augustine phrased it in his commentary on the Gospel of John: "Every Jew that slew the preachers of Christ reckoned that he was doing God service."

At one stroke, Augustine had defused the cries of "Enemy!" and "Murderer!" found in writers such as Justin and Tertullian. He had also mapped out a program for the future. The Jews, he argued, may personify carnality and evil, but in doing so they forever remind the faithful that evil is a condition from which man can never fully escape. Augustine thus was effectively restating Paul's basic principle that the Jews are constantly God's "friends" as well as his "enemies." This promotion of a modus vivendi with the Jews was not, however, free from pragmatic considerations. Augustine's teachings on the Jews reflect—in addition to Pauline thought—an accurate assessment of both tradition and change in Roman imperial political realities. By 429, if not earlier, Christianity had become a dominant force in the Roman Empire, at least in name and political clout, and in the process it had gained the upper hand over Judaism. In the hundred or so years since the emperors had adopted Christianity, imperial legislation had transformed the theology and polemical rhetoric of Jewish subservience into political and legal fact. If nothing else, the Jews could not freely speak out as before. Militant clerical anxiety thus lost much of its justification. At the same time, as Augustine in formulating his thought was evidently aware, despite its Christianization, the Empire, and even its now Christianized Roman law, had not entirely abandoned tradition. There were limits which that law preserved, and to which Christians had to defer.[19]

18. Reuther, 1974: 129; Langmuir, 1980: 362; idem, 1990: 288–290. See also Cohen, J., 1983.
19. Cohen, G., 1967.

Roman Law

In the year 313, the emperor Constantine made the historically momentous decision to accept Christianity. Prior to this moment, Christians in the Empire numbered no more than one in four. Christianity's popular appeal had been limited. Following its acceptance by Constantine, however, Christianity became the Empire's religion, which the majority of the inhabitants adopted, often more out of political prudence than out of sincere or knowledgeable belief. The early fourth century did not witness a sudden Christian awakening. The emperors, accordingly, proceeded with caution. The Edict of Milan in 313 indicates a tolerance in equal measure for Christians, Jews, and pagans.[20]

Christianity's uncertain position is illustrated by the events of the short reign (361–363) of the last pagan emperor, Julian, known as the Apostate. Julian viewed Christianity as inimical to the interests of the State; he well appreciated that even at that early date, devoted clergy held the interests of the faith superior to those of this-worldly institutions and authority. Julian's paganism was also of a sophisticated, almost monotheistic Neoplatonic variety.[21] The actual threat to imperial Christianity that Julian posed was resolved only two years after he took the throne, when he was killed by the arrow of a Parthian (Persian) archer. Nevertheless, the memory of his plan to reconstruct the Jerusalem Temple—certainly for political purposes—left uneasiness in its wake. To convince contemporaries that God opposed both Julian and his plan, chroniclers wrote that crosses were seen amid the flames which even during Julian's reign consumed the new Temple's foundations. However, nobody wrote of taking revenge on the Jews themselves. Jews had always enjoyed political security, including, on occasion, political advantage—for example, when they were clients of Julius Caesar.[22] Even when segments of the Empire's Jewish population had rebelled, in 66, 115, and 132, the Jews were not generically outlawed. Accordingly, there was no reason to exclude the Jews from Caracalla's edict of 212, which conferred Roman citizenship on all the Empire's residents. Nor did the emperors feel impelled to cancel the limited Jewish self-rule exercised in Galilee by the *Nasi* (Patriarch), the great Pharisaic leader who was a direct descendant

20. Baer, 1961a.
21. Avi Yona, 1976: 185–204; see also Ehrhardt, 1959.
22. Levy, 1968.

of the House of Hillel. The authority of the *Nasi* was restricted, but real. He held Roman rank and could invoke the aid of Roman soldiers.

This affront to the teachings of Jewish subservience led various churchmen to press for change. The emperors responded. Nevertheless, their response was limited. True change in the Jews' status, as expressed in new legislation, did not occur until the close of the fourth century. Only at that time, too, did the *Nesiut* (Patriarchate) lose power, becoming extinct when, in 425, the last *Nasi* died a natural death and no successor was appointed.[23] Yet even this new legislation did not recklessly trample on the legacy of the past. The Jews remained Roman citizens, and their right to practice Judaism and observe its rituals was restated. Imperial activity vis-à-vis the Jews thus was ambivalent. On the one hand, it moved in the direction of Christian desires; the gap between the metaphoric Jewish Esau and political reality was constantly narrowing. On the other hand, imperial legislation renounced extremes.

The earliest restrictive legislation, already in the 330s, is of a religious nature and deals with conversion. Jews were neither to hinder pagans from converting to Christianity nor to entice Jewish apostates back to Judaism. Jewish proselytism was strictly forbidden. By the turn of the fifth century, Jews were losing civil ground. They were forbidden to buy Christian slaves, prevented from serving as officers in imperial cohorts, and forbidden to obtain "honorific" political appointments—that is, any office bearing aristocratic *dignitas*. More significant, monies that had once been sent to the *Nasi* were now to go into the imperial treasury. Jewish ordinary jurisdiction in civil affairs was abrogated. The *Nasi* himself was reprimanded and stripped of much of his authority for daring to judge Christians.[24]

What truly diminished Jewish legal status were laws prohibiting the erection of new synagogues and edicts threatening the curtailment of all privileges, should the Jews insult Christianity. (This they were thought to do every year at the Feast of Purim, when they hanged the archenemy, Haman, in effigy. Christians, perhaps correctly, perceived the effigy as symbolizing Jesus and the crucifixion.) Jewish religious expression thus was made dependent on imperial will. Judaism also became legally despicable. The law forbidding the purchase of Christian slaves stipulates: "We consider it abominable that very religious slaves should be defiled

23. Avi Yonah, 1976: 225–228.
24. *Codex Theodosianus*, 1954: bk. 16, title 8; Linder, 1987: passim.

by the ownership of impious [Jewish] purchasers." Imperial attitudes worsened as time went on. The emperors viewed the law more and more as a Christian Roman law resting on Christian theological underpinnings. In prefacing the Novels (new laws) that accompany his Code, Theodosius wrote: "Among the other anxieties which Our love for the State has imposed upon us for Our ever watchful consideration, We perceive that an especial responsibility of Our Imperial Majesty is the pursuit of the true religion."

Such statements do not mean that Church pressure had vanquished the emperors or convinced them to forsake the Roman past. Recent studies have shown that specific laws, like those forcing Jews to assume the decurionate (local posts whose prime function was to spend money for the feeding and entertainment of the lower classes), were enacted together with other legislation that canceled ecclesiastical exemptions in general, including those of Christian priests.[25] In addition, the restrictive laws of the Theodosian Code are balanced by others protecting basic Jewish rights. The Code reaffirms Jewish citizenship, indicates that Jews (in the autonomous regions of Palestine) are to set their own market rules and prices, specifies that Jews exercise ordinary jurisdiction in ritual matters (apparently throughout the Empire), and grants recourse to arbiters in civil matters. It outlaws attacks on synagogues, and forbids summoning a Jew to court on the Sabbath. Most important, the Code forbids the arbitrary cancellation of Jewish rights, thereby enunciating a doctrine of due legal process. Jewish status would not endlessly deteriorate. For "no person shall be trampled upon when he is innocent, on the ground that he is a Jew, nor shall any religion cause any person to be exposed to contumely."[26] Augustine's insistence on "loving the Jews," enunciated only nine years before the promulgation of the Theodosian Code, thus went hand in hand with imperial policy.

Yet this was only logical. Both imperial policy and Augustine's teachings were compatible with the writings of Paul, a font from which both had imbibed, whether directly or indirectly. And thus the foundations were laid for the policies of Gregory the Great. His theology echoed that of Paul and Augustine, his spiritual mentors; his political and legal attitudes depended fully on the Theodosian Code, which he often cited; but between his theology and his politics, Gregory himself correctly saw

25. Linder, 1987: 212–215.
26. *Codex Theodosianus*, 1954: bk. 16, title 8, law 18.

no caesura. Indeed, had Gregory's policy continued to function through-out the Middle Ages, and had all ranks of medieval society accepted it, the outcome of the medieval Jewish experience in Latin Europe might have been different. Jews would not have participated in medieval society as equals. Far from it; they still would have endured increasingly greater disadvantages. But neither would they have undergone attacks, expul-sions, and forced baptisms. Where Gregory the Great's policy did con-tinue to function, namely in Rome itself, Jewish life continued uninter-rupted. The Jews were the first to appreciate this fact.[27]

Chrysostom, Ambrose, and the Emperors

The real course of events was different. Outside Rome and the papal estates, the policies of Gregory the Great were rarely applied. In limited ecclesiastical circles but especially in lay society—paradoxical as it may seem—the tradition of Romans and Augustine was gradually submerged by that of Galatians. Already in the late fourth century, certain church-men initiated extraordinary measures to stamp out purported Jewish improprieties. In 422, the monk Bar Sauma led attacks on Jewish houses of worship and pagan altars in Galilee; his object was to purify the land. Bar Sauma did not advocate physically assaulting Jews, yet his attacks weakened the remaining Jewish hold on the Land of Israel. That hold was further weakened by churchmen who advocated that Christians "settle" there. The remains of church foundations, like the spectacular one at Avdat in the Negev, indicate the breadth of this activity. Bar Sauma himself campaigned to have churches built in Jerusalem. The call to abolish the Nesiut followed naturally. It proved a final blow to organized Jewish existence in ancient Palestine.[28]

For the most part, the negative Pauline tradition crystallized as verbal and literary invective. Eusebius of Caesarea, a prime exponent of Chris-tian settlement in the "Holy Land," passionately decried the Jews' imp-ious perversity.[29] However, the first to formulate a full-blown doctrine of a Jewish threat in precise and extensive detail was the later fourth-century bishop of Antioch, John Chrysostom. Chrysostom was convinced that Paul's anxieties in Galatians and Corinthians had materialized. For one thing, the Jews' substantial and socially well-established presence in the

27. Stow, 1986b; see also Stow, 1976.
28. Avi Yonah, 1976: 220–224.
29. Eusebius, 1965: 6,16; see also Avi Yonah, 1976: 50–52.

population of Antioch violated the rule of Christian superiority and perverted the social order. That some of the Hasmoneans (Maccabees) were said to be buried in the precincts of Antioch's synagogues only worsened the situation. Recently converted Christians, who often distinguished Judaism from Christianity only with difficulty, were venerating these graves and the bones they contained as relics. These Christians also habitually consulted Jews for medical advice and potions, including love potions—many of whose recipes, incidentally, have survived. In Chrysostom's opinion, such activities bordered on Judaizing and threatened Christian salvation, as Paul had warned. Accordingly, in his eighty sermons on the Gospel of John, Chrysostom portrayed the Jews as the arch-symbol of evil. And in his Eight Orations against the Jews of Antioch—delivered in the fall of 386 and 387 for the explicit purpose of stopping the veneration of Maccabee bones and the resort to Jewish healers—Chrysostom frontally assaulted the Jews.[30]

The synagogue, he said, is the habitation of demons, a house of prostitution, and a veritable theater, where Jews carry on like drunken dogs; it is a place of "disgraceful behavior . . . [and] indecorous dances, . . . ruled by gluttony and licentiousness." To enter a synagogue endangers a Christian's state of Grace, and other Christians must prevent this from happening. They must view themselves as members of an army, bound to maintain discipline at all costs. Should they see their "brother being dragged unjustly and iniquitously to the pit of destruction . . . by the Devil" [for "the souls of the Jews are the dwelling places of demons"], they must rescue him. Or else he will "be[come] a slave just like she [the synagogue] is" (Gal. 4:25). Surprisingly, Chrysostom said nothing about aggressive action. Every line of the Orations revealed his pent-up rage. At one point he reiterated what he had previously said in his *Demonstration of the Gospel,* only this time he made no secret of his innermost wishes: "When animals are unfit for work, they are marked for slaughter, and this is the very thing which the Jews have experienced. By making themselves unfit for work, they have become ready for slaughter" (Orations 1 and 2). But Chrysostom knew that neither the emperor nor local authorities would tolerate violence. Accordingly, he concentrated on successfully convincing the Antiocheans to consecrate as churches the synagogues containing the Maccabee relics.

The authorities were not always so pliant. When the bishop of

30. Simon, 1962; Meeks, 1978.

Callinicum, a town somewhere between the Tigris and Euphrates rivers, illegally sanctioned the burning of a synagogue in the year 388, the emperor Theodosius the Great ordered it rebuilt and the bishop punished. This decision infuriated Ambrose, the bishop of Milan. The great rhetor and teacher of Augustine emotionally appealed to the emperor to rescind the order, demanding that he not "give this triumph over the Church of God to the Jews." "Which," he asked, "is of greater importance, the show of discipline or the cause of religion?" The law should not support an institution in which the name of God is sullied and polluted, "a home of unbelief, a house of impiety, a receptacle of folly, which God himself has condemned." The right order of the State, Ambrose was saying, depends less on discipline than on the cause of religion. In preferring the honor of the Jews to that of the Church, Theodosius had acted against the best interests of the State; by the same logic, he had also given aid to its enemies.[31]

This appeal did not at first sway Theodosius. Before Theodosius acquiesced, Ambrose had to excommunicate the emperor de facto, by refusing to say Mass in his presence. Ambrose's victory was also incomplete. In 393, Theodosius declared attacks on synagogues to be a major crime. Nevertheless, the affair of 388 boded ill. Rome, after all, had traditionally viewed State and Church, temporal and spiritual entities, beliefs and practices as closely interrelated. The welfare of the Empire depended on proper service to the gods. In this context, Ambrose's claims made sense. If God bestowed kingship and Empire—the same Empire which the early sixth-century Justinian said "was delivered to Us by His celestial Majesty"—then imperial policy must implement God's will. In the long run, therefore, Theodosius may have been more persuaded that Ambrose was right than he was cowed by the bishop's threats. Ambrose's arguments were made especially cogent by their congruence with traditional Roman mentalities. Roman views may even have been influenced by originally Jewish ones. Virgil's epic poem, the *Aeneid,* for example, views the Romans as a chosen people. Romans also applied exegetical methods to their sacred texts.[32]

The fusion of political and religious concepts that marked imperial legislative activity during the fifth century and at the beginning of the sixth century therefore occurred on well-prepared soil, the same soil on

31. Marcus, J. R., 1965: Ambrose; Parkes, 1934: 166–168.
32. Hadas, 1959.

which eventually grew the doctrine of Caesaropapism. The emperor would stand at the head of both Church and State, just as he had always functioned as the *pontifex maximus* (high priest) of the old pagan cults. To protect the faith was no less an imperial duty than was protecting the Empire's borders. For the Jews, this Caesaropapist doctrine was a threatening one. Given sufficient reason, as apparently Theodosius was in 388, emperors might bend tradition to the Jews' disadvantage, or even worse. The actions of the early sixth-century emperor Justinian vividly illustrate this point.

Justinian believed it was his imperial duty to labor for the faith. He strove to convert pagans and control heresy, even through violent means. He composed theological tracts. But most of all, as part of his overall project to codify and preserve the fruits of hundreds of years of legal activity and teaching, he devoted enormous energies to religious legislation. "If for the general welfare," he wrote in his introduction to his Code, "we have taken measures to render the civil laws more effective, with whose execution God, through His good will toward men, has entrusted us, how much more reason is there not for us to compel the observance of the sacred canons and Divine laws." The product of these "measures," which encompass both civil and religious law, is the monumental *Corpus Iuris Civilis*. What immediately strikes the reader of the Code, the second of the *Corpus'* four parts, is its method of organization. Its first "book" concerns religious issues—the same religious primacy advocated by Ambrose. Its "titles" (chapters) are "The Holy Trinity," "The Holy Faith," "Concerning the Holy Church," "Concerning Bishops," "Concerning Heretics," and "Concerning Jews." In this context, the line distinguishing civil from religious legislation, concerning the Jews or others, was fully blurred. Justinian's editorial procedures blurred that line even further. Although many laws concerning Jews in the Justinianic Code repeat those found in the Code of Theodosius nearly a hundred years earlier, Justinian's legal editors sometimes altered their meanings. For example, Theodosius' law had said that Jews are Roman citizens; they must bring their disputes over civil matters before state tribunals. Religious issues they were to adjudicate themselves. Justinian's editors changed the wording (Code 1,9,8), depriving the Jews of religious jurisdiction too.[33] Justinian also exploited an older law to indicate that the Jews as a group no longer had corporate status (Code 1,9,1). Without

33. Ferrari dalle Spade, 1956; *Corpus Iuris Civilis,* 1906: Code, bk. 1, title 9, law 8.

such a status, later commentators explained, the Jews possessed no true self-rule whatsoever, thus fulfilling the Christian interpretation of Genesis 49:10 (a central verse of later polemic), which Christians interpreted to mean that with the Messiah's arrival, Jewish political power would cease.

Nevertheless, the tenor of the Code as a whole remains Pauline and Augustinian. There is no reference to a Jewish threat, no attempt to segregate the Jews, no attempt to coerce them to convert. At the most, there is tension such as that introduced by churchmen like Ambrose. One may legitimately read into the edited Code the idea that Jewish honor or power is incompatible with the security of the State. Still, the balance evident in Roman tradition remained in place. Eventually, however, Justinian pushed that balance off center. His Novel 146 from the year 553 (one of hundreds of legal innovations that comprise the fourth part of the *Corpus Iuris Civilis*) violated the Jews' right to unhindered ritual expression by dictating which vernacular translations they might publicly read to accompany the Hebrew reading of the Torah in their synagogues. Justinian was convinced that the Greek Septuagint translation in particular would lead the Jews to Christianity, once the supposedly anti-Christian Hebrew Midrash, which the Jews normally read, had been prohibited. On another occasion, Justinian reportedly ordered the Jews to postpone their observance of Passover until Eastertime. In the words of the contemporary historian Procopius, the source of this report, the emperor had caused the Jews "to neglect the divine service and to transgress their laws." These edicts, it must be stressed, were acts of imperial initiative. Justinian had no doubt concluded that the free observance of Judaism ran counter to Rome's best interests. He had identified civil welfare with spiritual welfare, and in so doing had turned the State into the Jews' greatest foe.[34]

It remained for the emperor Heraclius, in the 630s, to show just how dangerous the State could be. In 607, the Parthians had captured Palestine from the Romans. In 629, it was recaptured. Christians living in Jerusalem accused the Jews of assisting the Parthians—indeed of leading a rebellion—and called for reprisals. Heraclius responded by virtually outlawing Judaism and applying conversionary pressures. Then, in 634, at the start of the Arab invasion, he decreed a forced conversion. Nobody knows precisely the intended scope of this order or its actual results; the

34. Avi Yonah, 1976: 243; Scharf, 1971: 23; Linder, 1987: 338, n. 10. See also Brown, 1972; idem, 1982.

Arab conquest in 638 brought the episode to an abrupt end. There are also questions about its stimulus. The Christian community of Jerusalem, especially its clergy, had called for action, but not for so drastic a step. To be sure, in 613, the Visigothic king Sisebut had decreed a forced conversion in his realms. Yet despite their many common elements, the episodes in Spain and Byzantine Palestine were not the same. One thing, however, is certain. In a moment of great trial, in his rage and incomprehension at seeing parts of his Empire so quickly dismembered by so unexpected an opponent as the Arabs, Heraclius decided to violate tradition. The continued presence in his realms of unconverted Jews, he must have believed, endangered not only religious welfare but the entire political and social fabric; and it did so even more perniciously than Ambrose and Chrysostom had feared. Whatever was the real nature of Jewish behavior, and especially Jewish loyalty, Heraclius appears to have invested both with a mythical dimension.[35]

Is it any wonder that Jewish polemic now became furtive and esoteric? The Antitrinitarianism in the verses of Yosi ben Yosi, for example, is expressed only by allusion: there was "none after" and "none before" Him.[36] Fantastic legends, like that of Sefer Zerubbabel, also made their appearance. Zerubbabel, descendant of the House of David, is guided to the gates of Rome by the angel Michael, also known as Metatron. There, from the lips of the Messiah, who is sitting at the gates binding his wounds, Zerubbabel hears a marvelous tale of two Messiahs. The first, the Messiah ben Yosef, would perish in battle; the second, the Messiah ben David, would defeat the archenemy, the emperor-like Armilus—perhaps to be identified with Heraclius himself.[37] The Jews had obviously come to appreciate that their security was never more jeopardized than when lay leadership assumed the role of religious guardian and then, in that guise, violated the limits which Roman law and Christian theology had set. This was a truth that experience would repeatedly verify throughout the Middle Ages.

Early Medieval Continuity

The responsibility for escalating the danger to the Jews did not belong to the State alone. Ambrose and Chrysostom were not one-time phenom-

35. Avi Yonah, 1976: 270–275; Scharf, 1971: 47–57, esp. 53.
36. See Shirman, 1979: 1:22–36.
37. Dan, 1974: 35–46; Levi, 1914: 131–144,144–160.

ena. The calls of the Jerusalemite clergy for Heraclius to punish the Jews make this point clear. Many churchmen in Latin Europe during the early medieval centuries followed suit. Even in his own day, Gregory the Great did not dominate attitudes. The recipients of his letters included bishops who participated in forced baptisms or did nothing to stop them. Other bishops confiscated synagogues, most often on the pretext that Jewish ceremonies were disturbing Christians at prayer. To be sure, Gregory's position was recognized as the correct one. Gregory of Tours, writing around 583, credits Bishop Avitus of Clermont with trying to stop a mob from burning a synagogue. Whether Gregory of Tours's accuracy may be relied on is another matter. Gregory also lauded Avitus for offering the Jews of Clermont the choice of leaving his city or converting.[38] The earlier medieval centuries were not a time of consistent, principled action. In the time immediately following that of Gregory the Great, even the popes were unpredictable.

In about 770, Pope Stephen IV complained to the archbishop of Narbonne about the lifestyle of the city's Jews. The intolerable Jews, he wrote, possess large estates in the Frankish kingdoms, and on their estates these enemies of God arrogate to themselves unwarranted rights. They force Christians to serve them in hard labor, and, worse, they have female Christian domestics who live under Jewish roofs. Male and female Christian slaves are in their company both day and night, in the towns and in the countryside, where they are exposed to the Jews' vile speech. Pope Stephen's complaints would be repeated on dozens of occasions throughout the Middle Ages; the prooftext the pope used to justify his demands was almost unique. This Jewish behavior must cease forthwith, Stephen wrote, for "can light consort with darkness? Can Christ agree with Belial, or a believer join hands with an unbeliever? Can there be a compact between the temple of God and the idols of the heathen?" (II Cor. 6:15–16). This prooftext was to be used again only once. In 937, Pope Leo VII reportedly instructed Archbishop Frederick of Mainz that should his conversionary sermons fail, he might legitimately expel the Jews from his city. "Do not," Leo said, "unite yourselves with unbelievers; they are no fit mates for you. What has righteousness to do with wickedness?" (II Cor. 6:14). Both Pope Stephen and Pope Leo no doubt intended that they be understood literally. So did Adrian I (ca. 795), who cited I Corinthians 5:9–13 to berate Christians for joining with Jews in table fellowship:

38. Gregory of Tours, 1927: 174–179,234–239.

"[You] must have nothing to do with [Christian] loose livers . . . You should not even eat with any such person . . . [but should] root out the evildoer from your community." The practice of Christians' sitting down at a common table with Jews apparently was a frustratingly common one. Church councils had unsuccessfully fought it since the sixth century.[39]

Mindful of Paul in Galatians, early medieval popes and councils were anxious to halt all social contacts between Christians and Jews. These contacts were insulting to both Christians and Christianity. Leo VII's instructions to Frederick of Mainz summed up this thinking by citing Matthew 7:6, "Do not give dogs what is holy." Five hundred years earlier, in a mixed society, Chrysostom had demanded of Christians that they absent themselves from the company of Jews in order to preserve their salvation; now, when the Jews were a tiny minority, church leaders demanded the reverse. Jews must withdraw from the company of Christians. Even for the popes, the Jews had come to incarnate and symbolize the antithesis of the Christian ideal. Pope Adrian I referred to the iconoclasts—Byzantine "heretics" who sought to abolish the reverence of images—as Jews, effectively equating heresy with "Judaism" (not, as is often said inaccurately for a later period, Judaism with heresy). As phrased by the exegete Rabanus Maurus (776–856), "Anyone who corrupts Christian doctrine is one who teaches a doctrine resembling that of the Jews." Rabanus Maurus also said that Jews and heretics were one in their union to persecute the Church. The patristic theme of the Jew as enemy was still in vogue.[40]

In the tradition of Church Fathers like Tertullian and Chrysostom, many early medieval churchmen feared that contact with Jews compromised Christian purity. However, the object of their concerns was no longer individual Christians; it was the "Christian community" as a whole. This sense of "community" helps explain the tenor of their remarks. The demise of the Roman Empire had brought with it a loss of institutional stability and legal standards. In addition, masses of barbarians had converted, but they had entered the Christian fold only nominally. By their very presence, Jews generated confusion. That confusion was amplified by the Church's uncertain place within early medieval society. Was the Church an independent body, in control of its own

39. Synan, 1965: 57–62; Blumenkranz, 1963: 142–144,219.
40. Blumenkranz, 1963: 174–178.

affairs, or should it be subject to royal supervision? The clergy itself was divided on this subject. Bishop Hincmar of Rheims (ca. 850) argued that the clergy should submit even to the judgment of the Carolingian Charles the Bald, who had sworn to defend the Church and its canons. In the opposing camp, Bishop Hincmar of Laon argued that only bishops may judge one another.[41]

The second Hincmar was reflecting a tradition that had grown out of early Christian reform movements, one of whose important authors was Augustine. Through reform, the Christian ascended to perfection. Initially this reform took place on a personal, spiritual level. Augustine held up as the clerical ideal the priest who monkishly gave himself over to religious devotion. By the early Middle Ages, reform had become a communal issue. The fully Christianized community was coterminous with the *populus dei,* the people of God. Its constituents were the limbs of the sanctified *Corpus Christi* (an image which, like so many others, originated with Paul).[42] Already in the late sixth century, Gregory the Great had admonished Queen Brunhilda of Neustria that Jewish ownership of Christian slaves was tantamount to "giving the boot" *(calcanda)* to the limbs of Christ. Ninth-century exegetes expanded on this image and made the sanctity of the entire community dependent on the continued purity of its individual constituents. The vision of the people of God united as the limbs of Christ in pure, Christian communities, under the stewardship of monkish priests, must have been very attractive in an era of constant instability. To those convinced of the primacy of spiritual over social and political values, this vision must have seemed objectively right. Its influence, together with that of the Ambrosian view it expressed, would increase over the following centuries. Ultimately the papacy would demand that the totality of Christian society unite under its exclusive spiritual leadership and, to a large measure, its political leadership as well.[43]

Already in the ninth century some popes were picturing their ideal world in terms of a society of the faithful, a *societas fidei.* Numerous reform clerics were seeking to make this ideal a fact. Various privileges bestowed upon the Jews by lay rulers, these reformers said, worked to the detriment of the Christian community. These privileges so favored the Jews that their behavior was threatening not only the faith but Christian society itself. Worse, there were bishops, like Hincmar of Rheims, who

41. Morrison, 1964: passim.
42. Ladner, 1967a: 153–283.
43. Ullmann, 1962: 413–446.

defended royal actions and called them just and congruent with Church standards. The reformist clergy must have felt enormously betrayed. In the third decade of the ninth century, Agobard—Saint Agobard, archbishop of Lyons—declared a verbal war against his opponents. A few years later, in 833, he participated actively in a revolt against the Carolingian emperor Louis the Pious,[44] motivated in no small part by the emperor's policy toward the Jews. Agobard correctly perceived a direct challenge in Louis' insistence that this policy did not violate ecclesiastical law.

In letters to the palace clergy, to Louis the Pious himself, and to the archbishop of Narbonne, Nibridus, Agobard deplored royal behavior. The king had supposedly issued a rescript saying that "no one may baptize the slave of a Jew without the consent of his master. At this, we stand dumbfounded that a decision has gone out from the court of the most Christian and most pious emperor which is so contrary to the law of the Church." Following the decisions of earlier church councils, Agobard assumed that a slave of a Jew who desired baptism would automatically receive it, and that he or she would also be freed. In fact, Roman law was hazy at best about slaves who were owned by Jews and who became Christians. Gregory the Great had said that such slaves became free, but then he added that had these slaves previously been *colonii* (a rough equivalent of the later medieval serf), they remained attached to the soil and must continue to work even the estates of Jews. Quite possibly, Louis the Pious had this ruling of Gregory the Great in mind when he issued a charter to Jews and condemned as violators of Church law those Christians who argued that baptized slaves of Jews became free, even if their owners refused to let them go. Wholly opposed to any such position, Agobard demanded that the emperor "remove this *impedimentum* from the holy Church."[45] Under no circumstances was the latter to forsake his foreordained soteriological role. Indeed,

Omnipotent God has long since prescribed and preordained that you should serve as the pious rector in the future time of perils . . . in the End of Days, . . . [and] matters have at this moment reached that juncture . . . Your *missi,* not acting as your agents in all matters but for the part of another, have showed themselves fierce to Christians and kindly to Jews, especially at Lyons, where they [the *missi*] have construed a persecution against the Church.

44. Bressolles, 1949: 62–63.
45. Gilboa, 1964; Stow, 1974.

This, in turn, emboldened the Jews, who spoke freely before Christians about their religion. For Agobard, this was blasphemy: Jews were corrupting the Christian community. They were allegedly kidnapping young Christians and selling them in distant Spain, as well as "perpetrating many evil deeds" against Christian women they had purchased. These offenses, said Agobard, must not continue. The emperor must start obeying the laws of the Church and reign in the Jews, as

> the most reverend governors of the Gallican Church [prescribed in former times] . . . [They] forbade all social fraternization with Jews . . . prohibited . . . anyone who has become impure through fraternizing and dining with the Jews from breaking bread with any of our priests . . . , [and called it] a sacrilege for Christians to partake of foods coming from . . . Jews; [further, since Jews call our food impure], we Catholics should begin to be inferior to the Jews, if we partake of those things which they serve to us . . . [It was also ordained] that Jews be denied the privilege of free concourse in streets and markets from Maundy Thursday to the first day of Easter.

The forceful opposition of Louis the Pious' *missi* had ensured that none of this ecclesiastical legislation would be observed. Agobard's frustrations accordingly grew. And so did the urgency of his pleas. "Who can doubt," he wrote, "that for all their deeds the Jews are most properly deserving of the greatest hate . . . They are a match for the evil of the Antichrist, presuming to deny that Jesus was Christ . . . They persist in being the sons of the Devil . . . despising the law, spurning the prophets, persecuting the Church, and blaspheming the very son of God." Agobard, when all is said and done, was horrified by the presence of Jews in society.

Yet Agobard did not insist on extreme remedies, even though his accusations embrace nearly every charge that would be leveled against the Jews during the rest of the Middle Ages. He even accused the Jews of flouting their own law. This charge would lie at the root of the attack on the Talmud in the thirteenth century. Agobard also anticipated the eventual host and blood libels by referring to Jewish sexual misconduct and, apparently, to the sexual mutilation of Christian slaves.[46] Agobard did not demand that Jews wear special clothing; that was a device Christians discovered only later, by observing Muslim precedent. But he did object to sexual contacts between Jews and Christians. The prevention of such contacts would be one of the principal reasons dress codes were later put into effect. Agobard's rhetoric would not be surpassed.

46. Blumenkranz, 1955: 572–582; Linder, 1988: no. 117.

Nonetheless, Agobard did not speak of expulsions, nor did he hint at physical violence. All of his emphasis fell on the observance of the law. To that end, he had his "secretary," Florus, collect a large body of past legislation, culled in particular from the edicts of Church councils. Agobard apparently hoped to insert these laws into an even more encompassing body of imperial law, a constitution, in which "there is neither barbarian nor Scythian, neither Aquitanian nor Lombard, neither Burgundian nor Alemanni, neither serf nor freeman, for all are one in Christ." Agobard must have dreamed that once instituted, this constitution would revive the age of the emperor Justinian.[47]

This resolve to consolidate rather than to violate the law underlies Agobard's prudent stricture in his letter to Louis the Pious. "Since they [the Jews] dwell among us, we ought not be malignant to them, nor should we threaten their lives, safety, or property. Let us observe the convention ordained by the Church, which is explicit in defining how we must be at once cautious but humane in our dealings with them." With this stricture, Agobard, at least formally, placed himself midway between Gregory the Great and John Chrysostom. His stance may well be called emblematic of the future. Many ecclesiastics would become as exercised about the Jews as Agobard, some perhaps even more, others less—as is evidenced by reports that the Jews publicly mourned the death of Adelbert of Metz (1004) and Bardo of Mainz (1051),[48] bishops who apparently fell into the latter category. However, few churchmen were to challenge the principle that Jews must be treated "humanely" *(pie tracterentur)*. The principle had been established, after all, by Paul himself. Ecclesiastical demands about regulating the Jews would have their limits. At the same time, those who set the limits were frequently ambivalent about observing them. And the limits themselves were sometimes so narrowly defined that they left the Jews very little room to maneuver. Agobard's missionary activities illustrate this dilemma very well.

In an epistle written sometime before 840, Agobard called upon Louis the Pious to fulfill his spiritual duties. On every Sabbath, Agobard said, he had been sending preachers into the synagogues of his diocese to deliver missionary sermons (surely against the Jews' will), and a number of Jewish young people had asked to be baptized. Jewish parents had reacted by sending their children to Arles, bringing them there from

47. Cited in Langmuir, 1980: 351.
48. Aronius, 1902: nos. 1004,1051.

Macon and Vienne as well, "secretly and especially at night." Hearing of these movements, Agobard summoned to him the remaining Jewish young people of Lyons, of whom as many as fifty-three eventually expressed a desire to convert. Agobard then asked Louis the Pious to pressure the bishop of Arles, so that the children hidden there too might be baptized. He also wanted the emperor to order that the remaining Jewish children in Lyons be raised as Christians. Yet, strangely, Agobard did not see himself as promoting forced conversions. He stressed that he was doing nothing counter to the law, that his actions had harmed no one, and that in fact the emperor had sanctioned his missionary endeavors. In addition, he had returned to their parents the Jewish children of Lyons who refused baptism; the children were untouched both physically and by the oil of the catechumen.[49] Louis the Pious was not convinced, nor, apparently, was his son, Charles the Bald, who may have had a similar encounter with Amulo, Agobard's successor at Lyons, another bishop whose premonitions of living at the End of Days (novissima tempora) and convictions about the Jews' supposedly demonic nature were instrumental in shaping his views.[50]

How often clerics resorted to forced conversions is a matter for conjecture. Surviving accounts of ecclesiastically sponsored forced baptisms in the early Middle Ages are few. Apart from Gregory of Tours's report about Avitus of Clermont and the supposed instructions of Leo VII to Archbishop Frederick of Mainz, and three or four sketchy accounts like that provided by Gregory the Great, only the fantastic tale of Archbishop Eberhard of Trier has survived. As the *Chronicle of Trier* tells us, in 1066 Eberhard "initiated a persecution and then decreed that unless the [Jews] became Christians on the following Sabbath, they would be expelled from the city." In response, the Jews fashioned a waxen image, which they had a renegade monk baptize. Then they burned the image, and when it was half burned the bishop became ill and died. This occurred at just the moment that the bishop was to initiate the mass baptism.[51] This tale has a Hebrew counterpart, purportedly about events in 992. A renegade Jew is said to have accused the Jews of Limoges of placing (once again) a waxen image of the local noble in the ark in their synagogue, alongside the Torah scrolls, and then of crucifying it. Nevertheless, the Jews were miraculously saved. Both of these tales are surely polemical fictions, as perhaps other accounts of forced conversions are, too. Their link with

49. Blumenkranz, 1960: 134–138; idem, 1955: 250–252.
50. Blumenkranz, 1960: 143; idem, 1963: 195–200.
51. Aronius, 1902: no. 1066.

reality can never be known. Jews and Christians preserved them, however, for to the Jews they offered reassurance, and to the clergy they served as a vehicle for expressing their radical will.[52]

In practice, most radicals, even mercurial and litigious ones like Ratherius, the bishop of Verona, understood that they could see their will fulfilled only in fantasy. In 965, Ratherius wrote bitterly to the German emperor Otto I, complaining that Otto's judges were favoring Jews. One of these judges, it appears, had imposed a stiff fine on a cleric for killing a Jew. Worse, the emperor had allowed this fine and had thus become "worse than the Jews . . . [For] he who loves the Jews, who deny God, denies God himself." Jews and Christians in Verona were also publicly discussing and debating their beliefs. The existence of open debates had always bothered clerics, since such debates seemed to put Christians and Jews on a par (although, contradictorily, in many accounts of saints' lives, victory in debating a Jew was often a *de rigueur* element in proofs of sanctity). Stirred up by these debates, Ratherius expressed his outrage: "Do I not have the right," he said, "to fly into a rage when the children of the Devil contest the divinity of Jesus?" Nevertheless, he went on, "I do [not] brutalize them, I would not dare to." That, even Ratherius admitted, Paul's teachings had forbidden, as well as had the canons.[53]

But not all clerics knew how to observe limits. The fictional entries concerning Jews in the diaries of Abbot Guibert of Nogent—who lived toward the end of the eleventh century and about whose relatively normal early life much is known—are violently pornographic. Guibert tells, for example, of the Jewish procurer of Count Jean of Soissons. The use of Jews to provide unsavory services was a tradition in the count's family. His mother had hired a Jew to poison her own brother. This Jew, says Guibert, was burned. (If this is true, it is the first known account of a Jew suffering this punishment, which likely originated at Orleans in 1022 to punish heretics—which Jews were not.) The count's mother then died of paralysis, in a state of filth, like a pig. Following in his mother's footsteps, the count himself "practiced the perfidy of the Jews and heretics to such an extent that he said blasphemous things about the Savior." So crude was he that "although he had a pretty young wife, he scorned her and was in love with a wrinkled old woman. He had a bed in the house of a certain Jew and often had it laid out for him, but he could never be restricted to a bed, and in his raging lust he thrust himself and

52. Haberman, 1971: 11–15; cf. Chazan, 1970.
53. Blumenkranz, 1963: 228–231.

that filthy woman into any foul corner, or, at any rate, some closet. And he ordered a certain parasite to go and lie with his own wife." The count "did not even except nuns or holy women from his abuse." Guibert had successfully fused the Jew's religious image with a social stereotype. As indicated above, medieval reactions to Jews were not motivated solely by religious concerns.[54]

Still, for Guibert, the right order of society hinged on religiosity and its appropriate expression. No vengeance, he said, would sufficiently punish a certain Jew, skilled in medicine and magic, who agreed to be a "mediator" between the Devil and a monk eager to learn the "black arts." For through this Jew's intervention, the monk made to the Devil "a libation of [his] sin," which he then "taste[d] . . . as a celebrant [of the sacrament]," thus "renouncing his faith." Through his cunning, this Jew had turned the world, Guibert's world, upside down. Should not Guibert have rejoiced a short time later when, as he himself reported, hundreds of Jews perished in the massacres that accompanied the First Crusade? Was this not the vengeance he had called for?[55]

Fortunately, Guibert did not represent the norm. By the eleventh century, many clerics were openly calling for restraint. The times were less turbulent, the invasions of the Northmen and the Magyars had been substantially checked, and feudal turmoil had lessened, especially with the appearance of Church-sponsored Truces of God.[56] The Church itself had grown immeasureably stronger as an institution. It was about to assert its independence from control by secular rulers and, through the papacy, to dominate Christian society. Internally, too, the Church was getting its own house in order. Within a short time, in about 1140, it would have a textbook of canon law and then a full-blown legal code, both of which also specified the limits of Jewish behavior. Furthermore, the Church had come to recognize its real enemies, the heretics and Muslims. One launched crusades against them, not against Jews. There were also the first stirrings of a renewed Christian mission, this time to the east. Europe itself was on the way to full Christianization, not only in name but also in terms of a commonly accepted system of values and ideals. Perhaps in reaction to this Christianization, Jews themselves were growing circumspect. If they proselytized, they did so discreetly, and if they debated Christianity's truth, they kept their emotions in check. It would have been hard for Christians to pursue the inflammatory rhetoric

54. Benton, 1970: 134–137,209–211; McLaughlin, 1974.
55. Guibert of Nogent, 1981: 246–248; Golb, 1985: app. 3:5.
56. Southern, 1963: 80–98.

of Agobard, Amulo, and Ratherius and claim that the Jews, in their "public flaunting" of Judaism, posed an active and continuing threat to Christian society. Jews were also maintaining a lower profile. They seem to have turned inward to consolidate their own communities and to establish strict guidelines governing contacts with the outside world. These were momentous changes which many in the Church, perhaps especially Pope Alexander II,[57] well understood.

In 1063 Alexander dispatched letters to the archbishop and viscount of Narbonne and to the body of Spanish bishops. In response to an earlier papal request, these churchmen had restrained the warriors under their command and prevented a Jewish slaughter during recent military operations in Spain. With the indisputable intention of turning this precedent into a rule, the pope specified that the protection of Jews was proper. "The matter of the Jews was entirely different from that of the Saracens: the latter actively engage in war against Christians; the former are everywhere ready to be subservient." By "subservient" Alexander II meant inferior and willing to accept domination. Like Gregory the Great before him, Alexander was repeating the threat of the Theodosian Code that Jews who showed contempt for Christianity would lose their privileges and be considered the Church's adversaries. At the same time, Alexander's letters also reaffirm Paul's teachings about the Jewish soteriological role. The point of these letters is thus a contractual one: if the Jews accept Christian sovereignty, the pope will ensure that the tenets of Christian theology be observed. Moreover, Alexander II was not alone in accepting these contractual terms. The concept that the Church should receive the Jews into Christian society because they were "everywhere prepared to be subservient" was about to gain the widest acceptance. It would become the central principle governing papal-Jewish relations during the next five hundred years. The "contract" itself would be reinforced, first, in the canon *Dispar nimirum est,* which memorializes Alexander II's letters, and, later, in the canon *Sicut iudaeis non,* ultimately named the "Constitution of the Jews." So fixed did these canons become that even the vociferous Dominicans of the thirteenth century reaffirmed them, and two hundred years later the Franciscans, albeit paradoxically, did as well. The argument of the latter, that the Jews ought to be expelled from the cities of northern Italy, rested on the claim that the Jews had violated Alexander II's contractual terms.

Yet in all of this, one item deserves special notice. However much

57. Stow, 1988c: 77–78.

Alexander's letters reflected broad contemporary issues, their immediate stimuli were most likely events of a strictly local nature.[58] In approximately 1041, a certain Baruch of Rome converted to Christianity, married a noble from the Frangipani family, and founded the house of Pierleoni, which numbered among its direct descendents the antipope Anacletus II (1131–1139). His relatives included popes Gregory VI and Gregory VII. By Jewish law, and canon law, too, the Pierleoni were Christians. But for the popular mind and for contemporary political opponents, they were something else. In the 1060s one bishop, Benzo of Alba, spoke condescendingly of Leo, the son of Baruch, saying, "He was a Jew, and he talked like one, too." Remarks like this did not pass the Jews unnoticed. They may also have affected the Pierleoni. Seeing that even after twenty years many Christians were unwilling to forget the family founder's Jewish ancestry, the Pierleoni may have responded positively to a Jewish call of distress. The Pierleoni may in any case have been fulfilling their obligations. The Roman territory controlled by the family embraced the traditional Jewish zone of residence near the Teatro di Marcello. Following normal medieval civic patterns of organization, in which clans, clientage, and areas of residence often overlapped, the Jews of Rome must certainly have been Pierleoni dependents who had to be protected. In addition, Alexander II may have been attracted to the idea of protecting the Jews of Spain for his own reasons. He could use his letters to prove that his war in Spain was a "just war," and, indirectly, he could cite the acceptance of his demands as proof of the feudal sovereignty that he was then claiming over Spain. But these issues were at best secondary ones. The deciding issues were those of patrons and their dependents, not the least of whom was the pope himself. Without the active intervention of the Pierleoni in a disputed election, Alexander II would have never been elected pope. Once elected, refusing a Pierleoni plea to help the Jews was nearly impossible. Important political decisions sometimes have unexpected origins.

As for developments within the Church after Alexander II, we must postpone discussing them until we have looked a bit more closely at the Jews themselves. Up to now, we have considered them only from the Christian viewpoint. With the exception of Paul, we have not met a single Jew face to face.

58. Stow, 1981a: 5–8.

2   Early Medieval Realities

Jewish settlement in early medieval Europe was sparse. Jews dwelled for the most part on the Mediterranean littoral, where they had lived since late antiquity. They clustered along a line leading roughly from Barcelona to Narbonne and Marseilles. Jews also lived in the regions of Sicily and Apulia (the heel) in southern Italy. By the late sixth century, they had moved north to what is now central France, although no records have survived to indicate what happened between that time and the late eighth century, when Jews first reached the edge of the Rhineland. Subsequently, Jewish traders appear to have followed the rivers Moselle, Main, Danube, and, perhaps, sections of the Elbe on the Polish frontier. How permanent their encampments were cannot be specified. The earliest true settlers of the region east of France probably came from central and northern Italy, places which themselves had only recently been settled.[1] The best-known of these settlers was Moshe ben Kalonymos of Lucca, who is often associated with the founding of Ashkenazic culture in the Rhineland.[2] If any of the information concerning him is reliable, it is probable that he migrated north sometime in the tenth century. No Jews are known to have reached England until 1066, and only after that did they permanently settle in the Low Countries.

The number of Jews in any settlement was always small. If Agobard's claim that fifty-three Jewish Lyonnais accepted baptism is correct, then the community of Lyons may have contained hundreds of Jews. It is doubtful that any settlements were larger, except perhaps the oldest of them, in the regions of Marseilles and Narbonne, or towns like Otranto

1. Schwarzfuchs, 1966, 1966a; Blumenkranz, 1966.
2. Grossman, 1981: 55.

and Oria in Apulia. The Roman Jewish population may have been larger yet, but there is no tool for accurately measuring. This lack of precise information about communal size is particularly frustrating. Gravestone inscriptions from contemporary Apulia sometimes indicate age at death, one of the demographer's most important data. By contrast, later on, when better indications about communal size are available, age at death is never mentioned. The language of the Apulian inscriptions, too, is noteworthy: Greek and Latin were used throughout the seventh century, but Hebrew thereafter. The orientation of Jewish culture was clearly changing, turning inward and perhaps becoming introspective. References in these inscriptions to public offices are also informative. Regrettably, there is no way of knowing if these offices were communal, curial, or truly administrative posts. Jews holding administrative office, as well as those who had appointed them, would have been violating Roman and ecclesiastical laws. Almost all of this information, it should be stressed, postdates the seventh century. Concrete data for earlier periods can at most be inferred from documents such as the letters of Gregory the Great, the conciliar decrees cited by Agobard of Lyons, and the chronicle of Gregory of Tours. Circumspection is essential in any efforts to draw firm conclusions.[3]

Some issues are not in doubt. There were Jewish landowners who worked large estates and had Christians in their service. Gregory the Great, in his role as Byzantine regent, determined that pagan slaves of Jews who had converted to Christianity must remain on the Jews' estates as *colonii,* if they did not depart within three months of their conversion. Jews still owned estates in the Narbonne region in the later eighth century, as Pope Stephen IV complained.[4] These Jews, too, had Christians in their service. But whether these Jewish landowners numbered two or two thousand cannot be determined. The same caution applies to the number of Jewish merchants. Jews certainly were active in international commerce, but whether Jews dominated this trade until the mid-tenth century, when Italian merchants initiated their long-lived commercial hegemony, is another matter. Ninth-century commercial charters refer to "Jews and other [international] merchants," but they supply no figures about the proportion between the two.[5] For earlier periods, information is even scarcer. No more is known about attitudes toward these Jewish mer-

3. Colafemmina, 1980: 199; Scharf, 1971: 87–89,122–123.
4. Synan, 1965: 62–63; Linder, 1988: 54:709.
5. Lopez and Raymond, 1955: 31–33.

chants. Should we take the attitude of Gregory of Tours as representative, when he said that Jewish merchants were "crafty," or was he merely reflecting ancient prejudices about commerce?

Jewish merchants unquestionably contributed to Jewish welfare. They performed a vital service by linking together the communities they visited. They also served as intermediaries between Jewish communities and distant civil authorities. Even in the confusion following the rise in Italy of the Lombard kingdom in the late sixth century, Jews could summon help from great distances. It was from traveling Jewish merchants that Gregory the Great learned about forced conversions in Arles and Marseilles. Within their communities, Jews had definite organizational forms. The letters of Gregory the Great, for example, indicate that at Palermo the community possessed a number of public buildings, including perhaps a ritual bath. The Jews of Apulia may have had an elaborate communal structure. But before the late eighth or early ninth century, no more than this is certain.

The Jews: An Early Medieval Political Force?

Despite the scarcity of information, the early medieval period has always been considered a politically favorable one for the Jews, to the extent that they may have even enjoyed real political power. In Septimania (southern France on the Catalan border), a Jewish prince may have ruled a third of the city of Narbonne.[6] Seventh-century Spanish rulers are said to have been forever wrestling with the choice between an alliance with the Jews or a war against them.[7] Jewish political strength has also been made responsible for Agobard's many woes.[8] None of this is wishful thinking. Jews had a clearly demarcated and stable political and social status, which only in later centuries began steadily to erode. In the ninth century, the emperor, the *missi*, and the specially appointed Christian *magister iudaeorum* (Jews' magistrate) formed a united front against reformers like Agobard. However, in defending the Jews, imperial authorities were not necessarily responding to Jewish political pressures. Just how much power, therefore, did the Jews really possess? The answer to this question will determine our understanding of the tenor of early medieval Jewish life, as well as its future implications.

6. Zuckerman, 1972.
7. Bachrach, 1977.
8. Blumenkranz, 1960: 379–381; see also Agus, 1965: 16.

The best proof of royal support and Jewish political power is that provided by descriptions of a Jewish princedom in Narbonne. A late twelfth-century text, an addition to the *Book of Tradition* composed by the Spaniard Abraham ibn Daud in the year 1161, tells a remarkable story. When the city of Narbonne was captured in the mid-eighth century, its conqueror, a certain King Charles (whose identity is unknown), divided the city into three equal parts. One he gave to the ruler, Don Aymerich, a second to the local bishop, and the third to a Rabbi Machir, whom he made a "freeman" to signify the rabbi's high status. In addition, "in his love, he gave the Jews and the city broad privileges and good laws, as it is written in the Christian charter (sealed by the king)." This story, which was written at least four hundred years after the event, would alone have attracted little attention. The charter it mentions is no longer extant. Without the charter, the entire argument suffers. However, the story's claims are repeated in a twelfth-century Latin chronicle, the *Gesta Karoli Magni ad Carcassonam et Narbonam*. According to this chronicle, when the Christians under King Charles stormed Narbonne—roughly the northernmost point of Muslim incursion in Europe—Rabbi Machir swore loyalty to the king in the name of the Jewish community. Once he had captured the city, the king bestowed a third of it upon the rabbi as a reward for his actions. The chronicle appears to be especially credible, since its real intention is to disparage the Jews. The seeming praise of Machir is tempered by the implication that the Jews were less than loyal subjects. Cleverly, the chronicler made his point by having Machir stress that he was free to transfer his allegiance to the king, because neither he nor the Jewish community had sworn an oath of loyalty to the Muslim ruler. This is an obvious allusion to the recurrent Christian theological motif that the Jews are as disloyal to man as they supposedly are to God. But on one crucial point the parallel between the Latin and Hebrew stories breaks down. The Latin contains no reference to the all-important charter. If there was a real Jewish prince in early medieval Narbonne, his existence cannot be proved.[9]

Yet the leader of the Jewish community in Narbonne was called the *Nasi,* or prince. In the twelfth century, he headed the Yeshiva in the city, and his title was transmitted hereditarily in the Kalonymos family. The travelogue of Benjamin of Tudela, dating from about 1160, gives a full description of the *Nasi,* his family, and his family holdings.[10] Jewish

9. Zuckerman, 1972; Grabois, 1966; idem, 1983.
10. Zuckerman, 1972: 58–62; Adler, 1907.

landholding in Narbonne was not something new. Stephen IV had referred to it angrily in his letter from about 770 decrying Christian domestic service to Jews. But the pope's complaints do not necessarily reflect on the *Nasi*. Indeed, the latter's true origins will probably remain forever unknown. It has been suggested that the *Nasi* was the descendant of a Rabbi Natronai. According to the Letter of the Gaon Sherira, written in Baghdad about 987,[11] Natronai was sent west in the late eighth century to bring the text of the Talmud to the communities of southern Europe. But this story may be an apocryphal one. Moreover, it is one question whether Natronai or his descendants became the *Nesiim* (princes) of Narbonne, and another one entirely whether the *Nasi* exercised jurisdictional powers.

The real political strength of early medieval Jews may be inferred from the letters of Gregory the Great. Jews occasionally owned land and controlled pagan slaves and Christians, including Christian domestics. Some Jews, thanks to their business skills, gained entry into royal circles. Others knew how to use weapons. But the evidence substantiates no more than that. One may point to the presence of the Jew Isaac in the delegation sent by Charlemagne to the Caliph Harun al-Rashid in 801. Isaac was the sole returnee from this mission, and he is fabled for having brought with him an elephant, a gift from the caliph to the Carolingian monarch. Yet Isaac was not Charles's ambassador. That post was reserved for a Christian.[12]

Two centuries earlier, about 580, another Jew, Priscus (like Isaac, a royal familiar), was said to be one of the few Jews at the Frankish court who resisted King Chilperic's attempts at forcible conversion. Priscus carried a sword and had a band of armed retainers in his service. But in contemporary terms, this made him only a rich and perhaps influential man. When he was assassinated by a certain Fatir, a converted Jew, his family did not even possess the leverage necessary to prevent Fatir's eventual pardon.[13] There were, of course, Jewish physicians of renown (Jewish physicians, as Chrysostom had lamented, were already active in fourth-century Antioch) and occasionally a Jewish customs official, especially in ninth-century France. The first that is heard about Jews engaged in this activity afterward is when Gregory VII complained about it to Alexander VI of Iberian Leon in the later eleventh century. Most notable Jews were no more than rich merchants. The daring of these merchants

11. Levin, 1972: 104.
12. Aronius, 1902: nos. 68,70,71.
13. Gregory of Tours, 1927: 6:5,10.

was astounding, even legendary. A ninth-century Abassid geographer, Ibn Khurrdadhbih, left an account of their journeys from western Europe to central Asia and as far as China, preceding the Marco Polos of Venice by centuries.[14] Nevertheless, many of these Jewish merchants may have resided permanently in the East. Their weight in European Jewish affairs would have been only marginal.

Had the Jews exercised real power, somebody would have said so. Stephen IV did not;[15] neither did Agobard, except to say that Jews had great influence with the *missi* and the *magister iudaeorum*. References to political power are also the exception in canons promulgated at Church councils from the fifth through the ninth centuries. Agobard cited a large number of these canons in order to demonstrate that his position was a venerable one which merited both royal and episcopal support. But he cited only three canons relating to the subject of Jewish power, one from the Council of Orleans in the later fifth century forbidding Jews to summon Christians to court, another from Macon in 581 stating that no Jew could serve as a judge or customs official, and a third from Paris in 614 declaring that Jews could not be government officials.[16] Had these edicts been frequently repeated, Agobard would have said so. His search for canonical support was also thorough. He failed to note only three canons restricting Jewish political activity, which were passed at the councils of Clermont (in 535), Reims (in 624), and Clichy (in 626). The last repeated verbatim the Parisian canon of 614. In 850, after the time of Agobard, a council at Pavia enacted similar legislation.[17] In any case, these canons essentially renewed decrees found in recensions of the late Roman law. Their presence in the conciliar codes may have been solely a pro forma one. The only early medieval conciliar edicts that unquestionably do reflect real problems are the numerous ones that prohibit mixed dining, social contacts, and control over Christian servants and slaves. The existence of these problems is corroborated by various papal letters. But they are problems of social ascendency, not jurisdiction.

Moreover, chronicles from the late sixth and early seventh centuries record that this was a time of extreme Jewish trial. In the 590s, King Chilperic is said to have expelled the Jews from France, and King Dagobert is said to have done likewise in the 620s. In 661, Pertaric

14. Lopez and Raymond, 1955: 30–31.
15. Zuckerman, 1972: 50–58.
16. Blumenkranz, 1955: 568–569.
17. Linder, 1988: 75:832, 76:839, 90:869.

expelled the handful of Jews residing in the Lombard realms of central and northern Italy.[18] Yet these expulsions, especially in France, were temporary in nature and limited in scope, circumstances that suggest Jewish weakness. Had the Jews wielded real political or military power, it is likely that their expulsion would have been permanent, or, more probably, they would have been physically destroyed. On the other hand, it may be countered that expulsions in the seventh century do not preclude the Jews' acquisition of power by the ninth century, a time when Jewish merchant activity attained its greatest importance. But to take this position requires making the unwarranted assumption that the Jews turned defeat into victory. It is no less problematic to argue, as has been done,[19] that throughout the seventh century, the Jews of Visigothic Spain, who were not few in number, were sufficiently powerful and influential to resist—sometimes forcefully—a sustained royal conversionary policy. Matters were far more complex. In fact, nearly everything about the Visigothic episode—however indicative it was of future developments—was unique.

In 613, the Visigothic king Sisebut ordered that all the Jews of his realm be baptized. During the following ninety-eight years, prodigious but unsuccessful efforts were made to have this order enforced. Only the Arab conquest of the Iberian peninsula in the year 711 brought these efforts to a halt.[20]

The events of these years have fascinated generations of historians.[21] For one thing, the events themselves were anomalous. In the future, kings who wanted to be rid of their Jews expelled them. Possibly, this was the solution preferred by the Visigoths' Gallic contemporaries, Chilperic and Dagobert, although Gregory of Tours claims Chilperic tried forcibly to convert the Jews connected to his court. The only two monarchs who truly repeated the Visigothic experiment were King Manuel of Portugal in 1497 and the Roman emperor Heraclius, whose decree of 634 ordering forced conversion followed that of Sisebut by twenty years. The Visigothic policy was also a fierce one. Those who escaped the Visigoths' edict fled for their lives. By contrast, in 1492 Ferdinand and Isabella gave all the Jews of Spain the choice of conversion or exile, and,

18. Baron, 1952: 3:53–54, 4:24–25.

19. Bachrach, 1973.

20. Blumenkranz, 1960: 107–108; Rabello, 1983: 52; cf. Parkes, 1934: 345–370.

21. E.g., Ben-Sasson, 1976; Rabello, 1983; Juster, 1976; Thompson, 1966; Glick, 1979; Bachrach, 1973; Baron, 1952: vol. 3; Blumenkranz, 1960.

like Edward I of England in 1290, they insisted that their decree of expulsion be justly executed. In addition, the Visigoths uniquely tried to legitimate their policy by anchoring forced conversion in law. They also created a "Jewish problem." In order to ensure that the forcibly converted Jews observed Christian ritual, the Visigothic kings instituted a host of regulatory measures and appointed the clergy as overseers. The converted Jews became a constant, as well as a highly visible, preoccupation.

The story begins in the mid-fifth century with the Visigothic conquest of Spain. The conquerors found themselves confronting the native Hispani, who were Romans by culture and law and Catholics by faith. The Visigoths were Arians, Christians who did not believe in the equally divine status of all members of the Trinity. The friction between conqueror and conquered never dissipated. The Jews of Spain, whose settlement was ancient and surely a large one—perhaps running into the thousands—identified culturally and civically with the Hispani. Jews, after all, were legally Romans. The Breviary, an abbreviated compendium of Roman law which King Alaric II issued in 506, specifically included Jews among those whom Roman law governed.[22] Of course, the Jews did not enjoy first-class legal status. The Breviary included many of the restrictions codified by Theodosius in 438. To these, local Church councils added limitations of their own, such as those concerning sexual contact and mixed marriages. In 306, even before the conversion of Constantine, the Council of Elvira demanded that Christians not summon Jews to bless their crops. But it is doubtful that anyone enforced these restrictions. The status of the Jews in early Visigothic Spain must have been similar to that enjoyed by their southern Italian counterparts.

In the year 587, the Visigothic king Reccared embraced Catholicism, and almost at once he prohibited Jews from owning Christian slaves and holding public office. Reccared also participated in the Third Toledan Council of 589, which elaborated on existing laws forbidding concubinage between Christians and Jews by demanding that the children of such unions be raised as Christians. Nevertheless, it was only in 613, a quarter of a century later, that Sisebut issued his revolutionary edict. The specific stimuli that motivated Sisebut are not known, nor, for that matter, are the details of what occurred during the subsequent twenty years. But in 633, the Fourth Toledan Council decreed that all Jews who had become Christians "ought to be forced to preserve their [new] faith."[23] Only

22. Colorni, 1945: 25.
23. Rabello, 1983: 56–59.

thirty years earlier Gregory the Great had assumed that forced converts would inevitably return to Judaism, yet he had suggested no counter-measures. The decree of the 633 Toledan Council thus set a new course. Throughout the seventh century, councils met at Toledo, issued ever more threatening decrees, and instituted increasingly harsh penalties for apostasy, which was rife. In desperation, the Seventeenth Toledan Council of 694 ordered that all Jews be enslaved and their property confiscated. Their children were to be removed, placed in Christian households, and eventually given in marriage to Christians. However, it was not the council but King Egica who devised these measures. The Toledan councils had in fact always been summoned and presided over by the kings. Thus, it is unclear whether the force behind the Toledan decrees, like that behind the policy they were intended to shore up, was a royal or an ecclesiastical one.

The policy's effects are equally uncertain. Not only was it generally ineffective, but the decrees issued to enforce it refer to even converts as "Jews," suggesting that converted Jews, just as they would be in Spain eight hundred years later, were being treated as a separate class of Christians.[24] Indeed, the term "Jews" in these decrees—conforming to Visigothic taxonomies—may refer to cultural identity, not religious beliefs.[25] Such provocative as well as unresolved problems have stimulated divergent, sometimes partisan explanations. For example, it is has been said that the kings or the churchmen—or the two working in concert—acted out of religious zeal and, possibly, outright hatred. Alternatively, the kings are pictured as initiating a conversionary policy for "reasons of state," but then as falling into an ecclesiastical trap. A more troublesome explanation is that the kings cynically made the Jews into scapegoats to detract attention from their own failure to unite and rule the country. More weight may be given to the views that forced conversion was intended to end Jewish economic competition and Jewish political power and that the kings wished to halt unacceptable Jewish missionary activities. Yet although these explanations may be factual, they do not consider the politics, mentalities, and shape of Visigothic society as a whole. Even the primary question of responsibility, of who initiated the conversionary policy, remains unresolved.

At first blush, the initiative seems to have been an exclusively royal one. Apart from isolated bishops, such as the roughly contemporary ones

24. See Yerushalmi, 1971: 1–50.
25. Cf. Albert, 1990.

of Arles and Marseilles, no body of ecclesiastical officials ever ordered forced baptisms, and it strains probability to argue that clerics adroitly manipulated the kings into adopting a purely clerical policy. Royal involvement after 613 also increased. In 636, King Chintilla forbade all non-Catholics from residing in Spain and categorized nonbaptized Jews as criminals. In the 640s, King Chindaswith declared circumcision to be a capital offense. And in 654, King Recesswinth abrogated the Breviary of Alaric, placing the baptized "Jews," together with the Hispani, under the jurisdiction of the Visigothic laws. To ensure that these "Jews" behaved like Christians, Recesswinth and, later, Erwig instituted *placita,* or professions of faith. "We will not," the Jews had to affirm, "choose wives from our own people, but in the case of both sexes we will always link ourselves in matrimony with Christians. We will not practice carnal circumcision, or celebrate the Passover, the Sabbath or the other feast days connected with the Jewish belief. We will not keep to our old habit of discrimination in the matter of food."[26] "Jews" also enjoyed limited rights, continuing to be prohibited, as they were before baptism (according to the Breviary) from holding public office. For all that, there was considerable imprecision. For a time, the laws distinguished between "Jews," "baptized Jews," and "sincere converts," until in 694 the "Jews" aligned themselves with royal enemies, and King Egica eliminated these distinctions and lumped all "Jews" together as traitors. The measures to ensure their conversion had failed. The Jews were fleeing en masse the embrace of Christianity and its sacraments.

The Jews' flight from Christianity should have particularly aroused clerical ire. Why should ritual and creedal deviance have so deeply troubled the kings? Yet at least during the first two decades of the forced conversion policy, the clergy was ambivalent. In 638, Bishop Braulio of Saragossa wrote to Pope Honorius I, expressing his reservations about abandoning the permissive stance toward forced converts espoused by Gregory the Great.[27] Previously, at the Fourth Toledan Council of 633, where the Church Father Isidore of Seville was the dominant ecclesiastic, clerics argued that forced baptism was illegal. Isidore himself questioned the "hazy zeal" that inspired Sisebut. Nevertheless, at this same council, clerics also insisted (setting a lasting precedent) that irrespective of the circumstances of their baptisms, former Jews be indiscriminately made to practice Catholic rites. The council members further directed that chil-

26. Parkes, 1934: 394–395.
27. Blumenkranz, 1963: 103–105.

dren of apostates be taken from their parents. Despite some initial diffidence, therefore, the clergy appears to have initiated many of the strong measures that reinforced Sisebut's original edict. Succeeding Toledan councils even enlarged on the Fourth Council's decrees. In violation of the canon that baptism creates a "new man," the Sixth Council of 638 ordered Christians to refrain from dining or bathing with Jews, and from visiting Jewish physicians. However, by "Jews" the council meant those who had been baptized. Isidore's protests about force aside, the council could not have been referring to actual Jews in feigned ignorance of Sisebut's decree, nor, under the circumstances, was it mechanically repeating earlier edicts, as sometimes occurred. Churchmen, in fact, seem to have become increasingly radicalized. At the Council of 638 they demanded that whoever attains the crown of the kingdom in the future is not to enter his palace until he swears "not to aid [the Jews] in their treason."

The clergy's most provocative act was to participate in formulating the Visigothic laws. Only clerics were sufficiently educated, as well as ready, to perform this service. No lay Hispanus would have willingly participated in the dismantling of the legal and constitutional system under which he had lived for centuries. Bishops like Ildefonse of Toledo, who called the synagogue a barn and the Jews themselves a bad limb that required amputation, had sufficient motivation.[28] Indeed, attitudes like his have persuaded some historians that in Visigothic Spain, it was the clerics who led and the kings who followed. The latter adopted a clerical program because in order to unify the Visigothic kingdom, they needed Church aid. But if so, then why was it the kings who presided over the Toledan councils, and why did they outdo the clergy in calling circumcision an "abomination," in labeling Jewish customs a "contagious plague [which] has infested the lands we rule," and in prefacing the Visigothic laws by saying that it was the royal duty "to uproot the entire error of the Jews"? To be sure, the sixteenth-century Jewish chronicler Joseph Ha-Cohen reports that between 621 and 631 Swinthila summoned back from exile the Jews who had fled Spain in 613 and allowed baptized Jews to revert to Judaism. And such information has led to the conclusion that Visigothic policy shifted, as did the alliances the kings made or broke with the supposedly politically and militarily powerful Jews.[29] Practicing Jews who fled Spain in 613 for southern France are even said to have

28. Blumenkranz, 1963: 111–116.
29. Bachrach, 1973.

been readmitted. Yet even were this reconstruction true, it does not explain why no Visigothic king annulled Sisebut's original edict, nor does it account for the enormity of royal piety.

Moreover, piety did not mean the same thing for kings and clergy, nor did both react equally to its imperatives. However great their zeal, most churchmen would not have exceeded the limits set by Ambrose and Chrysostom and would not have actually counseled or participated in forced baptisms. Converts who returned to Judaism were another matter. A society blemished with heretics and backsliders could not realize Augustine's Idea of Reform, which surely served as an ideal for Visigothic churchmen no less than it served Agobard two hundred years later. The sources of royal piety were much more complex. On one level, the Visigothic kings stood at the head of their church and considered themselves responsible for religious order in their kingdom. But that order required only the formal piety expressed by rigorously enforcing restrictive canons. There was no need for extremes, particularly to curry clerical favor. The clergy was not in a position to help the king unify the kingdom; power in Visigothic Spain was in the hands of local counts, including some who chose to ignore the forced conversionary order. Nor did issues of economic piety have to be addressed. Jews might somehow have been suspect because many of them were merchants, but conversion did nothing to remedy this fact. Indeed, as Christians, their economic clout might actually increase.

In one area alone did the Jews create a dilemma severe enough to push the kings to extremes. Together with the Hispani, the Jews possessed social, cultural, and legal structures that competed with those of the Visigoths.[30] As long as this institutional gap remained open, it was impossible for the latter to dominate Spanish society and anchor their authority. Even if they succeeded in pacifying the unruly nobility, they would always, and visibly, remain conquering outsiders. The gap had to be closed, and this the Visigoths first tried to do by converting to Catholicism. The next, in fact unavoidable step was forcibly to convert the Jews. But as the Visigoths soon learned, in the later sixth century uniformity of religion did not necessarily produce an equal uniformity of society, law, and culture. That could be achieved only by imposition from the top down. Accordingly, in 654, the Visigoths abrogated the Breviary of Alaric and made the Visigothic laws universally binding in their place. The

30. Glick, 1979: 14,27-33,289.

Hispani and others who had lived by the now-defunct Roman law, particularly the (even converted) Jews, lost their legal and constitutional distinctiveness. Their cultures, too, were threatened. Indeed, the formal professions of Christian faith which in 654 Spanish Jews were forced to make effectively affirmed their amalgamation into the new Visigothic institutional and cultural (religious) order. By instituting a single body of law, therefore, the Visigoths were seeking to erect a homogeneous social pyramid, from whose apex they proposed to reign supremely. Put another way, Visigothic policy toward the Jews was integral to overall Visigothic aims. The emotional royal response its failure evoked—expressed in terms of pious outrage—was only to be expected.

The Visigothic failure was in fact a total one. Its example and memory may have even helped persuade subsequent medieval European rulers who sought social, institutional, and religious homogeneity in their realms to opt—as did most notably Ferdinand and Isabella in 1492—for expulsion over forcible conversion.[31] The decree issued at the Fourth Toledan Council against backsliding also endured, to be reiterated first in the ninth century by Gregory IV, and then in 1298 by Boniface VIII, who conferred upon it canonical status. Only those who could prove that they had vigorously resisted baptism were exempted from this rule. Such persons were obviously few.[32] Finally, there is the issue of Jewish political loyalty. Both medieval chroniclers and modern historians have said that in 711, the Jews rushed to the aid of the Muslims who invaded Spain.[33] In fact, the Jews had much to fear. There is no certainty that Spanish Jews knew of their Islamic status as a tolerated People of the Book, which exempted them from being forced to convert (as were the other peoples the Muslims conquered). Spanish Jews may instead have heard that Mohammed had massacred the Jewish tribes of Medina.[34] What would happen to them in Spain was not clear. More tangibly, the Visigothic kings had harassed the Jews, but much of the nobility had not; on the contrary, it had aided them in avoiding the royal decrees. Why should the Jews now turn their backs on these longtime friends? The contention of later chroniclers that the Jews went to war against the Christians was thus a probable fabrication. Following medieval practice, these chroniclers were describing theological topoi, not events: to wit, the claim of

31. Baer, 1936: 404–408; Kriegel, 1978b.
32. Grayzel, 1989: 209.
33. Zuckerman, 1972: 47–48; Rabello, 1983: 79–80.
34. Stillman, 1979: 3–22.

the author of the *Gesta Karoli,* who intimated that in 759 the Jews of Narbonne deserted the Muslims, because the former were no more loyal to man than they were to God.[35]

Such typological fantasizing, in the context of the actual events of Visigothic Spain, does not strengthen claims about Jewish power. If the Jews escaped the effects of forced baptism, it was only because the kings were weak and the nobility, which protected the Jews in order to flout the king and derive political and commercial advantage, was strong. Jewish participation in the revolts at the end of the seventh century—such as that of 673, when they sided with the lords of Septimania against Wamba—cannot have been weighty. A more accurate measure of Jewish strength at this time is provided indirectly by the Chronicle of Gregory of Tours.

Gregory of Tours: Reliable Barometer of Opinion

The chronicle of Gregory of Tours, *The History of the Franks,* is our most descriptive source for the early Middle Ages. It tells of Jewish merchants, the presence at court of Jews such as Priscus, and King Chilperic's possible involvement in an episode of forced baptism. But Gregory's Jews do not have clout. Wealthy Jews with court connections carried swords and had armed retainers, but this act no more made them warlords than did the defensive stationing of armed Jews on the walls of Arles in 508 and on those of Naples in 536. Gregory's stories do bespeak an intimacy between Jews and kings. That intimacy must be understood in its proper context. Usually it is said that from the fall of the Roman Empire through as late as the twelfth century, in Carolingian and Capetian France, as well as in eleventh- and twelfth-century Christian Spain, Jews and kings accommodated each other in what has been been named a Jewish royal "alliance."[36] Attention has been given to the threatening nature of late sixth-century and early seventh-century royal initiatives, and even to purported incidents in the early eleventh century of forced conversion, principally the one attributed to the Capetian king Robert the Pious. Nevertheless, these events are viewed as interruptions in an otherwise consistently positive royal-Jewish relationship. After all, in the sixth and seventh centuries, even while Chilperic and Dagobert were expelling Jews or

35. Zuckerman, 1972: 379; and see Ravid, 1983; Ben Sasson, 1976: 409.
36. Chazan, 1973: 12.

possibly pressuring some to convert, other rulers, such as Brunhilde Queen of Neustria, allowed Jews to possess Christian slaves. Hence, with few exceptions, an appealing symmetrical reconstruction has been made. In the early Middle Ages, motivated by economic and other practical needs, secular rulers fostered Jewish settlement and commerce and re- sisted ecclesiastical pressures. In the High (later) Middle Ages, because the Jews no longer were valuable, secular rulers acceded to these pres- sures and made Jewish life exceedingly difficult, and worse. Yet does this reconstruction really reflect the course of events? The tales of Gregory of Tours suggest that it may not. Indeed, Gregory's descriptions of the Jews' early medieval vicissitudes suggest that their situation was far less envi- able than has often been argued.[37]

Gregory's kings (mostly powerful lords, not royalty) hold the Jews in disdain. They are an odious bunch of sycophants, who merit little ɔn- sideration. King Guntram remarks cynically to his familiars that the Jews of Nevers are deceitful. They have come out to greet him, because they hope he will order the rebuilding of the synagogue a local mob destroyed; but he, Guntram, intends to disappoint them. Chilperic, too, keeps the Jews under his thumb. Priscus' spirited argument against the virtues of Christianity does not prevent Chilperic from ordering him to be baptized. Priscus delays this eventuality by pleading that he must go to Spain for his son's wedding (an indication of how extensive the network of Jewish relations was). But he swears to become a Christian immediately after- ward. In fact, Priscus intended to remain precisely what he was—namely a Jew so observant that, scrupulously obeying the halachah (Jewish law), he went to synagogue on the Sabbath (as Gregory of Tours put it) "carrying no iron."

Gregory, of course, should rarely if ever be taken at face value.[38] For example, in 576, Avitus, bishop of Clermont, presided over the mass baptism of five hundred Jews. This ceremony, with the Jews all dressed in white, took place only ten days after the violent destruction of the Jews' synagogue by the people of Clermont. One Jew had agreed to convert, but during the procession to the baptismal font, another threw rancid oil onto his head. At the first opportunity, the populace rioted. Nevertheless, Avitus pressed on with his sermons until nearly the whole of the Jewish community decided to embrace Christianity. The remaining

37. E.g., Baron, 1952: 3:24–27, 4:36–53; Agus, 1969: 12–18; Blumenkranz, 1960: 1–64,294–306; cf. Schwarzfuchs, 1966: 125; Parkes, 1934: 330–339.

38. Gregory of Tours, 1927: 6:11, 6:10; see also Gurevitch, 1988: passim.

Jews, who refused baptism, left Clermont for Marseilles. Yet even assuming that the number five hundred is an exaggerated one, a massive voluntary baptism at this time and place seems doubtful. These doubts grow upon seeing how Avitus persuaded the Jews to convert simply by invoking the eschatological vision from John (chapter 10) that speaks of a future union of all mankind into a single flock under a single pastor. The story conveyed by the Avitus episode is thus a subtle one. It is a hagiography, a saint's life, as well as a chapter in the world's progress to salvation, a theme all medieval chronicles shared. The backdrop of white purity and the spontaneous perception of eternal verities by five hundred Jews are thus foregone conclusions. But why is it that so many Jews leave for Marseilles? Possibly because this story was really one of a forced conversion, in which Jewish eyes were opened not by Avitus' sermons but by the threats of expulsion—and perhaps worse—which, in an unguarded passage, Gregory admits were made. At the same time, this story may also have been wish fulfilling, invented out of whole cloth. Traditional methods of preaching, as Gregory himself learned five years later, when he failed to convert Priscus, rarely worked. In which case, doubt may also be cast on the amount of pressure applied by King Chilperic to this same hapless Jew.

These stories have yet another level. Gregory may inflate reality and cast it in typological terms, but unlike Agobard later, Gregory does not invest every event with cosmic significance. Accordingly, Gregory's stories may be discriminatingly read as an approximate mirror of social opinion. Most often, Gregory's Jews are simply unpleasant types. They are the sniveling sycophants of the Guntram story, the crafty businessmen who trick Bishop Cuttino, a priest who spends his time trading with Jews rather than preaching salvation to them, and the physicians who heal by cupping. Their worthless medicine brings back blindness to Leonast, archdeacon of Bourges, when in his lack of faith he turned to the Jews rather than to prayer. Gregory's Jews are also anxious creditors—with Christian partners—excessively badgering Frankish nobles to pay off their debts and viewed with too much contempt for anyone to bother testifying when subsequently they were murdered.[39] Moreover, whatever services, especially commercial ones, that Jews provided could be just as easily provided after baptism as before. There was every reason to encourage if not actually to pressure Jews into taking this step. Of course,

39. Gregory of Tours, 1927: 4:8, 5:6; see Dietrich, 1991.

the events at the courts of Guntram and Chilperic—and at those of Dagobert in the 620s and of Pertaric in the 660s—were too sporadic and too loosely related to be identified with the consistent policies of the Visigothic kings of Spain. But they do reveal a royalty that willingly ignored the fundamental obligation no Roman emperor had ever eschewed—namely, of ensuring that Jews enjoyed the protection of the laws and were allowed to observe their rituals unmolested.[40] The early Middle Ages were certainly not the time of a royal Jewish entente.

Carolingian Balance

Our understanding of the stories told by Gregory of Tours would be fuller if we knew more about what happened between the years 600 and 800. Did the negative image of the Jews, so widely entertained in the period of the Merovingian kings, persist during these two centuries and survive into the age of the Carolingians, the descendants of Charlemagne? Regrettably, except for the events of Visigothic Spain, we remain in near if not total darkness about this time. To compound the problem, what information we do have from the ninth century must be carefully filtered. Agobard's lament is not reliable as a source of hard facts. And the so-called Laws of Charlemagne, which restricted the Jews economically, religiously, and judicially, are probably a fiction from the later ninth century at the earliest.[41] They say nothing about Charlemagne's actual policies. At the same time, the little that is known shows that the major parameters of Jewish life were unchanged. There were still Jewish landowners, perhaps in numbers similar to those of earlier centuries, and there were merchants, whose number and importance probably increased in the wake of the Muslim invasions, although not in geometric terms. Ecclesiastical attitudes remained fairly constant. The differences between Agobard of Lyons and Avitus of Clermont are ones of sophistication and restraint. The Carolingian age also continued Roman law traditions; some that had fallen into disuse in the seventh century were even reinstated. No shift in the Jews' constitutional status took place; in fact, it was restabilizing in the direction of the status the Jews had been assigned in the time of the late Roman Empire. However, legal and constitutional stability should not be confused with permissiveness; past legislation was

40. *Corpus iuris civilis*, 1906: Code, bk. 1, title 9, law 14 (13).
41. Aronius, 1902: nos. 73,76,78.

not jettisoned, and Jewish activities were still severely circumscribed. For example, as had already been the case in late antiquity, Jews could not openly solicit proselytes. Nor could anyone desert Christianity in favor of Judaism without endangering himself. This point is made incontrovertibly by the story of the conversion of Bodo, a deacon at the court of Louis the Pious. The events took place in the year 839.[42]

Contemporary reports do not explain why Bodo embraced Judaism. Typically, he was accused of being "seduced by the Enemy of Mankind." And more informatively, he was called "a prisoner of *cupiditas* [passion]," in this case surely that of a sexual kind. Yet the latter was principally a criticism of Judaism's more open sexual teachings. For Bodo to have converted in order to enjoy the sexual prerogatives of marriage would have made little sense; in the ninth century, he could have done so nearly unhampered even as a priest. Bodo's probable motives were sincere. After his conversion, he embraced Judaism wholeheartedly, underwent circumcision, and grew a beard. There would be a trickle of converts to Judaism throughout the Middle Ages, especially among clerics. Besides Bodo, other clerical proselytes were Vecelin, André the archbishop of Bari, and Obadiah the Norman, famous for his musical compositions and known in Hebrew literature as Obadiah the Proselyte. Jewish proselytes also perished in the massacres of the first Crusade.

Conversion to Judaism is a subject about which too little is known.[43] Possibly, Jewish proselytizing efforts remained intensive almost to the time of the Crusades. Gregory the Great, for example, complained that some Christians were refusing to work on the Jewish Sabbath, and the Council of Coyaza in Spain in 1050 ordered Christians not to live together with Jews in one building.[44] Apparently, these Christians were being subjected to Jewish influences. But this does not mean the Jews were actively proselytizing, let alone winning converts. Actual conversion to Judaism was probably limited to those few individuals who somehow voluntarily persuaded themselves that Judaism rather than Christianity was the way of God's People. To be sure, in the Khazar kingdom on the northern shore of the Black Sea, the entire population, or at the least its ruling strata, converted to Judaism sometime around the year 900. But the Jewish missionaries who may have proselytized in this kingdom must have come from the Byzantine Empire or the Muslim East. The Khazar

42. Blumenkranz, 1963: 184–185.
43. Goitein, 1953; Golb, 1965; idem, 1965a; Blumenkranz, 1963a.
44. Blumenkranz, 1960: 173,176.

episode would also have stirred few to emulation. Toward the end of the eleventh century, the kingdom was conquered and all traces of Judaism wiped out.[45]

Converts to Judaism were indeed socially intolerable. Deserters, as converts were—from the flock of the freewoman Sarah to that of the slave Hagar—posed for Christians a true psychological threat. As a rule, therefore, converts were forced to flee, often to the Muslim East. Bodo went to Saragossa in Muslim Spain, where, renamed Eleazar, he engaged in a testy religious debate with one Paolo Alvaro, a debate made notable by Alvaro's lament that Bodo's knowledge of the Hebrew Bible gave him a significant advantage.[46]

The story of Bodo leaves no doubt that imperial authorities felt obligated to protect the Christian faith. Yet the criticisms Agobard of Lyons leveled at Louis the Pious imply that Louis selectively defined his obligations, apparently preferring the secular welfare of his realms to that of the faith. The charters of privilege that Louis the Pious granted to Jewish merchants—the forerunners, in fact, of all others the Jews in medieval Europe would receive—reveal that Agobard was far off the mark.

Perhaps the most important technical characteristic of the Carolingian charters is their nature as grants of privileges to individuals. They are not constitutions defining the rights and privileges of a people as a whole. Charters issued from the eleventh century onward would be precisely that. It is important to make this distinction, since the wording of the later charters differs little from that of the Carolingian ones. The individual nature of the Carolingian charters may be seen in two ways. First, they are addressed to specific individuals or companies of individuals. They contain no hint that their paragraphs apply to a larger group than that which the individuals represent. Second, three variants of Louis the Pious' charters are known by way of a formulary. Formularies were the medieval equivalent of present-day printed legal forms, and documents were included in them to simplify their reissuance. The clerics of Louis the Pious' court who copied the Jewish charters into a formulary must have assumed that the emperor, or his successors, had every intention of issuing more of them. And quite possibly this occurred. Frequent repetition is not characteristic of constitutions.

The Carolingian charters grant privileges to their addressees in three

45. Dunlop, 1967, passim.
46. Blumenkranz, 1963: 184–191.

separate spheres: commerce, slave trading, and protection. The words of the charters are clear enough to let them speak for themselves. Here is one example:

> May all people know that we have taken under our protection [*defensione*] the following Hebrews, R. Domatus and his nephew Samuel. Accordingly, neither you nor your juniors nor your successors should presume to disturb these Jews illegally or to cause them physical harm. Nor should you at any time presume to seize from them any of their private property or to take any of the possessions they now legally own. Do not presume to exact from the above Hebrews taxes, horse fees, residence fees, and road tolls. In addition, we permit them to trade and freely to sell their possessions to whomever they will. They have the right of living by their own laws. And they may hire Christian [men] to work for them, except on Christian feast days and Sundays. They are also free to acquire foreign slaves and to sell them within our borders. If a Christian has a dispute or litigation with them, he must bring in his behalf three acceptable Christian witnesses, in addition to three acceptable Hebrew ones, and thus argue his case. If Jews have a dispute or litigation with a Christian, they must produce Christian witnesses in their behalf. These Hebrews complained to us about certain Christians, who, to the detriment of the Christian religion, have induced slaves of the Hebrews to despise their masters and to have themselves baptized, as if this were a Christian principle. More precisely, they urge these slaves to be baptized in order to free themselves from their masters. The sacred canons in no way ordain such manumission; in fact, they decree that perpetrators of this [crime] be punished by excommunication. Thus, we desire that you do not presume to do this thing [and allow manumissions] in the future, nor should you permit any of your subordinates to do so. Be aware that whoever perpetrates such an act will not escape, once we are informed of it. He will endanger his life and his possessions. Further, you are to make it known that anyone who plots against their lives [of these Jews] or actually murders one of them will have to pay our "palace" ten pounds of gold, for we have taken these Hebrews into our protection [*mundeburdo et defensio*] so long as they remain faithful to us. Under no circumstances do we wish that these Jews undergo judgment by trial—that is, by fire, boiling water, or the rod—except where their law permits it.[47]

The commercial clauses pose no interpretative difficulties. They confirm what has been said so far, including what has been said about the clauses exempting the Jews from tolls to expedite the movement of merchandise. The slavery clauses are not so transparent. The Jews are permitted freely to engage in this trade, to which no one attached opprobrium at this time,

47. Aronius, 1902: nos. 81,82,83.

on the condition that they purchased the slaves, presumably pagans, outside Christian lands. But what then happened if these slaves requested to be baptized? Agobard claimed that this automatically liberated them. The Theodosian Code said Jews could possess Christian slaves, although they could not purchase them; it also ordered provincial judges to be wary of those who claimed otherwise. Gregory the Great took a midway position, preferring liberation but noting exceptions to the rule. In the time of Louis the Pious, there seems to have been no fixed Church law or precedent establishing whether slaves who accepted baptism must be liberated. When Louis the Pious rejected Agobard's demands and claimed the "sacred canons" made no provision for the liberation of baptized slaves, he must have been convinced that he was acting justly and that he was not weakening the faith in favor of commercial advantage. His insistence that Jews not employ Christian men on Sundays conformed to long-standing ecclesiastical demands. Such demands also explain the apparent obligation of Jewish litigants to prove their cases against Christians by calling *only* Christian witnesses. Since the fifth century, Church councils had protested against Christians' being convicted by Jewish testimony. Louis the Pious thus responded to ecclesiastical demands when he deemed them justified. His was not a policy that may be called "favorable" to the Jews. If Louis favored anything, it was the rule of law, ecclesiastical or otherwise.[48]

It was his commitment to law that explains why, despite clerical protests, Louis also stipulated that Christian litigants had to produce Jewish witnesses. This stipulation set precedent. It reappeared in charters given as late as the thirteenth century, and even the popes accepted its legitimacy when Jews were accused of such alleged crimes as ritual murder—although not in civil or criminal disputes.[49] The charters of Louis the Pious also paraphrased the cornerstone of Jewish legal protection, the Roman law *nullus*. No one was to disturb the Jews or to seize their property without due legal process. Punishments and distraints were a monopoly of the authorities. For this reason, anyone attacking a Jew who possessed a royal charter paid a fine to the royal "palace." These fines signified not Jewish dependence but rather a royal commitment to maintain peace and avenge wrongs. They were a function of the special relationship that existed between privileged merchants, or other privi-

48. Lotter, 1989: 35–36; Blumenkranz, 1960: 354.
49. Grayzel, 1989: 116,118, n. 3.

leged individuals, and the royal court. Jews were not the only ones whose death was avenged by a fine paid to the king. Such fines were a characteristic of the institution of *tuitio,* or royal protection and wardship, which was a desirable privilege for Christians as well as for Jews.

Tuitio—or its alternate, *defensio,* which appears in the text above—is the most important operative term in Louis the Pious' charters.[50] It reoccurred in charters given Jews throughout the Middle Ages, and ultimately it signified Jewish constitutional alienness. However, from the time of its Ostrogothic origin—with no relationship whatsoever to the Jews—*tuitio* signified not alienness but its precise opposite. Its bestowal guaranteed (in return for loyalty) special protection, which only permanent residents of a realm were entitled to receive. The appearance of the terms *tuitio* and *defensio* in the charters of Louis the Pious signals that Jews were considered a fixed element of Carolingian society, despite their different beliefs and despite their legal disabilities. They were not foreigners living by a "A Law of Foreigners," as legal historians at the turn of the twentieth century and afterward argued.[51] They resided in the Carolingian domains on the basis of firm and venerable legal principles. Consequently, they had no cause to doubt the permanence of their status. The Jews who had special merchants' privileges were secure in their enjoyment of them so long as they remained *fideles,* by which Louis seems to have meant actively engaged in commerce to his benefit and to that of his kingdom. This security and stability no doubt made Carolingian Jews confident, and, quite possibly, it was this confidence that Agobard called presumptuousness.

Moreover, *tuitio* was a privilege that only certain individuals needed. Even without this special privilege, Jews enjoyed well-established rights, such as due legal process, exemption from trial by ordeal, and the unhindered observance of Jewish ritual; these rights were reiterated in the merchants' charters for emphasis. This is also true of the stipulation that Jews had the right to live by their own law. As permanent residents of the Carolingian Empire who were considered a *genus,* or one of its peoples, Jews were entitled to this right as a matter of course. In the early Middle Ages, each *genus* lived by it own or personal law.[52] Territorial law, that which today is called the law of the land, reappeared only in subsequent centuries. The law of the Jews was especially complex. Its

50. Colorni, 1945: 27–30.
51. Scherer, 1901: 3–7,64,67; Stobbe, 1968: 3–8.
52. Colorni, 1945: 34–43.

principal component was Jewish law, perhaps already Talmudic law of some variety, but it also included surviving elements of Roman law found in abbreviations of the Theodosian Code. Felicitously, but not accidentally, the Theodosian Code, unlike the later Justinianic one, sanctioned the observance of Jewish law in internal affairs[53] alongside the observance of Roman law in matters concerning the State and the Christian populace. This combination of laws and the constitutional status it bespoke afforded the Jews ample protection.

The constitutional status of the Jews in the Empire of Louis the Pious was therefore not unlike that of the Empire's other peoples. Jews were permanent residents, they constituted a *genus* which lived by its own law, and Jewish merchants were eligible for grants of *tuitio*. The existence of this status justifiably enhances the impression that Jews were active participants in early medieval society, particularly during the reign of Louis the Pious. At the same time, the Jews' *legal* status indicates that their participation was a limited one. In distinction from Christians, Jews had to submit to the canonical restrictions the emperor imposed upon them. They were also excluded from the benefits Christian religious law accorded to members of the "community of the faithful." Agobard intended his proposed corpus of restrictive statutes to institutionalize this exclusion. Jews were further set apart by the direct jurisdictional bond created between them and their sovereign through the medium of the *magister iudaeorum,* the Christian royal official specially appointed to oversee their behavior and their rights. This bond worked to the Jews' advantage in the mid-ninth century, and it would continue to do so as long as the laws being enforced were those in the tradition of Rome, which encouraged stability and due process. When Roman law disappeared sometime in the tenth century, however, the Jews' legal status assumed an increasingly precarious aspect. From this time onward, Jews came to be dependent on their rulers not only for law enforcement but also for law itself. In a process that reached completion only in the mid-thirteenth century, the law of the Jews—distinctly unlike that of Christians—became more and more the law which their rulers arbitrarily designated.

The Jews' constitutional status would also destabilize. *Tuitio* ceased to be an additional privilege of the few—as the charters show it to have been during the time of the Carolingian Empire—and evolved into the

53. *Codex Theodosianus,* 1954: bk. 2, title 1, law 10.

essence of Jewish status. From the late eleventh century onward, Jews no longer resided in a given territory by inherent right. Instead, their residence came to hinge on a charter that the ruler offered the entire Jewish community, which he took under his *tuitio,* now literally protection, and to which he granted a body of laws. Nevertheless, in format and wording, these new charters would differ little from the charters of privileges that Louis the Pious had issued. This continuity is not accounted for by the conservatism of legal formulas alone. Rather, the Carolingian formulas endured because their wording anticipates the future dependency of the Jews on their rulers, even as it makes room for the concept that in dealing with their Jews, rulers must guide themselves by sacred needs alongside profane ones. In this context, the security of the Carolingian period must not be confused with a royal Jewish alliance, or its stability with entente.

Moreover, throughout the early medieval period, rulers agreed that Jews must not offend Christianity. Some rulers, like the Visigoths, interpreted this principle radically. Others, like Louis the Pious and Charles the Bald, took a more flexible position. They ratified neither Agobard's Jewry statutes nor the especially restrictive decrees issued at the Council of Meaux in 845. Rather, they based their actions on an accommodating clerical legal exegesis that enabled them to reconcile religious and secular goals. Carolingian religiosity did not demand the complete identity between the goals of kingdom and the cult that had been pursued by the Visigoths. Nevertheless, the rejection of extremes in favor of balance does not mean that early medieval rulers never acted from a sense of religious obligation. The direct involvement of kings in promoting the welfare of Christianity at Jewish expense may have been typical, as is often said, of the later Middle Ages, but it was also a factor of the early medieval period. There was more continuity between early and late medieval royal Jewry policies than is normally assumed.

Nevertheless, we are hard pressed to demonstrate the stages in this continuity. We know far too little about Jewish fortunes in transalpine Europe between the time of Louis the Pious and the eleventh century. About Jewish life south of the Alps, we know somewhat more.

3 Cultural Beginnings

The first European Jewish records—in the form of inscriptions on grave-stones—appeared in southern Italy about the time of Gregory the Great. More significant writings, including poetry, biblical commentary, scientific writings, and chronicles, were produced in subsequent centuries, first in southern Italy and later at Rome, as well as at Lucca in Tuscany. Eventually, Italian writings made their way north, into the Rhineland and France, where they deeply influenced Ashkenazic culture.

The political history of Italian Jews was somewhat different from that of their transalpine counterparts. Large portions of southern Italy remained under direct Roman Byzantine rule until the tenth and even the eleventh centuries, when they were conquered by French Normans. Until that time, the tense equilibrium achieved in the fifth century between the Jews and the Roman Empire continued to prevail. Accordingly, in southern Italy the Jews' right to reside in the region and freely practice Judaism was not challenged, as it was in Visigothic Spain. And their legal and constitutional statuses were even more firmly rooted in Italy than they were in the Carolingian Empire. The Italian Jews were *cives* (roughly, "citizens") who "live according to the Roman law." Representatives of the Byzantine authorities, such as Gregory the Great, who also held sway over the vast estates of the Church in central Italy and Sicily, enforced the laws of the Theodosian Code itself, not the revised versions that are found in the collections of barbarian Roman law. This legal structure did not deteriorate. Long after the end of Byzantine rule, Italian legists affirmed that the Jews were *de populo romano* (part of the Roman people), that they had an almost unimpeachable right to reside in Christian lands, and that they were *fideles,* accepting at least the temporal authority of the Roman Church Militant.[1] Jewish settlements in Byzantine Italy were also too ancient for anyone to question. At the same time, the Jews had to submit to a body of severe restrictions imposed to protect Christianity. The source of these restrictions was Roman civil law, no less than the canons. The rigor of the law could be tempered only in a setting such as that of the Carolingian Empire, where the sovereign was convinced that he had harmonized religious with secular needs and where the palace clergy actively supported his legal policies and saw in him the protector of the Church. Yet southern Italian clergy rarely repeated the radical demands that transalpine and Spanish clergy made on Jewish behavior. So long as the restrictions Roman law imposed on Jewish activities were enforced, the Italian clergy had less reason for anxiety.[2]

In this atmosphere, Jewish life and culture flourished. It did so in large part because the Jews learned how to moderate their behavior. They made it flexible and responsive enough to meet the challenge of everyday exigencies, as well as of extraordinary religious and political pressures. Italian Jews even survived a time of extreme stress between the years 873 and 936, when the Byzantine emperors temporarily rejected the norm and espoused a policy that verged on forced conversion. Jews also had to adjust to brief periods of Muslim rule in Apulia and to the extended Muslim dominion in Sicily. Muslims conquered the island in the ninth century and held it until the arrival of the Normans in the eleventh century. In addition, some Jews lived in the Lombard north. In the late fifth century, Theodoric the Ostrogoth—resident in Ravenna—had been the first ruler to grant charters of *tuitio*. Presumably, he had granted these charters to Jews, as well as to others, just as would occur later in the Carolingian Empire. But instead of stability, the Lombard conquest at the end of the sixth century created uncertainty. The Lombard ruler Pertaric may have expelled Jews from northern Italy in 661, and so too, it appears, did the son of Louis the Pious, Lothair, in 855, after the region had passed into Carolingian hands. Lothair's order is found in a collection of royal laws, not in some unreliable monkish chronicle. Yet the only evidence that he enforced it is the absence of all references to Jews in northern Italy over the next fifty years. In any case, Jewish residence in this region was always sparse. Only from about the thirteenth century did Jews begin extensively to settle in the north. In the early Middle Ages, Jewish

1. Stow, 1977: 102,104.
2. Colorni, 1980: 242; Colafemmina, 1980: 199.

settlements beyond the Byzantine dominion were on its border, in places like Benevento and Capua. Jews also lived in Rome and surrounding areas, as far south as the port city of Gaeta. North of Latium, Jews reappeared in the tenth century in Ancona and Verona. Verona eventually became a center of learning with close connections to schools in the Rhineland. The best known new northern center was Lucca. Charters given to the Jews in the years 1000 and 1003 refer to them as being *ex genere hebreorum*, "of the Jewish people." This reference indicates that the Jews were permanent residents of the city, entitled to live by their own law. The constitutional and legal statuses of the Carolingian Empire had apparently been put into effect. The mid-tenth-century complaints of Ratherius of Verona to Emperor Otto I support this conclusion. It is noteworthy that the individuals who received these charters signed the notary's record book in Hebrew. Jewish culture had become Hebrew culture. However, it was in the south, not the north, that this culture produced its first and most enduring achievements.[3]

Culture

Hebrew rhymes appear already on late seventh- and early eighth-century lapidaries. Real poetry appears in Apulia at the turn of the ninth century. This poetry excelled in its ability to combine religious and secular themes with elegance. A wedding takes place simultaneously on both earthly and heavenly levels: the wedding feast is prepared on the days of Creation; the bride and groom unite under the wedding canopy. Poets wrote of the Creation, and they wrote of the Messiah. They also wrote epics that trace the history of the world from the Creation to the times of Moses, and, in wedding elegies, they described the life cycle from birth to death. In addition, they wrote dialogues, like that between the grapevine and the trees which disputes the virtues of wine as opposed to its vices. The vocabulary of this poetry is biblical and the language is Hebrew. The terminology reflects the mysticism that was so influential in learned Jewish circles of the day. The form betrays the cultural influence of the classic school of religious poetry from the Land of Israel. The poets themselves and at least one of their subjects are independently mentioned in the *Megillat Ahimaaz (Genealogy of Ahimaaz* or *Scroll of Ahimaaz)*. The poetry of Amitai and Shefatiah of Oria, who lived at the end of the

3. Roth, 1966: 100–121; Milano, 1963: 52–66.

ninth century, is the first solid evidence of a fully developed internal Jewish culture in Europe. The hymn 'Enqat Mesaldekha, by Silano of Venosa, is still recited as part of the Ashkenazic High Holy Days liturgy, as are other products of this southern Italian school.[4]

In Rome, there were at least twelve authors of religious poetry (who were called payyetanim) active between the eleventh and thirteenth centuries. The best-known is Solomon the Babylonian, who lived in the mid-tenth century. His poetry is a central feature of the Ashkenazic holiday prayer book. One scholar has proposed that "Babylonian" is a pejorative nickname that refers to Rome itself. However, Jewish toponymics often reflect the city a person traveled to, in this case Baghdad, rather than his place of origin. Solomon's nickname, therefore, most likely indicates either his eastern origins or his openness to eastern Jewish cultural influences.[5] From the late ninth century, the culture of the Jewish academies of Baghdad, the schools of the Geonim, was making ever greater inroads into Italy.

Solomon's poems display a great sensitivity to Jewish Christian frictions. He wrote of the bitterness of exile, confrontations with Christians, conversionary pressures, and physical attacks. Perhaps these themes reflect recent Byzantine conversionary pressures in the south. A letter sent to Spain indicates that at least one Jew from Bari martyred himself rather than convert and that others were massacred.[6] Not long after Solomon's day, there are reports of Jews being attacked at Aterno in Umbria for disfiguring a crucifix (1062). The prince of Benevento, Landulf, forced a number of Jews to convert (1065), and even in Rome (1020) Jews supposedly suffered for attacking an image. One would like to know more about these incidents and whether there were others like them. Had the distrust seen in the stories of Gregory of Tours matured into violence as the concept of a societas christiana, which had once animated only the radical clergy, penetrated the lay populace?[7] Regrettably, Solomon the Babylonian's references to Jewish suffering are too generic to say whether they were evoked by specific stimuli, a general change in Christian behavior, or the overall exilic condition that at one time or another produced Christian extremes and Jewish despair. Moreover, of the incidents

4. Klar, 1974: 56–59; Shirman, 1979: 2:9–43, esp. 9–29 and 30–43.
5. Shirman, 1979: 2:21; Roth, 1966: 119.
6. Mann, 1931: 11–16.
7. See Becker, 1981: 19–58.

mentioned above, only that of the forced conversions in Benevento can be reasonably verified.[8]

Besides writing poetry, Jewish scholars in Rome gave shape to the order of prayers. One of them, Judah ben Menahem, created a prototype of the Roman rite that survives today in its original geographic setting. Originally, Italian ritual was heavily influenced by the Palestinian model, based primarily on religious poetry. There may also have been a Palestinian form of blessings and prayers, but it has been lost. All current Jewish liturgy goes back to the *Siddur,* or Order of Prayers, compiled in the ninth century by the Gaon (Babylonian Academy head), Rabbi Amram, and sent to communities throughout the Diaspora. Each Diaspora community had to reconcile this *Siddur* with its own existing form of prayer. The result was two basic rites, the Italo-Ashkenazic one, known as the Palestinian rite because of a supposed underlying Palestinian influence, and the Sephardic one, with Babylonian (Iraqi) origins. In fact, the rites are quite similar. Nevertheless, a visitor to the Roman synagogue is struck by the similarity between Roman and current Ashkenazic rites. The Sephardic service, especially when overlaid with oriental melodies, gives a very different impression. This is true even though Sephardic-Spanish motifs dominated new Roman synagogal poetry from the time of Benjamin Anau in the mid-thirteenth century. The original Roman rite arranged by Judah ben Menahem was remarkably resilient. Paradoxically, in Ashkenaz, where there was no Sephardic influence, the products of early Italian synagogal poetry have best survived.[9]

The most well-known product of the Roman school is the *'Arukh* (or *The Order*), a talmudic dictionary completed in 1101 by Natan ben Yehiel. Natan was the son of the *payyetan* Yehiel min ha-Anavim, a member of one of Rome's legendary Jewish families that trace their origins in the city to the times of Julius Caesar. In the *'Arukh,* Natan displays a vast erudition, the result of a truly international education. He studied in such far-flung places as Bari, Sicily, and Narbonne. His Sicilian teacher, Mazliah ibn al-Bazaq, had studied in the east, under the Gaon Hai. That Natan cited Hai 138 times in his dictionary is not coincidence. But Natan also cited Rabbi Hananel of Qairowan (near modern Tunis in North Africa) 142 times. The *'Arukh* is thus a compendium of all

8. Synan, 1965: 68–69; Roth, 1966: 120.
9. *Encyclopaedia Judaica,* 1971: s.v. "Prayer Books"; Baron, 1952: 7:105–118.

talmudic study in Natan's day. It is an international work, and for that reason, copies of it quickly spread beyond Rome and were cited by scholars in the north. Indeed, talmudists today still derive benefit from the *'Arukh;* a leading scholar toward the end of the nineteenth century believed his updated reissue of the work would well serve his contemporaries.[10]

The advanced scholarship of the *'Arukh* was paralleled by commentaries intended for a wide audience, including women. Commentaries on traditional texts were written in Judeo-Italian, which is neither a language nor a dialect but what sometimes is called a linguistic mode. The *'Arukh* itself is full of Judeo-Italian usages. The Judeo-Italian commentaries formed a linguistic bridge over the centuries. The terms they employ transmitted from one generation to another linguistic elements that were no longer used in spoken communication. These terms survived as late as the early fourteenth century. One of the most interesting of them appears in a commentary on the legal code of Maimonides, the *Mishneh Torah,* a work that was composed in late twelfth-century Egypt but that swiftly reached the far corners of the Jewish world. The commentary's author, Judah Romano, an important student of philosophy and cousin of the well-known storyteller Immanuel ha-Romi, tried to explain just what the *Mishnah* meant when it referred to a flat bread that might be kept heated for consumption on the Sabbath. The term for this bread, *hararah,* was an obscure one, and in the eleventh century, Rashi (whom we will meet again further on) explained it as "flat cake." Judah Romano was more succinct. He used one word only, spelled (in Hebrew letters) *peh-yod-zade-heh;* that is, *pizza.* This is the first known written attestation to this now international term. Judah Romano's pizza and the kind eaten today may also have a more than superficial resemblance.[11]

Roman Jewish culture migrated northward. It did so through both literary transmission and the movement of scholars. Members of the Kalonymos family, one of the most noted of all medieval Jewish families, migrated from (perhaps) Rome to Lucca, and from there to Mainz in the Rhineland. Their settling in Lucca is itself noteworthy, since it provides one of the first indications of a Jewish presence in northern Italy after the "expulsion" by Lothair in 855. The second migration, to Mainz, occurred between 917 and 950. Moshe ben Kalonymos—probably the son of

---

10. Kohut, 1878.
11. Stow, S. D., 1983; idem, 1986; idem, 1990; Sermoneta, 1976.

Kalonymos of Lucca (called "Kalonymos the Roman" in a late source)—is reputed to have been taken to Mainz by none other than Charlemagne. More probably, Moshe migrated of his own will; the Ashkenazic Jews who chronicled the event introduced the Charlemagne motif to enhance the importance of this already distinguished individual. Moshe's son, Kalonymos ha-Zaqen (the elder), is another central figure in Rhineland lore, but we know little about him, since few of his writings have survived. Reputedly, they were censored for ridiculing Christianity. Finally, Meshullam ben Kalonymos (the elder) also settled in Mainz, although he lived much of his life in Italy, where he was a student of Solomon the Babylonian and where he composed many of his important works.[12]

Apart from attesting to migration history, albeit with a rather hazy explanation of its causes, the stories associated with Kalonymide wanderings transmit chains of learning-traditions. One such chain that also contains a version of the Charlemagne legend is found in Eleazar of Worms's early thirteenth-century *Sefer ha-Roqeah* (or *Book of the Perfumer*). Eleazar traces, name by name and generation by generation, the members of the Kalonymos family, to which he himself belonged and which he associates with the liturgic and mystical traditions that were most influential in shaping the culture of the Ashkenazic north.[13] These traditions first appeared in poetry on subjects such as sin, the suffering of the exile, and repression at the hand of the Jews' enemies. The *'Amitz Koah* of Meshullam ben Kalonymos, which describes the ancient High Priest's unique ritual of atonement, remains even today a staple of the Yom Kippur liturgy. Another Kalonymide, Moshe ben Kalonymos, was instrumental in transmitting to future generations the *sod tiqqun tefillah* (secret of how to pray with mystical affect). Moshe had learned these secrets from his father, who, in his time, had learned them from a figure clouded in enormous mystery, Abu Aaron. According to the *Megillat Ahimaaz,* Abu Aaron arrived at Gaeta from Babylonia, bringing with him Babylonian traditions. These traditions were now to be amalgamated with preexisting Palestinian ones, whence a specifically European Jewish culture would be born.[14]

Palestinian culture had long been rooted in Italy. It is reflected in a

12. Grossman, 1981: 44–48,54–55; *Encyclopaedia Judaica,* 1971: s.v. "Kalonymus"; Grossman, 1980: passim.

13. Klar, 1974: 46; Dan, 1966: 283.

14. Bonfil, 1987; idem, 1989; Ta Shema, 1988a.

singularly distinctive midrashic creation, the *Tanna de-vei Eliyahu,* which appeared (some say was composed or redacted) in Italy in the late ninth or early tenth century. Unlike most midrashic collections, this one has a principal unifying theme: the progress of world history from the Creation to messianic redemption. The world is said to exist on the basis of six principles: the Torah, Gehinnom (a kind of netherworld), Gan Eden (or paradise), the Throne of Divine Glory, the Name of the Messiah, and the Temple. History is divided into epochs: two thousand years of confusion, two thousand years of Torah, two thousand years of the Messiah, the inauguration of an age of peace, and the World to Come. Many of these ideas reappeared in Jewish and non-Jewish literature throughout the Middle Ages. Some of the individual midrashim go on at length about the "Act of Creation" and the "Act of the Chariot," two central mystical topoi. There are also various halachic references; they are clearly to the *halachot* of the Land of Israel.[15] Their presence in the Italian work attests to ongoing contacts. When Babylonian traditions met those of the Land of Israel in southern Italy, they met not a vague shadow of Palestinian Jewish culture but that culture itself, in its full flower.

That the Jews of Italy were so heavily influenced by Palestinian traditions is not surprising. After all, learning activities in the Land of Israel never ceased. Admittedly, following the editing of the authoritative legal compendium, the Mishnah, in about 200 C.E. by Judah ha-Nasi (the Patriarch), the principal center of Jewish learning became the schools of Babylonia. However, as late as about 375 C.E., the Jerusalem Talmud was compiled in the Land of Israel (albeit with a heavy Babylonian input), and schools of learning continued there even afterward, if on a much diminished level. These schools reawakened in the early Muslim centuries. About the ninth century, the strength of the Jerusalem Academy was such that Egyptian Jews viewed its halachic decisions as binding.[16] The late ninth century was also the time when Jerusalem became the center of the Karaite sect. Born of urban intellectual revolt, this sect's influence peaked when first Benjamin Nahawendi and then Daniel al-Qumisi moved its schools to Jerusalem, emphasized the use of Hebrew, and called upon Karaites to migrate to the Holy City. There was then much in contemporary Palestinian learning, both rabbanite and Karaite, from which Italian Jews could benefit.[17]

15. *Encyclopaedia Judaica,* 1971: s.v. "Tanna de-vei Eliyahu."
16. Goitein, 1971: 2:8–14.
17. Ankori, 1959: chap. 1; Nemoy, 1952: 30–41.

Italian Jews benefited equally, if not more, from Babylonian traditions, which were brought to them by travelers going west or gleaned in their own travels east. The ninth and tenth centuries witnessed a large-scale commercial expansion in the Arab empires that was accompanied by a westward migration. Commerce with Latin Europe also grew. By the late tenth century or the early eleventh, a grand trading axis linked Spain with Alexandria, in Egypt, and then, by way of overland routes, with the cities of Iraq and places as far away as India and China. The products being carried were no longer limited to luxury goods, as they had been one or two hundred years earlier. The merchants as well as their means of transport were increasingly European. Italians from Genoa, Pisa, and Venice were carrying heavy cargoes, such as wood and iron. The East was sending back cloth and coloring agents. The Jewish role in Mediterranean commerce, especially commerce with Latin Europe, was declining. Nevertheless, European Jewish merchants were still prominent. Some of them even owned their own ships. Exactly what routes these Jews sailed has not been clarified; it has been suggested that Jews from southern Italy were trading with the East and with North Africa, but not with Greece.[18] Yet coastal vessels normally touched at numerous ports of call. A boat that sailed from Brindisi, at the southern tip of the Adriatic, would surely have made port at Corfu, on the Greek side of the Ionian. Such landings promoted the growth of a tightly knit network of contacts that ensured the rapid spread from place to place of Jewish culture and thought. In the East, a most potent force for cultural transmission was the so-called Merchant's Agent,[19] a respected Jewish figure found in every major port who oversaw the affairs of both local and visiting merchants. But this person also ensured that legal questions (and their accompanying donations) addressed to the Baghdad academies were expeditiously forwarded to the next city on the chain. The Gaon's responses, too, passed through his hands; and both questions and answers were copied and preserved for local use. This renewed commercial and cultural interchange helped set the stage for the appearance of scholars such as Shabbetai Donnolo (ca. 913–982), one of the first European Jews who can be singled out as a student of philosophy.

Donnolo's origins were as complex as the man himself. His family may have been the victim of an Arab *razia* (raid) on the city of Oria in the

18. Goitein, 1967: passim; cf. Lewicki, 1980; Ashtor, 1980: 428.
19. Stillman, 1970: passim.

year 925. He wrote that he was redeemed from captivity in the city of Taranto, yet his parents were sent to Palermo and North Africa. What befell them in those ports, and what Donnolo's own lot was as a youth (he was twelve at the time of the raid) are total mysteries. No less mysterious is his name, Donnolo, which apparently means "little lord." Nicknames did turn into family names much later on, but in the tenth century such an adoption must have been extremely rare. Perhaps the name stuck because Donnolo was an imperiously inquisitive type? In any case, the Jews he met could not satisfy his thirst for knowledge. As Donnolo wrote in the introduction to his *Sefer Hakhmoni* (or *Enlighten Me*), he had to turn elsewhere.[20]

The *Hakhmoni*, principally an exegetical commentary on the problem of divine creation, probes the secrets of a work called *Sefer Yezirah (The Book of Creation)*, a mystical tract that rests on the mysticism of the *merkavah* ("chariot") and the *heikhalot* ("palaces") and whose purpose is to describe the heavenly world, the *ma'aseh bereshit* ("work of creation"), and the *ma'aseh merkavah* ("articulation of the divine chariot," of Ezekiel 1). The origins of *Sefer Yezirah* are cosmological and cosmogenical mystical teachings on the origins and structure of the universe propounded chiefly in the Land of Israel from the third through the sixth centuries. This speculative mysticism, which has a strong secretive gnostic element that influenced early Christianity as well as Judaism, also embraced doctrines of the *shi'ur qomah* ("measurement of the body of God"). These measurements are literal and anthropomorphic ones that embarrassed later thinkers, including Donnolo, who tried to purge them by reinterpreting them in astrological and physiological terms that draw parallels between parts of the body and the created universe. Donnolo also reinterpreted the measurements of *Sefer Yezirah* by conferring upon them mystical and theological equivalents. Perhaps for this reason, Donnolo's writings influenced principally mystics.[21] In such as the *ma'aseh merkavah* philosophers saw metaphysics, not the mystical seven heavens.[22]

The *Hakhmoni* reflects the problems Jews were about to confront as they wrestled to maintain intact their own intellectual world while selectively absorbing a most attractive external one. Donnolo claims to be a scientist. In contemporary terms, he probably was one, but his methods

20. Sirat, 1975: 378–380.
21. Scholem, 1938: 84; *Encyclopaedia Judaica*, 1971: s.v. "Donnolo"; Dan, 1966: 290.
22. Scholem, 1974: 10–13,14–20; Dan, 1966: 289–290.

and conclusions are far from inductive and systematic. Fire, he says, is generated by water.[23] At other times, Donnolo acutely observes psychological conditions such as melancholia and nightmares. Donnolo's knowledge of Arab medical science, as well as of Arabic, was incomplete, but he knew enough Latin and Greek to compose his *Antidotarium (Book of Drugs)*, which lists one hundred liquids, powders, bandages, applications, and ointments to put on the skin, all with a vegetable base. Acquiring this knowledge was not easy. Jews, apparently, were uninterested in natural science; they may also have had anxieties about it. For all that Donnolo searched, he could find no suitable Jewish teacher. He thus set out "and travelled through the lands to find the wise men of the peoples," until he found "a man from Babylonia called Bagdesh," who taught him what he wanted to know.[24]

This "Babylonian," whose identity is a complete mystery, may have taught Donnolo the rudiments of philosophy besides those of natural science. The philosophical ruminations of Shabbetai Donnolo did not of course include Aristotelianism, which had still to be absorbed by the Arabs—from whom it was then transmitted to North African and eastern Jews, who, in turn, transmitted it to the West by way of Spain, in the form of translations from Arabic, usually via Hebrew, into Latin. However, Donnolo's career reflects the start of a serious problem. How much could one absorb of non-Jewish culture without endangering Jewish principles? Christians and Muslims had to face the same issue. Donnolo reports that he had contacts with Christian monks, but they were apprehensive about his teachings. Still, with regard to science and mysticism, the problem was solvable. External mystical influences, especially gnostic ones, were transformed and so particularized that they could no longer be confused with anything foreign; science in its pure form was too neutral, and too limited an issue, to present insuperable difficulties. On the other hand, philosophy, with its close links to theology and the common questions it posed in similar terms to all three faiths, was a source of unending conflict. How much could be adopted and absorbed, and how much had to be resisted and rejected?

A pattern of adopt and resist, in varying measures and proportions, recurred frequently in the history of southern European Jews, some of whom denounced all speculative thought[25] while others rejected only the

---

23. Zinberg, 1972: 2:138; Zimmels, 1966: 297–301.
24. Shabbetai Donnolo, 1968; Sirat, 1975: 378.
25. Baer, 1961: 1:96–110.

naturalism of pure Aristotelianism, which could not be reconciled with theories of revelation.[26] Intellectual fights concerning the merits and demerits of speculative thought were thus often bitter. They reached their peak at the turn of the fourteenth century in Provence (southern France), where they sometimes took on strong political and factional hues. Ashkenazic Jews resolved the philosophical problem by shunning the subject entirely. However, this does not mean that they closed themselves off from outside culture. Some of them were expert in non-Jewish biblical and legal exegesis.

Italian Jews seem to have alighted on the same balanced middle way with regard to speculative thought as had luminaries such as Meir ha-Levi Todros Abulafia, in Spain, and Maimonides and Saadya Gaon, in the east, all three of whom were also halachic authorities. Paradoxically, the Italians' way to balance was through reliance on the works of Christian philosophers and theologians, who had already "domesticated" Averroes. Jacob Anatoli in the thirteenth century made frequent use of the works of Michael Scot, an enigmatic figure Anatoli knew personally from their meetings at the court of Frederick II in Sicily. A few decades later, Judah Romano translated numerous Latin works into Hebrew, including those of Boethius, Albertus Magnus, Alexander of Hales, and Giles of Rome, whose forte was political theory.[27] Notably, translations often appeared within a few years of the original. However, if Jews did participate in mainstream culture, they did so through the medium of Hebrew. Here, once again, was the pattern of adopt and resist.

Jews were not alone in following this pattern. Thomas Aquinas did not hesitate to cite the philosophical learning of one Rabbi Moise Aegypticus—that is, Maimonides. The Jewish role in European intellectual life, which began in ninth-century Italy, was a far more active one than scholars have hitherto thought. Jews were not simply the *Dolmetscher*—"middle men" in transmitting Greek and Arabic philosophical thought to the West—that Moritz Steinschneider, the late nineteenth-century Jewish historian and bibliographer, called them.[28] Christians even developed a great interest in rabbinic literature. Agobard and Rabanus Maurus apparently had some knowledge of it in the ninth century,[29] although their observations on the subject were far from flattering. Three hundred

26. Septimus, 1982: 104–115.
27. Sirat, 1975: 379–383; Sermoneta, 1965.
28. Steinschneider, 1893.
29. Merchavia, 1973: 42–70.

years later, monks became avid recipients of rabbinic biblical commentaries and talmudic midrashim. At first, their teachers were often contemporary Jewish scholars, but these Jews soon gave way to converts from Judaism. Christians, the Jews discovered, were studying rabbinic literature primarily in order to exploit it in debates and conversionary sermons.

Chronicles, Institutions, and Individuals

Shabbetai Donnolo was acutely aware of the novelty of his learning. His experiences with both Jewish and Christian men of letters taught him that. Possibly for this reason, Donnolo made it clear that no one was to copy his books without crediting their author. He did not suffer from a desire for anonymity, as many in the Middle Ages are said to have done. The author of the *Megillat Ahimaaz,* Ahimaaz ben Paltiel, was also interested in publicizing himself, as was to a lesser extent Yosef ben Gurion, nominal author of *The Book of Yossipon.*

Yossipon is ostensibly a translation of Josephus Flavius' *Jewish War,* prefaced by sections of his *Antiquities,* which are the primary sources of information about Jewish life in the Land of Israel at the end of the Second Temple period.[30] Yet the medieval Yosef was careful to make it clear that he had graced his Hebrew translation (from the Greek original or a Latin version) with significant additions. These additions turn the *Yossipon* into an original work of Jewish political theory.

Yosef ben Gurion in fact left his personal imprint on *Yossipon* in many ways, one of which is his language, which is filled with Greek usages resting on a Judeo-Italian base. There may also have been linguistic traces reflecting the contemporary Arab presence in parts of southern Italy. Yosef ben Gurion's knowledge of antiquity, which he derived from Latin chronicles, is reinforced by descriptions of the wonders of medieval Rome; his familiarity with southern Italy is beyond that which anyone except a resident could have possessed; and his intimacy with specific events and court protocols leave no doubt that *Yossipon* is a product of the Byzantine south. The book has been dated to precisely the year 953.[31] Yosef ben Gurion was also a typical historian of his day. As if anticipating the advice to chroniclers given in 991 by Gerbert of Aurillac, the future

30. Flusser, 1979; Hominer, 1978: esp. chaps. 15,23,84.
31. Flusser, 1953; Baer, 1985c.

Pope Sylvester II, Yosef treated history and literature as indivisible. He believed that it was legitimate to enhance his stories with invented detail, and he valued the importance of rhetoric.

Yossipon's story begins sometime before the founding of Rome and continues through the destruction of the Second Temple in the year 70 C.E. and the fall of Masada three years later. Most of the book describes the events of the Jewish War, and there is also a lengthy discussion of the Hasmonean Dynasty. However, *Yossipon*'s high point is unquestionably the unorthodox history of the founding of Rome that appears in the first three of the book's eighty-nine chapters. According to *Yossipon*, the Kittim, one of the early biblical peoples, settled in the Roman countryside. They were later joined by Zepho, a grandson of Esau, who was fleeing Egypt, where he had been a prisoner of Joseph. Zepho fled west and arrived in Carthage. From there, together with the mythical Aeneas, Zepho arrived at Rome, where he married a local woman. His grandson Latinus founded Roman culture (chapters 1 and 2).

What *Yossipon* had done was to conflate the Roman myth—in which Aeneas marries the daughter of Latinus—with a rabbinic midrash (B. Sota 13a) which says that Zepho wandered "west"[32] but does not specify where. *Yossipon* also expanded on the midrash to argue that Zepho was followed west by others of Esau's progeny, who likewise united with the Etruscans, consequently turning Latin culture into a derivative of that of Esau. But if this were so, then Christians could not claim that as the descendants of the Kittim, the offspring of Noah's son Yefet, they were not the descendants of Esau. This was significant; for Esau is exactly what the Jews said Christians were. The Jews even used Esau's other name, Edom ("ruddy"), referring to his complexion, as a synonym for Christianity and Christian lands (as in the biblical Land of Edom itself). Accordingly, *Yossipon* had to establish the identity of Edom with Christianity, and by extension with Rome. The first step was his revised history. The second was to produce what in his day passed for an airtight ethnographic explanation. The Arabs, he said, called the Christians (the people of Rome, or the *Ahl al-Rum*) the *Banu Asfar*, which in cultured medieval Arabic means "sons of the Red One." However, Asfar is also the Arabized form of the Greek translation of the name Zepho as it appears in the Septuagint, a translation the Christians considered holy. How then could the Christians deny *Yossipon*'s historical revisions? Moreover, how could

32. Cohen, G., 1967: 40–44.

they continue saying, as they had been since the time of Paul, that not they but the Jews were Esau's heirs?

Yet in order properly to combat all Christian claims about the identity of Edom, *Yossipon* also had to show that Rome was the Fourth Kingdom spoken of in the book of Daniel, whose fall would mark the advent of the Messiah. In its early days, he thus wrote, Rome protected itself from the power of the Jews. Romulus even signed a pact with King David, and, accordingly, when the ancient Babylonians defeated the Jews, Rome turned its defenses toward Babylon. But Rome did not actually have to defend itself until the Persians, who met and defeated the Babylonians, were themselves destroyed by the Greeks. And even then, Rome acted only when Antiochus Epiphanes tried to destroy Judaism (chapter 13); and very soon afterward, Rome once again sought a covenant with a Jewish ruler, Judah Maccabee (chapter 21). These episodes all have one common theme. Each of the four kingdoms who are their protagonists either defeated the Jews, destroyed those who defeated them, or threatened the Jews with extinction. The victories were also divinely orchestrated. These four kingdoms, therefore—Babylonia, Persia, Greece, and Rome—perfectly fit the criteria established by Daniel; they, and no others, are the four kingdoms of Daniel's visions.

But if the succession of kingdoms proceeded according to divine plan, then the Jews, too, must accept its justice. The ancient Jews were wrong to violate the covenant Judah Maccabee made with Rome. Their rebellion of 66 C.E. brought down upon them God's anger, for they ignored the fact "that now is the hour of [divinely appointed] Roman rule" (chapter 78). The Jews of tenth-century Italy, who had survived the conversionary pressures applied by the Byzantine emperor Romanos I only three decades before *Yossipon* was written,[33] should thus learn and take heart. For, as *Yossipon* quickly added (putting his words, of course, in the mouth of the original Josephus), "Behold, the elder will rule the younger, and there is no disgrace or shame to the younger if he must serve the elder . . . You now are the younger who is bowed before the Roman . . . But your time will come, and you will return to God with all your heart, and then you will rule the Nations." The divinely ordered soteriological scenario—God's choice of the Jews—had not been altered. It remained intact, even if Christianity currently held Judaism under its heel. Thus, the midrash said that on the same day Solomon married the

33. Scharf, 1971: 82–94.

daughter of Pharaoh, Rome was founded, eventually to serve as God's instrument to punish the Jews for their sins. If Rome—Christian Rome, that is—was now punishing the Jews, it was not, as Paul had said, because the Jews had rejected Jesus but because one of them had committed a "crime" long before Jesus was born.[34] Here, of course, was not only consolation but practical political advice. For did not the law of Rome, Byzantine Rome, guarantee the rights of law-abiding Jews but threaten those who grew haughty and did not know their proper place (lex nullus)? It behooved the Jews, accordingly, to observe the law of both God and man. In doing so, they would gain not only eternal rule and glory but also security and peace in the here and now. Theories like this one facilitated Jewish survival in the threatening Christian world. A similar, though more traditional, theory of Jewish behavior appears in the Megillat Ahimaaz.

In its simplest terms, the Megillah is a family chronicle.[35] It was composed in the year 1054 by one Ahimaaz ben Paltiel upon his return from Capua (where he had lived for the first thirty-seven years of his life) to his ancestral city of Oria. Apart from memorializing his ancestors, Ahimaaz was also pragmatically seeking recognition for himself as a descendent of an illustrious family. This especially personal aspect of the Megillah may explain why it has survived in only one manuscript copy. And even that was accidentally discovered in the 1890s in, of all places, the library of the cathedral of Toledo in Spain. Nevertheless, the Megillah is an excellent guide to medieval Jewry's cultural world.

The Megillah was composed in a particularly memorable year. In 1054, the Eastern and Latin Catholic Churches definitively split in two. This was also the year that the Normans invaded Sicily and southern Italy. Within a short period, Latin (rather than Byzantine) culture and institutions would dominate the south, to be further entrenched in the twelfth century with the arrival of the German Hohenstaufens, whose architectural imprint in particular is still visible throughout Apulia in the shape of cathedrals and fortresses. The world which Ahimaaz records, of Italian-Jewish culture's first blossoming, was soon to disappear. The year 1054, furthermore, was a time of serious political struggles in Rome. The victors were the Pierleoni faction that supported the papal candidacy of

34. Cohen, G., 1967: 31–32,43.
35. Klar, 1974: passim; see also Yassif, 1984.

Alexander II. Alexander's decrees, it will be recalled, marked the first step toward a consolidated and balanced papal policy toward the Jews.[36]

Ahimaaz, of course, was not a modern historian. Issues such as precise dating or the historicity of events or persons did not trouble him. Thus, Ahimaaz depicted his grandest hero, Paltiel, as the Vizier of Al-Muizz, the tenth-century Muslim who ruled parts of southern Italy, Sicily, and present-day Libya. Often, Paltiel is identified with Jacob ibn Qillis, a convert from Judaism to Islam, who became the vizier of the Egyptian Fatimid caliphs.[37] Yet, more probably, Paltiel was a creation of Ahimaaz's imagination whose feats and deeds were modeled on those of the contemporary Samuel ibn Nagrela, the Nagid ("prince"), vizier of the Muslim kingdom of Granada and general of its armies. Paltiel's portrait may also contain elements drawn from the life of the later tenth-century Hisdai ben Shaprut. The *Megillah* is a hagiography—a saint's life—and it must be read as such. Its heroes must conform to ideal types, no matter how much interpolation is needed to realize this end. Ahimaaz's motifs are also polemical ones. Hananel debates the bishop of Oria. The debate takes the form of a wager: Hananel's Judaism against a horse. A similar story appears in the hagiographic biography of Wazo of Liege. But here, the Jew, who had wagered a finger against a barrel of wine, lost. Only Wazo's magnanimity saved this Jew from a cruel fate.[38] Wazo also, if inexplicably, did not try to convert him. The victory was sufficient reason for praise. In Ahimaaz's version, Shefatiah wins, but only because God directly intervened on his behalf.

For all these strictures, and perhaps in many ways just because of them, one can still see Ahimaaz himself and his society in real terms. The route Ahimaaz followed from Capua to Oria traversed the ancient Appian Way that began in Rome and stretched hundreds of miles southward to Brindisi on the Adriatic coast. It took him through Benevento in the Appenines, Venosa at the edge of a treeless and wide plain leading from the Appenines to the Ionian Gulf, Materna, which looks down on the sea, and Taranto, the great Ionian port, to Oria, about halfway between Taranto and Brindisi, and then on to Brindisi itself. From there, Ahimaaz could move a short distance south, down the coast to Otranto, only a few miles from the tip of the peninsular heel, or back north to the centers

36. Stow, 1981a; Chodorow, 1972; Stroll, 1987.
37. Cohen, M., 1980: 12–14,21–27.
38. Blumenkranz, 1963: 263; King, 1985: 6:64–71.

of Bari and Trani. From Trani, he would retrace his course over the Appenines, perhaps stopping at Melfi rather than at nearby Venosa, and detouring a short way south on the Tyrrhenian coast to Amalfi, and possibly even to Salerno. At long last he would return to Capua, not far north of Naples. Christian and Muslim travelers, too, followed this route, whether they were traveling for commercial or for other purposes. It was in the cities and towns along this route that much of the Jewish poetic, legal, and scientific writings of this period—some of which Ahimaaz mentions by name—were composed.

Although Ahimaaz wanted his readers to consider Oria, his ancestral home, the center of events, it was not the only place he viewed as important. He makes Babylonian culture enter Italy at the distant Gaetan peninsula (about halfway between Naples and Rome) on the Tyrrhenian coast. Ahimaaz's point, of course, is that southern Italy was a unified cultural domain. Yet the most significant people in that domain were also Ahimaaz's ancestors, the poets Silano of Venosa, and Amitai and Shefatiah of Oria. The route one follows in reading the *Megillah* of Ahimaaz, therefore, is that of cultural and institutional diffusion, along which are revealed the thought, the priorities, the ideals, and the methods used by Ahimaaz's fathers for coping with both internal and external political vicissitudes, and even with domestic strife.

No quality typified Ahimaaz's first ancestors more than their cultural foundations. That culture rested on mystical teachings. Halachic knowledge came mostly from what is called legal midrash. Amitai the poet, founder of the family, did not know the Talmud at first hand, since it reached Europe only sometime in the ninth century. Nevertheless, even without the Talmud, Italian Jews established their own institutions. When the full measure of Babylonian talmudic learning arrived, it brought the preexisting culture to fruition.[39] Specifically, Ahimaaz writes, the new learning enabled the Jews to mete out death sentences for capital crimes. Italian Jews under Byzantine rule certainly exercised no such powers. Ahimaaz was writing metaphorically, and his contemporaries no doubt understood him perfectly. Metaphor also served Ahimaaz in his description of Abu Aaron, the Talmud's mythical bearer. Supposedly, Aaron—a scion of Gaonic stock—had been exiled for three years by his father because, improperly using mystical knowledge, he had yoked a lion to a millstone. Sailing from Jaffa to Gaeta, Aaron at once displayed his

39. Bonfil, 1987: passim.

prowess by uncovering the acts of a sorceress. Only in Oria did he reveal himself as a great legal master. More important, however, Rabbi Amitai and his sons, Shefatiah and Hananel, were able to appreciate the depths of Aaron's learning, for they themselves had previously "established schools" and were themselves "masters in public discourse and of learned discussions of the law, distinguished scholars."

With its keen interest in Aaron's knowledge of mysticism and even magic, this story is decidedly Italian. But it also rings loudly of the founding myth of Jewish learning in Spain. Like Abu Aaron, a Rabbi Moses arrives by sea and is quickly made chief rabbinic judge out of deference for his knowledge of arcane talmudic—indeed, extratalmudic—texts; the story takes place in the later tenth century, when the Talmud itself was already well known in Europe. Like Abu Aaron in Italy, an outsider brought learning to its full measure in Spain. One wonders if Ahimaaz was acquainted with the kernel of this Spanish myth, which, in the twelfth century, received an elaborate updating and literary reworking by Abraham ibn Daud.[40] The parallels do not end here. In both myths, the mastery of new learning goes hand in hand with eventual independence. In the Spanish version, Rabbi Moses' son, Hanoch, marries into the ibn Falija family of Spanish-Jewish grandees. But the couple has only a daughter, who marries a maternal cousin. Whence the family retained the name of ibn Falija, meaning that the descendants of the foreign Rabbi Moses do not form a dynasty of outsiders that rules Spanish intellectual life. Likewise, in Italy, the days of Aaron's leadership come to a close when his exile ends and he mythically disappears, setting sail for the East in a boat of supernatural dimensions.

Yet the Italian founding myth seems to diverge from the Spanish one over the issue of the Land of Israel. The Spaniards never had real links with Palestine; ibn Daud did not have to consider them. Ahimaaz did, as becomes evident from the tale—told immediately after Aaron's arrival— of the ban placed by the Palestinian Academy on Rabbi Silano of Venosa for tricking their *shaliah* (their representative). The unwitting fellow found himself—in the middle of a midrashic lesson—recounting a somewhat ribald story (secreted into his prepared written text) about the oversized oven paddles used by local women to strike men from outlying districts who were (it seems) reneging on promises of marriage. Only when another Venosan scholar read before the Palestinian worthies a

40. Cohen, G., 1960: passim.

penitential prayer that Silano had composed was the ban on Silano released. Ninth-century Italian Jews were very dependent on their Palestinian brothers. Abu Aaron thus brought Italian Jews more than one treasure. His arrival bestowed upon them not only Babylonian learning but also the capability to break their Palestinian ties.[41] In the story of ibn Daud, the arrival of Rabbi Moses has a parallel effect. The Jews of Spain free themselves from their dependence on the Geonim and the Babylonian academies. Despite their diversities, European Jewries shared many common problems.

Spanish Jewry capitalized on its independence by creating formal institutions, which ibn Daud discusses under the rubric of "the Rabbinate"—a term that he reinterpreted to mean "institutional heads." The Jews of Italy had a limited institutional life. Their schools of learning remained small, quasi-private affairs; they did not become centers of communal leadership, as occurred in Spain. In Italy, leadership was the province of prominent individuals, called *hashuvim*, "important people." This term was common in Ashkenazic circles, too. It had about it an aura of power and prestige, but nothing more official than that. Yet even with their informally structured leadership, the communities did function. Ahimaaz's claims about criminal jurisdiction were no doubt exaggerated, but Italian Jews certainly had courts of arbitration. They also had to represent themselves before governmental authorities. No one seems to have been more expert at this task than Rabbi Shefatiah of the later ninth century, perhaps Ahimaaz's most believable hero.

Like so many other Jewish communal authorities—even through early modern times[42]— Shefatiah combined in himself learning, wealth, and power. Best described by his wife, Shefatiah was "a great man . . . in Torah and Mishnah, Holy Scripture and Law, in Wisdom, in the Midrash—Sifra and Sifre, in textual exposition, and in Gemara (Talmud), in less and more difficult matters, in mystical understanding, in knowledge and cunning, in wealth and greatness, in courage and power, in laws and commandments, in fear and modesty, and in all the good virtues." Shefatiah also headed a yeshiva peopled by notable scholars *(haverim)* and pupils *(talmidim)*. Shefatiah's wealth no doubt came from his commercial involvements, not from land. The yeshiva and his scholarly prestige were Shefatiah's only institutional base, making him a *hashuv*.

41. Cf. Bonfil, 1989.
42. Israel, 1985: 194.

But this base was sufficient for Shefatiah, and others, to overcome challenges of several kinds. Shefatiah's son Amitai excommunicated a certain Rabbi Moses—possibly the scholar Moses of Pavia, whom Ahimaaz calls a "teacher of children"—for mocking a funeral elegy and challenging Amitai's ritual competence. This was a society where ritual created the spiritual underpinnings of communal life and was believed to unlock secret cosmological knowledge. Hananel, Shefatiah's brother, used mystical and ritual secrets to manipulate the written letters of God's ineffable name in order temporarily to restore to life his cousin, Papaleon, and Abu Aaron undid a similar act. A certain Baruch improperly used a book of *merkavah* mysticism, and as a result he died in a divinely ordained plague. In this context, Moses' slur was unforgivable.

Ritual issues could also be ones of life and death. The Muslim invader Sudan would have executed Shefatiah had he journied on the Sabbath, as he returned to Oria following negotiations that saved the city from attack and pillage. Negotiating skills served Shefatiah well on another occasion, when he averted a decree of forced baptism issued by the Byzantine emperor Basil. The key to Shefatiah's success was the emperor's esteem, which Shefatiah won for exorcising a demon from Basil's daughter. At Oria, Shefatiah had once prevented a pair of witches from cannibalizing an unfortunate boy. The emperor treated Shefatiah royally, even serving him kosher food in his Byzantine palace. What brought the two men together, one suspects, is that Basil loved his daughter "like the apple of his eye," and Shefatiah "cherished" his own daughter. Shefatiah, it was decreed, would not be made to endure conversionary pressure; neither would the Jews of Oria.

This reprieve, like the entire narrative of the encounter between Shefatiah and Basil, was surely the product of wishful thinking. The half century from about 876 to 935 was a trying time for southern Italian Jewry, whether because of Byzantine conversionary pressures or Muslim raids. Some Jews must have converted, and others were killed. If Shefatiah did save the Jews of Oria from Basil's decree, he saved only them, not those elsewhere in Apulia. As for the decree itself, it is not clear how persistent Basil and his successors were in using outright force, violating Roman law. Still, the Jews must have wondered exactly what the emperors intended. Jewish leadership, in addition, had been generally ineffectual against both emperors and Muslim invaders. Ahimaaz had to explain this failure, which he did through fanciful tales that at once paper over the truth and reinforce Ahimaaz's image of the correct political—

and personal—ideal. Shefatiah and Basil are thus made into equals. Even their deaths occur simultaneously, with Shefatiah telling the loving crowd around him that he, Shefatiah, "has been summoned by God Himself to . . . confront Basil, who is on trial [before God] for his evil deeds."[43]

Ahimaaz would in fact like his readers to believe that under his ancestors' stewardship, relations with the authorities had been cordial. Yet even he admits that any such cordiality masked a fragile truce, including that with the Christian populace as a whole. The story of Theophilo, whom Abu Aaron had condemned to death for adultery, recalls events told by Gregory of Tours. Nearly lynched on his way to execution, Theophilo was saved by the imperial adjutant in Oria, but only at the price of his Judaism. Furious when Theophilo reneged shortly after, the adjutant cut off Theophilo's hands and feet and threw him into prison to die in agony.

Jews were truly secure only in their family life, which Ahimaaz describes in unexpectedly rich detail. Shefatiah tells the emperor Basil's wife that he has three children, two daughters and a son. This in fact was above the norm; brief life expectancy and death in childbirth made larger families a rarity. Perhaps to explain so many deaths,[44] children are said to be the easy prey of demons and quick to be possessed by spirits. Parents, nevertheless, grieved for dead children, and like Shefatiah (and Basil) they cherished living ones. At times, these emotions conflicted with halachic teachings. Shefatiah, for example, knew that it was advisable to betroth his daughter Cassia when she reached puberty. His wife knew this too, but she did everything to prevent a betrothal, declaring all of Cassia's suitors to be unworthy. One suspects that the mother, whose name Ahimaaz does not know, wanted to delay her daughter's exposure to childbirth. Cassia probably was fourteen or fifteen years old (befitting a society with scant medical technology, in which the onset of the menses is frequently late).[45] Yet why the mother and not Shefatiah held off the suitors is unexplained. Does this suggest maternal power, or is it only a device to make the story flow? For when Shefatiah discovers the truth, he immediately betrothes Cassia to Hasadiah, his nephew. Literary device or not, Ahimaaz could have been writing only from experience.

Experience also taught Ahimaaz that even the saintly Shefatiah perceived marriage as more than a framework for giving birth. On discov-

43. Klar, 1974: 82–103; Bowman, 1985: 9–11.
44. Dan, 1974: 153–155, and see 170–175.
45. Levy, 1965: 50–55.

ering that Cassia had reached puberty, Shefatiah responded simply that the "time had arrived for making love." Allusions to sexuality, obliquely hinting at the sexual maturity of the offended women, may also be present in the verses Silano inserted in the sermon of the Palestinian *shaliah*. Medieval Jews were not constrained to repress sexuality, an attitude perhaps encouraged by the independence the Jewish marital bond created. Cassia married a first cousin, which Jewish law allows, but this was not a foregone conclusion, as her many suitors—and the qualities of learning and wealth Cassia's mother sought in them—reveal. In theory, Cassia might have married an outsider. When she married, like other Jews she would also have left her parents' home to form an autonomous conjugal unit.[46] Shefatiah and his brother Hananel maintained separate households. So Ahimaaz says, and so figuratively say also the narrow single-family dwellings, fronting on even narrower alleys, that survive in Oria's Rione Giudea (Jewish Quarter) even today.

An underlying curent of realism thus bears Ahimaaz's ideas along. His messianic hopes, however, rest on a wishful (and admittedly unconvincing) fiction. God, Ahimaaz seems to be saying, sends His people the Jews ever greater leaders: first Amitai, then Shefatiah, and finally Paltiel, who—achieving nearly everything that Gentile society had forbidden—guided Al-Muizz, bested the snub of a Byzantine ambassador, and ultimately became the nagid, or vizier, of Al-Muizz's son. Ahimaaz's message is barely disguised: if God has given the Jews a Paltiel, surely that greatest of all leaders, the Messiah, himself will not long tarry. Provocatively, Samuel the Nagid, the probable real-life model for Paltiel, played an equally premessianic role in the work of Abraham ibn Daud, once more suggesting a parallel between Italian and Spanish myths.[47]

Yet in the final analysis, patterns of individual behavior mattered far more to Ahimaaz than did messianic speculation. What defined Jewish life were acts of learning and piety, without which there would be neither leaders nor followers. Knowledge propelled Shefatiah to power; its absence, or misuse, destroyed Baruch. Piety brought Theophilo to unexpected reward. Over his family's objections—on the eve of Yom Kippur, the Day of Atonement, "when sins are forgiven"—Theophilo the *hashuv* betrothed his daughter to the pitiful *'aluv* ("lowly one") who unfailingly served him in prison. And in return, "God secreted him away, and

46. Stow, 1987: 1090–94.
47. Shirman, 1951: 185; Cohen, G., 1968: 76.

forgave him his sins." Yet were not Theophilo's decision to forgo conversion and suffer physical pain, his life in prison, the Yom Kippur aura, and, finally, the gift of his daughter to a devoted although lowly servant acts of repentence *(teshuvah)*, prayer *(tefillah)*, and charity or good deeds *(zedaqah)?* Consequently, the Theophilo story contains the germ of the eventual concept sanctified in the High Holiday liturgy, that "*teshuvah, tefillah,* and *zedaqah* avert the evil decree" and permit Jews spiritually to surmount earthly sufferings. However, the prayer which says just these things, the *Unetaneh toqef,* was composed in the Rhineland, and its author was a descendant of Kalonymos of Lucca. It would appear that the ideals depicted by Ahimaaz became part of the cultural baggage that Italians migrating northward took with them and transmitted to their disciples, so laying the foundations for later developments. The chains of scholarly tradition composed by these disciples as much as two hundred years later freely admit this much.

Yet Italian-Jewish culture spread in more than a northerly direction. Ibn Daud's "Story of the Four Captives," which prefaces his myth of Spanish foundation, commences with a portentous event. Four scholars, setting out by ship to reach the Academy of Babylonia, are captured by pirates and then ransomed. This seemingly fortuitous event leads directly to the establishment of great yeshivot in Fustat (Cairo), Qairowan (Tunis), and Lucena (Cordoba). The port these scholars embarked from was Bari. The story, of course, is a fiction, but it is built on what people believed. Did not the towering twelfth-century scholar Rabbi Jacob Tam remark that not "from Zion" but "from Bari will come forth the Torah, the word of the Lord from Otranto"? As we have seen, this playful biblical paraphrase (Isa. 2:3) was far from being empty hyperbole.[48]

48. Klar, 1974: 47 (citing Jacob Tam).

4 Maturing Culture and Politics

The earliest references to Jews in Ashkenaz (specifically, the German Rhineland and its environs) concern merchants and their activities in the eighth and ninth centuries. Stable Jewish settlements were probably not founded until sometime around the year 850. Shortly afterward, in the year 888, a church council at Mainz—the city that would soon become the center of Jewish life—prescribed rules to ensure that Christians maintained a proper distance from the Jews and their negative influence. All too little is known about the origins of these new Jewish communities. Jews settled in towns along the Rhine and other rivers, principally at Mainz, Worms, and Regensburg. They also settled in numerous small villages where they continued to dwell for hundreds of years.[1] The geographic distribution of Ashkenazic settlements was an unpredictable one. Jews settled in Speyer on the Rhine river only when they were invited to do so in the year 1084. They had lived in Cologne, Mainz, and Worms, just to the north, since the tenth century, if not earlier. There is no way of knowing whether the late settlement in Speyer reflects hesitancy, hostile conditions, or simply that Speyer lagged behind other Rhenish towns in developing its commercial potential. Jewish commercial activities may have included the production of goods and not only trade in those goods. A twelfth-century renewal of charters given the Jews of Speyer and Worms[2] permitted them to deal freely in "colors and ointments." These Ashkenazic Jews, like their Sicilian and Spanish contemporaries, may have been involved in the arts of dyeing and the preparation of medicinal compounds. Their production and distribution would have benefited

1. Blumenkranz, 1966: 62–74.
2. Linder, 1988: 44:557.

considerably the commercial expansion of the city. Indeed, in his charter of 1084, bishop Rudiger Huozmann said that he was inviting the Jews to dwell there specifically "to add to the city's [commercial] reputation."[3]

Surprisingly much is known about the social structure of these new communities. An overall homogeneity of interests and a single class structure went hand in hand with the appearance of wealthy individuals, a scholarly elite, and a body of communal leaders. These three were most often one and the same. Possibly the Jewish population as a whole in the tenth and eleventh centuries came close to imitating this pattern, although there surely was considerable uncouthness and even violence.[4] The truth probably lies somewhere in the middle. Some Jews must have been poor and some may have engaged in service or menial occupations. But these Jews were not submerged by the kind of wealthy, patrician Jewish households known in places like Nuremberg in the late fifteenth century. They also did not have to compete against the power blocks created by alliances of learning and wealth such as those that distinguished eastern European Jewish society in early modern times.[5] Distinguished rabbinic families, too, were not a caste apart, although the offspring of these families frequently married the children of other rabbis. Furthermore, rabbinic families were no larger or smaller than others in the community. In fact, family standing in the Rhenish communities cannot be distinguished on the basis of family size, as is normally the case. The homogeneity in Jewish family structure suggests a homogeneity of attitudes and perhaps of wealth, at least in the broad center strata of the communities. Male literacy, necessitated by the Jews' disproportionate commercial involvements, was no doubt exceptionally high. Many women, too, needed this skill, for the same reason. However, whether not only commercial writings but liturgical and halachic ones as well were being widely read is moot; the absence of multiple copies of manuscripts may have made it necessary for the latter to be memorized.

Jews could not imitate the manorial, feudal patterns of governance that characterized much of northern medieval society from the tenth century onward. They had no feudal aristocracy that claimed right through might and through the possession of large estates. The only governmental procedures to which they had access were those they had learned from the Jews of Italy. But these soon proved to be inadequate, and Ashkenazic

3. Linder, 1988: 49:600.
4. Agus, 1969: 7–11,310–318; Grossman, 1981: 20–23.
5. Toch, 1980; Katz, 1971: chap. 15; Israel, 1985: 190–194.

Jews were forced to develop new procedures of their own. This they did in part by adapting specifically non-Jewish practices and remolding them to conform to traditionally Jewish perspectives. In the words of Gershom of Mainz: "What the *kehillah* [the community] has decreed is a valid edict; and its acts are *faits accomplis*."[6] These edicts and acts were to be enforced by the *kahal*,[7] a term that normally refers to an informally selected body of more worthy—although not specially privileged—citizens, called the "men of the city" or, alternately, the "good men of the city" or the "important ones." All or most (male) individuals nevertheless took part in communal life, for the *kehillot* were small in size. As late as 1096, the number of Jews in Mainz did not exceed eight hundred, and no community was larger. Within this restricted physical context, as well as within an equally limited conceptual one, we may easily understand Gershom of Mainz's emphasis on collective commitment when he ruled that "whoever has lost an object has the right to insist that the *kahal* make the Cantor cease his benedictions until *all* enter into a *herem* ["ban" = oath, or pact] requiring anyone with knowledge of the object to notify one who is *tsanua* ["modest"] from among the *'anshei ha-'ir* ["(important men) of the city"]. No one may say: 'I will not join the *herem* but will only litigate [possibly before non-Jews].'"[8]

The physically small Jewish community thus predicated its functions on consent, as, in fact, European Jewish communities were still doing as late as the seventeenth and eighteenth centuries, when their character had also become a distinctly oligarchic one.[9] Communal order was established through binding oaths sworn by each communal member to perform specific acts. Anyone who violated these oaths would be excluded from the community and denied its services. The powers of the *kahal* in this process were essentially indirect. The *kahal* could enforce discipline only by resorting to such devices as allowing aggrieved parties to interrupt communal prayers.[10] The reliance on these roundabout tactics indicates how weak and unstructured communal governmental organs actually were. The interruption of prayer is especially revealing. In Ashkenaz, as in Italy, prayer was considered to be far more than simple verbal communication between a Jew and his God. It was endowed with secret meanings, and its uninterrupted recitation was believed necessary to

6. Grossman, 1981: 131; idem, 1988.
7. Grossman, 1975: 189.
8. Finkelstein, 1972: 120.
9. Israel, 1985: 192.
10. Finkelstein, 1972: 15–18.

preserve communal well-being. The *kahal* would not have sanctioned interruptions had it possessed more concrete jurisdictional powers. The absence of these powers may also partly explain why it was necessary for the community to rely on consent, and why, wherever possible, it circumvented litigations, which encouraged the unwanted intervention of outside authorities in internal disputes. The absence of governmental authority may be seen again in the opinion of Joseph Bonfils (Tov Elem) of Limoges that one community had no right to obligate the members of another, even to share the expenses involved in ransoming captive Jews.[11]

These details about communal life may be known because for the first time we have access to a corpus of nonliterary Jewish sources. Hundreds of legal responsa—questions about specific disputes, together with detailed answers—have survived from as early as the tenth and early eleventh centuries, the period of Gershom of Mainz and Joseph Bonfils. What we know from these responsa is amplified by textual commentaries and later legal codes. There are also chronicle sources that describe the events of the Crusade period. Yet even these sources leave many gaps in our knowledge. More than one historian has been ready to fill in these gaps by speaking of an underground origin to Jewish communal structures.[12] These structures purportedly emerged into the open only in the eleventh century, when the Jews were granted autonomous powers, including those of taxing their fellows. One is apparently to assume that the structures themselves were always there. This was simply not so. Rather, as the dicta of Gershom of Mainz indicate, structures evolved slowly, gropingly, and perhaps in ways that were beyond the awareness of contemporaries themselves. Even at the time of the First Crusade, these structures were far from being formalized. This is not surprising. Before about the end of the eleventh century, nobody, neither Christians nor Jews, had begun to define such things as the nature of elected office and the powers that elected officials (like bishops) exercised after election and before consecration.[13] Just when the Jews began to reflect on the nature and substance of their political institutions is hard to determine. The inchoate Rhenish institutions of the tenth and eleventh centuries were animated less by formal structural considerations than by a series of highly creative academic and communal leaders.

These leaders built on Italian foundations. The pivotal figure in trans-

---

11. Agus, 1965: 173–175; see also Grossman, 1975: 180–181; Saperstein, 1986.
12. Agus, 1969: 186–190; Schwarzfuchs, 1966: 125.
13. Benson, 1968: passim.

ferring Italian culture to the north was most likely Meshullam ben Kalonymos, who remained in Lucca for most of his life but whose teachings and followers moved northward.[14] Meshullam's responsa were treated as binding legal decisions in southern French communities such as Arles and in Rhenish ones such as Mainz. Mainz was a magnet community. Scholars emigrated there from as far away as French Anjou. They were attracted by Mainz's new schools and by the probing method of textual commentary and learning that these schools were developing. The reputation of these schools grew as they sent complex and learned questions to older centers like Rome and even to Rabbi Hai Gaon in Baghdad in the early eleventh century. The great masters of these schools, whose structures were small and intimate—in the manner of a tutor surrounded by his immediate pupils—were often newcomers. The earliest of them, Shimon ben Isaac, may have immigrated from Le Mans, just as Abun the Great may have somewhat later. Rabbi Leontin, the teacher of Gershom of Mainz, was an immigrant of indeterminate origins, as was Rabbi Gershom himself, who may have come from Italy or more likely France. From no later than the time of Rabbi Gershom (ca. 960–1028), Mainz became the center of northern Jewish learning. The city boasted not only schools but also an informal aristocracy of learning in the form of five major rabbinic families, the Kalonymos, the Machiri, the Abun, the ha-Cohen, and the ha-Levi, which cross-fertilized each other culturally and through intermarriage.[15] The outsider, Rabbi Gershom, towered above them all.

Gershom of Mainz, known as Rabbenu (Our Rabbi) Gershom, the Light of the Exile, is most famous for the *taqqanah* (meaning "ordinance" or "innovation") correctly attributed to him, stipulating that Jews may not marry more than one wife at a time. This *taqqanah* formalized within European Jewish law a reality that had existed since the closing centuries of the Roman Empire, when the emperors forbade the Jews to practice bigamy. The perceived need to make written Jewish law congruent with practice may reflect the conscious emphasis eleventh-century Rhenish Jews placed on the monogamous conjugal family unit. It has also been suggested that the ordinance reflects the anxiety that while traveling abroad for extended periods, Jewish merchants might violate the norm and take a second wife.[16]

14. Grossman, 1981: 60.
15. Grossman, 1981: 27–29,79–105; idem, 1988a: 23–25.
16. Westreich, 1988: 118–164; Grossman, 1981: 131; idem, 1988.

Gershom's *taqqanah* on monogamy was not the only one he issued. He has been credited with a whole series of communal ordinances, including one that prohibits divorcing a woman without her consent; another, designed to prevent rent gouging, orders Jews not to rent houses from Christian landlords who have forced out former Jewish tenants. Gershom also composed sacred poetry, or *piyyutim* (this was a scholar's "cultural obligation"), as well as textual glosses, legal decisions, and responsa. Ten of his *piyyutim* have survived, as have more than seventy-five of his responsa.[17] Nevertheless, Gershom's greatest legacy is his contribution to the development of the methodology that characterized the Rhineland schools. Learning in those schools took place in an atmosphere of intensive dialogue between master and pupils. The subject of this dialogue was the text of the Talmud. Even in the eleventh century, the Talmud was in many ways still an obscure work for northern Jewry. Its text had to be elucidated and made into a flexible instrument to serve as the basis for ongoing legislation and communal direction. Without the teaching skills of scholars like Rabbi Gershom, this transformation would not have occurred.[18]

But the Jewish schools of the Rhineland were not free to pursue their labors undisturbed. Rabbi Gershom was forced to issue a *taqqanah* regarding the status of those who had been (forcibly or willingly) converted to Christianity and who later sought to return to Judaism. A similar text was issued at the beginning of the twelfth century by Solomon Itzhaqi, better known by his acronym, Rashi.[19] On more than one occasion, the Jews had to interrupt their studies to deal with matters of security and with their political status. The greatest interruption of all was that caused by the First Crusade, in 1096, which nearly brought the Jewish settlement in the Rhineland to an abrupt end and certainly affected the course of Jewish cultural life.

Political Fortunes

Rabbenu Gershom's apparent references to forced baptism, together with reports that his own son had been forcibly baptized, have sometimes created the impression that the early eleventh century was a time of violence. Accounts in Christian chronicles alluding to attacks on Jews

17. Ta Shema, 1988a: 45; Grossman, 1981: 161–164.
18. Ta Shema, 1988a: 29–31; Grossman, 1981: 424–434.
19. Katz, 1958.

have strengthened this conviction, to the extent that this purported violence has been labeled the "initial crisis of northern Jewry."[20] Such a pessimistic opinion, however, is not easily verified. The chronicled accounts are so stylized and problematic as to put their credibility in doubt.

According to the Quedlinberg Annals, for example, King Henry II of Germany expelled the Jews of Mainz in 1012. Yet if this expulsion occurred, it was nullified within a month of its promulgation. Jewish sources do not mention it at all. Jewish sources are also silent about the multiple attacks reported by Raoul Glaber, who said that in the year 1009 "all the peoples of the world united in a common will" to punish the Jews for persuading the Caliph Al-Haqim to destroy Jerusalem's Church of the Holy Sepulcher. But Glaber is notorious for blending fantasy with fact.[21] Indeed, nearly twenty years before Glaber's chronicle, Ademar of Chabannes—also describing the Holy Sepulcher's destruction—said nothing about an attack on the Jews. Not that Ademar's chronicle itself lacks peculiarities. No other source corroborates Ademar's claim that in 1020 Pope Benedict VIII burned twenty Roman Jews at the stake for desecrating a holy image and causing an outbreak of plague. Had this event occurred, it would have been unique in the history of the relations between the Jews and the medieval papacy. An anonymous Hebrew text implicitly contradicts Ademar by crediting an early eleventh-century pope, possibly Benedict VIII himself, with saving the Jews of northern France from a persecution initiated by King Robert the Pious. Yet even if this contradiction is discounted, and we accept the argument that this text—which traditionally has been given full credence—is a thirteenth-century fiction, Ademar's claim remains unconfirmed.[22] In short, our knowledge of the so-called crises and violent episodes of the early eleventh century derives exclusively from clerical narratives that often substitute literary topoi for real events.

Yet these narratives do reflect the mood of the late tenth and early eleventh centuries. Jews had reason to feel that Christian negativity was becoming ever more firmly entrenched. That feeling is conveyed in Meshullam ben Kalonymos' condemnation of Christianity as the true fourth kingdom of Daniel—a kingdom "with legs of iron and hoofs of brass that consumes, destroys and tramples all with its feet."[23] Possibly,

---

20. Chazan, 1972.
21. France, 1989: xlviii–xlvix.
22. Chazan, 1972; cf. Stow, 1984: 27–29.
23. Grossman, 1981: 63.

Meshullam was alluding to episodes of episcopally initiated forced conversions (as distinct from mob or royally sponsored violence), like the
one that Glaber alleged to have taken place in Limoges in the year 1010.
Moreover, was not Pope Leo VII, in 937, supposed to have counseled
Archbishop Frederick of Mainz to expel those Jews whom he could not
persuade to convert through preaching? Did not a letter of 936, attributed
to the Venetian doge Pietro Candiano, urge the German King Henry I to
order all the Jews of his empire to accept Christianity or be expelled?
And were not the contents of this letter adumbrated in a missive reportedly sent in 932 by the patriarch of Jerusalem to the Synod of Erfurt,
over which Henry himself presided?[24] Yet it is also possible that the texts
recounting these conversionary pressures are once again the products of
monastic fiction, founded on the difficulties which the Jews in the Byzantine Empire then were facing, and perhaps all growing out of one
original literary source. Indeed, Leo VII's consent to expulsion appears
as a codicil—and hence may be no more than a later interpolation—in a
letter whose basic subject is the archbishop's appointment and authority.

Regardless of the use of force, the truth is that Jews converted to
Christianity throughout the Middle Ages, many apparently willingly and
convinced of Christian truth. Hermann of Cologne's early twelfth-century
autobiographical memoir of his route to Christianity—although it, too,
has been accused of being a monkish invention—abounds with affirma-
tions of his beliefs.[25] Conversions like his, it goes without saying, were
rarely mentioned by Jews. But in at least one instance, stemming from
the late tenth century, Jews constructed a parody to relieve the anxieties
and apprehensions that these conversions must have generated. A certain
Sehoq ben Esther Israeli is said to have converted for venal reasons and
then endangered the community of Limoges (or Le Mans) as he self-
servingly wove his way back and forth from Christianity to Judaism. His
name, meaning "Joke, the son of Esther," makes it clear that this tale is
a fiction. No wonder that like all versions of the original Purim story, this
one, too, ends with the Jews' escape from danger.[26]

The Jews could not escape the effects of the new canon law collections
that were being produced in the eleventh century. The *Decretum*, composed in 1012 by Burchard of Worms, contains a fully structured Jewry

24. Linder, 1988: 56:724.
25. Cohen, J., 1987: cf. Saltman, 1988.
26. Chazan, 1970; Haberman, 1971; Stow, 1992a.

law whose nature is both restrictive and pejorative. More than thirty other canon law collections also adopted the *Decretum*'s texts.[27] The Church, in other words, was beginning to codify the rules for dealing with the Jews. Paradoxically, the establishment of commonly agreed upon boundaries to limit Jewish behavior eased the way toward accepting the Jews' right to coexistence and to the uninhibited practice of Judaism. Nonetheless, from the Jews' own point of view, collections like that of Burchard were at best a mixed blessing.

A further difficulty was that—to a greater extent than Guntram in the sixth century and Louis the Pious in the ninth—eleventh-century secular rulers were becoming imbued with a sense of duty to Christianity. The German emperors were anointed kings who considered it their obligation to protect the Church and to function as guardians of Christian piety. Ideas like those expressed by Agobard about a pure Christian community whose borders were coterminus with those of society itself[28] were beginning to penetrate lay circles. To be sure, the late eleventh-century papacy challenged this conception of monarchical supervision of the Church and demanded in its stead what it termed ecclesiastical liberties. But this challenge did not vitiate the sense of piety and duty to Christianity that rulers felt. Indeed, if late eleventh-century rulers sometimes overlooked notable canonical restrictions concerning Jews, this was because the ninth-century charter of Louis the Pious continued to set the tone in these matters through as late as the thirteenth century and even the fourteenth.[29]

Fundamentally, royal attitudes were shifting toward enforcement. In 1090, Emperor Henry IV reacted ambivalently to the problem of forced baptisms, threatening perpetrators with severe penalties but saying nothing about helping victims return to Judaism.[30] Only when hundreds of Jews were forcibly baptized during the massacres of 1096 did Henry consent to their lapse from Christianity. Jews could no longer feel secure about royal actions in matters regarding Christian belief. And as time progressed, Jewish distrust was increasingly justified.[31] Secular rulers were also becoming uncertain sources of day-to-day support, a fact likely reflected in the praise of the early eleventh-century rabbi Shimon ben

27. Gilchrist, 1988.
28. Tellenbach, 1970: chap. 3.
29. Lotter, 1989: 48–49.
30. Lotter, 1989: 38–39.
31. Stow, 1987a: 104–110.

Isaac for "laboring for the communities and seeing to the cancellation of evil decrees and tolls."[32] The Jews' constitutional stability had indeed begun to erode. The charters of privileges given to the Jews of Speyer in the year 1084 by Bishop Rudiger Huozmann and to those of Worms in 1090 by Emperor Henry IV, although granting the Jews broad privileges and stressing their continuing participation in the Rhenish economy, nevertheless reveal notable discontinuities with the past.[33]

Structurally, the charters of Rudiger and Henry IV resemble those of Louis the Pious. Exemptions from road tolls encouraged the expansion of Jewish trade, and other privileges made the Jews' private lives more comfortable. Jews were given a place to establish a cemetery, opportunity for the kosher slaughtering of animals, and the possibility of selling to Christians the nonkosher hindquarters of the animals they slaughtered. Churchmen had long protested this practice, and, as a rule, they would continue to do so whenever it was sanctioned during the Middle Ages (until the fifteenth and early sixteenth centuries, when the popes themselves allowed Jews to engage in it). Churchmen protested more vigorously Jewish employment of Christian wet nurses, which Rudiger's charter also permitted. It is unclear how Bishop Rudiger balanced his episcopal obligations with his secular responsibilities as the head of a city. Throughout the Middle Ages, many other churchmen found themselves in a similar predicament.[34]

The eleventh-century charters, especially the one of Henry IV, went a step beyond those of Louis the Pious in allowing Jews to summon Jewish (alongside Christian) witnesses to testify against Christians in court. Louis, as well as the later pseudo-Charlemagne capitularies, had apparently followed the canonical ruling specifying that Christian witnesses alone would have to suffice. Henry IV's innovation was adopted by succeeding German rulers until as late as the fourteenth century. But this change did not reflect a preference for secular over ecclesiastical advantage. More likely, Henry was moved by the highly developed medieval sense of law and justice.[35] Even canon lawyers accepted that Jewish testimony might at times be permissible.[36] Besides, at least one clause in Henry's charter displays sensitivity to ecclesiastical needs. Louis the Pious

32. Grossman, 1981: 95; and see Cohen, J., 1986.
33. Graetz, 1939: 297; Ben-Sasson, 1976: 412–413; Linder, 1988: 49:602.
34. Lotter, 1989: 37–42.
35. Linder, 1988: 49:603.
36. Pakter, 1974: 145–161.

had threatened "the life and the possessions" of those who enticed Jewish slaves to desert their masters and adopt Christianity. Henry reduced the penalty to a moderate pecuniary one and insisted that baptized slaves be allowed to practice their new faith, even while returning to their Jewish masters, as Henry required them to do. Louis the Pious may have observed (what he considered to be) the letter of Church law; Henry IV appears to have observed—at least in part—its underlying spirit.[37]

Yet Henry's concession to the Church regarding the Jews' slaves did not annul the effects of the other privileges granted by either his charter or that of Rudiger. Perhaps the most beneficial was the one that virtually gave the Jews de facto primary jurisdiction over internal disputes, saying: "Their [Jewish] *archisynagogus* [a title borne by communal heads even in late antiquity] shall judge in any dispute which occurs among them and against them, just like the city tribune among the townspeople." Jews may also have had no choice about appearing before the *archisynagogus*. As Henry IV said, "If it should happen that one of them, a perfidious person, should wish to hide the truth of something done among them, the man who governs the synagogue for the bishop shall make this person confess the truth according to their law."[38] Previously, the Jews had not possessed such coercive powers. The charter of Louis the Pious[39] says, in contrast, that "if any of them, Christian or Jews, should wish to hide the truth, the [Christian] *count* of that place shall make each of them reveal it, through appropriate investigation and according to his law." Henry and Rudiger thus granted the Jews unique jurisdictional and legal privileges. When Rudiger said that nowhere in the past or in any other German city had the Jews attained privileges like those he had bestowed upon them, he was correct. Rudiger's stated motivation for granting these privileges is also above suspicion. He acted not from Christian charity or some other possibly episcopal virtue but because, as he said, "When I wanted to make Speyer into a great town, I though I would add immensely to its luster if I would bring Jews to dwell in it."

Nevertheless, although the *archisynagogus* was chosen by the Jews themselves, his status was that of a tribune. He was a regent who only "governed the synagogue *for* the bishop" and at his behest. The *archisynagogus'* jurisdiction was also vulnerable, since appeals were heard by

37. Blumenkranz, 1960: 338,340.
38. Linder, 1988: 49:603.
39. Linder, 1988: 47:573; see also Stow, 1987b.

the bishop himself. Dissatisfied Jews could circumvent his decisions. Moreover, because jurisdictional authority resided solely in the hands of the *archisynagogus,* the system of justice organized around him defended primarily short-run, individual Jewish interests, not necessarily those of the organized communities. It certainly did not bestow upon the communities a recognized "corporate" status[40] or true primary jurisdiction. In addition, the obligation to appear before the *archisynagogus* may have been imperfectly enforced. Why else would Jewish leaders have constantly sought new means to prevent Jews from looking for redress to outside sources? Finally, there was a potential for conflict between the community and the *archisynagogus.* The *archisynagogus* is probably identical with the person called the *parnas* ("the provider") in Hebrew sources. In the later eleventh century, the *parnas* invariably belonged to one of the leading rabbinic families, such as the Kalonymides, who headed the communities. Certain charters even refer to members of this family by name.[41] So long as this unity of persons persisted, the *parnas-archisynagogus* and the communities functioned complementarily. In later centuries, when the *archisynagogus* evolved into either a governmentally appointed "state rabbi" or a secular head chosen by wealthy nonrabbinic Jewish factions, his existence, all too frequently, promoted tension and conflict.

More serious in contemporary terms, Rudiger's charter to the Jews differs little from those given at that time to foreign settlers. In 1106, the bishop of Hamburg—considering "that it would be profitable to us and to our successors"—entitled a group of Dutch colonists to enter his regions and polter (drain) the swamps, using techniques developed in the Netherlands. In return, the Dutchmen were to pay a fixed annual rental. The bishop also empowered the Dutchmen to establish their own courts, for they feared the "injustice of foreign judges," although the bishop himself was to take cognizance of appeals.[42] In addition, the lands the Dutchmen reclaimed were physically set apart from the rest of the town. Rudiger prefaced his charter to the Jews by saying that he was settling them in a walled *faubourg* (suburb) to protect them from the insolence of the worst mobs. As these parallels between Dutch and Jewish charters reveal, Rudiger was treating the Jews like outsiders, not indigenous residents. Their previous status under Roman law had thus expired. Even

40. Baer, 1985b.
41. Grossman, 1981: 401.
42. Reisenberg, 1958: 136.

the diluted version of it that had continued into the Carolingian ninth century was no longer valid. In addition, Rudiger's charter is not a grant of special commercial privileges to a select group of denizens, but a constitution for an entire community and the sole legal justification for that community's presence in Speyer. The charters of Henry IV and of subsequent German rulers are identically structured.[43]

Despite its broad privileges, therefore, and despite the clear desire it expresses to bring Jews to Speyer, Rudiger's charter and its subsequent ratifications mark a watershed in medieval Jewish history. Between the tenth and the thirteenth centuries, the Jews' constitutional status of Roman citizenship, with its unimpeachable right to live in Christian society, was exchanged for the status of personal dependence.[44] Wherever Jews resided, they did so increasingly at the arbitrary pleasure of their rulers, often with severe consequences. These rulers had in effect become the Jews' direct, and exclusive, feudal lords. However, unlike Christian dependents, the Jews had no set rules governing their feudal bonds. The result was that laws, guarantees, and conditions of residence could be, and not infrequently were, changed at will, as in the case of the "evil decrees" Shimon ben Isaac succeeded in having annulled in the early eleventh century. The privileges accorded by Rudiger's and Henry's charters may have differed little from those found in ninth-century grants, but these privileges were now bestowed as favors, not as benefits that derived from the Jews' status as permanent imperial residents. The emperor's *tuitio*, too, had become a discretionary grant and was no longer a prerogative of faithful citizens. In the Empire, this dependence on imperial discretion eventually was named "chamber serfdom," and similar names were instituted in other kingdoms. The late eleventh-century charters of Rudiger of Speyer and Henry IV roughly mark the midway point in the transition to this new status.

Constitutional erosion was also accompanied by growing physical insecurity. The Jews of Speyer needed walls for protection, and Henry IV set the penalty for forcibly baptizing a Jew at the enormous sum of twelve gold pounds. Such baptisms nevertheless continued to occur, and with ever greater frequency. In 1096, the number of Jews forcibly baptized was exceeded only by that of Jewish martyrs. For the Jews of the Rhineland, the First Crusade, which occurred in that year, was a major trauma.

43. Linder 1988: 49:595.
44. Colorni, 1945: 43–66.

5   The Crusades

In the spring of 1096, bands of wandering vagrants, followed by the armed contingent of Count Emicho of Leiningen, destroyed the Jewish communities of Mainz, Worms, and Cologne. Communities were decimated in Treves and as far away as Prague. Jews in small towns were murdered or forcibly baptized. The entire population of Regensburg was forced to immerse itself baptismally in the Danube. Because of his faithfulness to commitments and his determined methods of defense, Bishop John saved all but eleven Jews at Speyer. There is some evidence of an attack in Rouen, but this is the only reference to violence outside the Empire (roughly speaking, Germany), where hundreds of Jews died[1] and probably no more than 30 to 40 percent of the Jewish populace escaped harm. The physical damage was matched by the deep scars the massacres left on Jewish memories. *Payyetanim* constructed detailed lists of martyrs. For hundreds of years afterward, these lists were ritually recited in synagogues. Chroniclers composed accounts of the events. Responsa dealt with the delicate problem of forced converts, their behavior, and the terms for their possible return to Judaism. These accounts are an open window onto twelfth-century Jewish mentalities and outlooks. The words of Solomon bar Samson, written shortly after 1140, speak for themselves:

> They arose . . . that awful nation . . . French and Germans, and set their hearts on going to the Holy City. To seek the grave of their disgrace[d one] and to expel the Ishmaelites . . . They put a foul sign on their clothing, a woof and weave . . . until they were like a throng of locusts, men, women, and children. When they passed the cities where Jews dwelled, they said: Behold, we are going far away, to take our vengeance on the Ishmaelites.

1. Baron, 1952: 4:105.

The Jews live among us, whose fathers unwarrantedly slew and hanged him on the cross. First, we will take our vengeance on them, and blot them out. The memory of Israel will no longer exist. Otherwise, let them be like us and confess the son of treachery.[2]

For Solomon bar Samson, the First Crusade was not a great moment in European history. It was a plague ("locusts") brought upon the Jews by men, women, and children drawn from many lands ("France and Germany"). It was the act of a mob that had set out to take vengeance on the Muslims for conquering the Holy Land, and especially Jerusalem, a city that had become as holy for Christians as it was for Jews.[3] Although Solomon was incapable of putting it in just so many words, he correctly intuited that the Crusade was also a pilgrimage in pursuit of sanctity. The attacks on the Jews, as he saw it, were intended to do far more than chastise; their purpose was radically to purge Christian society and purify it. The Jews must be eliminated, then the Muslims, unless both first accepted baptism. The crusading passion was also all-embracing. At one point or another, it swept up everyone along its path. Solomon concluded that only unilaterally, and with sword in hand, could the Jews guarantee their protection.

But were Solomon bar Samson's perceptions—formed fifty years after the events themselves—accurate? Had the world in which the Jews lived been transformed?[4] And had attitudes toward them become only negative? Had the Jews become vulnerable to capricious violence[5] whenever the emotions of prejudice boiled over,[6] making Jewish life into a "Vale of Tears"?[7] Or were the Crusades in fact an isolated event, indicative of a progressive erosion in status but no more than that?[8]

The truth is that the massacres of 1096 do not indicate that Jewish security had totally collapsed, nor were they necessarily a prelude to subsequent unremitting assaults. They were also unforeseeable, presaged by neither the policies of pre-Crusade rulers nor possible earlier episodes of forced baptism. On the eve of the Crusades, Rhenish Jews had no reason to believe that their position was a precarious one; the attacks

2. Haberman, 1971: 24.
3. Linder, 1985: 1–22.
4. Chazan, 1987; Schwarzfuchs, 1989: 251–268; see also Chazan, 1972.
5. Ben Sasson, 1976: 414.
6. Allport, 1958: 56–61.
7. Hakohen, 1895.
8. Kisch, 1949: 135–153.

took them by surprise, as the Jewish chroniclers say. In addition, it is arguable that the Crusades altered the course of Jewish creativity. They did provoke an intellectual crisis. Yet the creative epoch in the Ashkenazic schools had peaked before 1096.[9] The towering figure of the times, Rashi, was a Frenchman who had studied in Mainz but then returned to establish his academy at Troyes in Champagne (France). Moreover, following the First Crusade, the Rhenish communities themselves revived, as evidenced by the flowering a century later of the Hasidei Ashkenaz, one of medieval Judaism's most creative expressions. Just where, then, should the line between continuity and change be drawn, if at all?

The Crusades themselves were many things. They were a pilgrimage to the Holy Land, a mission to free captive holy places, and a renewal of the Christian ideal of settling the Holy Land, first enunciated by Eusebius in the late fourth century. The Crusades provided military aid to an embattled Byzantium that had almost fallen to the Muslim sword earlier in the eleventh century, and also provided lands to younger sons who could neither inherit their fathers' estates nor marry and found households of their own. The Crusades were a logical escalation of the three-century-old war for the reconquest (or conquest, depending on one's point of view) of the Iberian peninsula from the Muslims, which by 1085 had reached the city of Toledo. As such, the Crusades signaled that with regard to the Islamic world, Europe had shifted from the defensive to the offensive. Indicatively, merchants in the Mediterranean now began to prefer Italian over Egyptian ships to move their goods.

The Crusades personified the abstract ideal of *Christianitas* (Christendom), the belief that the Latin world was united by a common culture and in pursuit of a common religious ideal. They were an expression of popularized piety, of the aura of religiosity permeating even realms that possessed no distinctive religious aspect,[10] and of the unquestioned belief by many at the time of the Crusades "in a superior, supra-empirical reality, which they designated by Christian symbols."[11] Agobard of Lyons' ideal of a Christian people living in a pure Christian society seems firmly to have taken root, at least in certain segments of the population.

The Crusades concretized messianic hopes. For many, the earthly and the heavenly Jerusalem had become indistinguishable, as Crusader maps and previous iconographic depictions of the Holy City testify.[12] To take

9. Marcus, I., 1989: 687.
10. Becker, 1981: 19–58.
11. Langmuir, 1980: 366.
12. Kuhnel, 1978: passim.

Jerusalem and to purify it of all non-Christians, even by fire—as the Crusaders did—was to cleanse the world in readiness for the Second Coming of Christ. Expectantly, and as though he were paraphrasing the contemporary Jewish poet and thinker Judah Halevi, Bernard of Clairvaux wrote that his heart was in the East, even while he dwelled (physically) in the West. Godfrey of Bouillon, the crusading Duke of Lower Lorraine and direct descendant of Charlemagne, crowned himself not king but "guardian" of the Holy Sepulcher, with a crown of thorns in memory of Christ's passion. To take the Holy Land was an *imitatio christi* ("imitation of Christ"). In the words of Urban II, who preached the Crusade, it was also an act worthy of eternal glory; to join the crusading army took precedence over all earthly concerns. The terms the Crusaders used to describe themselves and their mission fully reflect their aspirations. They were "Catholic Soldiers, Warriors of the People of God, and the Troops of the Eternal Kingdom" (*milites catholici, pro populo Dei pugnatores, belligeratores regis aeterni*).[13]

In an electrifying address in the fall of 1095, Urban II preached the Crusade in the French town of Clermont. In the words of the monk Robert, who reported the speech, Urban told of a "cursed people [the Muslims], alienated from God," which had attacked and pillaged Christian lands, forcibly converted their inhabitants, and destroyed churches. "When they want to torture anyone by a base death, they perforate his navel, drag out the extremity of the intestines, and bind it to a staff; then, by blows they compel the victim to run around the stake until the viscera gush forth."[14] Such barbarity demanded revenge, even if that meant leaving behind worldly affairs, families, and children to pursue eternal glory. Christians had to love God above all. Their recompense would be the soil of the "Land of Milk and Honey" that had been given to the Children of Israel. The land sought its liberation, and, liberated, it would belong to those who lacked land in Europe. To go to the Holy Land was to do penance for sin. The "Holy People," the spiritual army of Christ, the spiritual family of the Church, would thus conquer as had Joshua, and would build a sanctuary as had Ezra and Nehemiah. It would fulfill the monkish vision of exchanging the this-worldly for the spiritual kingdom, to realize on earth the *populus dei*.

For more than two centuries this vision lured Crusaders, including the greatest princes and kings. Its power measures the Christianization of a

13. Riley-Smith, 1982: 62.
14. Roberti Monachi, 1963: 200–202.

Europe that was coming to maturity in the twelfth century. In 1096, Duke Godfrey of Bouillon took the Cross. In 1146, he was followed by the French king Louis VII and the emperor Conrad III. Quite probably, Louis VII himself helped initiate the Second Crusade. In 1188, the Third Crusade was led by kings Richard the Lion Hearted of England, Philip Augustus of France, and Emperor Frederick I Barbarosa. Richard was captured in Austria and Frederick drowned. In 1204, the crusading ideal was perverted when the Venetians turned the Fourth Crusade into the conquest of Constantinople by Western knights. In 1248 Louis IX left France for the Holy Land, and in 1270 he died in Tunis; his entire reign, in fact, has been compared to an extended Crusade.[15] Louis' younger contemporary Emperor Frederick II, the *bête noire* of the High Middle Ages, also spent years in the East.[16]

Crusades to the East were paralleled, in fact anticipated, by those at home. The battles of the Spanish Reconquista in the mid-eleventh century were fought under the papal banner of Alexander II, who also set forth rules to govern the Crusaders' conduct toward Jews. In the thirteenth century, Pope Innocent III preached a Crusade against the Albigensians, Christian heretics of southern France, many of whom were massacred at Montségur. Gregory IV preached a Crusade against Frederick II. Boniface VIII called for a Crusade against his local enemies, the Colonna family of Palestrina. Yet even this mockery did not destroy the crusading ideal. In the early fourteenth century, plans were made for a new Crusade, to recover at least Acre, the last Crusader stronghold in the Holy Land, which had fallen in 1291. These plans were never implemented. Nevertheless, the idea of unity and redemption through battle continued to animate western Europe. Possessing such great power, the crusading ideal could obviously do enormous damage, as well as good. The Jews, who were believed to be an obstacle to its fulfillment, suffered bitterly.

The Crusaders' attack on the Jews was more than an accidental outgrowth of the attack on the Muslims. It was, like the latter, integral to that idealized quest for a pure Christian society which had been restated in the eleventh century—albeit with no reference to the Jews—by such seminal Christian thinkers as Peter Damian, Cardinal Humbert, and the monk Hildebrand (Pope Gregory VII). The impulses that drove Christians to attack the Muslims also drove them to attack Jews. If Muslims were

15. Jordan, 1979.
16. Lopez, 1982: 23–26.

polluting the distant Holy Land, Jews were polluting Christian territories at home. If Muslims were fighting Christ's army of warriors, Jews stood opposed to Christ's mystical family, the Church. If Muslims in the East symbolized mythical unknowns, the Jews did so all the more in the West, because of the latter's unique "sacred history." As Christians failed to distinguish the real Holy Land from the mythical one depicted on maps, so, it seems, they also failed to distinguish their real enemies, the Muslims, from their imaginary ones, the Jews. Were not the Jews, moreover, deserving of punishment for murdering Christ? At the time of the Crusades, this was being said ever more frequently.

Not every Christian entertained such hostile thoughts, however, and only a few were prepared to act them out. The events of 1096 were not those of Spain in 1391, when nearly an entire society rose up to rid itself of the Jews or forcibly convert them.[17] Moreover, violence in 1096 did not come from the highest levels of society. Neither royalty nor bishops participated in the massacres. The official crusading army, made up of ranking nobility and led by a papal legate, the bishop Adehmar of Le Puy, appears pointedly to have avoided harming Jews. Adehmar was no doubt guided by the letters issued in 1063 by Pope Alexander II (praising those who refrained from attacking Jews and censuring others who forcibly baptized them), which, just two years before the First Crusade, Ivo of Chartres had included in his influential canonical collection. Ivo himself was the confidant of another Frenchman, Pope Urban II, about whom an anonymous (albeit fourteenth-century) Hebrew manuscript says that he issued a bull decrying violence. Popes in the early twelfth century likewise took steps to prevent the repetition of violence. If Solomon bar Samson condemned "the Satan, the pope of Rome," for his failures, he was probably referring to Clement III, the antipope appointed by Emperor Henry IV, who had protested the return to Judaism of the forcibly baptized.[18]

Violence instigated at the top of society, or connivance at that level, would indeed have been unprecedented. Visigothic kings resorted to enslavement, and other early medieval rulers to expulsion. The sole story of violent royal persecution, concerning the early eleventh-century French king Robert the Pious, is a much later fabrication. In 1096, kings did not alter their ways. However, Emperor Henry IV—in whose lands the mas-

17. Kriegel, 1979: 1391.
18. See Leibeschutz, 1959; Stow, 1984: 17–18.

sacres occurred—failed to protect his Jewish subjects. His charters threat-ened violators of the Jews' peace with corporal punishment, and he did punish a few culprits. Yet isolated and belated reprisals such as these did nothing to keep the attacks from starting. This failure was to be expected. At the time of the First Crusade, the emperor was bogged down in southern Italian Apulia, as he had been since 1090, with problems that threatened the continuity of his rule. Henry's most effective act was to respond to the request of Kalonymos, the *parnas* of Mainz, and persuade Duke Godfrey of Bouillon (who was also bought off by large sums of Jewish money) not to fulfill his oath to begin his pilgrimage by murdering Jews. Henry also mitigated his failure by opposing Clement III's refusal to allow the forcibly baptized to reenter the Jewish fold.

Before the massacres, the Jews believed that their best hope for protec-tion was the Rhenish bishops. In fact, these bishops accomplished little. This failure has been attributed to political loyalties. Bishops appointed by Henry IV supposedly made great efforts on the Jews' behalf, while those loyal to the pope in his protracted struggle with the emperor (over control of the Church) were at best lukewarm.[19] Yet were not the French bishops who headed the crusading army and kept it from attacking Jews direct papal appointees? Moreover, on closer inspection, only one Rhen-ish bishop, John of Speyer, truly prevented a massacre, and even in Speyer eleven Jews died. The other Rhenish bishops were either too weak—or threatened—to be effective. "The archbishop of Mainz," says Solomon bar Samson, "gathered his officials and appointees, great men of the land, to aid us. At first, he intended to save us with all his might." But his Christian soldiers refused to kill Christian attackers in order to save Jews. "The bishop himself had to flee his abomination [his church]. Some had threatened to kill him for speaking well of the Jews." In Treves, the bishop, who had refused all bribes, was powerless, since "he was a stranger in the city . . . He had no kin or allies there." He had said, "I intended and I properly ought to keep faith [my pledge] with you . . . [to protect you] until not one community remains in all of Lotharingia. [But now they are all destroyed.]" The bishop's only advice was that the Jews save themselves through baptism. Their subsequent acts of martyrdom, *Kiddush ha-Shem* ("The Sanctification of God's Name") horrified him, as they previously had the bishop of Mainz: "He heard that the rabbi had slaughtered his son; he grew furious, and said, 'I surely have no further wish to aid you.'"

19. Schiffmann, 1930/1931: passim.

The case of the bishops is mirrored by that of the townsmen. Little is known about German town life at this time—and about the middle class in particular—but once again Solomon bar Samson is instructive. The attacks did not come from the townsmen themselves, nor were they caused by economic jealousies more typical of a much later period.[20] On the contrary, "The idolatrous wanderers gathered, . . . some of the important townsmen opposed them," and for doing so they were killed. Still, some townsmen were willing to open the gates, and others may actually have joined the attack. Did not Rudiger's charter refer to a "turbulent crowd" already in 1084? Yet the basis for this supposition, the episode in the anonymous Hebrew "Story of the Ancient Decrees," which describes townsmen arousing popular fury by parading an exhumed Christian corpse through the streets of Worms and accusing the Jews of "boiling it in water and pouring the water in our wells to kill us," has been called a later insertion in the text.[21] One cannot so easily explain away Solomon bar Samson's claim that villagers near Treves joined the members of the wandering bands in their pillage and slaughter.

It was indeed these wandering bands which first assaulted the Jews, motley crews—as they are unflatteringly described by the contemporary Latin chronicler Albert of Aix—of ignorant and illiterate men, women, and children from France, England, Flanders, and Lotharingia, all of whom had spontaneously set out to join the Crusade.

> These people burned with the fire and with the love of God. They took with them all their money and possessions. But along the route wild goings on commenced and knew no limit. For these would-be Crusaders did not keep their distance from deceitful men, from sinners and from criminals. This bunch sinned further, and disgustingly; this crowd of pilgrim fools. They spoke of a goose as though it had the spirit of God upon it, and they said the same of a goat. Then a spirit of cruelty came upon them. Perhaps this was the will of God, or the fruit of confused thinking. They took vengeance on the Jews and carried out an awful slaughter, especially in Lotharingia (the Rhineland). And they said that this was the beginning of their pilgrimage and the first fulfilling of vows to fight against the enemies of the Christian faith.[22]

Jewish chroniclers accepted the accuracy of Albert's report. Solomon bar Samson, for one, drew details from it, including, notably, the story of the revered goose. The Jews understood that the establishment disapproved

20. Spufford, 1988: 344–348.
21. Riley-Smith, 1984.
22. Krey, 1921: 54–55.

of these rootless marginals. Albert and other Christian chroniclers in fact viewed the decimation of the wandering bands in the Hungarian swamps as a justly deserved punishment. Nevertheless, these wanderers were not mindless. They were aware that they had embarked on a crusading pilgrimage and that their attacks on the Jews stemmed from a crusading ideology, however primitive it may have been. Yet the zeal of these wanderers was not wholly beyond control. The first and perhaps the largest of their bands, which inundated the Rhineland in successive waves, refrained from attacking. Its leader, Peter the Hermit, a man of some renown, was too disciplined to allow pillage. At the same time, discipline did not put Peter above soliciting letters from the Jews of France informing their Rhenish brothers that it would be wise to contribute substantially to the provisioning of Peter's flock. Other wandering bands turned whatever discipline they had into destruction, and none inflicted more than the band led by Emicho of Leiningen.

Unlike other bands, which simply "encountered" Jews, that of Emicho deliberately set out to find and destroy them. Emicho attacked from the south and moved northward, beginning at Mainz and reaching Cologne. Emicho also differed personally from many of the Jews' other actual or would-be assailants. He was not a rootless vagabond but a powerful local noble, as, in fact, other members of his cohort were, too.[23] In common with the the vagabonds, however, Emicho and his noble followers must have suffered from great personal insecurity. For just as the former were surely anxious and perplexed by recent social transformations that had left them bereft of land, work, and often food, so Emicho and his followers no doubt felt threatened by the increasing feudalization of Europe and by the growing consolidation of its great fiefs and kingdoms. Local nobles like them were in constant danger of being swallowed up by large regional dukes and counts, and if they sat by passively, they chanced being dispossessed and degraded to the margins of noble society. It thus seemed natural that they should apply to themselves the words of the French monk Baldaric of Bourgueil: "Would you not avenge your blood relative? How much more ought you to avenge God, . . . whom you see reproached, *banished from his estates*, . . . begging for aid?"[24] In this sense, Godfrey of Bouillon, too, was threatened. He was a great duke and a direct descendent of Charlemagne who hoped to become a

23. Riley-Smith, 1986: 50–57.
24. Haberman, 1971: 26–27; Langmuir 1990a: 97–98.

king in his native Lotharingia. But his hopes were constantly dimming; he had to react. And like Emicho, Godfrey sought to do so—in the wake of Urban II's preaching—by setting out to conquer Jerusalem. Emicho fell on the way; Godfrey achieved a crown. Yet the crown that Godfrey placed on his head was literally one of thorns; the title he preferred was *advocatus* ("protector"), rather than "king." Is it any wonder that Godfrey was determined to "avenge the blood of the crucified one" by killing the Jews before he set out on his way?

The potential for nobles like Emicho and Godfrey to react to outside threats by choosing a course identical to that of the rude vagabond bands had fearful implications. At one time or another, any medieval Christian might feel similarly threatened. Reduced to possessing less land, wealth, power, or status than he believed was his due, he might displace the blame for his plight away from personal inadequacies and project it onto "the other," the Jew, who by way of ecclesiastical teachings had come to personify the essence of all frustration and opposition. The increasingly common desire of Christians to make reality congruent with ideals exacerbated the dangers, to the point that even those who opposed attacking Jews were pressured into deserting them in moments of stress. Accordingly, counseled Solomon bar Samson, Jews should henceforth trust themselves alone. Yet self-defense was not always sufficient. In 1190, the Jews of York, England, who had taken refuge from a raging mob in the king's tower, eventually committed mass suicide. William of Newburgh, the principal chronicler of this massacre, described it in terms that recall 1096: the town patriciate disassociated itself from the massacre; the initiators were heavily indebted members of the middle and even upper knightly class, motivated by fears of foreclosure; the spark that set off the massacre was the impending Third Crusade, whose army many of the attackers eventually joined.

The York violence was also a "rebellion of the king's debtors."[25] Formally, the Jews held the notes of indebtedness, but foreclosures benefited the king. He was the real creditor, controlling the redistribution of forfeited lands, as well as directly profiting through taxes on the interest collected by his vulnerable middle men, the Jews—the "royal usurers," as William of Newburgh himself called them.[26] The fear that these "royal usurers" might reduce them to penury impelled the knights to fury, a fury

25. Dobson, 1974: 37.
26. Langmuir, 1963: 223.

so great that the royal chancellor, the bishop of Ely, made no attempt to punish the ringleaders but took the more prudent, if pusillanimous, course of feigning ignorance about their identity. Any actions he took might have incited the knights to rebel. After all, at least one cause of the great rebellion in 1215—this time principally by the English magnates— would be resentment against royal manipulations worked through Jewish lending.

Tragedies at Blois and Brie[27] in France, in 1171 and 1192 respectively, escalated noble involvement in attacks one notch further. The Blois affair was spawned by a libel that the Jews had killed a Christian boy. But Count Thibaut of Champagne's subsequent burning of thirty Jews resulted mainly from his wish to avenge himself on his repudiated Jewish mistress, much to the delight of the countess, his wife—or so, at least, the Hebrew chronicler Ephraim of Bonn reports. At Brie, King Philip Augustus himself ordered Jews burned. He was furious—once again Ephraim of Bonn says—that the Jews had convinced (and paid) the local countess to execute a royal dependent guilty of murdering a Jew.[28] The Jews of both Blois and Brie, it would appear, were victims of comitial and royal anger. The count and the king, however, had also acted to restore a disrupted social order. The count had to repent for having taken a Jewish mistress; the king could not accept passively the news that his dependent at Brie had been accused and paraded to his execution, "crowned with thorns."[29] Indeed, ten years earlier, in 1182, Philip Augustus had expelled the Jews from his own royal domains, ostensibly to punish the offense to Christianity created by Jewish lending,[30] but even more because he believed that the Jews were guilty of ritually murdering a Christian boy.[31]

To be sure, in episodes like these, neither kings nor counts acted alone. At York, Brie, and Blois, clerical invective was crucial. A Premonstratensian monk urged on the rioters at York. The incitement of an unnamed Austin friar led directly to the fiery denouement at Blois. The royal chronicler Rigord also lauded Philip Augustus for expelling the Jews from the royal domain. Yet the chronicler who emotionally condemned the York riot, William of Newburgh, was an Austin friar. Unrestrained cler-

27. Jordan, 1989: 35–37; Chazan, 1970a.
28. Haberman, 1971: 124–126,128.
29. Chazan, 1968; 1969.
30. Chazan, 1980: 288–289 (trans.).
31. Jordan, 1989: 30–32.

ical animus seems to have been personal, not institutional. Bernard of Clairvaux, who protected the Jews at the time of the Second Crusade, and his pupil Rudolph, whose agitation Bernard quashed, were both Cistercians. If Ephraim of Bonn pointedly dubbed Bernard of Clairvaux "a priest with integrity" *(komer hagun)*, he had good reason for doing so.

By contrast, Ephraim was most dissatisfied with lay noble and royal behavior. His liturgical poem comparing the Jewish martyrs of Blois to the boys in the furnace in the Book of Daniel noted the role of the Austin friar, but placed the onus of blame on the count. Similarly, in 1146, Ephraim's censure of the monk Rudolph pales before his unreserved condemnation of the crusading king Louis VII. If Ephraim is to be believed—and it seems he should be—Louis caused the Jews great losses. According to Ephraim, "The Jews lost great sums of money, for the king of France commanded that all those who volunteered to go to Jerusalem should have quittances for any interest they owed the Jews; and most Jewish loans were contractual [literally, 'by faith'] ones."[32] In plain terms, Louis VII had released Crusaders from their obligations to Jewish lenders beyond the repayment of the principal. The Jews had also been unable to recuperate any lost interest through the profits that pledges—in particular, landed ones—generated, since most Jewish loans in mid-twelfth-century France were made on the basis of contract(ual oaths). From the mid-thirteenth century, incidents like this one became the norm; thirteenth-century kings, especially in France, regularly canceled the interest as well as the principal of loans. One hundred years earlier, Louis VII's action had been unparalleled. According to Ephraim of Bonn, Louis VII had also been its sole instigator.

One might have imagined that this role would have been played by a churchman. Eventually, a large number of ecclesiastics did vehemently object to Jewish lending. Yet no church law and no pope ever went beyond demanding that a moratorium be placed on the interest owed by absent Crusaders, and the first demand of this kind was not made until the year 1198, in the bull *Post miserabilem*. In 1146, Peter the Venerable, abbot of the great monastery of Cluny, did argue that Jewish wealth—which, he said, was the product of theft from Christian victims of usury—ought to be confiscated and used for a Crusade.[33] But confiscation

---

32. Haberman, 1971: 121.
33. Friedman, 1978; see also Berger, 1972.

is far more devastating than a moratorium or a calculated cancellation of interest. And Peter the Venerable was out of favor at the Capetian court. His proposal remained a dead letter. On the other hand, Pope Eugenius III's bull *Quantum praedecessores* was effectively forcing Christian lenders to release their debtors from *oaths* of repayment, thus automatically canceling the interest Crusaders owed. Yet neither Eugenius nor any subsequent pope ever pretended that it was possible to make *Quantum praedecessores* apply to Jewish lenders. Aware of this limitation, in 1146 Bernard of Clairvaux called upon the kings to apply to the Jews at least the "spirit" *(tenorem)* of the bull. Referring most likely to moratoria, Bernard should have been at least indirectly held responsible for Louis VII's edict. Nevertheless, it was the king's royal initiative that in the final analysis caused the Jews great losses. Louis alone had the power unilaterally to go beyond moratoria—as he did—and arbitrarily cancel oaths. This king, said to have treated Jews well in other respects,[34] wholly reversed his policy in the face of a Crusade, one he may himself have also originally proposed. It was this pattern of potentially unstable royal behavior and willful ignorance of the law that Ephraim of Bonn wanted to stress.

It is true that, secure in his royal status, Louis subdued the Jews by fiat, not brutally through physical force. But what has been called Louis' underlying sense of mission[35] was not far different from the emotions that motivated the Emichos and the wandering bands. Yet the vision these two shared of a correctly ordered society was not necessarily one that ignited conflagrations. Without a direct stimulus, the pent-up aggression of those who attacked the Jews in 1096 and 1146 might not have been unleashed. That stimulus was provided by the very act of crusading. For the Crusade was a pilgrimage and the Crusader was the *peregrinus,* the pilgrim par excellence, and pilgrims often traverse the thresholds, the *limina,* of behavior and judgment, conflating issues and violating norms that they would otherwise unfailingly observe.[36] This is precisely what occurred in 1096, as the crusading pilgrims lost sight of the distinctions separating Jews from Muslims, saying (in Solomon bar Samson's words), "First, we will take our vengeance on the [Jews]."

But not all pilgrims traverse *limina,* and neither did all Crusaders. Episcopal leaders like Adehmar of Le Puy diffused and channeled aggres-

34. Jordan, 1989: 9; Stow 1987a: 109–110.
35. Pacaut, 1964: 33–35; Grabois, 1984.
36. Turner, 1978: 1–39.

sive crusading fervor by converting the official crusading army into a disciplined *militia Christi,* unlike the unruly Rhenish levies. However, even this army, once it had entered the mythified sanctity of the Holy Land—under Godfrey of Bouillon's baton—was carried by its instincts across the threshold of restraint. In 1099, during the sack of Jerusalem, it set fire to the rabbinite synagogue, killing all the Jews who had fled to its sanctuary. No Crusader, it appears, was immune from traversing forbidden bounds.

The Crusades thus were a microcosm of medieval Jewish disasters. The events of 1096, 1146, and 1188 reflect a pattern that would recur in nearly all subsequent debacles: the Jews' antagonists were pilgrims, physically embarking on a Crusade, setting out to reform society, or mentally reaching within themselves in search of higher levels of personal piety; these pilgrims' goal was to purify space, the inner private one of their own minds or the outer public one of an entire society or land. The Crusades also bespeak the potential for explosion inherent in the meeting and fusion, in the late eleventh century and afterward, of the maturing concepts of the pilgrimage and the *societas christiana*—concepts to which all medieval Christians were coming to subscribe. In this sense, the Crusades may be said to signal a psychological divide. In its newly militant posture, Christianity was beginning to question whether it should, or could, harbor non-Christians in its midst.

Yet so far as the Jews were concerned, Christian society's growing militancy marked not the birth of radically new ideas but the diffusion of formerly elitist ones that the Jews already knew well and that in any case they had always viewed as inimical. In concrete terms, too, the Jews had no reason to exaggerate the effects of the Crusades. Their legal status did not abruptly change, and neither did the quality of their physical security. The Rhenish communities themselves revived within three or four decades of 1096. There was no universal European Jewish disaster. On the other hand, the Rhenish Crusade massacres of 1096 left the Jews with much to reconsider.

Jewish Reactions

Jews, in particular, had to rethink the matter of protection. In 1096, the Jews of Mainz perished because the bishop's soldiers failed them. The Jews of Speyer survived because, secure in the walled defensive perimeter given them by Bishop Rudiger, they deterred the attackers by force of arms. Jews throughout the Rhineland, and elsewhere, remembered this lesson. In 1104 and 1146, they retreated into stone towers and closed out would-be Christian defenders, as was pointedly described by Ephraim of Bonn, speaking from personal experience: "[The Jews of Cologne] sent away the governor of the fortress by means of many gifts. It was left to them alone, and no uncircumcised stranger was among them . . . And the Jews who had all gathered together there [were no longer persecuted]."[37] But this defense also failed, at York, in 1190, and (in the face of new storming procedures) again at Frankfurt am Main, in 1198. Paradoxically, well-meaning secular rulers were its real nemesis. From 1103, so-called Landpeaces were legislated in the Empire to protect women, priests, and other defenseless people, notably Jews. Yet a Landpeace presumed that defenseless persons did not bear arms. Jews (or others) who elected to use force in their own behalf theoretically forfeited the Landpeace's benefits. They might even be considered the aggressors, a principle which in the early thirteenth century may have contributed to imperial Jewry's being prohibited from bearing arms.[38] Landpeaces were also ineffective. Jews were massacred in various German cities in the 1240s and once again during the Rindfleish massacres of 1298 and the Armleder uprising of 1336.[39]

Yet did most Jews in 1096 have the means to defend themselves? Solomon bar Samson, after all, critically observed that the Jews had been weakened by fasting and prayer. Their hands wielded the sword to no effect, because they relied exclusively on God and trusted in the "[ritual] skills of their fathers," rather than on themselves. However, such trust did not reflect a resignation to fate. Jews, like eleventh-century Christians, lived by religious ideals. According to Solomon bar Samson, 1096—the eleventh in the cycle *ronu* ("sing out")—was one of messianic expectations. But when deliverance was replaced by wholesale slaughter, the Jews sought a redemption of their own making: They took their lives "sacrificially" as martyrs for the "Sanctification of the Holy Name" and as members of a "chosen generation," a choice they reaffirmed by their deaths, traversing, as it were, *limina* in their inner pysche, pilgrims directing their violence against themselves. Ironically, Christian pilgrims, too, called themselves members of a "chosen generation."[40] The two chosen peoples and their parallel ideals, it seems, were bound to collide.

37. Ben-Sasson, 1976: 420.
38. Kisch, 1949: 109–110,132–134.
39. Ben-Sasson, 1976: 186.
40. Gilchrist, 1988a: 714.

There were precedents for this martyrdom in the tenth century; a letter to the Spanish Jewish grandee Hisdai ibn Shaprut[41] refers to Jews' being slaughtered with a *ma'achelet,* a knife used in Jewish ritual slaughtering. But an articulated ideology equating martyrdom with the sacrifice of Temple ritual developed only in 1096. These Jews were like Isaac at the 'Aqedah ("the binding"), except that the sacrifice of Isaac was stopped, whereas theirs was fulfilled.[42] As recounted poetically by Ephraim of Bonn, Abraham "with steady hands slaughtered [Isaac] according to the rite . . . [And when] down upon [Isaac] fell the resurrecting dew, and he revived, [the father] seized him to slaughter him once more . . . The Lord [then] called Abraham, even a second time from heaven [only so preventing Abraham from killing his son again]."[43] Israel had truly become the holy people, a nation of priests, itself the *agnus dei,* as if in open competition with the Christian claim that Christ alone was the perfect sacrifice.

Nobody has successfully explained the appearance of the ideal of martyrdom. Had the Jews gained access to the Greek Books of the Maccabees, with their accounts of those who preferred death to profaning God's name and his commandments?[44] Or had they discovered Josephus' report of the mass martyrdoms at Masada? The Jewish ideal of martyrdom may also have been nourished through contact with Christianity—in particular, with medieval Christian pietistic movements.[45] The roots of the specifically Ashkenazic ideal may lie in the teachings of that Jewry's Italian ancestors. The literary person of Theophilo in the *Genealogy of Ahimaaz*—who penitentially sacrificed his life rather than accept Christianity—is possibly a conceptual precursor of the Rhenish martyrs. But the martyrdoms of 1096 featured a new element: fathers slaughtering sons and mothers killing daughters. Christians were horrified; Jews saw this as an act of ultimate piety. It was also a demonstration of family solidarity. Chronicles and memorial lists record the martyrs' names in absolute family—nuclear family—order (and would continue to do so throughout the Middle Ages). Jewish familial and spiritual ideals had interpenetrated. The Jew sacrificially immolated his family on God's altar and thus penitentially accomplished his "pilgrimage." In Christian soci-

41. Mann, 1931: 1:12,24.
42. Mintz, 1964: 87–97; Marcus, 1982.
43. Spiegel, 1969: 147–149.
44. Spiegel, 1969: 13–14,113–120.
45. See Grundmann, 1961; Benz, 1934.

ety, the reverse seems to have been true. The potential Christian martyr was told to leave his family and set out for the East. Only centuries later, it seems, did familial piety and Christian piety become interchangeable conceptions.[46] In the late eleventh century, the Christian's biological family was in conflict with his spiritual one—that of the Church and of *Christianitas* as a whole.

The spiritual elation of *Kiddush ha-Shem* ("The Sanctification of God's Name") was offset by the despair of forced conversions. The limited number of forced converts before 1096 increased during the massacres to an extent that will never be known. Nor will it be known whether the forcibly converted came from the ranks of Jews who would have preferred to die or of those who left Judaism in fear. In either case, the convert's fate was not an enviable one. The Jews inside the bishop's keep in Mainz, on the eve of their suicides, called to their forcibly baptized ex-coreligionists outside, "We will be together in death and in life!" Spiritually, the converted had already perished. Only in the future life, *after* death, would both the converted and the martyrs be reunited. Moreover, as early as 1096, Christian society was shabbily treating even voluntary converts. Authorities routinely violated the canonical admonition that the status of converts must improve *(melioris conditionis)* by confiscating their property, and numbers of them were reduced to petitioning the popes—who protested these confiscations—for redress, or at least a modest pension.[47]

The general Christian populace did not take converts to its heart. The derision that even voluntary converts encountered is epitomized by the plaint of one known as Master Andreas.

> You will look around you; people from every part will come before you. One will say: "Take good care of your comings and goings," and another: "May your coming be a blessing." A third, however, will say: "What you have begun, finish;"—a fourth: "Be on guard for your soul;"—a fifth: "Be on the watch not to ruin your reputation among us;"—a sixth: "Be strong and a man;"—a seventh: "If you are false to our 'Torah,' you will pay with your life;"—an eighth: "Guard your tongue and what you say, and keep yourself far from trouble." There are also those among them who will whisper, saying: "See how great is our wisdom and how clever we are; they have brought us an *'ish 'ivri* ["Jewish man"] to mock us. But [Jews like him] are the lowly and the despised, the rash and the foolish. They are gluttons

46. Herlihy, 1983: 127–129; cf. Chavarria, 1988.
47. Grayzel, 1966: 16–18; idem, 1989: 57,82,142,191.

and drunkards, as we can plainly see. And when they are naked, barefoot, and worked up into a lather, they will go to a place where they are not recognized, and there they will return to their Jewish origins."[48]

Jews, too, were suspicious of forced converts. Reality was not always congruent with the halachic principle that conversion did not sever a Jew's ties to Judaism. Forced converts who wished to be reconciled with Judaism in this world—not only "after death"—found the return path strewn with obstacles. Rashi and other rabbinic leaders were compelled to stipulate that converts must neither suffer discrimination nor be reminded of their ordeal.[49] Diffidence in accepting "repentant" converts who had rejoined the Jewish community was matched by a diffidence toward the few proselytes who entered the Jewish fold from the outside. Once again, reality sometimes belied principle. The story of Johannes of Oppido, a Norman priest who converted, fled to the East, and became an esteemed scholar and composer of music,[50] was balanced by that of Jacob ben Sulam, a martyr in 1096: "There was a good man," wrote Solomon bar Samson, "Jacob ben Sulam. He was not from a family of yeqarim [vaguely, 'well-regarded ones' or even 'noble ones']; his mother was not of Israel [although now he was]. He called stridently to those near him, 'Until now, you made fun of me; now see what I do [as he martyred himself to sanctify God's name].'" Jews never overcame their ambivalence to the Jacob ben Sulams in their midst. Without an act of total commitment, there were too many reasons for skepticism. There was also danger.

The edict of the Fourth Toledan Council stipulating that even the forcibly baptized must remain within the faith was being increasingly accepted. When, in the late twelfth century, Alexander III followed Gregory the Great in assuming the contrary, his stance was exceptional, as was that of the archbishop of Canterbury in 1189, who colorfully put it: "If he [Benedict of York] will not be a Christian, let him be the Devil's man."[51] The Church was determined to retain converts. It was also determined to punish those who aided them to relapse, a determination that grew as in the twelfth century and even more in the thirteenth the number of converts—forced or otherwise—sharply increased. Jews who proselytized, however furtively, jeopardized their lives.

48. Stow, 1987c: 228.
49. See Katz, 1958.
50. Golb, 1965; Goitein, 1953.
51. Dobson, 1974: 24.

Enormous challenges, therefore, awaited the Jews and their leaders who would have to rebuild on the ruins of the Rhenish communities. Yet who would the leaders be, and what new programs would they advance? The leadership in the great center of Mainz had been decimated. Families like the Kalonymides did regroup and emerge in sensitive positions in later decades. But the Kalonymides and the four other pre-Crusade rabbinic families had lost their preeminence, a political change that would provoke complex transformations in religious, cultural, and intellectual leadership as well. The nature of that leadership, and of the changes it wrought—especially of what for more than a century has been the most historiographically controversial among them,[52] the Hasidei Ashkenaz, or the Pietists of Ashkenaz—will now occupy our attention. Yet it must be said that these Hasidim were not the only source of high medieval Jewish creativity. Whatever toll the Crusades took, and however indelible their memory, they did not permanently stifle Jewish cultural innovation.

52. E.g., Graetz, 1939: 3:297–310; Marcus, 1981.

6　Hasidei Ashkenaz

What the Hasidei Ashkenaz were is something that nobody knows for sure. It is certain only that they were a limited constituency led by descendants of the Kalonymos family, that they set for themselves especially strenuous halachic and pietistic goals, and that they came into existence partly if not largely in reaction to the events of 1096. An early thirteenth-century chain of learning traditions, stretching back to eighth-century Italy, is the only extant documention of the Pietists' origins and historical growth. Otherwise, they left no written records until the end of the twelfth century; and these records themselves are principally cast as short moralizing stories called exempla, none of whose realia are rooted in specific time or events. The small number of speculative and halachic works they produced are equally barren of historical detail. In the absence of this detail, historical imagination has been especially fertile.

Some have maintained, for example, that the essence of Pietism was a social movement—one, moreover, that was heavily influenced by parallel movements of Christian reform, including that of the mendicant friars.[1] Pietism supposedly strove to establish stringent ethical standards for all Jews, and even more so for the Pietists themselves, which also entailed ameliorating the conditions of the poor (a class from which many of the Pietists—although not their leaders—purportedly emerged)—a determination, it is said, that eventually made the Pietists popular and influential. In fact, the Pietists were the first to admit that instead of being popular, they were despised. Their social program's existence, let alone influence, is arguable at best. What they seemed to stress was their elitism, their

1. Baer, 1985a.

view of themselves as set apart from and superior to other Jews. So convinced did they seem of their unique merits that they apparently considered themselves accountable only before the *Din Shamayim* (an unwritten Law of Heaven) and not before the normative halachah.[2] That they set for themselves distinctive halachic standards is beyond dispute.[3]

This elitist attitude went hand in hand with esoteric, mystical ideals that perhaps gave the Pietists their distinctive flavor.[4] Pietistic mysticism was certainly unique, combining traditional ideas, indigenous to the Rhineland, with others emanating in the twelfth century from such southern French and Catalonian writers as Abraham ibn Ezra and Abraham bar Hiyya. The Pietists also drew heavily on an early, imprecise paraphrase of the *Beliefs and Opinions* by Saadya, the philosopher and head of the Babylonian academy of Sura. However, unlike the mystical Kabbalah, which grew directly out of southern French and Catalonian thought, pietistic mysticism is highly unsystematic. It also lacks the Kabbalah's fully developed symbolic structures. Pietistic mysticism represents the limits of Ashkenazic speculative thought. It is restricted to resolving specific problems such as the anthropomorphic references in the Bible and the nature of God's intervention in worldly events. The closest it gets to pure speculation is in its characteristically mystical distinction between a passive, hidden Creator *(Bore)* and the revealed divine Glory *(Kavod)*, whose emanations marvelously produced the physical world and whose traces may be discerned in nature by those who know the *sodot ha-tefilah* ("secrets of prayer")—or at least so wrote the Pietist leader Judah in two works, of which only fragments are extant. The resemblance between this concept and the similar, more elaborate one of the Franciscan mystical philsosophers—for instance, Saint Bonaventure—is accidental; it almost surely does not bespeak mutual influence.[5]

But there was more to Pietism than these mystical teachings. Pietism must be grasped within its specific historical setting, that of the changing political, rabbinic, and intellectual constellations within the Ashkenazic communities during the century following the First Crusade.[6] Yet its roots may also be partly traceable to early medieval esoteric and mystical

2. Scholem, 1938: 94.
3. Soloveitchik, 1976: 354–355.
4. Scholem, 1938: 80–118.
5. See Dan, 1968; Idel, 1983; Bonaventura, 1953.
6. Soloveitchik, 1976; Marcus, 1981.

teachings,[7] as well as to developments in eighth- and ninth-century Italy. The Pietists were extremely attentive to their historical roots. The chain of learning-traditions transmitted by the eminent Pietist Eleazar of Worms—who was known as the *Roqeah* ("the Perfumer"), after the name of his major composition—eloquently makes the point.

> They received the secret of ordering the prayers and the other secrets from Abu Aaron, . . . who came to Lombardy, to the city of Lucca, where he found R. Moshe [ben Kalonymos], who wrote the *'Eimat nora'otekhah* and passed onto him all the secrets. He was R. Moshe ben Kalonymos ben R. Meshullam ben R. Kalonymos ben R. Yehudah. He was the first to leave Lombardy, he and his sons R. Kalonymos and R. Yequtiel, and his cousin R. Itiel, and other worthy people whom King Charles brought with him from Lombardy and settled in Mainz. There they flourished [until 1096]. Then we were wiped out, except for a few who remained of our family [our relatives], along with R. Kalonymos the Elder. He passed [the secrets] on to R. Eleazar, the Hazzan of Speyer, as we wrote, and R. Eleazar . . . to R. Samuel the Pietist, and [then] to R. Judah the Pietist [his son]. From him, I [his cousin] received the secrets of prayer and other secrets.[8]

Regardless of any specific inaccuracies, the overall reliability of this chain of traditions is unquestionable. Ashkenazic Pietism was indeed founded on an uninterrupted line of scholars, their esoteric lore, and pietistic teachings. That line began with the mythical yet representative Abu Aaron—whose learning was rooted in the traditions of the Babylonian Gaonic academies—and extended to the three seminal thinkers of the late twelfth and early thirteenth centuries, the Kalonymides Judah, Samuel, and Eleazar. All of Pietism's fundamental ideas or principles, it appears, originated prior to the First Crusade. Yet only following the Crusades did pietistic lore and teachings mature and Pietism itself emerge as a solidified and recognizable entity. The fruits of this process, approximately two thousand mostly opaque moralizing vignettes, constitute the *Sefer Hasidim* (or *Book of the Pietists*), whose principal authors were Samuel the Pious and his son Judah the Pious. These vignettes, often rephrasing earlier teachings that had been the private or near private possession of the Kalonymides, are cast in a form that presupposes a loose fellowship of individuals gathered around a leader called a *hasid hakham* ("pietist sage"). To this Sage, Samuel attributed a vital social

7. Schaefer, 1989.
8. Klar, 1974: 46.

role. Samuel's son Judah went farther and depicted him as the head of a sect or, possibly, of Jewish society as a whole. In the *Sefer ha-Yirah (Book of Awe [before God]),* which prefaces the whole of the *Sefer Hasidim,* Samuel describes the Sage, his role, and his responsibility.

> To "Fearers of the Lord" will I write . . . to show them how to fear the Lord; and they will teach their sons [and daughters]. Not that I am [a greater] *hakham* than anyone else of my generation; my good deeds and learning are insignificant. Indeed, in this generation, there are *hakhamim* in matters of Torah and in all *hokhmah* ["wisdom"] and deeds. There are also those who fear more than I do. Yet because of their great wisdom, they juggle [literally, "make (sometimes overly) fine logical distinctions in"] the [talmudic] text, whose wisdom is infinite. So it appears to me that [one must distinguish] between those who [indiscriminateiy] fear the Lord . . . and Pietists. There is [also] the Pietist Sage. . . He [bears that title because] he learned [wisdom and pietism] from his Rav ["teacher"]. What his fellow failed [to achieve in these realms] was caused by the fact that he did not learn from a Rav.
>
> [Now] we have learned in the Torah that each one who is capable of [learning and] understanding—even though he has not been [explicitly] commanded to do so—is punished for shirking his responsibility. Consequently, one should be clever [resourceful] in knowledge (*B.T.,* Berachot 17a). For he is punished, if he does not know what he should have been learning and studying. Before the Ruler [of the Universe], one cannot say: "It was an accident." It was for this reason that I set out to write a book for the "Fearers of the Lord," [to warn them] lest they be punished and think [their punishment] was without justification . . . [They must also be warned] that if a fellow *haver* is punished and he [the Fearer] does not [fore]warn him . . . all the punishment will be ascribed to his [the Fearer's] account, since it is the same as if he [the Fearer] had killed him [the fellow].[9]

The Pietist, as an individual but even more as a Sage, was existentially responsible for the transgressions of his fellows, indeed for the transgressions of Jewish society as a whole. Wherefore he vowed to know and—with an unprecedented rigor and discrimination—to observe God's precepts, including those which he had not been explicitly "commanded" to heed. He took it upon himself to suffer for not forewarning his fellows. And above all, he swore to instruct those complete enough in their own observances to have reached the level of Fearers, so that they in turn might warn their fellows. He was also to prevent the credulous from uncompromisingly trusting in "conventional" rabbinic scholars, would-

9. Wistinetski, 1924: par. 1; see also Marcus, 1981: 27.

be leaders, whom the Pietists superciliously called "jugglers." The element of political apology is undisguised.

The Pietist Sages—invariably descendants of the Kalonymides—had to respond to insinuations made in the mid-twelfth century by such as Solomon bar Samson. The Kalonymides, Solomon seems to have been saying, had proved inadequate as leaders: "the ways of the fathers"—repentance, prayer, and acts of righteousness—which they had urged upon Rhenish Jewry, had *not* averted the evil decree. The Pietists' response was a brilliant one: they took upon themselves the enormous responsibility of special practice and of being clever or resourceful in observance. Coupled with their assuming the task of being spiritual guides—indeed, asserting that only they were fit to function properly as such—the Pietist Sages were at once accepting the blame for past tragedies and making a case for their continued leadership. The concept of enlightenment and renewed legitimacy as the explicit product of original failure was sometimes almost flatly stated: "Most persecutions befall the community because people are insolent and do not properly punish those who violate the ban. The Holy One, blessed be He, brings them together and in the end causes them to be persecuted and killed."[10] To wit: the "insolent" pre-Crusade Kalonymides had "not properly punished" their flocks, and their failure had guaranteed the massacres of 1096, as well as their own demise. Would it not then (one must extrapolate) be enormous folly, indeed wickedness and an invitation for renewed persecution, were the communities to follow the newly "insolent"—that is, the scorned rabbinic "jugglers," who had unjustifiedly laid claim to both spiritual and political leadership? By implication, trust should be placed only in the new generation of chastened and enlightened Kalonymide Pietists.

Yet no community could stake its future on such rationalizations and existential flights, no matter how sincere the protagonists. What counted were stone towers, a well-disciplined sword, and less fasting on the eve of attacks, despite the reverence for martyrs and martyrdom. It was also necessary to have a fuller knowledge of the Christian leadership and its policies. A new generation of more practically minded and perhaps more self-serving leaders, many of whom did not belong to the now decimated five rabbinic families, could not take seriously Samuel's program.[11] Their rejection of Samuel's rationalizations and demands may well be that

10. Marcus, 1981: 57.
11. Soloveitchik, 1976: 339–343,350–351.

mockery to which his son Judah constantly refers throughout the *Sefer Hasidim*—although it must be noted that mockery may have been the traditional lot of Jews who lived by extravagant ideals.[12] Rejection also left Judah with little choice but to turn inward and cultivate theories of Pietist practice and esoteric teachings. Judah may even have organized communities of Pietists, who either lived among other Jews or retired to closed communities in small villages.[13]

Within such communities, Judah's followers could more easily have observed their distinctive (and perhaps sometimes outmoded) halachic interpretations.[14] The Pietists were also deadly serious about fulfilling their spiritual ideals. Nevertheless, Pietist spirituality was closely entwined with Pietist politics. In response to the new generation of non-Kalonymide leaders in the Rhineland and in response to the overwhelming influence enjoyed throughout the twelfth century by the towering halachic scholars of France, the Tosafists, the old leadership, represented by the Kalonymides Samuel and Judah, was trying to reassert its primacy, or at least some part of it. And one way in which it did so was by setting elitist standards and by claiming legitimacy for only those who met them, even if this required withdrawing physically from the community as a whole. These standards, it goes without saying, were based on stringent interpretations of the most traditional norms of Jewish comportment, which, by definition, only Pietists were entitled to make. Only they putatively possessed the exclusive knowledge of that secret lore on which (they said) communal survival depended—as well as the ability exegetically to manipulate it, which they did by creating new midrashim. In a society where halachic acumen, an intimate knowledge of liturgy, and political leadership had heretofore been virtually synonymous, this posture might have been a successful one. Its watchword seems to have been Judah's division of Jewish society into "Pietists" and "non-Pietists," whom he labeled the "good" and the "bad."[15]

Judah's reasons for adopting this precise terminology are unclear. Did he intend to castigate those who spurned Pietism and to warn Pietists against them, or was he lauding the select few who adhered to his ways? In either case, this was a distinction that could not endure. Social frictions, it has been suggested, may even have brought Judah himself to flee

12. Schaefer, 1989: 11–13.
13. Marcus, 1981: 87–106; Wistinetski, 1924: pars. 1300–1301.
14. Ta Shema, 1977.
15. Soloveitchik, 1976: 334–338.

his home in Speyer and to settle in Regensburg; his followers may have fled once again, to achieve prominence among Poland's first Jewish settlers.[16] The tensions that arose between Pietists and the rest of Jewish society may also have been instrumental in convincing Eleazar of Worms to reject his cousin Judah's separatist communal ideal. Instead, Eleazar sought to normalize Pietism by framing its tenets within standard halachic forms and formulations. To be a Pietist in the full sense remained as praiseworthy as before, but people no longer needed to isolate themselves to attain pietistic ideals. In fact, it seems that Eleazar was himself ambivalent. He identified with the claims of Judah, for he, too, was a scion of the Kalonymides. He also rejected the new styles of learning and observance imported from France that were constantly gaining ground on traditional Rhenish ones and on their underlying ideals. Yet as a signer of the Rhenish Ordinances *(Taqqanot Shum)*, the closest thing the Rhenish communities had to a constitution, Eleazar had bridged at least the communal gap and made common political cause with the new leaders, many of whom traced their roots to regions beyond the Rhineland. Such a stance naturally blurred the Pietist distinction between "good" and "bad." It also prepared the way for at least some of the Pietists' teachings to acquire a broad, albeit tacit social influence.[17] What, then, we would like to know, was the precise content of the Pietist ideal? What ideology so exercised the Pietists that they were ready to do political battle on its behalf? What did it mean to be a "Fearer of the Lord"?

The Hasidic Ideal

Pietism's most central tenets concerned the *Rezon ha-Bore* ("Will of the Creator"). It was the first duty of the Pietist to obey this Will, which imposed upon him or—most emphatically—her a neverending series of obligations. Yet however demanding these obligations were, they expanded on the halacha, never contradicting it, even when the Pietists said they were obligated to follow the *Din Shamayim* ("Law of Heaven"). Pietistic elitism did not condone disregarding the norms that bound all other Jews, a point that has special cogency with respect to the suggested mutuality between the Pietists and Christian reformers. Christian discussions of personal legal liability, such as that found in the contemporary

16. Ta Shema, 1988.
17. Marcus, 1981: 109–110.

Summa Coloniensis, indicate that there is a "personal law" *(lex privata),* usually pertaining to pious acts, that might occasionally be preferred to the "public [normative] law" *(lex publica).*[18] In his famous *Testament,* Saint Francis, in particular, seems to have counseled the virtues of this alternative. The *Din Shamayim* offered the Pietists no such choice, but was an integral element of the *Rezon ha-Bore,* urging the Pietist ever more strongly to achieve the Fear of the Lord through a nearly superhuman devotion to normative Jewish precepts. The Pietist, that is, was "to develop to the utmost the Law that had been revealed, and to seek out those Divine prescripts embedded elsewhere—in history and Scripture . . . He sought . . . to endow transactions of the soul with a significance equal to those of the body."[19]

The Pietist's devotion expressed itself in two spheres: one esoteric and mystical, the other perfectionist. The former had mostly to do with prayer. By knowing the secrets of the prayers, specifically, by knowing the proper method for penetrating the meanings behind the letters in liturgical wordings, the Pietist could rise spiritually toward communion with God (not a union—which never occurs in Jewish mysticism). Parallel to his increasing proximity to the divine, the Pietist increased his capacity for behavioral perfection, which allowed him to seek out prodigious challenges. He might, for example, deliberately flirt with the *yezer ha-Ra* ("evil impulse"), man's physical drive, in a continuous process of retesting. By spending entire nights in the company of prostitutes, yet resisting their charms, the Pietist won both a behavioral and a psychological victory. This victory would be no less precious were it the result of a battle waged in the Pietist's dreams. Adherence to the Will of the Creator was as compulsory during states of unconsciousness as it was during wakefulness. In fact, acts of wholly inner devotion—which the Pietists, most notably Judah himself, freely discussed—seem to have added considerably to one's pietistic standing.[20]

Hardly a page goes by in the *Sefer Hasidim* without Judah's admonishing the Pietists to be resolute in the face of jibes and jeers, steadfast in self-assurance, and oblivious to social ostracism. For all their commitment to modesty, Pietists must have stood out like sore thumbs and appeared to outsiders as effete snobs. Many outsiders, as well, must have doubted the Pietists' sincerity. The Pietist, as described by Eleazar of

---

18. Kuttner, 1969: 1:39.
19. Soloveitchik, 1976: 319,325.
20. Dan, 1982: 85–120; Marcus, 1986b: 19; idem, 1986a: 356–366.

Worms in his *Hilkhot Hasidut (Laws of Pietism)*, was to speak truth in his heart, refrain from despising those beneath him, act piously at all times, and be humble to the point of self-effacement. Fewer persons could have conformed to such demands in practice than did in thought. And fewer yet would have responded to Judah's insistence that the Pietist regularly divulge his transgressions to a Sage, much as to a Father Confessor, who would prescribe suitable penances. There was outright provocation in the argument that the Pietist should speak to a "modest Sage, who will instruct him as to which penance he must undertake to set himself on the path to the World to Come." That world apparently was to be peopled solely by an elitist Pietist minority.

What impelled the Pietist to shoulder such awesome commitments may have been the conviction that by fulfilling the *Rezon ha-Bore* he was vicariously sacrificing himself to Sanctify God's Name. He was Isaac at the Binding, who, in one traditional midrash,[21] tells Abraham: "Father, hurry to do the Will of thy Creator." But he was also Abraham, applying to "Isaac" the penances and acts of atonement that Judah so emphasized. In doing the *Rezon ha-Bore*, the Pietist was at once accepting punishment for past failings, like Isaac, and making himself worthy, like Abraham, of leadership and of future honor in the World to Come. In spirit, the Pietist saw himself as a member of the "Chosen Generation" of the First Crusade massacres. However, any such Pietist identification with the Crusade martyrs and with Isaac at the Binding was possible only because of the Pietists' midrashic inventiveness. Their ability to transform older midrashic concepts into new ones with meanings specifically tailored to their own needs is perhaps the keystone of the Pietist exegetical method.[22]

The Pietists themselves would have denied their innovative tendencies, insisting, as did Eleazar of Worms in his chain of tradition, that their lore and methods harked back to early medieval Italy—in particular, to the esoteric knowledge transmitted to their Kalonymide ancestors by Abu Aharon. The ideal of deliberate flirtations with sin and subsequent drastic penances was prefigured in the drama of Theophilo in Ahimaaz ben Paltiel's *Genealogy*, as was also the Pietists' attraction to such bizarre, magical happenings as the cannibalizing of children or their transformation into animals.[23] Yet the Pietists brought all these images up to date by abstracting them to relate to the Jews' immediate predicament. They

21. Spiegel, 1969: 148.
22. Soloveitchik, 1976: 322–323, 354.
23. Dan, 1971: 273–289.

did the same with regard to their perception of the cosmos, its structure, and its functions, whose ring is so much that of the late twelfth and early thirteenth centuries that it is possible to compare Pietist perceptions and contemporary Christian cosmological visions.[24] Contemporary Christian parallels also exist for details found in pietistic exempla, such as witchlike figures flying in the air and (once again) the cannibalizing of children.[25] Sometimes it seems that Pietism would have flourished differently, had the Pietists not been living in the specific Christian cultural milieu of the twelfth and thirteenth centuries. Paradoxically, Pietism, that most peculiar of medieval Jewish expressions, most convincingly demonstrates how medieval Jews absorbed contemporary (Christian) culture—its sense of piety, esotericism, and even its romantic notions—yet at the same time cultivated their own individuality.[26]

Pietism also reflects internal transformations, the growing size and sophistication of Jewish society, and the need to compete with professional scholars and rabbis possessing a new brand of powerful dialectical learning. Yet grasping the particulars of Pietism is difficult. Nothing in *Sefer Hasidim* is transparently said.[27] No constant interpretative pattern can be adopted as a key to the meaning of specific exempla. Still, the opacity of *Sefer Hasidim* does not render unknowable, at least in their generalities, such things as how the Pietist was to confront his sexuality, his family, his Jewish neighbors, communal authorities, and non-Jews. In its technical aspects, the formula for doing so was always the same: the Pietist was to subject himself to an unending progression of probings and testings, to grapple with potential limits and conflicts. It is this process that *Sefer Hasidim*'s exempla repeatedly illustrate. The Pietist asks whether a son should respect the choice of his parents in marriage or follow the ways of his heart. Both are goods; how does one choose between the two?[28] The exemplum itself proposes no solution. What the reader of *Sefer Hasidim* cannot know is whether the exempla's author, most often the Pietist teacher Judah, was describing reality or figuratively portraying man's unending confrontation with ambiguous choices. In this particular exemplum, Judah may have intended a little of both. The same

24. Soloveitchik, 1976: 315–316,320.

25. Foa, 1980: 10–20; Sinanoglou, 1973: 499; Dan, 1974: 170–176; idem, 1971: 273–289.

26. Southern, 1963: 219–257.

27. Soloveitchik, 1976: 332.

28. Wistinetski, 1924: pars. 930,951.

does not necessarily apply to exempla that query such issues as whether one should marry only from among the "good" or whether dire consequences will ensue from matches with the "bad."[29] Exempla like these have fueled a modern scholarly debate over the open or closed nature of Pietist communities.

Pietist sexuality is one of *Sefer Hasidim*'s most fully explored subjects.[30] Sexual imagery already appears in the book's opening sections within the context of just penances. Pietists are told to sit in ice-cold water in order to cool down, literally, their sexual passions when they "burn like a furnace." Pietists are also described struggling to control themselves when aroused during prayer. To achieve sexual control was to withstand a trial. It was to seek out yet withstand temptation—a constant Pietist theme—just as it is also a leitmotif (albeit in significantly different guise) in contemporary Christian romances of courtly love.[31] One potential Pietist adulterer "embraced, kissed, and fondled [his beloved's] entire body but refrained from having intercourse," despite their mutual desire.[32] How far could the Pietist allow himself to go without losing control? How great a battle could he wage against his "evil impulse" and still emerge victorious? There is also a secondary message here about the virtues of passion itself. The Pietist is continent, not abstinent. In the battles of the Pietist with his sexual drive, not passion but its inappropriate expression is condemned. Appropriately directed sexuality, as the halachah says, leads to personal sanctity, or holiness.[33] By sexually tempting himself, therefore, the Pietist's degree of sanctity significantly increased.

But would the Pietist's sanctity also be increased through appropriate social actions?[34] Just what did Judah mean when he spoke of children dying because their fathers cheated Christian clients? Was he preaching a universal morality? Or was he not more likely making another statement about the Will of the Creator—that its demands are complete and that no exceptions can ever be made, not even for the Gentiles?[35] On the other hand, far from bespeaking an overall social ethic, Judah's insistence

29. Wistinetski, 1924: pars. 949,950.
30. See Soloveitchik, 1976: 324; Stow, 1987: 1105; Marcus, 1981: 42–43,46–47, 79.
31. Harris, 1959: 13–44.
32. Wistinetski, 1924: par. 33.
33. Abraham ben David, 1964: 122–126.
34. See Marcus, 1981: 93,109; cf. Soloveitchik, 1976: 325–326.
35. Wistinetski, 1924: 661; Marcus, 1981: 15,88.

on preserving the ancient tradition that exempts Sages and scholars from paying communal taxes appears to be unabashedly self-serving. It also appears to be duplicitous when measured against his reprimand of lay communal "heads" who either hold back their full share of taxes or who themselves pay, but wink at others who scoff at the law. At the same time, Judah tells the Pietist not to inquire about his neighbor's tax rate. He is to pay willingly in order to secure his place in Paradise. In exempla such as these, just as in his apparently sincere condemnations of such vices as profiteering on the sale of grain, Judah's sense of social responsibility seems to be wholly unambiguous.[36] That lack of ambiguity extends also to his occasionally literal, rather than his normally figurative, invocations of the terms "good" and "bad." The nature of Judah's social program, if indeed he had such a program at all, remains clouded.

A similar cloud obscures the parallels between the Pietists and contemporary Christian reformers—in particular, the mendicant friars. Real points of contact between the two did exist; mostly they moved in opposite directions. The Christian religious movements, especially the Franciscans, arose, like the Pietists, in an urban setting. Their members devoted their lives to piety and to stimulating others to follow their example. That example had an ethical component, yet that component was no more a central feature of the Franciscan ethos than it was of that of the Pietists. The Franciscans' principal concern was Apostolic Poverty, their belief that Jesus and the Apostles possessed literally nothing, and that the true Christian religious (clerics and monks) must live and preach as mendicants according to the apostolic example. The latent challenge to the Christian religious establishment, which did not subscribe to this doctrine, was obvious. Indeed, when in 1322 Pope John XXII declared Apostolic Poverty a heretical teaching, large numbers of otherwise moderate Franciscans broke off to make common cause with those on the order's radical fringe. During the rest of that disturbed century, radical Franciscans were a constant source of social unrest.[37] By contrast, with the exception of Judah's possibly sectarian venture, Pietism never threatened normative Jewish communal institutions, let alone normative Judaism. Rather, through the intermediacy of Eleazar of Worms, Pietism became ever more normalized.

Also at odds with Franciscan behavior was the Pietist social and

36. Kriegel, 1989.
37. See Bullarium, 1898: 5:552–554.

behavioral platform. The former preached abstinence, the latter continence. The Pietists had no doctrine of poverty. Most important, the Pietists emerged from the ranks of a former leadership and pursued a clearly demarcated political program of restoring their lost communal primacy. The actual content—the substance—of their religious ideals came from the traditional Jewish center, that which had grown to flower in Italy and traveled north to the Rhineland. The idea of reform that animated the Franciscans had known distinguished exponents, including Saint Augustine, but prior to the High Middle Ages it remained at the fringes of Christian religiosity, championed by clerics such as Agobard of Lyons and Ratherius of Verona. Nevertheless, Pietists and Franciscans did have things in common, most notably, their taste for nonsystematic theology. Both spoke in quasi-mystical, Neoplatonic terms of divine emanations, and both sought traces of God in the universe. Both also eschewed the rigorous brand of theology and philosophy that arose with the entrance into Europe of Aristotelian writings and which was espoused by the Franciscans' archrivals, the Dominicans. Yet what Pietists and Franciscans really shared was a flattering self-image, for both believed themselves to constitute an elect and a perfected few, pursuing truly elitist ideals, from whose fulfillment no earthly authority might rightfully deter them.

But in the long run, Pietists and Franciscans each had a sharply different social impact. Franciscanism, or at least its radical branch, promoted extremes. Indeed, opposing the will of the ecclesiastical establishment, the Franciscans eventually became the Jews' most dangerous adversaries, as instigators of forced conversions, campaigners to halt Jewish lending, and supporters of ritual murder libels, like that in the northern Italian city of Trent, in 1475, with which Saint Bernardino da Feltre was closely associated. By contrast—and perhaps just because Jewish Pietism was rooted in the old mainline establishment—Pietist radicalism soon ebbed, allowing the movement's influence to become considerable. The Pietists' existential doctrine of justification for Jewish misfortunes, albeit not a new one, enabled Jews to live with the fact of continuous suffering. It also militated toward the acceptance of the ideal of *Kiddush ha-Shem*, whether in a literal or a vicarious form. To this day, the climactic synagogal prayer of the Jewish High Holy Days intones that the evil decree will be averted through "prayer, repentance, and worthy deeds."[38]

38. Cf. Rubin, 1965: 161–176; Marcus, 1981: 159.

Most of all, Pietism added a mildly ascetic and strongly devotional flavor to Ashkenazic life. An individual did not necessarily pursue the Pietist ideal of *Rezon ha-Bore* in its purest sense, but he did seek religious meaning in all his actions. Jewish pietistic radicalism thus eventually bred moderation and commitment. Through the medium of its new midrashic techniques, Pietism was instrumental in making Jewish life viable, even competitive, in the broad new medieval world of the late twelfth and thirteenth centuries. However, we must be wary of exaggerating. Pietist midrashic innovation did not stand alone. It was matched by a broad spectrum of exegetical innovations produced contemporaneously by non-Pietist scholars. This new exegesis, by Pietists and non-Pietists alike, provided medieval Jews with important tools. With their help, Jews defined their distinctiveness and successfully coped with a difficult outside world.

7 Exegesis

Exegesis was the fulcrum of medieval existence, for both Jews and Christians. Through exegesis medieval people molded their identities, expressed their ideals, defined their goals, created their plastic culture, topoi, and iconography, and even shaped their politics. Exegesis was indispensable for theology, law, and religious controversy. Because no text from Scripture either directly or indirectly—that is, interpretatively, exegetically—justified forced baptism, Gregory the Great reproved the bishops of Marseilles and Arles for having subjected Jews to just this. For medievals, all actions had to be rooted in the exegesis of revealed sacred texts, much as was done by the Hasidei Ashkenaz. The entire Pietist structure effectively depended upon the exegesis of the phrase *Rezon ha-Bore*. Unusual textual interpretations like those of the Pietists also fueled heterodoxy. Their exegetically sophisticated urban intellectual milieu stimulated the Jewish Karaites, who in the ninth and tenth centuries flourished in the Muslim East, to dispute normative Geonic teachings.[1] Christians, too, exploited exegesis to substantiate variant cultural expressions, including those of heterodoxy and heresy.[2]

Exegesis also conferred legitimacy. Popular, as well as learned, magical beliefs of both Jews and Christians—such as those contained in the Jewish *Secrets (Razim)* literature—were validated through their integration into normative exegetical discussions.[3] Much to the chagrin of some,[4] these beliefs became the subject of orthodox debates. In the twelfth century, the Spaniard Abraham ibn Ezra argued against those

1. Ankori, 1959: chap. 1.
2. Stock, 1983: 88–230.
3. Ta Shema, 1988a: 27.
4. Septimus, 1982: 86–87.

whom he called the "refuters" and denied that the verse "One should not damage the upper and nether millstone" (Dt. 24:6) referred to a groom's withholding intercourse from his bride; in doing so, he seems to have been rejecting the widespread and perhaps ancient belief (also associated with verses like this one) that bewitchments may "tie" a groom's genitals and make him impotent—a belief that was cited by both Jewish and Christian authorities throughout the Middle Ages.[5] Exegesis also legitimized less controversial practices—in particular, local customs that diverged from the practices specified by the codified halachah. As put by one eleventh-century Rhenish scholar, "They are not doing anything wrong, because that is their custom, and they have proof[texts] and [other textual] support [for what they are doing]."[6] Such divergent customs were justified by Rashi himself, again on exegetical grounds. He condoned the common use of the ungrammatical liturgical phrase ha-melekh ha-mishpat ("the king the justice"), instead of melekh ha-mishpat (the king of justice), by noting its resemblance to similar usages found in several biblical verses.[7] Exegesis, it thus appears, blurred the lines between learned and popular Jewish medieval culture—so thoroughly, in fact, that truly popular Ashkenazic culture has for the most part eluded scholarly detection.

Exegesis was as versatile as it was ubiquitous. Through its manipulations, Jews successfully inverted, transformed, and defused external threats. Perhaps no medieval decree should have more disturbed the Jews' pyschological equilibrium than that issued by the Ecumenical Fourth Lateran Church Council of 1215. Jews were ordered to distinguish themselves from Christians by wearing special clothing. Yet the sole written Jewish reference to this edict during the thirteenth century, that of Isaac Or Zarua (citing Samson of Coucy), discusses the round wheel that French lay authorities required the Jews to sew on their outer garments as an object of exegetical, halachic inquiry. Would wearing it on the Sabbath be considered a violation of the rule forbidding Jews "to carry" on that sacred day? Apparently, it would not. The frighteningly new and unknown was thus integrated into Jewish domestic usage—although it must be admitted that Or Zarua justified his decision by saying that the

5. Targum Yonathan (and its Perush), Deut. 24:6; Bazak, J., 1968: 52–56; Le Roy Ladurie, 1973: 136–149.

6. Ta Shema, 1988a: 38, citing Zedeqiah ben Abraham, 1987: 2:59; cf. Soloveitchik, 1987.

7. Ta Shema, 1988a: 37, citing Elfenbein, 1943: sec. 18.

wheel was "like the 'seal' [sewn onto the garment] of a slave and worn there throughout the week." The *double entendre* is self-evident. This simile appeared again—this time contemptuously—in later medieval Christian legal commentaries.[8] Even for Christians, the Jewish "badge" had to be validated exegetically.

There was thus à medieval exegetical consensus. Justly, the rejection of exegesis in favor of reason by the mid-seventeenth-century Dutch Jewish philosopher Benedict Spinoza has been called a watershed between the medieval and early modern worlds.[9] No medieval, no matter how radical, would have openly considered, much less dared—or wanted—to go that far.

The normal object of medieval exegesis was, of course, biblical and legal texts. Specifically Jewish exegetical activity in northern Europe, about whose social (as distinct from its specifically scholarly) implications relatively little has been said,[10] began in earnest in the tenth century with the migration to Mainz of Meshullam ben Kalonymos. The most formidable of the early Rhenish scholars in the generation paralleling and immediately succeeding Meshullam was Gershom, the Light of the Exile, the pupil of a somewhat obscure figure, Judah ben Meir ha-Zaqen, known as Leontin. Gershom was not a member of the Kalonymos family but a Machiri, another of the five Rhenish rabbinic families, whose origins apparently are to be traced to Metz, on the Mosel (in Alsace, to the west of Mainz), and perhaps to further south in France. Later generations viewed Gershom as a kind of superauthority. In his own day, he was more a "first among equals." Even in the yeshivot of Mainz, where Gershom lived, his influence was balanced by that of the Kalonymides.[11] Gershom's teachings became widely disseminated only a half-century later, through the efforts of Rashi, who traced directly back to Gershom his own intellectual pedigree. This fact suggests competition between schools and families, even at this early date, or, at the least, the existence of two mildly disparate exegetical traditions. Gershom thus was praised by the (Kalonymide) Pietists; he did not figure in their chain of esoteric traditions.

Northern learning activities grew out of early Italian midrashic and talmudic studies, which rested on a Palestinian base. To this was added

8. Isaac of Vienna, 1862: "Hilkhot Shabbat," 84:3; de Susannis, 1558: pt. 1, chap. 4.
9. Cohen, G., 1968a.
10. E.g., Ben-Sasson, 1976: 459–461,525–527; Baron, 1952: 6:55–56,296–298.
11. Grossman, 1981: 94–96,116–119; idem, 1988: 5.

a Babylonian, Gaonic superstructure and perhaps some peripheral influences from the nearly dialectic exegesis created by that structure's Karaitic opponents. This external learning arrived in Europe together with the text of the Babylonian Talmud sometime in the ninth century—perhaps to the displeasure of the Babylonian authorities, who wished to preserve their textual monopoly and teaching authority.[12] By the time of Meshullam ben Kalonymos in the mid-tenth century, the Italian schools had declared their independence from both Palestinian and Babylonian schools. The Talmud was already on its way to becoming a pliable instrument in Italian scholarly hands. The knowledge that one could pierce the Talmud to expose its most nuanced meanings was perhaps one of the major Italian contributions to future study. Similar intellectual discoveries were being made in the southern French school of Narbonne, as well as at other centers in that region, such as the one at Arles. The regrettably little-known products of these schools also made their way north to the Rhineland.

The European schools began at a great disadvantage. The Talmud, especially in its Babylonian version, was composed in an agrarian environment, edited in the sixth and seventh centuries, and subsequently polished in the cosmopolitan urban atmosphere of the Abassid Caliphate. Its text and exegesis were the carefully guarded property of two academies, the yeshivot of Sura and Pumpeditha, whose heads, the Geonim, were determined to establish their universal halachic supremacy. This they did in part by teaching through a method of authoritative lectures summarizing broad problems. The Geonim might ask for the opinions of other academy members and debate with them about interpretative subtleties, but ultimately it was the Geonim who unilaterally decided all academic and legal questions that were directed to their individual academies. Geonic literature frequently assumes a similar apodictic format.[13] What all this meant to European scholars was that the Talmud was transmitted as a virtually foreign product, written in an ambience wholly different from that of feudal society and lacking a key for its interpretation. Geonic lectures, although thorough, did not provide students with the requisite tools for continued independent investigation.[14]

The Jews of Europe countered by elaborating an exegetical method based on precise lexicographic distinctions. Only one Geonic-style talmu-

---

12. Grossman, 1985; idem, 1988a; idem, 1989.
13. Assaf, 1942: pt. 2.
14. *Encyclopaedia Judaica*, 1971: s.v. "Saadya Gaon."

dic summary, prepared by Gershom of Mainz, seems to have been made.[15] The lexicographic method first appeared in southern Europe. Its immediate origins may have been in the non-Jewish Arab world,[16] although the method really goes back to the Jewish philosopher Philo and to the schools of ancient Alexandria. The Geonim of Babylonia and Eretz Yisrael, as well as their Karaite opponents, were also familiar with philological debate.[17] Still, it was in the small yeshivot (or, more precisely, bate midrash) of the Rhineland that this near-dialectical exegetical method was perfected.

In size and structure, the Rhenish yeshivot were diametrically the opposite of the Babylonian ones.[18] The latter had at least seventy fixed members and perhaps scores of informal habitués. As late as the end of the twelfth century, the Rhenish yeshiva of Eleazar of Worms was so small that Eleazar's wife, Dolcia, easily catered to the physical wants of all the students. Preparatory schools, too, were small. Didactic manuals cautioned teachers of young children to accept no more pupils than they could comfortably supervise.[19] The goal was to familiarize the youngsters with the basic texts and to stimulate them to ask questions. This method, it was hoped, would ready a select few for the rigors of the yeshiva, where the primary activity was to absorb and ponder the master's glosses on individual words and phrases of the talmudic text. These glosses were always open to challenge and frequently were modified following vigorous debates. Students then wrote down the accepted glosses in their notebooks (quntresim). By the mid-eleventh century, a process of editing had commenced, whose products were known as the Quntres Magenza (Mainz) and perhaps, too, the Quntres Wormiza.[20]

The mid-eleventh century was also a period of summarizing in other centers. Italian scholars produced a Sefer Romi, also a form of quntres, and the Narbonnais schools a consummate sage in Moshe ha-Darshan ("the preacher"). In 1101, Natan ben Yehiel of Rome composed his talmudic dictionary, the 'Arukh (Order). All these authors and their works were cited in the ultimate of quntresim, that of Rashi (an acronym for Rabbi Solomon ben Isaac). Indeed, from Rashi's quntres, as well as

15. Grossman, 1981: 165.
16. Makdisi, 1974: 640–662.
17. Twersky, 1957.
18. Neubauer, 1895: 2:86–88.
19. Assaf, 1925: 1:9–15.
20. Berliner, 1969: 179–181.

from his extant responsa, it becomes clear that by his day, Jewish learning within Europe had acquired an international flavor. Responsa questions traveled from as far north as Paris to Rome in the south. Geonic responsa from Babylonia, too, were well known. This internationalization of Jewish learning paralleled a similar process in Christian society.

Rashi's *quntres* differed from all previous ones. Rashi edited his glosses three times, assuring that he had elicited all applicable lexicographic and interpretative principles, compared every appearance of a word or phrase in a given talmudic tractate, and located these words and phrases in what he believed was their immediate real context; on occasion, he cited *aggadot* to elucidate appropriate talmudic passages. Sections of all three editions of the *quntres* have survived.[21] Rashi himself—who died at age sixty-five in about the year 1105—did not complete the editing and polishing; these were done by his disciple, Simha of Vitry, and his son-in-law, Judah ben Natan.

Rashi, who was a relative by marriage to the family of Rabbi Gershom, came from afar to study in the Rhenish centers, like many other Jewish contemporaries. Significantly, he first studied in the yeshiva of Yaacov ben Yaqar, Gershom's disciple in Worms. It is possible that Rashi knowingly was avoiding the Kalonymides of Mainz—although it was at Mainz that Rashi completed the first edition of his *quntres*. Rashi's eventual return to his native Troyes in Champagne sometime before the First Crusade was really a forgone conclusion. What could not be foreseen was that partly in response to the Crusades, but more likely in response to the educational impact of Rashi himself, students in the next generation stopped migrating from France to the Rhineland. Pride of place during the next century was taken by the schools of Champagne and northern France; it was to these French schools that German Jewish students now migrated. There, on the basis of Rashi's finely edited *quntresim*, his son-in-law, Judah ben Natan—followed by his three grandchildren, Samuel, Isaac, and especially Jacob ben Meir—initiated new schools and a new epoch of Jewish learning, that of the Commentators (*Ba'alei ha-Tosafot*, literally "the Supplementers").

The work of the Tosafist Commentators, going far beyond that of the earlier Jewish Glossators, dealt principally not with textual problems but with halachic ones. Yet without Rashi's *quntres,* the Tosafists could not have performed their task, a fact that medieval Jewish scholars as far

---

21. Ta Shema, 1988a: 50–52; Lipschutz, 1966: 78–95.

away as Spain acknowledged.[22] Rashi had that rare ability succinctly to unify vast amounts of material without sacrificing clarity; many of his glosses consist of no more than a brief two- or three-word phrase. Moreover, once Rashi had established the meaning of a talmudic word or phrase in one location of the Talmud, that meaning could usually be applied to the word's repetition elsewhere, or Rashi would indicate otherwise. Often, Rashi's interpretations decided the precise reading of the talmudic text itself. His fame rapidly spread. Within fifty years of his death, Rashi's glosses had penetrated every Jewish community in Europe; within one hundred years, they were known and used universally, including by Christian Hebraists. They were first published in 1522 by the Jewish Italian printer Gerson Soncino. Copying his page design from that already used by Christian printers to publish the legal works of Christian Glossators and Commentators, Soncino placed Rashi's glosses on facing inside margins, flanking the talmudic text, and the commentaries of the Tosafists on the outside margins. This design has endured; even today, Rashi's glosses remain indispensable for anyone who wishes to understand the primary meaning of the talmudic text. Every Jewish child since Rashi's day who has received a talmudic education has been exposed to these glosses. Advanced students, too, rely on their support. Few scholarly works have ever become so essential, and fewer yet have been so universally studied over so many successive generations.

Rashi's glosses on the Bible were even more widely disseminated than were those on the Talmud. They were known by all Jews, everywhere, either at first hand or through their incorporation into synagogal sermons. In 1475, they were set in movable type as the first Hebrew printed book. These biblical glosses differ sharply from those on the Talmud in both style and content. For one thing, the text of the Bible was known and circulated freely. Unlike the Talmud, its basic text did not need establishing. Jews also had limited access to Latin translations and to their own Aramaic ones to help elucidate obscure scriptural passages. In any case, biblical material is principally narrative or poetic, not legal, and therefore requires different exegetical techniques. These techniques were primarily midrashic ones. In fact, by Rashi's time, Jews were privy to a large body of midrashic exegesis that had grown up and been transmitted over the generations by a group of mostly anonymous exegetes known as the *Karaim* (roughly, "Biblicists"—not to be confused with the Kara-

22. Urbach, 1955: 15.

ites of the East). In Rashi's own day, these Biblicists included Menahem ben Helbo and Joseph Kara. Rashi's problem, therefore, was not to reveal the unknown but to select and anthologize from a wide selection, which he did with consummate skill. Rashi also marks a turning point in medieval biblical exegesis. From the twelfth century, Jewish exegesis would deemphasize midrash and stress the *peshat*, or "plain sense," of the text. There was a growing awareness that even the Bible's text was not so transparent as it had once seemed.

This awareness was a by-product of the impetus given in the late tenth and early eleventh centuries to Hebrew grammatical and philological studies by Spanish students such as Dunash ibn Labrat and Menahem Seruq. *Peshat* also had special advantages, as is pointed out by the *Sefer ha-Brit (Book of the Covenant),* a polemical tract composed in the mid-twelfth century by the Provençal writer Joseph Kimhi. Literal textual meanings often precluded Christian allegorical interpretations, especially ones such as those that see in the "suffering servant" of Isaiah a prefiguration of Christ. Sometimes it is difficult to decide whether Kimhi's tract is really a polemic or a medieval-style advertisement for the virtues of *peshat.*[23] Nor was the message of such advertisements wasted on contemporary Christian Biblicists, who likewise soon turned to *peshat.* Northern Jewish exegetes were slow to be convinced. The height of *peshat* was achieved in the commentaries of Samuel ben Meir, Rashi's Tosafist grandson. Rashi himself took a halfway position, which in later life he said he regretted and for which his grandson did not hesitate to chide him. But Rashi was deliberate in his ways. He was by profession a teacher par excellence, and as such, he had a highly developed aesthetic and didactic sense. One taught, especially in the Middle Ages, by reference and allusion; these, rather than the "plain sense," instilled values. Besides, the sermon was the prime medieval entertainment, sometimes lasting for three or four hours. Only midrash made this kind of sermon possible; *peshat* is a vehicle for orators of few words.

Rashi, accordingly, mixed his exegetical methods. Commenting on Genesis 3:8, he wrote, "There are many *midrashei 'aggadah* [that discuss this verse]. Our rabbis have set them all in order in *Bereshit Rabba* [the standard midrashic collection of commentaries and *'aggadot,* or legends, concerning Genesis]. My intention is only to discuss the *peshat* of Scripture and the *'aggadah* that clarifies the scriptural sense." Thus, Rashi surveyed the various *'aggadot* on the verse: "They [Adam and Eve] heard

23. Joseph Kimhi, 1972: 39 and passim.

the voice of the Lord walking in the garden along with the daily breeze." These '*aggadot* all try to explain exactly what Adam and Eve might have heard: perhaps it was the sound of oak trees, as God was walking through the garden; perhaps it was the song of the angels announcing that God was walking through the garden; or perhaps it was the Divine Presence that had briefly descended to earth. Rashi seems to have rejected all three interpretations. "What they 'heard,'" he said, "was the voice of the Holy One Blessed Be He, Who was betaking Himself through the Garden." "'Along with the daily breeze'—that is, the same westerly breeze that comes from the direction of the sun; for in the evening, the sun is in the west, and Adam and Eve sinned at the tenth [evening] hour." This literal—even anthropomorphic—understanding obviously responds to the midrashim of the '*aggadot*. Nonetheless, it too is aggadic, relying, as it does, on the midrashic interpretation "rise and descend" to explain just what it meant for God "to walk."

Jewish and Christian Common Ground

Interpretations like these may appear to have been quintessentially Jewish. In fact, they shared much in common with Christian approaches to the Bible and to textual understanding. Like Jews, medieval Christians operated within a frame of reference in which forms, symbols, and topoi were often more meaningful than the hard matter of reality. No Christian could do without the interpretative tools that were being developed in the primarily monastic schools scattered throughout western Christendom. Moreover, one of the hallmarks of the developing unified Christian culture of the High Middle Ages was the wandering of scholars from one country to another and from one school to another, much like the Jewish scholars who easily moved between Italy, Germany, and France. In terms of both purposes and structures, Jewish and Christian higher culture had many similarities. To be sure, the small yeshivot never flowered into the full-fledged universities that eventually replaced the monastic schools. But that may have been primarily a function of numbers, not structural differences. The methods of learning in both university and yeshiva were roughly identical; terms like "gloss," "commentary," "question," and "distinction" apply equally to both, as perhaps does also the term sometimes applied to the great revival and expansion of high medieval learning, the "Renaissance of the Twelfth Century."[24] Intellectual cross-fertil-

24. Southern, 1963: 203–218; Urbach, 1955: 74–76.

ization must have been common. On at least one occasion, Jewish educational standards themselves were envied. The Jews, wrote a pupil of the philosopher Peter Abelard, send all of their sons—and even their daughters—to school (in fact, to primary school), "moved by piety and by the love of the law of the Lord"; this was not the practice of Christians, who "send [only some of] their sons . . . for lucrative reasons."[25] This claim was no exaggeration; communal ordinances dictated charitable distributions to educate the children of the poor.[26] How diligent these children were as scholars (there is so little information to rely on) is another matter. With regard to those who were not, *Sefer Hasidim* warned against throttling them with a book.[27] It was more efficient, and honorable, to use a strap—and such straps, incidentally, became broader as the Middle Ages progressed.[28]

Christian influences on Jews are hard to measure, although Jews must have sensed the contemporary Christian intellectual expansion. Samuel ben Meir knew at least parts of the Vulgate, responding on more than one occasion to its text and to specific interpretations.[29] The formalization of Jewish exegetical techniques under the rubrics *peshat, derash, remez* (literally "hint," with the rough meaning of "philosophy"), and *sod* (literally "secret," meaning roughly "mysticism") may also correspond to a parallel formalization of similar rubrics by Christians.[30] Nevertheless, Jews did not directly borrow from Christian culture, least of all from works such as those of the Parisian philosophical and theological schools. Christians, on the other hand, were willing to borrow from Jews. From the middle to the end of the twelfth century, the school at the Abbey St. Victor in Paris, in particular, was noted for its reliance on Jewish teachers, who taught Hebrew and Jewish exegetical methods.[31]

Christian Biblicists were most interested in the *peshat*. It was the Jews' prime polemical weapon, and it had to be known before it could be opposed. *Peshat* also opened possibilities of defending Christological interpretations. Christians were convinced that these interpretations were far more than allegorical, tropological, or anagogical (that is, spiritual,

25. Grabois, 1975: 633.
26. Morris, 1977: 2:181.
27. Wistinetski, 1924: par. 662; Marcus, J., 1965: 377 (trans.).
28. Horowitz, 1986: 80–82.
29. Talmage, Frank, 1986; see also Grabois, 1975: 632.
30. Scholem, 1969: 61.
31. Smalley, 1964: 83–195.

moralizing, or eschatological) in nature. As viewed by Hugh of St. Victor, the first of the Victorine Biblicists, they expressed the Bible's literal meaning. But such an argument could be sustained only by students who knew the Bible's original language. Accordingly, Hugh's disciple Andrew turned to Jewish teachers, and others followed his example. The virtues of knowing the plain sense of Scripture were championed by Peter the Chanter, a leading late twelfth-century Parisian intellectual and noted teacher. Jews, Peter noted, made little of Christians who had to rely on allegorical and spiritual interpretations even for the New Testament. If the New Testament could not be understood in its plain, literal sense, then why should anyone accept Christianity as truth?[32]

Knowledge of Hebrew also opened the door to the study of non-Biblical Jewish texts, often through the agency of Jewish intermediaries. One of the first such texts to be studied was Rashi's glosses. Andrew of St. Victor may have been familiar with the writings of Rashi's disciples and followers Samuel ben Meir, Joseph Kara, and Joseph Bekhor Shor. The special emphasis all three placed on the *peshat* may have led Andrew into accepting untraditional interpretations of such critical verses as Isaiah 7:14, "Behold a virgin will conceive." Christians had always understood this verse as referring to the virgin birth; Jewish scholars argued that it referred to an attack made by the king of Israel against the king of Judah in Isaiah's own day. Andrew's seeming agreement with this Jewish opinion led his contemporary Richard of St. Victor to accuse him of "Judaism," or Judaizing. Andrew's stance was a somewhat unusual one. On the whole, Christians studied Jewish commentaries in order to refute Jewish arguments more effectively. The postillae to the Christian biblical *Glossa Ordinaria*, composed around the year 1340 by the Franciscan Nicholas of Lyra, refers repeatedly to "Rabbi Salamonis," that is, Rashi, whose interpretations Lyra invariably disputes.[33]

From biblical commentaries, some Christians proceeded to the study of the Talmud and other forms of rabbinic literature, which were vaguely known to them as early as the times of Agobard of Lyons. By the twelfth century, Christians knew that some of the Talmud's passages might be considered offensive to Christianity, and by the thirteenth, converts from Judaism were revealing to them exactly what these offending passages were. Some Christians also acquired the ability to read rabbinic texts. In

32. Baldwin, 1958: 92–96.
33. Heilperin, 1963; Cohen, J., 1986a: 610–612; Berger, 1986.

Spain, an entire school of Christian scholars of rabbinic texts grew up around the Dominican Raymundus Martinus. Its main product was the voluminous *Pugio Fidei (Dagger of Faith)*, a tour de force of most likely legitimate midrashic texts[34] exploited both to verify Christianity and also to reveal contemporary Judaism as a satanic innovation.[35] These twelfth- and thirteenth-century developments were only a beginning. Similar Christian exploitations of rabbinic literature took place in subsequent centuries involving the *Zohar* and other mystical writings. One sixteenth-century Christian student of this material argued that there was a true and a false Kabbalah, the former proving Christianity, the latter confusing the Jews. Christian Kabbalists included the famous Pico della Mirandola; among the better-known Hebraists was the humanist Johannes Reuchlin. Both were convinced of the virtues of Hebrew as a conversionary device.[36] By contrast, monks at the Tuscan Abbey of Vallombrosa said the Office of the Blessed Virgin in a Hebrew translation, beginning this practice in the sixteenth century and continuing throughout the eighteenth.[37] Their aim was perhaps a return to the sources, a goal they may have shared with the Congregationalists of colonial New England, who likewise were ardent students of Hebrew. Yet ever since the initial contacts in the late twelfth and early thirteenth centuries, Jewish teachers of Christian Hebraists have been increasingly on guard. Chastened by attacks on the Talmud in the 1230s and 1240s, northern French Jewish intellectuals quickly retreated into purely Jewish intellectual precincts and concerns.

The Tosafists

During the century that Christian Hebraism was taking its first steps, Rashi's physical and spiritual descendants, the Tosafists, were engaged in expanding the boundaries of talmudic learning. Rashi had unlocked the talmudic text; his grandsons and their contemporaries in both France and Germany—beginning with the Rhenish Isaac ben Asher Halevi—turned it into a living work. They interpreted the Talmud's thousand-year-old dicta and juristic principles and made them applicable to contemporary, northern European Jewish realities. The Tosafists achieved this transformation by sharpening the dialectical tools of past generations, equipping

34. Merchavia, 1988: 203–207.
35. Bonfil, 1971.
36. Wirzubski, 1975; idem, 1977.
37. Stow, 1976a.

themselves to reveal the finest logical distinctions and draw the subtlest implications from the most obscure talmudic passages. In doing these things, the Tosafists may have inadvertently been reviving the methods used in creating the Talmud in the fourth through the seventh centuries: unlimited debate and induction that paradoxically culminated in deduction, analogy, and conjecture. It was as if they were filling in that which was missing from the talmudic text itself, saying what they felt the Talmud should have said, putting each talmudic dictum under a magnifying glass, comparing it with other dicta in a search for contradictions, and drawing radical conclusions through such devices as the *reductio ad absurdum*.[38] Yet in form, the Tosafist commentaries appear to be little different from the questions, cases, and dissertations being produced—or about to be produced—in Christian schools and universities. The Tosafist method and the Scholastic method have a great deal in common. Both were equally criticized by representatives of older learning traditions. The Pietists of Germany accused the Tosafists of disingenuously exploiting their finely honed pilpulistic argumentation. Cases of Tosafists' cleverly manipulating their dialectical skills to procure personal advantage were apparently not unknown.[39] Moreover, even the best-intentioned Tosafist interpretations sometimes left the plain, original sense of a passage far behind. Passages seemed to be emended, rather than explained, a practice that the more rigorous Tosafists, especially Rabbi Jacob Tam, strongly denounced.

Such excesses were perhaps unavoidable, considering the scope of the Tosafist endeavor. Prior to the Tosafists, the goal of the Sages was to gloss texts. The Tosafists welded commentaries, responses to juridical questions, and legal decisions into seamless wholes that have been described as "new Talmuds."[40] Their writings were produced by means of unfettered debates that took place in dozens of small yeshivot stretching from Tocques near the mouth of the Seine in Normandy to Nuremberg and Rothenburg in eastern Germany, and perhaps to Vienna on the Danube; they appear to have commenced during Rashi's lifetime, first in Germany and then in France,[41] and to have continued through the end of the thirteenth century, although their creative peak was reached about the time of Jacob Tam (d. 1171) and shortly thereafter. In the course of these

38. Urbach, 1955: 524–526.
39. Soloveitchik, 1976: 341.
40. Urbach, 1955: 525.
41. Grossman, 1989.

debates, no argument or opinion was considered above dispute. Rashi, for one, was constantly challenged and reversed, yet so too were the ideas of the Geonim, and of Talmudists in Spain, Provence, and Italy. Remarkably, the Tosafists believed that their methods were identical to those of the original talmudic Sages. Needless to add, they were unaware of the Talmud's many historical layers.

The Tosafists' enormous self-assurance derived from more than their perfected dialectical tools. They also possessed Jewish scholarly texts that their predecessors had barely known—in particular, Eastern Geonic writings, the commentaries of Rabbi Hananel of Qairowan in North Africa (which blend materials of Palestinian, Babylonian, and even European provenance), and the extended talmudic paraphrase containing primarily legal decisions produced in the eleventh century by Rabbi Isaac Alfasi, a peripatetic scholar who was born in Tunisia, studied in Fez (Morocco), and achieved greatness at the Spanish academy in Lucena. The Tosafists also had access to the grammatical and syntactic studies of Dunash ibn Labrat and Menahem Seruq, and they cited on more than one hundred occasions the 'Arukh talmudic dictionary of Natan ben Yehiel of Rome, with which Rashi may have had only a passing acquaintance. Perhaps most important, the Tosafists had before them the hitherto obscure Jerusalem Talmud, with its variant readings and additional dicta that shed light on difficult passages in the Talmud's normative Babylonian version. It is little wonder that Tosafist commentaries, so armed, extend beyond pure theorizing to embrace the practical. The two in fact are often indistinguishable. Abstract principles of contracts and torts are discussed alongside references to current practices of money lending. There are also abundant references to details of a personal, even intimate nature, as well as to popular customs, such as the way Jewish youths rode out on horseback to welcome arriving bridegrooms. Without fail, however, the practical, and especially the new, were firmly rooted in venerable tradition.[42]

For all that, the Tosafists rarely sought public acclaim. Most Tosafist commentaries are anonymous, known by their place of origin rather than by the name of their author. Even the *tosafot* of Jacob Tam and Isaac of Dampierre, both of whom are often cited by name, are in their present form reworked and revised versions of the originals. The best known *tosafot* are those of Sens and Tocques. The latter—actually a revision of

42. Katz, 1971: 24–47.

the former—were eventually included by Gerson Soncino in the margins of the Talmud he published in 1484, and in this way they became the standard Tosafist collection. Yet this somewhat ironic fact should not hide the existence of other minor collections, including that of Speyer, where many of the Tosafists were identified with the Pietists of Germany. The anonymity of the actual collections of *tosafot*, or of most individual comments, does not, however, mean that we have no information at all about the actual Tosafist scholars and their varied activities. Many are known by an acronym, such as RI for Rabbi Isaac of Dampierre, also called Ri Ha-Zaken (Ri the elder), a nephew of Rabbi Jacob Tam. Other notable Tosafists included Rabiah (Rabbi Eliezer ben Joel Halevi) in Mainz, and Raban (Eliezer ben Natan) in Bonn, as well as Judah ben Isaac Sirleon and Rabbi Yehiel in Paris. The last is famous for his role in the so-called dispute that preceded the burning of the Talmud in that city about 1240. Toward the end of the thirteenth century, at a time of summing up and consolidation, there were the Maharam (Meir ben Baruch) of Rothenburg and his pupil the Rosh (Asher ben Yehiel). Rabbi Meir died a prisoner of Emperor Rudolf, and Rabbi Asher migrated south to Spain, where he introduced significant methodological innovations. A notable Italian exponent was the RiD, Isaiah of Trani. The greatest of all Tosafists, Rabbi Jacob Tam (the "unblemished"), was the unofficial head of French and indeed of all European Jewry in the mid-twelfth century. Our concentration on the scholarly achievement of sages like the Tosafists—and of Rashi, too, for that matter—should not allow us to forget that frequently these learned men were also the political heads of their respective communities.

Legal Compendia

The scholarly Tosafist talmudic commentaries were paralleled by the Tosafist achievement in constructing legal codes. Theoretically, these codes were to be as free of controversy and conjecture as the Tosafist commentaries were supposed to be exclusively dialectical. In fact, no European Jewish compendium of *halachot* ("laws") ever approached the magisterial and supremely confident categorical order achieved in the late twelfth-century *Mishneh Torah* by Maimonides, who arrogated to himself the right to establish legitimate halachic practice for all time. European scholars considered the halacha to be a constantly evolving body of legislation, subject to continual reinterpretation. No Tosafist collection of laws was ever free of variant possibilities or theoretical reflections. The first of these collections actually grew within the framework of a *Mahzor,* the generic name for a comprehensive book of prayers. Its author, Simha of Vitry, for whom the collection is named, was a pupil of Rashi. Much of the collection reproduces halachic decisions made by Rashi himself. A second signal work was the *'Avi ha-'Ezri,* written by Eliezer ben Joel Halevi at the turn of the thirteenth century; this was a compendium of contemporary laws and *halachot* arranged according to the order of the talmudic tractates. The book's lack of a systematic order of presentation perhaps reflects the career of its author, who wandered from town to town in Ashkenaz, studying with all the greatest scholars, and devoting himself to both personal and communal affairs, including the ransoming of prisoners.[43] Somewhat different is the *Mordekhai,* named for its author, Mordecai ben Hillel Hacohen of Nuremberg, a pupil of Meir of Rothenburg. Composed toward the end of the thirteenth century, the *Mordekhai* is more a collection of opinions, decisions, and responsa than a code in the strict sense. Greater order was achieved in the code of Moses of Coucy, the *Sefer Mitzvot Gadol,* which sets out *halachot* according to a list of 613 positive and negative commandments. A similar order is followed by the *Sefer Mitzvot Qatan* of Isaiah of Corbeil. In complementary fashion, collections of local and regional customs began to be made.[44] The first full-blown example of these customaries was that of Jacob Molin of Mainz (d. 1427). Ashkenazic Jews placed enormous emphasis on customary practices, often giving them precedence over the strict letter of the halachah.[45] One may justly appreciate the ritual and practical world of these Jews only by studying the halachic codes and customaries together.

The most significant codifying achievement to result from the Tosafists' labors is really a post-Tosafist work, the mid-fourteenth-century *'Arba'ah Turim (Four Columns)* by Jacob, the son of Asher ben Yehiel. Written in Castile, Jacob's work integrates Ashkenazic and Sephardic learning. It brings together the fruits of northern exegesis—especially as represented by Jacob's father, who, as noted, was a pupil of Meir of Rothenburg—and such southern achievements as the *Mishneh Torah* of Maimonides. Reading through the *Tur,* as Jacob's work is known, is like perusing a digest

43. Urbach, 1955: 315–318.
44. Feldman, 1974: 10.
45. Soloveitchik, 1987: 212,220.

of all halachic study up to its day. The *Tur* is also remarkably lucid. One may commence with it and without great effort work one's way back into talmudic and subsequent exegetical literature. It is little wonder that indirectly the *Tur* eventually became the basis of normative Jewish religious observance. In the sixteenth century, Joseph Karo, a resident of Turkey and then of Safed in Eretz Yisrael, composed a commentary on the *Tur*, the *Beit Yosef (House of Joseph)*, which he later abridged, following the exact organizational order of the *Tur*, down to identical paragraph numbering. This abridgment, known as the *Shulhan 'Arukh (Prepared Table)*, underlies all Sephardic practice. With the supplement of Rabbi Moses Isserles, Ashkenazim, too, accepted this book as their definitive legislative collection.[46]

Yet all this was possible only because of the nature of the Tosafot as a textual bridge. The work of the Tosafists, preceded by that of Rashi, laid the groundwork for the Jews of northern Europe to tie their own textuality to that of Jews in communities as far flung as Spain, North Africa, Egypt, and Iraq. Had European Jews developed a textual system of great rigidity—as sometimes characterized eastern interpretation— their understanding of the Talmud might have become overly distinct from that which grew up in eastern and Sephardic circles. And despite underlying halachic unities, two parallel systems of Jewish observance might have developed. Communication and interaction would have been minimal, contacts and interchanges sterile. Instead, the dialectical flexibility of the northern exegetical masters made it possible to interpret any text in relativistic terms and to modify any custom in order to meet new exigencies; very little was absolute or unbending. No work better reveals this adaptability, as well as the applicability of the northern Tosafist system to southern custom, than does the *Tur*, along with its direct successor, the *Shulhan 'Arukh*. The legacy of Tosafist exegetical versatility remained alive over the centuries. Indeed, it was still operating among the Jews of Rome in the sixteenth century, many of whom had been recently drawn to settle there from the four corners of the Jewish world. Regardless of their initially differing customs, they were (with certain liturgical exceptions) able to unify practices within no more than three or four decades of their arrival, as witnessed particularly by standardized contracts stipulating the conditions of engagement and betrothal *(tenayyim)*, in which the origins of the bride and groom are

46. Werblowsky, 1978: 6–7; Adelman, 1987: 152–153.

wholly obscured. To be sure, not every halachic or intracommunal difference was so smoothly resolved. Yet it was no accident that in their communal assembly, Roman Jews frequently cited the continuing validity of ordinances issued four hundred years earlier by none other than Rabbi Jacob Tam.[47]

The Tosafists were thus enormously successful in creating exegetical methods that had the power to transform purely textual foundations into the arbiters of cultural and social realities; their labors enabled traditional culture to be absorbed and adapted to suit contemporary needs. Their literacy and their textuality became synonymous with northern Jewish medieval rationality.[48] But did Tosafist methods—like Jewish biblical exegesis and, for that matter, Jewish philosophy (whose great master, Maimonides, was both utilized and cited by the thirteenth-century Parisians William of Auvergne and Thomas Aquinas[49])—have any impact on Christian legal study?

In fact, there are distinct lines dividing Christian and Jewish concepts of law. In particular, the halachah, like Islamic Shari'a, is an all-embracing legal system. It does not distinguish or balance—as does Christian law— civil, criminal, and religious spheres but unites them into one whole. In the Jewish and Islamic legal systems, the origin of all law is divine. Christian law assigns diverse origins to divine, natural, and human law, and to what was known as the law of the nations. Jewish law was also "received" (into medieval Europe) as a completed whole in the form of the Talmud. This reception paralleled (although it chronologically preceded) the revival of Roman law, which was "rediscovered" through the unearthing of Justinian's *Digest* and its subsequent study at Bologna from the late eleventh century. By contrast, canon law was effectively "created" during the Middle Ages through a process that edited and combined sayings of the Church Fathers, conciliar decrees, and papal letters, culminating in 1234 in the *Decretals* of Pope Gregory IX. A similar process of development and editing took place with respect to local lay customary and written law—for example, in the thirteenth-century *Beauvaisie* of Philippe de Beaumanoir and the *Sachsenspiegel* of Eike von Repgow.[50]

Nevertheless, Christians, like Jews, viewed all law, whatever its origin,

47. *Archivio Storico Capitolino:* 45r,45v,75v; see Finkelstein, 1972: 305.
48. Stock, 1983: 30–34.
49. Stow, 1976: 130–132.
50. Kantorowicz, H., 1964: 152–155; see also Kuttner, 1960.

as the concrete expression of the divine virtue of justice.[51] Accordingly, law was to be analyzed and its implications drawn through a process of exegetical elaboration. The glosses of Rashi are thus paralleled by the *Glossa Ordinaria* of Accursius on the Roman law and that of Johannes Teuthonicus on Gratian's *Decretum* (1140). The commentaries of the Tosafists have their complement in the *Summae* and *Apparatus* of the Decretalists and the *Commentaries* of the legists. In form, structure, intent, and effect, the parallels are virtually complete.[52] Yet Jewish glossing and commenting procedures had become sophisticated long before those developed by Christians. Rashi died about 1105; Jacob Tam and the other leading Tosafists were active before 1170. In contrast, Accursius completed his work about 1228, and Johannes Teuthonicus finished his before 1217. The heyday of the Decretalists was the mid- and later thirteenth century; that of the Commentator-legists was the fourteenth. Christians might therefore have learned legal methodology, especially dialectical skills, from Jews. Regrettably, no evidence confirms that they did. On the other hand, it is not inconceivable that Jews profited from Christians. One Jewish scholar at least was intimately acquainted with the influential canonistic writings of Pope Innocent IV.[53]

The Rashbam

But accrued antipathies made the Christian intellectual world into one that Jews mostly sought out when they were forced to respond to its challenges. Jews preferred to immerse themselves in broadening their own, intrinsically Jewish textual understanding. The pursuit by Rabbi Samuel ben Meir (the Rashbam) of the plain scriptural sense is a case in point. Meanings of individual words, the Rashbam believed, were to be elicited by comparing their usage in different verses and chapters; one contrasted remote verses and portions of the biblical text in order to grasp their true import. For example, had God, in Genesis, not explained that he had completed the creation of the world in six days, we would not understand why, in Exodus, he commanded the Jews to observe the seventh day as the Sabbath. Genesis, furthermore, describes God's acts; Exodus explains man's participation in them and his assent.

51. Ullman, 1946: 36–38.
52. Twersky, 1957.
53. Stow, 1984: 35–37.

The underlying creedal basis of this seemingly forced interpretation did not prevent the Rashbam from also engaging in cold grammatical analysis. He did so when it brought him into open conflict with previous authorities and even to the verge of debating the fundamental Jewish belief that the world was created, not eternal. Twelfth-century Spanish Jewish exegetes, too, questioned this belief. Yet they did so quite openly and with the aid of rationalistic and philosophical tools that the Rashbam would no doubt have eschewed, had he known of them.[54] His perplexity was that of the scholar who doggedly insists on precisely understanding the text before him. What, the Rashbam asked, did the biblical text mean when it commenced with the word *bereshit*?[55] Some, he explained, interpret it as "In the beginning," as though the text read *ba-rishonah*. But that is not what the text says. Furthermore, and even more puzzling, the second part of this verse (Gen. 1:1) says *ve-ha-'aretz hayeta,* in the sense of "And [at that time] the land was"; and indeed the waters, too, were *already* in existence. Were we to accept this traditional interpretation, the Rashbam was saying, we would be left with something like: "In the beginning, God created the heaven and the earth; *yet* the land [already] was." But this was grammatically and logically impossible, the Rashbam claimed. Nor, he continued, would this problem disappear, if, as some would have it, the verse were read in the sense of "Prior to the Creation." Rather, we must read the word *bereshit* not as *ba-rishonah* but as a *davuk* (the modern *nismakh,* or construct genitive form)—that is, in the sense of "at the start of creation" *(be-tehillat bri'at ha-shamayyim)*. The whole verse should thus be read: "At the beginning of the creation of heaven and earth, that is, at the time when [*ba-'et*] the upper heavens and the earth already [*kevar*] were created—whether this occurred over a long or a short period of time—then ['az] 'the land,' which already was in existence [*benuyah*], was a void [*tohu va-vohu*]." Perhaps aware of such a possible interpretation, as well as of its inherent challenge to the doctrine of Creation, Rashi had admitted that the word *bereshit* should be read as a construct; yet he warned that the Bible did not intend to establish—as the Rashbam insisted it did—which act came first. The verse, Rashi said, ought best be midrashically understood. His grandson, the Rashbam, refused to budge from the plain sense. At the most, he was willing to concede that the verse (and, by extension, the entire creation

54. Septimus, 1982: 89–92.
55. Samuel ben Meir, 1969: Gen. 1:1.

story of Genesis) explained why centuries later at Mount Sinai, God insisted on the Jews' observing the Sabbath.

The commitment of the Rashbam to his textual methodology was such that he dared to apply it to Genesis 49:10, one of the two or three most critical verses debated in the polemic between Christians and Jews. Both had commonly understood the verse—"The scepter shall not be removed from Judah, nor the ruler's staff from between his feet, until Shiloh comes, and unto him [shall be] the obedience of peoples"—to refer to the Messiah. The Vulgate, the Latin translation of the Bible made from the Hebrew in the fourth century by Saint Jerome, had in fact emended "Shiloh" to read as though the Hebrew were *shiloah* and had rendered the text *qui mittendum est* as "he who was *to be sent*"—namely, Jesus. Jews, of course, rejected this reading. Rashi argued that the scepter referred to the leaders of the exile in Babylonia who, even in his day, still reigned. (Rashi, of course, had no way of knowing how much the Exilarchs' real stature had diminished.) "Shiloh" meant "King Messiah, to whom the [everlasting] Monarchy belongs" and who had yet to come; "Shiloh" might also be interpreted midrashically, following the Aramaic translation of Onkelos, as *shai lo*, "a gift to him." The Rashbam, however, knowing that this interpretation was open to Christian challenge, decided to divert the issue by reading "Shiloh" literally, and correctly, as a geographic place name. "The scepter will not depart from Judah," he wrote, "[that is,] until the King of Judah arrives, namely, Jereboam the son of Solomon, who would come to renew the monarchy at Shiloh, which is near Shechem; at that time, the ten tribes would turn their backs on him and name Reheboam as their king."

But such genius in diffusing so explosive an issue is not always appreciated. The *peshat* of the Rashbam, like his specific exegesis of Genesis 49:10, were soon overtaken by renewed midrashic interpretation. Having to confront the literal *peshat* of certain texts may have exacerbated, rather than soothed, the anxiety Christians suffered from no less than Jews. Andrew of St. Victor's interpretation that Genesis 49:10 referred to an event in the life of King Saul[56]—once more demythifying the verse—is a good illustration; it may well have contributed to the charge of "Judaism" leveled against Andrew by his fellow Victorine Richard. Midrash and allegory were much safer, for it was they above all that performed the hermeneutical task for which exegesis had been created in

56. Grabois, 1975: 621.

the first place. However *peshat*-oriented interpretation might logically triumph, it simply could not compete with texts such as Rashi's midrashic disquisition on the meaning of the opening verse of Genesis:

> Why did [God] begin with *Bereshit?* It was the power of his doings that he was revealing to his people, giving them the inheritance of the Nations. Lest the Peoples of the World say to Israel, "You are brigands, you conquered the lands of the seven nations [of Canaan]," they [the Jews] could reply, "All the world belongs to the Holy One Blessed Be He, he created it, and he gave it to whom he saw fit. By his will he gave it to them, and by his will he took it away from them and vouchsafed it to us."

If the Jews subsequently lost that land and were now subject to the Nations, Rashi was implying, they might rest assured. Just as in the past God had taken the "inheritance" from the Nations and bestowed it upon Israel, he would assuredly do so again, at the time of the Jews' repentance. The Jews remained God's Chosen People.

It was ideals like this one that medieval Jews desperately need to have restated. Only through the interpretative reiteration of ideals could they enunciate their separateness and retain confidence in their identity in the face of Christian claims, especially in the wake of such debacles as the massacres of the First Crusade. Yet exegesis allowed the Jews to reaffirm their identity on more than a purely abstract plane. By means of exegesis, ancient principles could be retained even in such mundane fields as economics and communal structure. How this was so will now occupy our attention. But the subject of purely abstract interpretation should not be left behind without a final note—namely, that in a society where both Jews and Christians professed to be the True Israel, the ideals one side stated, and the favorable interpretations an interpreter of one faith elicited, could with great facility be taken up by an interpreter of the other and be said exclusively to apply to him. Exegesis reveals to us, if nothing else, the intricacy of the struggle in which medieval Jews and Christians were perpetually engaged.

8 Community

However great were the virtues of exegesis, there must be no illusion that Jews allowed theory indiscriminately to govern practice. Texts and their commentaries served fundamentally as controls, permitting the endorsement of actions because they stood muster before hallowed theory. Rabbenu Tam's opinion legitimizing commerce with Gentiles makes this abundantly clear. In its setting, it is a model of Tosafist methodology.

A mishnaic text (*'Avodah Zarah* 2a) propounds that "for three days prior to their feast days, one may not do business [*laset ve-latet,* 'give and take'] with idolaters, [including] the lending and borrowing [of objects] and the lending to them and borrowing from them [of money]." According to Rashi, "This [prohibition] is because he [the idolater, would take the object or money and use it] to go and worship his idols on the feast day." Putatively, Rashi has supplied us with the original reason for the ruling, and in fact the succeeding lengthy *tosefet* (commentary) begins by incorporating Rashi's statement. It also expands on the rationale of prohibiting *memkah u-memkhar* ("bargaining," or "trading").

> However, there is a problem here. What [legal precept] justifies the fact that everybody [from the time of the *Mishnah* down to our day ignores the mishnaic ruling and] does do business [with idolaters, specifically, with Christians], even on the feast day itself and even granted that most of their [Christian] feast days are for their saints? On top of that, they [the Christians] have at least one feast day a week. [If we observed the mishnaic ruling, we would never be able to do business with them—which is why this passage is so problematic.] Moreover, Rabbi Ishmael has said that commerce [of the kind described here] is totally prohibited; you cannot say that the idolaters [in question] do not truly worship idols but are only following the customs of their fathers [out of filial piety].

Theory and practice had collided; and perhaps in desperation, one un-named authority suggested that the reason for ignoring the ruling was 'Eivah, or ill-feelings. One ought to avoid the idolator's holding a grudge. But (came the reply) how can refraining from a simple business exchange be considered an offensive act?

The matter could not rest there. A way out of the quandary had to be found. For, the text went on, "Jews today cannot say that I do not need to buy and sell, borrow or lend . . . Perhaps, therefore, the justifica-tion for circumventing the [mishnaic] ruling is that we are certain that idolators in our day [Christians] do not engage in true idolatry [and there are talmudic precedents for this reasoning]." But these explanations are really rationalizations. Worse, this last explanation—which is merely a variation on what has already been said—ignores the principle that Christianity is idolatry. In an atmosphere of vast Christian superiority and sometimes conversionary pressure, to ignore that principle was to destroy a significant barrier separating Judaism from Christianity, and so to weaken Jewish defenses.[1] This was a point that the Tosafists under-stood perfectly, especially Rabbenu Tam: "It is," he said, "forbidden to have business dealings with them specifically in matters that would be used for sacrificial purposes [midi di-tiqrovet]. But the [mishnaic] ruling does not at all apply to simple buying and selling . . . As for [the expression in the mishnaic text], laset ve-latet, that means to take [laset] the money and to give [latet] the sacrificial goods in return."

With characteristic brilliance, Jacob Tam had resolved the issue: cir-cumventing the mishnaic ruling did not entail equating Christianity with monotheism. As subsequent Tosafists explained, "Although it is the ac-cepted belief [minhag ha-'Olam] that they [the Christians] are idolaters," this fact poses no problem: Christian sacrificial offerings are in the form of money, and their "offerings [of food, goods, and so on]" are "for the pleasure" of the "priests and monks." Exegetical methods had thus validated current practice. There was no danger that a Jew might sell a Christian the midi di-tiqrovet which alone Jacob Tam had forbidden, and, consequently, there was no halachic objection to Jewish commercial relations with the surrounding Christian population. Moreover, in exe-getically validating Jewish practices, Rabbenu Tam was in good company. His grandfather Rashi had earlier exploited exegetical acumen selectively to condone the custom of using a Christian middleman to allow Jewish

1. Katz, 1971: 24–27, A.Z.2a.

creditors to accept interest from Jewish debtors that was normally prohibited.[2]

Yet even on a theoretical level, interpretations such as this one by Rabbenu Tam were meaningful only because medieval Jews considered exegesis their central means to rationalize social structures and communal institutions, as well as their primary tool to fashion suitable postures for confronting outside authority.[3] Largely by exploiting the halachah and its exegetical techniques as the building blocks of communal action, early Ashkenazic leaders like Meshullam ben Kalonymos, Gershom Meor ha-Golah, and Joseph Bonfils equated the community itself with a *Bet Din* (rabbinic court) and its leadership with rabbinic judges.[4] Only such an equation justified Rabbenu Gershom's tentative legitimization of communal government through the dictum "What the community has decreed is a valid edict."[5] That is, communal edicts were validated by exegetically likening them to the fruits of halachically rooted judicial process.[6]

Community and King

Jews functioned within two overlapping governmental systems: their own, and that imposed from above. Jews had to accommodate the latter, in the interests of constitutional consistency—and perhaps of their own emotional stability—to internal governing principles. Attempts to reach such an accommodation go back to the talmudic period. All of them revolve around the self-explanatory principle *Dina de-malkhuta dina* ("The law of the kingdom is the law"). European Jews began discussing this principle in the late eleventh century. Yet like their Christian counterparts, who also were taking the first steps toward constitutional definition, Jewish thinkers in the eleventh century were able to agree on only elementary principles—in particular, the need to find a rationale for accepting external rule. Between the time of Rashi and that of Rabbenu Tam, at least four distinct rationales were proposed. These ranged from stipulating that the halachah recede to make room for "royal practice" implicitly consistent with Jewish law to accepting preexisting or even

2. Soloveitchik, 1972.
3. Soloveitchik, 1987.
4. Grossman, 1975: 177–179.
5. Grossman, 1981: 131.
6. Agus, 1965: 536; Baer, 1985b; see *Babylonian Talmud*, Yebamot 89b.

new royal edicts that won common approval, regardless of their halachic congruity. A middle position said that new edicts were acceptable only with "unanimous ratification" or that "the land belonged to him," the king, leaving the Jews no choice but to acquiesce or be expelled.[7] Such contradictory proposals indicate the distance separating the Jews from theoretical sophistication. Not unexpectedly, it was the realist Samuel ben Meir (the Rashbam) who most unambivalently recognized the independent legitimacy of a royal authority which increasingly was asserting absolutist rights over the Jews. Jews also had to come to grips with their growing administrative—and eventually constitutional—isolation, initiated however tentatively in the ninth century when King Louis the Pious appointed a non-Jewish official, the *magister iudaeorum*, to oversee Jewish affairs.

The precise mandate of the *magister*'s office is unknown. Was he limited solely to protecting the Jews from excesses like those perpetrated by Agobard of Lyons, or was he empowered to deal with the Jews' internal leadership, interfere in communal affairs, and apply the ecclesiastical and other restrictions that King Louis chose to enforce? What is certain is that the *magister*'s existence created neither a sharp nor a formal division between the Jewish and Christian communities. Such a division is not visible before the later eleventh century, long after the office of the *magister* had disappeared. By then, the official who mediated between the Jews and the outside authorities had also become a Jew—the *archisynagogus*, or Jewish communal head. Alternately, he was called the *Episcopus Judaeorum* ("Jews' Bishop"), whose purview was the local region rather than the entire Empire (in contrast to the jurisdiction of the Carolingian *magister*). In England, a similar office was held by the Presbyter ("Jews' Priest"). Five such priests were appointed for "life" between 1199 and the Jews' expulsion in 1290. Unlike the *Episcopus*, the Presbyter had power over all English Jews. No Jew in France held a corresponding position, at least not before the end of the thirteenth century, and more likely not before the end of the fourteenth. The first French Jews who might cautiously be likened to a Presbyter, Mattityahu ben Joseph Treves and his son Johannan, were commissioned only in 1360, after some of the Jews expelled from France in 1306 were readmitted. Both men additionally served as chief rabbis. Indeed, Provençal and Spanish rabbinic authorities even certified Johannan's scholarly rabbinic creden-

7. Shilo, 1974: 59–62; Funkenstein, 1986.

tials and supported him when a certain Isaiah ben Abba Mari demanded that he be named rabbi of all French Jews in Johannan's stead. Yet whatever their titles and functions, or the geographic limits of their office, neither Johannan nor his father claimed authority over the Jews solely as royal appointees. Like the *Episcopus,* and possibly the Presbyter, both had been given power by the Jews themselves. Indeed, the *Episcopus* and the Presbyter were also *parnasim* ("providers"), those whom the community had entrusted with overseeing Jewish secular affairs.[8]

This union of externally appointed and internally chosen leaders was not an ideal one. For one thing, the *Episcopus,* or his equal, was an agent of Jewish constitutional isolation. His very existence enhanced the Jews' judicial uniqueness and cemented the portentously direct jurisdictional bond linking them to their rulers. He was an intermediary and administrator, serving the emperor, count, or bishop who conferred power upon him through a charter of privileges or a letter of appointment—irrespective of the de facto ordinary jurisdiction or the halachic primacy that he sometimes exercised. The *Episcopus* and his ilk could be made to coerce the Jewish community against its will, and against its best interests. This occurred most visibly in England in the thirteenth century, when the kings began to demand from the Jews abusive taxes and to use the Presbyters as their chief collectors. The English Presbyters were also directly answerable to a non-Jewish royal official, the *Dominicus Iudaeorum,* and eventually to a "Justiciar of the Jews," whose title is self-explanatory.[9] The Presbyters obviously had little autonomy, apart from those judicial prerogatives that rulers delegated to them. The same may more or less be said of the late fourteenth-century French chief rabbis and of the imperial *Hochmeister,* or *Landesrabbiner,* who began to function in 1407, about the time that local *Episcopi* stopped being appointed.[10] Their malleability in royal and baronial hands almost perforce made these governmentally appointed Jewish leaders into foci for intramural friction.

The problem was compounded for leaders whose authority was based on a solely external appointment. Rarely were Jewish communities prepared to give such appointees free reign over internal affairs. The Jews may grudgingly have tolerated them, but they vigorously condemned the all too common practice of Jews with no internal mandate accepting

8. Kohn, 1984; idem, 1988: 234–240; Levi, 1899: 85–94; see also Frank, 1935; Breuer, 1976: nos. 98,106.

9. Roth, 1964: 112.

10. Baron, 1952: 2:62; cf. Breuer, 1976: 26, nos. 99,109,126,140; and see Zimmer, 1978.

royal, ducal, or episcopal nominations to positions such as *Sheliah Tsibbur* ("the one delegated to lead prayers") or communal rabbi, whose prime task was to administer the halachah.[11] Even when the *Episcopus* was a respected rabbi, his initiatives might still be circumscribed. Rabbi Solomon ben Samson, the *Episcopus* mentioned in Henry IV's charter of 1090 to the Jews of Worms, unquestionably shared his headship with representatives of the five leading rabbinic families. In his role as *parnas,* he enjoyed no monopoly over internal rule that might have enabled him to consolidate any real powers which the outside government may have conceded him. Equally problematic, in the Rhenish communities through the early eleventh century, and possibly before that in those of France, *parnasim* such as *Mar* ("Master") Juda ben Abraham of Cologne were not always rabbis or scholars.[12] The ideal that Jewish community leaders ought to be rabbinic scholars possibly entered the Rhineland only about the year 1000, when such figures as Meshullam ben Kalonymos emigrated from Italy. The eleventh- and twelfth-century rabbinic attempt to define the community as a *Bet Din,* presided over by rabbinic judges, may have been just as much related to attempts to unseat lay *parnasim* and install rabbinic ones in their place as it was to justifying halachically the foundations of communal rule.

A unified leadership, simultaneously facing outward and inward, evidently succeeded only in the person of dominating personalities like Jacob Tam and Meir of Rothenburg. Not coincidentally, neither of these two men held direct royal or comitial appointments, but both of them were strong enough internally also to be recognized by the external, non-Jewish authorities. The period of their greatest influence was also a time of royal weakness, or at least indecisiveness. Rabbenu Tam may have been more hesitant about issuing the text known as *The Flowering of the Staff* (the phrase refers to the staff of Moses and is the *incipit* of the text) if the current French ruler had been the relatively strong Philip II Augustus—perhaps the true founder of a unified French kingdom—rather than his weaker predecessor, the crusading Louis VII. Jews, this text said, would at obvious royal expense be excommunicated for dealing directly with the government. Such dealings were to be pursued only through the agency of recognized communal leaders—meaning, of course, Jacob Tam

11. Breuer, 1976: nos. 52,57; Yuval, 1989: 332,161.
12. Grossman, 1975: 189.

and his close associates.[13] In the case of Meir of Rothenburg, lack of caution cost him more than his authority. In 1286, the Hapsburg emperor Rudolph arrested Meir and kept him imprisoned until his death in 1293. Meir, it seems, had opposed Rudolph's progressive consolidation of imperial sovereignty, which included asserting an exclusive right to tax imperial Jewry. By contrast, in the later fourteenth century, when the emperor's position deteriorated, his relationship with Jewish leaders was again reversed. He held no more power over the regional and communal rabbis nominated by counts, bishops, and sometimes city councils than he did over their Christian nominators. It was now the nominators' turn to determine the levels of Jewish strength, which in fact varied greatly.[14] In England, where the king had truly ruled since the Norman conquest in 1066, no dominant Jewish leader or rabbinic authority ever emerged; nor, for that matter, did close-knit communal or intercommunal organizations.

The authority of the Jews appointed by Christian authorities to govern the communities of northern Europe was thus constantly challenged and compromised. Neither the Presbyter nor any other royally appointed Jewish official in France or the Empire possessed the powers of the Castilian *Rab de la Corte* or the Sicilian *Dayyan Kelali*. These two, often laymen despite their rabbinic titles, stood astride their respective communities. The *Dayyan* was considered to be so dictatorial that in 1447 the Sicilian Jewish communities successfully petitioned the Aragonese king, who ruled the island, to abolish the office—just sixty years after its inception in 1386. The Castilian Court Rabbinate commenced in 1255 and continued until the expulsion in 1492. Its incumbent functioned as a judge in appeals (including the criminal cases over which Spanish Jews uniquely possessed jurisdiction), presided over intercommunal synods, and was normally a familiar at the royal court. He might also be the royal physician, chief financier, and collector of taxes from Jews and non-Jews alike. Occasionally he was a scholar, such as Abraham Benveniste. The last *Rab*, Abraham Seneor, converted to Christianity rather than be expelled.[15]

Surprisingly, the northern European Jewish leadership had much in common with that in the Muslim East. To be sure, the Muslim leadership

13. Finkelstein, 1972: 159.
14. Breuer, 1976: no. 140; Yuval, 1989: 149–151.
15. Ashtor, 1979: 220–221; Gutwirth, 1989: 169–229.

had become hereditary: the Babylonian lay communal head, the *Rosh Golah* (Exilarch) traced his descent, and office, to King David; and he had ruled more or less uninterruptedly since the fifth century B.C.E., although with ever-diminishing sovereign powers. The Egyptian Nagid ("prince"), who came into existence in the later eleventh century, traced his descent after the thirteenth century to Maimonides. Yet here the uniqueness ends. For as was often the case with their northern counterparts, the function of the Exilarch and the Nagid as intermediaries with the outside authorities was an extension of their preexisting communal offices. The caliphs ratified rather than initiated their appointments. The same applies to the *Episcopi*, the later German communal and regional rabbis, and even to the Treves—the two anomalous, and weak, French chief rabbis of the late fourteenth century. Only the English Presbyter and the later chief imperial rabbis, like the southern Spanish court rabbi and the Sicilian *Dayyan*, were purely royal inventions and functionaries. Once again like the northerners, the main reason Muslim authorities continued to support the Exilarch and the Nagid was the collection of taxes. The *jizya* ("poll tax") that the Exilarch and the Nagid collected was indispensable to ensure the Jews' continued toleration as *Dhimmi* ("protected peoples") in Islamic society. Furthermore, like the northerners, both Exilarch and Nagid were putatively expendable, or replaceable. They certainly had competitors. For example, members of the Baghdadi banking family, the Netiras, claimed that to guarantee the *jizya*'s payment, the Abassid caliphs had bypassed the Exilarch and turned to them. The Exilarch and the Nagid were also beset by the Geonim, the rabbinic heads of the academies in Baghdad and Jerusalem, whose spiritual primacy over the Jews of Babylonia and Egypt, respectively, intrinsically challenged the jurisdictional prerogatives of the Exilarch and the Nagid.[16] In Ashkenaz, competition between rabbinic leaders and *parnasim* was a permanent feature of communal life.

Internal Leadership

That competition had not always existed. Early medieval Jewish leaders in southern Italy were ideally scholars, rabbis, intermediaries with non-Jewish authorities, and successful men of affairs, at one and the same time. The Italian Meshullam ben Kalonymos had no doubts that

16. See Cohen, M., 1980; Grossman, 1988a.

parnasim should preferably also be *talmidei hakhamim* ("scholars"), an attitude he successfully propagated following his migration to the Rhineland. Lay *parnasim,* such as the early eleventh-century Juda of Cologne, quickly ceded their authority to men of learning. On the eve of the First Crusade in 1096, the *parnasim* of Worms and Mainz were both called "rabbi." The *parnas* of Mainz was a member of the leading Kalonymos rabbinic family.

This unity was likely a function of overall social homogeneity.[17] Rabbis and most other communal members shared common lifestyles, ideals, and goals. The number of rabbis in a single community may also have been large enough to create a powerful clique. In Mainz, in 1096, forty-one of eighty-five male family heads were called "rabbi."[18] By the same token, it was virtually impossible to distinguish rabbis from laymen on the basis of titles such as *tovim* ("good men") and especially *hakham* ("sage"). The latter, a normally rabbinic designation, was accorded to the lay *Mar Juda.*[19] However, social homogeneity was disrupted after the Crusades. Rashi unintentionally signaled the start of this process by identifying the *hakham* as "One appointed over the town and from whom [halachic] instruction is sought."[20] Toward the middle of the thirteenth century, Isaac Or Zarua more purposefully described the *hakham* as "What we *now* call a rabbi."

Jewish social change, like that in contemporary Christian society, was a product of greater political stability, widening commercial and urban boundaries, intellectual stimuli, and a slow but inexorable demographic expansion and social stratification, accompanying an ever-waning feudal violence.[21] A prime victim was the homogeneous Jewish society of pre-Crusade times. The result was competitiveness and a division of power. From about 1096, rabbinic leaders lost ground until, by the end of the Middle Ages, the main Ashkenazic communal leaders were lay *parnasim.* The latter never fully eclipsed the rabbis, but the rabbis were forced to join in an informal balance of power weighted to the *parnasim's* advantage.[22]

These dynamics are once again suggestive of the Muslim East, although

---

17. Grossman, 1975: 177–178; Breuer, 1976: 22.
18. Agus, 1969: 258–260,334.
19. Breuer, 1976: no. 18.
20. Breuer, 1976: no. 10.
21. See Lopez, 1971; Cantor, 1963.
22. Frank, 1935.

there the division and hierarchy of power was even sharper. The mid-tenth-century Netira and Pinhas banking families could make or unmake Jewish officials almost at will. A theoretical discussion composed toward the end of the century by a certain Nathan the Babylonian proposed that Jewish power be divided three ways,[23] assigning formal public roles to the Gaon and the Exilarch, with the Netira—mentioned by name—to be the (financial) power behind the throne. Indeed, the Netira, despite occasional boasting in which, with some justification, they cast themselves in the role of Mordecai in the Book of Esther, in fact preferred manipulating power to openly wielding it.[24] The Netira may also have shied away from attacking the entrenched interests of the few families[25] who controlled the Gaonate and Exilarchate. As events in contemporary and later Spain and Sicily would prove, openly pursued family rivalries could first dominate and then undermine Jewish communal strength.[26]

In Ashkenaz, the emphasis on a nuclear conjugal family unit obviated this kind of behavior, or at least its extremes. Nevertheless, by the thirteenth century the previously seamless and fluid Ashkenazic communal structures had given way to articulated and rigid ones. The *hakham* or *rav* (rabbi) was now most often a halachic overseer or the head of a yeshiva, while the *tovim* were reconstituted into communal directorates regularly composed of seven or alternately twelve men—never women— who functioned in conciliar frameworks. As time progressed, these councils grew ever more oligarchic, their membership being predicated on personal wealth or the payment of a high tax. Elaborate electoral systems, such as that put into effect at Worms in 1312, created a panel of *parnasim* chosen for life who controlled the exclusive right to appoint their successors.[27] The councils also absorbed the functions of the older *Episcopus,* whose place, as at Worms, was taken by the senior councillor known as the *hegmon parnas* ("bishop *parnas*"). *Parnasim* sometimes operated their own independent courts of arbitration.[28] These transformations were bound to provoke censure. *Parnasim* were charged with the misuse of wealth and with the evils of overweening haughtiness. The loudest complainers were of course those who, like the Kalonymides, saw their

23. See Ben Sasson, M., 1989; Neubauer, 1895: 83.
24. Harkavy, 1903.
25. Grossman, 1988a.
26. Kriegel, 1979: 131–134.
27. Frank, 1935: 342.
28. Breuer, 1976: 14.

authority slipping. Powerful rabbis, too, such as Meir of Rothenburg and his earlier contemporary Isaac Or Zarua, protested the ever-increasing conciliar encroachment on rabbinic prerogatives.[29]

How councils eventually controlled communal life is especially well illustrated by the example of the Roman Jewish *Comunità,* which was consolidated in the sixteenth century—a time when medieval Jewish governmental structures had reached their apogee—in order to cope with the doubling of the city's Jewish population, and its division into a number of quasi-independent bodies, following expulsions (in the late fifteenth and early sixteenth centuries) from Spain, Provence, Germany, Sicily, and the Kingdom of Naples. A preexisting structure of three *fattori* and a council—still traditionally known as that of the *VII Bonos Iudaeos* (seven good men)[30]—was wholly revamped. A unified community was now to be headed by a Factorate, composed of two Italians (including Sicilians) and a recent Spanish, French, or Ashkenazic immigrant (or one of their descendants). But the *fattori,* whose term of office was only six months, were chosen from and responsible to a broadened council containing sixty seats, which were equally divided between Italians and *Ultramontani* (as the Ashkenazim, French, and Spanish were called). This division, an apparent attempt to calm interethnic Jewish feuding,[31] in fact reflects a formal agreement to share political power in the newly amalgamated community. True ethnic rivalry would have more likely pitted Ashkenazim, Frenchmen, and Romans against Spaniards and Sicilians.[32] The division that set Ashkenazic, French, and Spanish Jews against those from Rome and Sicily was as ethnically improbable as the united front composed of all other Jewish groups that opposed the hegemony of the frequently Ashkenazic majorities in northern Italy.[33]

Those who lost most from these political feuds were the rabbis. At Rome, especially, rabbis retained little power. They held no office, participated in communal affairs only at the request of the council and the *fattori,* and even needed a mandate from the *fattori* to constitute themselves into a three-judge rabbinic court.[34] Formal rabbinic posts existed on the synagogal level alone. These posts were not attractive. Their

29. Breuer, 1976: nos. 38–40.
30. Esposito, 1983: 110.
31. Milano, 1935; Toaff, 1984: passim.
32. Stow, 1988b: 62–63.
33. See Bonfil, 1990: 108–109.
34. Stow, 1988b: 57; Bonfil, 1990: 235–246.

holders were little more than employees of minor communal dependencies burdened with time-consuming obligations such as weekly preaching, teaching children, officiating at daily and festival services, and performing weddings. Sixteenth-century Roman synagogal rabbis enjoyed even less prestige than did the Spanish *Marbiz Torah* ("Expounder of the Torah"), examples of which were to be found in contemporary Naples and Sulmona. The *Marbiz Torah* was recognized as the rabbi of his entire community, and often he held the important post of *Sofer Meta* ("Town Scribe"), whose job was to write wedding contracts, take down testimony, and keep records of communal affairs. In Rome, the *Sofer Meta* was invariably a respected rabbinic scholar, drawn from a notable family. But his scribal duties were his only official ones.[35]

Communal rabbis had greater powers in the heavily Ashkenazic communities of northern Italy, which had arisen since the later fourteenth century. With a mandate to supervise all matters pursuant to the halachah, the Veronese rabbi, for example, was numbered among the community's *fattori*. Yet his tenure was contractual, and he exercised fewer powers than did many of his contemporary transalpine Ashkenazic counterparts. In particular, he was denied the monopoly over excommunications that most if not all rabbis north of the Alps managed to retain until about 1600.[36] Like other Italian communal rabbis, he also fought a losing battle against the scholarly heads of yeshivot.[37] The sometimes ill-equipped communal rabbi of the fifteenth and sixteenth centuries[38] was no match for the acumen of such scholarly giants as Joseph Colon, Meir Katzenellenbogen of Padua, and Judah Mintz—all of whom were of German or French origin. Indeed, competition betweeen communal rabbis and the heads of yeshivot had long been a problem in the German north.[39] Heads of yeshivot like Moshe Mintz in the fifteenth century and Isaiah Horowitz at the start of the seventeenth century were the dominant rabbinic scholars of their day. These great scholars also dominated lay communal institutions. Jacob Molin (d. 1427) instructed the community of Mainz as to when its *parnasim* should meet in council, and, from distant Italy, Joseph Colon, in 1476, ordered the community of Regens-

35. Bonfil, 1990: 143–150; Stow, 1988b: 55.
36. Breuer, 1976: nos. 183,184.
37. Bonfil, 1990: 103–107.
38. Breuer, 1976: nos. 106,123.
39. Breuer, 1976: no. 179.

burg to pay a special tax levied to free those of its members who had been arrested and accused of ritually murdering a Christian boy.[40] Rabbinic scholars of this class looked askance at the excesses of their less qualified communal counterparts. And often they challenged the latter's right to issue such technical instruments as a *get* ("bill of divorce"), unless they had first been examined by a *gavra rabba* ("great scholar").[41]

However, his privileged position as the head of a yeshiva did not stop the adamant Moshe Mintz from defending the prerogatives of duly constituted rabbis, especially the newly ordained.[42] Indeed, the title *Mara de-'atra* ("Master of the Place"), which referred to northern communal rabbis, was not reduced to purely ceremonial status.[43] Even the community of Worms—ruled after 1312 by *parnasim*—conceded its rabbis exclusive power over excommunications. But not all of these concessions came at communal initiative. In 1445, the bishop of Wurzburg confirmed local rabbinic powers;[44] in 1372, the bishop of Cologne appointed the communal rabbi as communal head; in 1370, Dutchess Agnes of Schweidniz did the same. These concessions were not designed to create a class of rabbinic puppets, however advantageous it may have been to do so. More probably, following the numerous deaths and subsequent massacres of Jews during the first outbreak of the Black Death in 1348, rulers decided to circumvent the querulous and fickle council and restore order by relying on a single rabbinic official in its stead.[45]

These newfound rabbinic powers, especially over excommunication, did not last long. The *parnasim* quickly reinstated the balance existing since 1250, when a Rhenish synod had decreed that neither rabbis nor *parnasim* alone might issue bans.[46] Rabbis soon were embattled even further. In fifteenth-century Germany, communal rabbis threatened with dismissal by their constituents frequently curried favor by easing cumbersome halachic restrictions.[47] They were also pressed to share with lay courts of arbitration—run by *parnasim*—their cherished prerogative of judging according to the halachah. Their halachic authority was com-

40. Breuer, 1976: nos. 116,165,168; Zimmer, 1978: 45–46.
41. Breuer, 1976: no. 128; Yuval, 1989: 362.
42. Breuer, 1976: no. 160.
43. Ben Sasson, 1976: 597.
44. Yuval, 1989: 152ff.
45. Frank, 1935: 346–348; Yuval, 1989: 361–364.
46. Finkelstein, 1972: 228.
47. Yuval, 1983.

pletely usurped when councils of *parnasim* began unilaterally to decide upon new communal procedures.[48] Meir of Rothenburg's late thirteenth-century admonition against innovations without rabbinic consent had been conveniently set aside.[49] Yet this was all foreseeable. Meir himself had neither objected to hiring communal rabbis[50] nor contested conciliar dominance. On one occasion, he even outlined conciliar tasks. The council was to "choose heads, appoint the *hazzan* ['Cantor'], establish a communal charitable purse, nominate *gabbaim* ['superintendents'], maintain the synagogue, enlarge or purchase a structure suitable for weddings, and construct a bakery for bread; in sum, they shall care for all the needs of the Kahal."[51] Nevertheless, Meir's pupil Hayyim Or Zarua cautioned that nothing pertaining to *mili dishemayya* ("religious affairs") should be done without the consent of the *Gadol ha-'ir* ("Great Communal Rabbi").[52]

It was to reduce this tense situation, as well as competition between rabbis themselves, that a professionalized rabbinate came into being. The aim was also to monopolize activities such as officiating at weddings and preparing bills of divorce, thus keeping them in competent rabbinic hands.[53] The actual process of professionalization, which probably began in the later thirteenth century, as councils became dominant and rabbis were acquiring a communal character, culminated toward the end of the fourteenth century, when Rabbi Meir Ha-Levi of Vienna reinstituted formal rabbinic ordination. Confirmed by a diploma and by the concurrence of up to three leading rabbis,[54] ordination had the virtue of weeding out imposters and the ill qualified, but it also led to abuses.[55] Considering themselves immune, ordained rabbis sometimes threatened to inform the Christian authorities about Jews who scoffed at their fines and punitive decrees;[56] they too quickly granted halachic easements, or were overly concerned with exemptions from communal taxes and with their (halachically illegal but now formalized) stipends.[57] Some were also

48. Breuer, 1976: nos. 124,127.
49. Breuer, 1976: no. 78.
50. Breuer, 1976: no. 74.
51. Breuer, 1976: no. 88.
52. Breuer, 1976: no. 90.
53. Yuval, 1989: 324.
54. Yuval, 1989: 326; Katz, 1979: 48–52.
55. Breuer, 1976: no. 106.
56. Breuer, 1976: no. 134.
57. Breuer, 1976: nos. 22,129; Stow, 1988b: 57.

charged with having obtained ordination despite poor credentials, others with withholding ordination as a weapon.[58] Yet government by councils, too, was flawed.[59] Lay council members, for example, were halachically unequipped to oversee such complex issues as ritual slaughtering, inheritance, marriage, and divorce[60]—a task that could be performed only by great scholars and the heads of yeshivot, much in the way that contemporary Christian jurisconsults provided expert legal advice to the political leadership in Christian communes.[61] As a result, there developed what may be characterized as an informal three-tiered hierarchy. The lay council or the head of a yeshiva stood alternately at its top, while communal rabbis were either contractually or by virtue of their ordination (or their intellectual inferiority) subservient to both. At the same time, even the weakest of these rabbis normally succeeded in enforcing his excommunications.[62]

This arrangement was so efficient that by the end of the Middle Ages, those great scholars and men of wealth at the top of the pyramid were reinforcing it through marital alliances,[63] anticipating as it were the patriarchal regimes and the rabbinic dynasties of early modern central and eastern Europe.[64] However, the European rabbinate had not been so completely transformed that the original rabbinic model of southern Italy ever fully disappeared. Toward the end of the Middle Ages, a select few German rabbis like Jacob Molin, Israel Isserlein, and Yequtiel Ziskind still combined as individuals wealth, learning, and communal power, including that bestowed by a Christian ruler.[65] On the other hand, quasi-dynastic rabbinic families had existed since the days of the early Rhenish Kalonymides.[66]

Intercommunal Organization

No arrangement ever kept rabbis from encroaching on one another's jurisdictional spheres, as they so often did. In 1391, conflicting opinions

58. Breuer, 1976: 21.
59. Breuer, 1976: nos. 38–40.
60. Breuer, 1976: no. 56.
61. Stow, 1977: 74–79.
62. Breuer, 1976: 28–30, no. 140; Ben Sasson, 1959: 186.
63. Breuer, 1976: 29.
64. Katz, 1971: 141.
65. Yuval, 1989: 151.
66. Yuval, 1989: 264ff., 322.

from Spain and the Empire supported and opposed, respectively, the candidacy of Johannan Treves for the post of French chief rabbi, and in 1476 Joseph Colon of Pavia (Italy) directed Jews in Regensburg (Germany) to ransom their fellows accused of ritual murder. Such outside intervention was especially disliked by Christian authorities. The ban against studying Maimonides' philosophical writings, issued in 1305 at Barcelona by the notable Solomon ibn Adret, was most probably not published in neighboring Provence (as medieval Jews loosely and imprecisely named this part of Languedoc, as well as the regions east of the Rhone), because its proponents feared the wrath of first the royal seneschal and then of the French king Philip IV himself.[67] The English kings, too, issued a statute—similar to that called *praemunire* (which warned against ecclesiastical interventions from outside the realm)—outlawing rabbinic decisions imported to England from the European continent.[68]

Jews also circumvented local jurisdiction by appealing to higher rabbinic courts or by turning to Christian authorities. In 1314, the Jews of Nuremberg, recently decimated in the so-called Rindfleisch massacre of 1298, requested the city's Christian chief justice to renew their traditional right to refuse residence to undesirable Jewish immigrants *(herem ha-yishuv)*, in this case, the notorious Zalkind of Neumarkt, the unsavory leader of a band of Jewish ruffians.[69] Nevertheless, the chief justice actually supported Zalkind, who was permitted to acquire a residence, attend meetings of the communal council, and have the privilege of recourse to an outside rabbinic authority whenever he litigated with the Nuremberg community. The early Ashkenazic hope that recalcitrant Jews might be forced into submission by resorting to Christian courts was becoming ever more difficult to sustain.[70]

Such hopes, as well as other principles of communal and especially of intercommunal action, had originally been expressed in *taqqanot* (decrees and ordinances) issued at rabbinic synods which irregularly met at the behest of significant rabbis, and sometimes with laymen in attendance, between the twelfth and the sixteenth centuries. The synodal record is, on balance, an illustrious one. In France, Germany, Spain, and Italy, the existence of synods enabled rabbis with no formal claims to intercommunal powers to establish uniform behavioral codes for the Jews of large

67. Saperstein, 1986.
68. Roth, 1964: 116.
69. Avneri, 1960.
70. Finkelstein, 1972: 196,250.

regions. These codes were often violated, but this does not detract from their worth as indicators of ideal Jewish behavior. Synodal decrees regulated matters of ritual, described judicial districts, made rules for legislative innovation and enforcement, fixed norms to protect the rights of wives and children, placed stiff sanctions on physical violence, eventually enacted sumptuary laws, and even required all males to set aside a daily hour for study—preferably of the Talmud, but at least of the Bible or the Midrash. Synods often effectively imposed regional taxes.[71] Despite this activity, these synods never became regular parliamentary bodies, nor did they acquire actual or regional jurisdiction. Only after 1580 did the so-called Polish Council of Four Lands[72] veritably rule—as it would do by governmental grant for the next two centuries—a true Jewish "Super Community."[73] Catalonian and Castilian synods in 1354 and 1432, respectively, proposed ongoing regional governing bodies, but their efforts failed miserably.[74]

Synods in both the early and the later Middle Ages were especially effective when they were presided over by a *Gadol Ha-Dor* ("Great [Rabbi] of the Generation"). The *Gadol* often set the synodal agenda, and his prestige gave teeth to synodal decrees following their ratification. *Gedolim* also functioned outside the specific synodal framework by independently circulating legislative proposals, which they magisterially exhorted their lessers to endorse, and by sometimes unilaterally having decrees issued in their own names.[75] *Gedolei Ha-Dor* were not appointed. Their status was a purely honorific one, which perhaps made it all the more coveted. Nor did every generation have a *Gadol*. Saadya, the illustrious head of the Babylonian academy of Sura (ca. 940), was bold enough to call himself a *Gadol*. He may in fact have been responsible for remolding this originally talmudic term, since by his day the Gaonic title he bore had lost its unicity. Originally, it belonged only to the Gaon of Sura (in fact, the title was derived from the academy's formal name, *Gaon Yaacov*, "the Glory of Jacob"). By the tenth century, the title was being applied as well to the heads of the academies at Pumpeditha and at Jerusalem. In the late twelfth century, Maimonides argued that "all the (significant) sages . . . after the Talmud's composition . . . were called

71. Finkelstein, 1972: 291.
72. Weinryb, 1973: 148–150.
73. Baron, 1948: 1:293–299.
74. Finkelstein, 1972: 336–375.
75. Chazan, 1968.

Geonim," including those in Ashkenaz. Ashkenazic scholars agreed.[76] If, therefore, one desired or needed—as did the stormy Saadya—to assert his primacy, a grander title was required. Saadya chose *Gadol,* "the Great One."[77] Following Saadya, Maimondes likewise was recognized as a *Gadol,* in Egypt, where he lived, and throughout the Judeo-Islamic world. Whether anyone attained such recognition in the West is another matter.

To name a Jew *Gadol* in Latin Europe, which lacked the centralized institutions of the East, was primarily a matter of perceptions. Rightfully, Rabbenu Gershom should have been called a *Gadol,* and, within a generation of his death, he was. Rashi called Gershom "the great light" and the one who "enlightened the exile." Never, he added, had there "been a *Gadol* like him."[78] In his own day, the emigrant to Mainz from Metz was not so well honored. Rashi, too, was not immediately recognized, especially during his Rhenish sojourn. Yet even after his return to France, he was not catapulted into power. Like Rabbenu Gershom before him, Rashi was essentially the respected head of a local yeshiva and a man of limited public activity.[79] Only his responsa, commissioned by rabbis from near and far, reveal the extent of his contemporary material influence. Two centuries later, in changed internal and external political circumstances, Meir ben Baruch of Rothenburg had a wider constituency. At least until his imprisonment in 1286, Meir functioned not only as a scholar and halachic authority second to none but also as the unofficial political leader of central German Jewry, in close contact with imperial and local authorities. He also saw himself as a *gavra rabba* ("great man"). Perhaps no rabbi in the Empire was ever again to be so authoritative. The fourteenth century was a time of turmoil. By the fifteenth century, reference was being made to multiple, simultaneous *Gedolim,* none of whom equaled Rabbi Meir.[80] Indeed, no one could pretend to Meir's independence and influence in what had by then become a fully articulated system of rabbinic appointments in which both Christian rulers and Jewish *parnasim* manipulated appointees, and appointees themselves willingly sought a base for power. Subject to cancellation, the power of these rabbinic appointees was also unstable. Secure dominance was at-

76. Maimonides, Mishneh Torah, Introduction; Finkelstein, 1972: 195.
77. *Babylonian Talmud,* Pesahin, 49b: Gittin, 36b.
78. Finkelstein, 1972: 106,249.
79. Finkelstein, 1972: 37,148–149.
80. Breuer, 1976: nos. 124,166.

tained only by a few notable heads of yeshivot, like Meir Katzenel-lenbogen of Padua, or by rabbis like Jacob Molin or Israel Isserlein, whose halachic primacy and independent wealth freed them from the need for a communal or a governmental appointment.[81] The powers of the *Gadol*, like those of the preceding Gaon, had been deflated.

Moreover, the line from Meir of Rothenburg, especially with respect to Meir's political activities—but to some extent with respect to his halachic ones, too—led not to influential rabbis but to an emerging breed of layman, the *shtadlan* (intercessor with the government), best typified by Josel of Rosheim in the early sixteenth century. Originally, Josel was the *parnas* of the communities of Lower Lorraine, but in about 1530 he was named by the Jews themselves to be their "commander" and "regent" throughout the Empire. Josel's official status and his lack of rabbinic ordination are demonstrative of changes in Jewish internal leadership that had occurred over the preceding two centuries, changes which had led to the preferment of laymen and the rejection of noted rabbis such as Seligman Bing in 1456.[82] Josel's powers to represent imperial Jewry, which he retained for nearly thirty years, were virtually complete.[83] They were honored and confirmed in practice by the secular authorities, despite the existence since 1521 of an imperially appointed *Landesrabbiner,* Rabbi Samuel ben Eliezer of Worms. Indeed, had Josel not actively participated in the synod of Worms summoned by Samuel in 1542, its decrees safeguarding local Jewish courts would probably have gone unheeded.

Shtadlanim like Josel were also distinguished from earlier rabbinic *Gadolim* by the constitutional nature of their authority. The Jews elected Josel to his post; nobody elected Meir of Rothenburg. Meir's authority, whether in dealings with Jews or Christians, was a moral one based only on his command of halachic intricacies, and, accordingly, Meir's word was not always final, as Josel's would be. On at least one occasion, leading rabbis in both France and Ashkenaz adamantly opposed Meir. And Meir himself cautiously refrained from issuing decisions that might defy local ordinances, even though he believed that to do so was his right.[84]

81. Yuval, 1989: 151.
82. Zimmer, 1978: 37–41.
83. Stern, 1965; Zimmer, 1978: 59–66.
84. Urbach, 1955: 412–416, 420.

Meir's disciple Asher ben Yehiel, who fled Germany in 1298 and became the rabbi of Toledo, was not so restrained. Rightly, Asher has been called "formally and in fact" the chief rabbi of Castile.[85] Freely attacking Spanish customs that clashed with those he had brought with him from the north and willingly denouncing protagonists in Toledo, Asher likewise did not shrink from enmeshing himself in Spanish Jewry's internal power struggles, allying himself with Christian courtiers and Jewish court favorites. His apparently unequivocal acceptance of Spanish Jewry's unique right to impose death sentences for crimes such as informing suggests that in the long run he assimilated the magisterial traditions of the Andalusian "Rabbinate" as described by Abraham ibn Daud in his *Sefer ha-Kabbalah* (1161).[86] Nevertheless, Asher's attitudes were equally molded by his originally northern ideals. "In our day," he wrote, "it appears that the most important (the high court) of the generation is that called the Court of the *Gadol*. As Rabbenu Tam has said, 'They always appointed the *Gadol* of the Generation to be the *Nasi* (the ancient Palestinian Patriarch), . . . just as the Benei Bathira ceded their Patriarchate to Hillel'" (Asheri, *B.T.*, Sanhedrin 3:41). In contemporary Toledo, Asher saw himself as the *Gadol* and the heir to Hillel, and it was as such, far more than as heir to Spanish rabbinic traditions, that he ruled over Castilian Jewry and over its lay and rabbinic leadership. In assuming this posture, Asher was of course following his mentor, Rabbi Jacob Tam of Ramerupt in Champagne.

In the judgment of both posterity and his contemporaries, Jacob Tam (d. 1171) was the *Gadol*. His personal bearing, his wealth from lending and possibly viticulture, his authority over Jews in Champagne and beyond the borders of France, his attitude toward other rabbis, and his relations with Christian authorities—in combination with his enormous learning and halachic prestige—made his standing unique, yet one that he unflinchingly believed to be his due. Not unexpectedly, he had little truck with opponents; his outspokenly brusque reprimand of Rabbi Meshullam of Melun was proverbial. Arbitrarily, he decided the propriety of customary practices.[87] Almost alone of great rabbis, Jacob Tam issued decrees on his own authority or insisted that other scholars approve by countersigning them.

85. Baer, 1961: 1:316–325.
86. Cohen, G., 1968: 63–90.
87. Urbach, 1955: 65,69.

The same skills Jacob Tam demonstrated in showing that Jews could freely trade with Christians he applied in resolving other practical cruces. Women could henceforth not be divorced without their consent; widows could not be abandoned. Should a wife die without issue in the first year of her marriage, her dowry was to be returned to her father, "lest he lose both his child and his wealth in one stroke."[88] Should a Christian landlord evict a Jewish tenant by demanding an exorbitant rent, no other Jew was to lease the dwelling. These last two *Taqqanot* were still being cited in Rabbenu Tam's name in the sixteenth and seventeenth centuries.[89] His decisions on constitutional matters enjoyed a similar longevity. No communal member, Rabbenu Tam ordered, could exempt himself from the obligation of paying taxes. The presence of a scholar or a cemetery in a town was prima facie evidence that a court could be established there. Cases had to be tried in one of three nearby cities, so that defendants would not be dragged to far-off venues. Yet there had to be regional courts of appeal. Jews were to turn to gentile courts only in moments of necessity. Still, the king and his courts should not be approached by anyone who was not properly designated to do so. The extant versions of these ordinances no doubt contain revisions and interpolations made by near-contemporaries and later scholars. The ordinance regulating rentals has been ascribed to Rabbenu Gershom.[90] The essence in every case, however, is unquestionably the formulation of Rabbenu Tam himself.

So accepted was Jacob Tam's authority that he was conceded the right to determine disputed Talmudic readings. The language and style of his writings betray his awareness of his enormous power. He was the unofficial *comes iudaeorum,* so sure of himself that he insisted that innovations in communal practice be unanimously ratified,[91] meaning, of course, that his own initiatives were to be unanimously ratified. Yet such strength reveals the essential flaw in medieval Jewish self-government. It could be effective only when it was headed by a person who united in himself, as did Jacob Tam, all the powers of lay, spiritual, internal, and external leadership, and only when all these were exercised at an opportune moment. Given the inherent instability of Jewish governmental institutions, one could not expect otherwise.

88. Finkelstein, 1972: 171–204.
89. Stow, 1989: 45–53.
90. Finkelstein, 1972: 171.
91. Morell, 1971: 95.

Jewish Political Theory

In their striving for effective self-governance, the Jews' reliance on hala-chically learned, ofttimes charismatic leaders or, alternately, on inchoate conciliar oligarchies—at least through the late fourteenth century, and perhaps even after that—was the product of various factors. The most obvious of them was that when it came to obtaining their rights to self-government, the Jews depended exclusively on their secular rulers' sometimes inconsistent behavior. The Jews also suffered from the under-developed state of medieval political theory, both Jewish and Christian.[92] Conceptually, as well as in practice, the sovereign states of Christian Europe emerged only after an agonizingly long process that began about 1100 and ended about four hundred years later. Not before the middle of the thirteenth century did people in the western kingdoms of England and France begin to realize that they were living in a "body politic," not simply in the private holding of some king or other feudal lord. Nor did they picture the kingdom abstractly as an undying, ongoing entity, with both a real and an ideal nature, and one that was invested with transcen-dental attributes such as those of being the *communis patria* ("common homeland"), and the *corpus reipublicae mysticum* ("mystical—theolo-gized—body of the state").[93] Until well into the High Middle Ages, therefore, the Jews had no fully elaborated governmental theory or model to aid them in perfecting their own political institutions. Furthermore, the more Christian political thinking coalesced, the more precarious became the Jews' theoretical and constitutional hold on their right to reside in Christian kingdoms. It is indicative that the only instance in which the Jews of northern Europe were organized into a quasi-parlia-mentary framework with "estates" occurred in 1242, when the English king Henry III ordered the moderately wealthy English Jews to meet and ascertain the truly wealthy's capacity to be taxed. The initiative was royal—that is, not one made by Jews themselves.[94]

Still, Jewish political thought was not wholly static, nor are its origins all traceable to medieval Christian precedent. Jews in the late ancient period, and again during the Geonic Age of Babylonia, were already discussing the implications of the dictum *Dina de-malkhuta dina,* which rationalized submission to external authority. The protection of Jewish

92. Watt, 1965: 47–57.
93. Kantorowicz, 1957: passim.
94. Stacey, 1987; Baron, 1952: 11:62–63.

courts against gentile competition was also debated. Northern European Jews continued these discussions. They also—according to one of the most seminal and influential theses of modern Jewish historiography—conceptually reproduced the ancient ideal of the *Kenesset Yisrael* ("Assembly of Israel").[95]

This "assembly" is said to have reified "organic" political images much like those proposed first by Plato in describing his utopian polity and later by Paul (actually borrowing Jewish ideas) in perceiving his archetypal *ecclesia* as the all-embracing and unified body of Christ, the Church and its members. The *Kenesset Yisrael*, accordingly, was more a transcendental than a physical entity, whose ideal existence continued even when its physical one had temporarily ceased. This would explain why medieval Jews seem to have structured their contemporary political life along lines preexisting in the second century B.C.E.,[96] and even why the charter of autonomy given to the Jews of Judea in the year 198 B.C.E. by the Syrian Antiochus III—and eventually ratified by the Romans—seems to presage the charters given to the Jews of the pre- and post-Crusade Rhineland by their episcopal and imperial rulers. In these charters, moreover, both the ancient and medieval Jewish communities were granted a "corporate" status, which was unique but at the same time akin in structure to the indigenous *Genossenschaft* ("company of comrades") so common in early medieval German political life.[97]

In terms of early twentieth-century neo-Idealist German historiography,[98] which still invested ideas with extra-mental existence, this thesis was highly plausible. It made sense to speak of an immanent Jewish national consciousness, *toda'ah le-'umit*, here in the guise of the *Kenesset Yisrael*, which was constantly seeking avenues for self-assertion. Today, such ideas are difficult to sustain. The thesis itself is also factually controvertible. The Jewish community was not a corporation, certainly not within the limits of that term's medieval usages. Nor (as is also assumed) was its nature—or that of any other medieval body, for that matter—democratic.[99]

Only in the thirteenth century did the first real medieval corporations, the universities—in particular that of Paris—acquire the legally corporate

95. Baer, 1985b.
96. Ben Sasson, 1976: 501.
97. See Baer, 1985b: 14.
98. Walsh, 1958: 49–51.
99. Baron, 1952: 5:62–67; Agus, 1969: passim.

status of a closed body with precisely enunciated rights as delineated by ancient Roman law. Alternatively, Roman law viewed corporations as minors with guardians. A third medieval corporate type, that of the merchants' guilds, eventually dominated civic life in many regions. But like the universities, the guilds acquired their closed corporate structure only well into the High Middle Ages.[100] In other words, the Jewish communities that coalesced in the Rhineland about the time of Rabbenu Gershom had no contemporary corporate model to imitate. The Jewish communities also had little in common with the early German merchants' associations, the *Genossenschaften*. These were *voluntaristic* bodies founded by itinerant merchants for the purposes of self-defense;[101] from both an internal and an external viewpoint, Jews *had no choice* but to accept communal rule. The complexity of Jewish commercial law also made early medieval Jewish organizations statutorily far more sophisticated than were the *Genossenschaften*. Further, the rights and privileges that rulers granted Jews were far more consistent than those granted foreign merchants.[102]

The emperor Justinian had also canceled the Jews' corporate communal rights in the early sixth century.[103] The privilege granted Jews by royal and other charters of privilege to live by "their own law" did not reverse this fact. Indeed, when this privilege began to be bestowed upon the Jews as a group, it reflected their becoming not a "corporation among the corporations" but rather a constitutional isolate—"the Jews"—in an increasingly alien Christian world. Hence, it cannot be said that "Jewish autonomy fell within the framework of the corporations which were permitted to stand between the individual and the sovereign in the Middle Ages."[104] Nor may that community be likened to the hierocratically envisioned unified and papally dominated Christian world.[105] On the contrary, Ashkenazic sages pragmatically insisted that every Jewish community was a jurisdictionally autonomous court of law, hardly "a 'natural' unit, a cell of an ancient body, dispersed but not broken up."[106]

Politically, Ashkenazic Jews of the eleventh and the twelfth centuries

100. Lopez, 1962: 142–144; Miskimin, 1969: 106–111.
101. Ennen, 1972: 105–109.
102. Lotter, 1989: passim.
103. Stow, 1987; Linder, 1987: 107–110.
104. Ben Sasson, 1976: 502.
105. Ullmann, 1962.
106. Ben Sasson, 1971: 211.

proved themselves to be enormously creative. Taking the measure of Christian political institutions, they expropriated pertinent elements and transformed them through exegetical manipulations to make them appear purely Jewish. Jews seem in fact to have understood all aspects of Christian political life and thought. Eventually, at the time of the Renaissance, Jews even engaged in theoretical discussions on the relative merits of monarchies over republics, and vice versa.[107] In the Middle Ages, Jews were mostly intent on absorbing knowledge. How did Christian thinkers and practitioners deal with such relevant issues as communal jurisdiction, discipline, and the participation of various segments of the community in making decisions? The politics of the High Middle Ages were no longer typified by the combination of savagery and religious guilt, war and pilgrimage, that had once marked the careers of feudal barons such as Fulk Nerra of Anjou (d. 1040).[108] Rather, in both theory and practice, power was being vested ever more in the "body politic."

That body, it was said, realized the enduring and abstract ideal of the "crown," whose real-life wearers could modify its behavior and its strategies but not affect its essence. Rulers were responsible for dispensing justice, framing laws, and protecting the "commonweal" as both a secular and a religious entity—and most often as the two together. For, said John of Paris in 1302, the king's temporal authority was directly vouchsafed him by Christ himself. This authority was often tempered by the unwelcome interference of councils, whose original purpose was to advise but which sometimes grew strong enough temporarily to displace kings.[109] Churchmen, many of whom produced elaborate conciliar theories, especially in the fourteenth and fifteenth centuries, argued that an ecumenical, ecclesiastical council might be greater than the head—that is, the pope. The popes replied that they alone ruled the Church, and "could be judged by none."[110] This theorizing did not mean that the rule of force had been displaced. The king of France found himself either dealing with his barons as equals, or completely dominating them. The German emperor, like all elected figures, had to share his rule, which he did by conceding power in large parts of the Empire to regional and local electors.

Arguments for the legitimacy of power were drawn from the Platonic

107. Melamed, 1986: 146–147.
108. Southern, 1963: 108; Bachrach, 1984.
109. Hollister-Baldwin, 1978.
110. See Watt, 1965; Wilks, 1963; Tierney, 1964.

and Aristotelian corpuses, biblical verses, the sayings of the Church Fathers, those of Paul, and papal decrees. No instrument served medieval theorists better than did the principles of the Roman civil law, which in particular enabled theories of representation to be shaped. Whether in the English parliament or in civic councils in eastern Germany and southern Italy, representative institutions gave large segments of the populace a share in governance. In the thirteenth century, the English king tried with mixed results to dominate his "parliaments" (discussions) by summoning nobles, the clerical hierarchy, and finally the squires. By the late fourteenth century, the process was being inexorably reversed, until English sovereignty was eventually said to reside in the "King *in* Parliament" (as officially it still does).[111] The essential question distinguishing one type of representative institution from another was whether, like kings or especially the pope, delegates had *plenitudo potestatis* ("full sovereign powers") or whether they had only *plena potestas* ("full power") *to bind* those whom they represented.

The delegation of power was perhaps even more important for Jews than it was for Christians. Unlike the latter, Jews had no concrete boundaries in which to reify their body politic. Their "Holy Community," as they called it, was a name, which medieval Jews themselves had invented to signify their collective halachic foundations, if not their very political existence. Yet in reality, not even communal jurisdiction was true or lasting; Christian overlords could overturn the decisions of Jewish tribunals at will. The community's sovereign functions were no more solidified. No one ever properly defined the locus of communal authority or managed undisputedly to lay claim to it. Even formal supervision of ritual was not fixed until ordination was reestablished about 1370. The halachah created additional problems, failing as it does to distinguish secular spheres of governance from spiritual ones. Inevitably, Jewish intellectual and rabbinic leaders were pressed to challenge and then to seek a modus vivendi with the *tovim*, the *parnasim*, and the *benei ha-'ir*—that is, with conciliar boards and sometimes with the entire Jewish residential body. The definition of the community as a court over which only properly trained halachic experts could preside was a first step in this direction. A second was to exploit Christian governing devices, which was accomplished by adapting and conferring upon them a true Jewish identity. This process is especially evident in the case of the *herem*, which (as a word)

111. Stacey, 1987a: 93–131; Sayles, 1975.

originally meant excommunication, confiscation, or a prohibited territory or object.

By the early eleventh century, *herem* had assumed the meaning of an "oath to excommunicate"—effectively, a juridical convention. Rabbenu Gershom's contemporary Joseph Bonfils was already using *herem* in this sense. The members of a community, he said, were called upon to enter into a *herem* to ensure that lost objects be returned.[112] Yet by "entering into a *herem*," the community was also creating a de facto judicial district. Rabbenu Tam cited earlier French sages to say that "in a place where there is a tradition of a scholar's presence, it is almost certain that there existed a *herem bet din* ("jurisdictional venue"), so that one may hold court there [even today]."[113] These de facto venues and juridical conventions proliferated. Medieval Jewry's most well-known governmental mechanisms are called *haramot*; their content was often highly innovative. The *herem ha-yishuv*, for example—entitling a community to decide who might or might not dwell in it—was so innovative that about 1130, the Jews of Paris wrote to those of Rome asking whether the latter upheld it; they did not.[114] Additional new *haramot* governed the holding of pledges, the levying and collection of communal taxes, and the right to interrupt prayers in order to demand that a court of arbitration be appointed. By means of a *herem*, monopolies *(ma'arufyot)* were also distributed for doing business with gentiles.[115]

Logically, these innovations were anchored in talmudic texts and traditional practices. A precursor of the *herem* for "interrupting prayers" may have existed in ancient Palestine, from which it may have passed to northern Europe by way of Italy.[116] More broadly, the Talmud (Gittin 7b–8b) gives local communities the right to fix wages, to set prices, and even to levy fines. Past communities may have also exercised legislative initiatives. By reinterpreting a verse from the Book of Ezra (10:8) that allows the confiscation of property, the Gaon Hananiah (938–943) concluded that a *minyan zeqenim* ("requisite number of [local] elders") could *be-haskamah 'ahat* ("with one mind") pass new enactments.[117] Ashkenazic scholars, who may or may not have known Hananiah's commen-

112. Agus, 1969: 173.
113. Finkelstein, 1972: 193.
114. Baron, 1952: 11:57.
115. Finkelstein, 1972: 16–19.
116. Finkelstein, 1972: 16; Baron, 1952: 5:66.
117. Morell, 1971: 88; Grossman, 1975: 178.

tary, followed his interpretative lead—except, however, on one crucial point. By "elders," Hananiah meant a fixed oligarchy, just as the term is used in the report of Nathan the Babylonian. The Ashkenazim located the source of authority variously in the "upright," a "majority of the leadership," and occasionally in the community as a whole. They also borrowed a talmudic term, the *sheva tove ha-'ir* ("seven good men of the city") and ingeniously applied it to town councils, which normally decided issues by majority vote, rather than by unanimity as Hananiah had said.[118] In addition, Hananiah's legislative initiatives were surely meant to be ad hoc ones. His Geonic zeal to retain halachic supremacy would have prevented him from considering any other alternative. By contrast, the Ashkenazim empowered communal leaders to establish permanent juridical institutions—namely, the *haramot*. This was a sweeping change. Never before had the Jewish communal leadership assumed such wide discretionary powers.

Christian leaders had. Powers like those conferred by the *herem* were exercised in Christian society through the medium of the feudal institution known as the signorial *bannum*. Originally, the *bannum* was most likely a purely judicial right exercised by the Frankish kings.[119] With the demise of the Carolingian Empire in the ninth and tenth centuries, lay lords, anxious to consolidate control over their estates and over the peasants who resided there, appropriated this right for themselves. Eventually, they fused it with their preexisting signorial right "to issue orders and punish those who disobeyed" and then expanded it to include the right to make monetary exactions, demand rents and services, and acquire monopolies over such things as mills and wine presses.[120] The *bannum*, therefore—which, like the organized Jewish community, formally emerged about the year 1000—created spheres of jurisdiction, established coercive rights of taxation and punishment, and assigned monopolistic franchises within a circumscribed geographic district. The *haramot* did precisely the same. Some process of emulation and adaptation must have been taking place.

The *bannum* and the *herem*, nevertheless, were not identical. The former was created unilaterally by a signor; the latter was legislated by a communal panel. Jewish society was, after all, not a feudal one. Its

118. Baron, 1952: 5:60.
119. Evergates, 1983; Bloch, 1941: 1:262.
120. Ganshof, 1941: 1:333; Le Goff, 1988: 93–84.

leaders were not great lords and landowners; its constituents were not peasants. In the earlier Middle Ages, especially, community members were frequently near-equals, and a large percentage were persons of substance and learning. Such a community could not be despotically or oligarchically ruled.[121] Jewish sages, therefore, might have preferred establishing a strict pecking order, as did the feudal nobility and, for that matter, the Babylonian Geonim (as the sages probably knew). They certainly believed that communal headship was their right; and in the eleventh century, they in fact possessed that headship. Moreover, when they spoke of obedience to communal ordinances and of the right *lehasi'a 'al kizotam* (figuratively, "to punish"), and when they related these issues to the notion of the entire community as a court, which obviously the learned alone could head, they were, within halachic limits, effectively—perhaps intentionally—trying to behave like the lay (or ecclesiastical) Christian signor. Indeed, what these sages most probably desired was eloquently summed up at the end of the thirteenth century by Meir of Rothenburg: "The *qadmonim* ['early sages']," he said, "were in the habit of decreeing a *herem* on a settlement, by which [they] might force communal members [to obey] without [the need to go] to court."[122] Similarly, in the words of a responsum from the mid-eleventh century, "Even when *qatanim* ['the lesser in standing'] are greater in number than the *gedolim,* [it is the former's obligation to bow to the latter's will]; . . . the outcries of the former are as nothing."[123] But in reality, the sages had to compromise. Contrary to the claims of the responsum, the sages themselves admitted that when a *herem* was decreed, it became operative only after *each* member of the communal body swore an oath of personal obligation.

The acquiescence of the sages to share power with other members of the community did not, however, derive from democratic impulses. Nor was it related to long-defunct German tribal practices. Rather, the sages were bowing to the facts of the Jewish community's limited size and to its overall homogeneity, both of which may have persuaded them to take note of the contemporary example of Italian (Christian) communal behavior. Widespread communal participation at aristocratic expense was a hallmark of the partly aristocratic, partly popular rural and civic

121. Baron, 1952: 5:67.
122. Breuer, 1976: no. 22.
123. Grossman, 1975: 184.

associations that arose in Italy in the late tenth and early eleventh centuries and then gradually spread to northern Europe. At Verona, toward the end of the tenth century, for example, Bishop Ratherius wrote of "the civic assembly attended by the entire citizenry."[124] These Christian associations also gradually gained power over local signorial bans and rights. In the year 1070, the people of Le Mans, in France, made "an association which they called a commune; they joined themselves together by oaths, and forced the . . . magnates of the countryside to swear allegiance to their commune." In Lombardy in 1036, townsmen "prevented their lords from getting away with anything against their will."[125] The communes even began to call the countryside and the small villages they controlled the *banlieu,* a district where the *bannum* was valid.

In establishing jurisdictional *haramot,* the Jewish communities and their leaders thus were quite probably following the lead of the communes. The vehicle for carrying these new concepts of communal rule northward from Italy could easily have been migrant scholars like Meshullam ben Kalonymos, who came from Lucca, in Tuscany. It does not seem accidental that the preexisting talmudic term *tovim,* so prevalent in Rhenish Jewish texts, is effectively interchangeable with *boni homines,* the term often used to designate the leaders of Italian Christian civic associations. But the use of such terms as *tovim* should emphasize that what the Jews borrowed from urban Christian governmental behavior they also masked, often beyond recognition. To wit, as early perhaps as the mid-eleventh century, a rudimentary version of the concept of sovereignty was subtly woven into a normative discussion of the community as a court. "What the community has decided," two rabbis declared, "cannot be voided on a charge of discrimination or enmity; such limitations bind courts alone."[126] The community, that is, was not dependent, like a court, on judicial procedures. Its legislation was legitimate in its own right. Yet for this rudimentary statement of sovereignty, no Jewish prooftext was offered. None, in fact, was available. Possible Christian supports or parallels went wholly unmentioned. Jews, in fact, were ambivalent about adopting Christian practices. Accordingly, much of what they adopted they failed to develop, as the following ordinance on ma-

124. Ennen, 1972: 105–138; Fasoli, 1974: 194–198; Tabacco, 1977: 200–202, 208–209; and see Agus, 1952: 165ff.

125. Cited in Reisenberg, 1958: 115, and 43,45,105; see also Le Goff, 1988: 290–293; Sergi, 1990: 410–412.

126. Grossman, 1975: 186.

jority rule and the commentary on it by Meir of Rothenburg well illustrate. The ordinance, which likely originated in the mid-twelfth century, has been attributed to Rabbenu Gershom.[127]

> If the *qahal* or the *benei ha-'ir* [both here meaning "leadership"] have made an ordinance concerning the poor, or concerning any other issue, and the majority of the upright [leaders] have consented, the minority cannot void the ordinance by saying, "Let us go to court to settle the matter." For following the ancient custom, or the need of the hour, everything is determined by the view of the *tovei ha-'ir.*

Yet by what right do the *tovim* exert such obviously sovereign powers? Even in the ordinance's definitive codification, dating from about 1225, no explanation is provided. To remedy this lacuna, Meir of Rothenburg explained that the ordinance was valid because the "*tovim* are like the *Gedolei ha-Dor,*" meaning—in the original sense of the word—that the *Gedolim* constitute a High Court, whose decisions cannot be overturned.[128] Communal authority had once again been justified exclusively by the judicial paradigm.

But this retreat may have been a strategic one. By Meir of Rothenburg's day, the actual sovereign powers of the Jewish community had receded even as intracommunal tensions had grown. Ensuring that the community would abide by the decisions of the *tovim* was difficult enough. It was best to use well-tried, talmudically substantiated arguments to justify conciliar powers rather than to search out new ones with possibly non-Jewish origins. An adequate theory of representation or of conciliar limits, despite the traditional participatory element in Jewish communal activities, was simply not a desideratum. The many allusions to councils in ordinances and in various other texts do not even define how conciliar members are to be chosen, elected, or appointed. It apparently also seemed irrelevant to justify why a conciliar *majority* should make decrees rather than any other grouping, such as the majority together with a rabbinic patriciate, a unanimous council, or even the whole community. Jewish communities, accordingly, developed various practices. In 1264, Rabbi Solomon ibn Adret of Barcelona, reflecting on conditions in Catalonia and elsewhere, wrote that there are "places where affairs are entirely run by the advice of the elders and the councillors; others where

127. Finkelstein, 1972: 121.

128. Rashi, Babylonian Talmud, Baba Batra, 8b; Mordekhai, 1911: ibid; Morell, 1971: 89.

the *majority* [of such councillors and elders] can do nothing without consulting *all* the people and obtaining their consent; and still others where *individuals* are given the authority to do as they see fit in all general affairs."[129]

When about 1200 the Rabiah (Eliezer ben Joel Halevi) at last offered a rationale for majority rule, its ring was hollow: "[Tractate] *'Abodah Zarah*," he said, "[teaches that] 'a decree is not to be imposed upon the community unless the majority can endure it' . . . We thus learn that a decree goes into effect with the consent of the majority."[130] In context, as the Rabiah must have known, the Talmud primarily emphasizes the decree's justice, not its approbation. Equally difficult was the attempt of Rabbi Asher ben Yehiel of Toledo to apply to communal legislative practice the talmudic principle that majority votes are binding in courts of law (though such an application logically elaborated the idea of the community as a court). Asher himself seems to have anticipated opposition. So he pleaded, "If you do not say [that the Talmud's reference to judicial majorities also pertains to communal government], then there is never a possibility of communal enactment. For when will the entire *kahal* agree on one opinion?"[131]

By contrast, from about 1100, the issues of majority rule, election, and representation attracted ever-greater attention in the increasingly autonomous Christian communes.[132] Christian savants searched Roman law to find endorsements such as the "consent of 'the wiser and greater part,'" which seems alternately to have meant both the majority and the elite.[133] Roman law was also probed to explain how, when, and why town councils were to be formed. John of Viterbo (ca. 1228) wrote that "if the importance of the crisis demands yet greater counsel, others of the wiser citizens elected by the entire citizenry should be summoned to give it—that is, representatives [of the various civic strata] . . . The [Roman law] principle to be followed is that all shall approve matters which concern all: let the judgment of all decide the future of all [*quod omnes tanget ab omnibus approbetur*]."[134] Individuals, therefore, were to be able to express their will through elected representatives, whose election con-

129. Beinart, 1971: 227; see also Schwarzfuchs, 1986: 52.
130. Morell, 1971: 91.
131. Morell, 1971: 92.
132. Reisenberg, 1958: 49–50; Sestan, 1977: 194–195.
133. Mundy, 1973: 435,489; Ullmann, 1946: 59; Baer, 1985b; Fasoli, 1974: 205–207.
134. Cited in Reisenberg, 1958: 125.

ferred upon the latter "full power" to bind their constituents. *Approbare*
meant not solely "consent" but the right, and the obligation, to vote on
the issue and to ratify the proposed action. This concept appealed even
to kings. It was repeated verbatim in 1295 by King Edward I to justify
summoning to parliament the squires alongside the nobility and the
clergy.[135] Edward wanted his royal initiatives ratified and made binding
by common consent.

Common consent, however, did not necessarily refer to unanimity.
Normally, the majority will was decisive.[136] But sometimes majorities
were considered to be inadequate. Did not (Christian scholars asked)
Nova jura, new constitutions, taxes, and ordinances require unanimous
conciliar or even popular consent?[137] Among Jews, the issue of majority
versus unanimous consent—in the context of true representative theory—
seems seriously to have troubled only Rabbenu Tam and possibly Meir
of Rothenburg.

Discussing the talmudic passage authorizing communities *le-hasi'a 'al
qizotam* ("to punish those who violated their rules"), Jacob Tam wrote,
"The *qizot* [literally, 'conventions'] themselves are made *mi-da'at kol
tovei ha-'ir* ['with the consent of *all* the *tovim*']."[138] Enforcement of
existing rules may be determined by a conciliar majority, but new enactments require common conciliar consent. This does not mean that
Rabbenu Tam was advocating sharing his acknowledged supremacy with
councils, whose members might even include laymen. This was, after all,
the same Jacob Tam who issued decrees in his own name and brooked
no opposition, even from leading scholars. Rather, Jacob Tam understood
that the question of the majority versus unanimous consent was principally a theoretical one. As a dictum apocryphally attributed to Rashi
succinctly states: "One is not exempt from public decrees if they are justly
enacted; [namely] decrees [literally, 'a thing'] to which all the *kahal* has
consented [*hiskim*]."[139] But this, of course, is a paraphrase of the Roman
legal principle of "ratification": *approbare* and *haskamah/hiskim* alone
make an ordinance just and universally binding. Rabbenu Tam's formulation *mi-da'at kol tovei ha-'ir* ("with the consent of all the *tovim*")
makes the same point; one would not be surprised to learn that the author

135. Stubbs, 1900: 485 (trans.).
136. Mundy, 1973: 408.
137. Mundy, 1973: 439,435; Wilks, 1963: 107.
138. Morell, 1971: 90.
139. Grossman, 1975: 190.

of the above apocryphal dictum was none other than Jacob Tam himself. Like John of Viterbo after him, therefore, Jacob Tam required that "the judgment of all decide the future of all."

Nonetheless, Rabbenu Tam's concept of consent may have more closely resembled the one contemplated by Edward I or the Statute of Princes enacted at Worms in 1231 than John of Viterbo's more strictly conciliar thought.[140] For both Edward and the 1231 statute viewed conciliar approval as necessary to ratify specifically royal decrees. And as has been observed, the ordinances which Jacob Tam insisted that councils ratify were those proposed by the *haver ha-'ir* ("city's important sage")— namely, by Rabbenu Tam himself.[141] He would magisterially decree, and the *tovim,* the *kahal,* would approve. In calling for representation and consent, Rabbenu Tam was being thoroughly consistent with his personal style.

The sources of Rabbenu Tam's conceptualization are another matter. In his native Champagne, urban development lagged far behind that elsewhere. Indeed, in France, conciliar principles first appeared after Jacob Tam's death, in thirteenth-century treaties between the French kings and their barons.[142] Possibly, therefore, he was building on hints scattered in the commentaries of earlier Rhenish and Italian scholars aware of Italian civic practice. At the same time, Jacob Tam was enormously creative. He and the Christian exponents of representative theory may have been following fully independent lines.

Regardless of its origins, Rabbenu Tam's theorizing was subsequently either misunderstood or purposefully ignored. Most discussions were intended to ensure that councils had sufficient coercive power or that their enactments did not produce "gain for one and loss for another."[143] Disregarding the implications of representative theory, nearly all Jewish scholars[144] effectively and simply agreed with Asher ben Yehiel that only by majority rule, as opposed to unanimous rule, could communities successfully be governed. By contrast, Meir of Rothenburg seems to have understood Jacob Tam's designs perfectly. But Meir also seems to have intuited that only someone with Jacob Tam's authority could make a pure

140. Mundy, 1973: 435.
141. Baer, 1985b: 39; see Babylonian Talmud, Baba Batra 9a.
142. Baldwin-Hollister, 1978; Langmuir, 1960: passim.
143. Morell, 1971: 98–107.
144. Ben Sasson, 1976: 502–503.

representative theory work. The following statements reveal how discriminatingly Meir balanced theory with practice:

> If there is a dispute [between the members of your] *kahal*, and they *cannot* agree on leaders by *haskamat kulam* ["common consent"] . . . , it is my opinion that all the tax-paying *ba'alei batim* ["householders"] should gather and swear an oath [*berakhah*] that each will say his mind for the sake of heaven and for the right order of the town. And they will follow the [opinion] of the majority, to choose leaders, to establish a charitable fund, and to provide [for all the other *administrative* needs of the community].

Meir, it appears, was sustaining the relative merits of unanimity over majority decision while agreeing with Asher ben Yehiel that in practice majority rule was needed to make the community run effectively. Yet Meir had also written, "The majority or that segment of the *benei ha-'ir* who have gathered together and elected a leader not *mi-da'at kulam* ['by common consent'] . . . do not have the authority to make *new* ordinances [literally, 'things'] without *da-'at kulam*." This is Jacob Tam's version of representative theory, in Rabbenu Tam's own words—which Meir then proceeded to sharpen. Going beyond Rabbenu Tam, Meir of Rothenburg also demanded common consent in order *le-hasi'a 'al qizotam* ["to inflict punishments"], saying: "[Only] seven *tovim* who have been chosen *mi-da'at* ['by'] *all* the townsmen . . . are authorized *le-hasi'a 'al qizotam*."[145] In context, Meir was extending representative theory even to executive functions like inflicting punishments. However, Meir then pithily and abruptly qualified his statement. The seven unanimously chosen *tovim*, he said, have executive power, "except where there is a *gavra rabba* ['great man']." Whereas Jacob Tam had exploited the principle of "common consent" to subordinate councils even further to *Gedolim*, Meir—confronting the realities of Germany in the later thirteenth century—viewed councils and leading rabbis as two irreconcilably opposed camps. A blow for rabbinic authority's supremacy had to be struck. Indeed, given the unpredictability and instability of Jewish self-governmental institutions, as well as their lack of theoretical sophistication, Meir was probably correct. As events repeatedly proved, Jewish communal government worked best when a charismatic figure stood at its head—such as Meir of Rothenburg himself.

145. Breuer, 1976: nos. 78,88.

Theory to Confront the Outside World, Theory to Confront the Jews

The absence of Jewish governmental theory is not to be confused with an absence of practical political understanding, especially concerning external affairs. By probing, for example, the meanings of the dictum *Dina de-malkhuta dina,* Jews sought to make ideological peace with their political subjugation. They were well aware that no "alliance" existed between them and their secular rulers.[146] Ephraim of Bonn's blame of Louis VII for canceling Jewish loans during the Second Crusade was echoed, and amplified, in the mid-thirteenth century, by Meir ben Simeon of Narbonne, who asked why the king dealt with Jewish lenders so capriciously. The pope, by constrast, assiduously observed canonical and theological precepts, which is why Meir counseled French prelates to make the pope, rather than the king, their mentor in Jewish affairs.[147]

Meir's contemporary, the anonymous Jewish author of a fictional tale of persecution, forced conversion, and deliverance—all of which supposedly took place in the year 1007—also had grave doubts about kings. Yet he found the popes nearly as problematic. In this tale, the king Robert the Pious of France initiated a forced conversion (in real life, he did nothing of the sort), but an unnamed pope intervened to save the Jews only at the price of being allowed to supervise Jewish religious practice and to demand total Jewish acquiescence to papal sovereignty. Still, in the Jews' eyes the popes were reliable, while kings were not. Thus, in 1354, a Jewish synod at Barcelona called upon King Peter IV of Aragon to petition "the King of Nations, the Pope," to stop papal Inquisitors (not the later Spanish ones) from exceeding their mandate. Should the king fail them, the delegates warned, they would approach the pope on their own.[148]

In evaluating papal and royal policies, Jews were effectively shaping a "foreign policy." That "policy," it was hoped, would bolster their limited self-rule. Yet Jewish policies only marginally succeeded. Jews were disinterestedly supported by neither kings nor popes. Royal arbitrariness of the kind denounced by Meir ben Simeon was sometimes matched by a papal readiness to protect the "honor of the [Christian] faith" at heavy Jewish expense. Jews easily became confused. Following their expulsion

---

146. Chazan, 1973: 12; see also Baron, 1952: 4:36.
147. Meir ben Simeon, 17r–37v,60v–61r,214r–218v.
148. Finkelstein, 1972: 338; Stow, 1984: 26–48.

from Spain in 1492, there even developed the extraordinary theory of the good and gracious king.[149] This was far from realistic.

Kings in particular dealt with both the Jews and their communal organs primarily on the basis of pragmatic exigencies, whether these exigencies and the responses they evoked concerned finance, law, or the spiritual welfare of the body politic. This abandonment of any pretense to system and theory was signaled toward the end of the eleventh century, when the emperor Henry IV confirmed the Jews' right "to live by their own law" by issuing a "communalized" charter of personal privilege. Neither Henry nor the Jews could continue to rely on the status of citizenship Roman law had once conferred, as had Louis the Pious in the early ninth century. As a result, the Jews' civil status remained an ambiguous one, and that of their communal institutions even more so. After the eleventh century, Jews enjoyed firm self-rule only when that rule was congruent with royal goals, such as in 1242, when Henry III of England demanded that the Jews organize to pay an extraordinary tax. Strong Jewish self-government also depended on strong kings. When kings were weak, as the German emperors frequently were, Jewish communal powers flagged.

It would not be an exaggeration to say that Jewish self-government retained theoretical legitimacy only in the reinvigorated high medieval Italian schools of Roman law. Building on the precedents of Justinian's Code, Italian legists, as late as the sixteenth century, argued that Jews themselves were *de corpore civitatis* or *de populo romano*—that is, members of the "Roman people" and citizens in their respective towns of residence. Jews were also entitled to live by their own (Jewish) law, when *ius commune* (medieval Roman law as applied in the Italian cities) did not prohibit or contradict it. Jewish law, in other words, was judged compatible with such other medieval legal structures as the civil law, the canons, and even local statutes. Moreover, if Jewish law was legitimate, then the Jewish courts of arbitration that enforced that law must be legitimate, too.[150] Nevertheless, in the regions of northern Italy where this thinking was elaborated, there were few Jews before the mid-fourteenth century. The first northern Italian Jewish communities were also exceedingly small ones, built around a single family of bankers and its dependents, whose very presence, furthermore, was primarily regulated by a

149. See Yerushalmi, 1976.
150. De Susannis, 1558: pt. 2, chaps. 2–6; Stow, 1977: 118–123,157–161.

condotta, a commercial contract stipulating obligations and privileges, rather than by theoretical principles. Only once Jews had been admitted to a town were the rules of *ius commune* applied. In short, the theory of the schools did not describe reality—except possibly at Rome, with its normally stable ecclesiastical conditions, and where canon lawyers also studied Roman law.[151]

To be sure, Roman legal culture was likewise cultivated in southern France, whose Jewish population in the thirteenth century may have numbered in the tens of thousands. However, following the northern Capetian conquest in 1226, Jews were made to live by the rules enforced by the Capetian kings, rules that viewed Jews as wholly dependent *servi regis* ("serfs of the king"), not as *de populo romano.*[152] The Jews in Castile suffered a similar, if somewhat more ironic, legal fate. Here, the thirteenth-century Alfonso X (Alfonso the Wise) took the lead in culti- vating the study of Roman law. Every page of Alfonso's code, the *Siete partidas,* bristles with it, as well as with elements drawn from the canons. But in practice, this code as such was never applied, certainly not in Alfonso's time. When finally it was promulgated—in 1348—it was as additional (suppletory) law, never as a comprehensive legal corpus. Ref- erences to the Jews in the *Siete partidas,* moreover, invariably stress their servility.[153]

Nearly without exception, therefore, not theory but subjective factors, such as immediate circumstances, relative royal strength, and, most significantly, the royal will determined the fate of European Jewish com- munal institutions. Rather than being absorbed into the constitutional superstructures of the various kingdoms and duchies where Jews dwelled—as the Italian theorists of *ius commune* presumed they would be—these institutions were inexorably transformed into unassimilable appendices of increasingly diversified secular governmental apparatuses. This anomalous situation was emphasized by these institutions' inherent singularity: their halachic underpinnings; their fusing, wherever possible, of secular and spiritual functions; their penchant for using exegetical methods to mask borrowed elements so that they appeared to be purely Jewish; and their failure to develop an articulated representative theory that might have created at least an external resemblance to Christian urban or regional counterparts.

151. See Colorni, 1945: 66–95; and Quaglioni, 1983.
152. Jordan, 1989: 110.
153. See Carpenter, 1986: passim; Marcus, J. R., 1965: 34–40 (trans.); and Macdonald, 1985.

The fate of Jewish self-government thus promoted, as well as it concretized, the Jews' growing isolation from medieval society, an isolation
which, whether on a legal, political, or religious front, eventually played
a central role in the Jews' expulsion from nearly every medieval state.
But this isolation had social and economic aspects, too, as the following
examination of Jewish familial and economic life will make clear. Like
the behavior of Jewish communal institutions, that of the Jewish family
and economy was at once eminently medieval yet distinctively Jewish, a
combination that created no little confusion and considerable enmity.

9   Family

How distinctive was the medieval Jewish family? Medieval Jewish society itself was an essentially homogeneous one, composed of small clusters of city dwellers with shared outlooks, a common halachic status, and, with notable exceptions, a reasonably uniform economic and cultural level—if only because the majority of Jewish men, and many Jewish women, were literate and participated in various facets of trade, commerce, and finance. In addition, European Jews were urbanized throughout the Middle Ages, as, in fact, most had been before. The Jewish family was thus perforce an urban institution. And, of course, urban Jews were the ones who kept its records—including certain vital statistics—and wrote its manuals of behavior. The information these records furnish is rich. It is even possible to know much about the urban Jewish family in the earlier Middle Ages,[1] when knowledge is available for the families of Christian peasants and aristocrats alone.[2]

As early as the eleventh century the Jewish family looked—except perhaps for the status it bestowed upon women—much like that found in fourteenth-century Italian towns.[3] A most eloquent testimony to this family is provided by the late twelfth-century dirge composed by the Ashkenazic Pietist leader Eleazar ben Judah of Worms—the Rokeah—following the brutal murder, in 1197, of his wife and two daughters and the wounding of his son by Christian hooligans, perhaps self-proclaimed Crusaders. A song of praise to the "stalwart wife," replete with stereotypes, the Rokeah's dirge offers an unsurpassed description of an ideal

1. Shatzmiller, 1987; Stow, 1986; idem, 1989; see also Kanarfogel, 1984; Todeschini, 1990.
2. Duby, 1983: 20.
3. Herlihy, 1985.

Jewish family unit, as well as of an ideal wife. Dulcia, the Rokeah's wife, must have been a remarkable individual. Immediately prior to her murder she had purchased parchment to make account books, for it was Dulcia who handled the economic side of family life, freeing her husband to pursue his studies and teaching. Dulcia also took charge of such traditionally feminine pursuits as tending the house and rearing children, and her "motherly" activities extended to caring for the physical needs of the students in the yeshiva her husband headed. In addition, she taught *halachot* and ritual observances to the women of the community, and her attendance at synagogue services was constant, although this was not required of women. Beyond that, she labored at stitching parchments together in preparation for the writing of Torah scrolls, sewed dresses for brides, and provided food for guests at weddings. She even undertook the honored task of washing the dead and dressing them in shrouds prior to interment. Last but certainly not least, she evoked strong feelings and emotions from her husband.[4] The poem says less about Bellette and Hannah, the daughters. But it is clear that their education included reading and writing and was not confined to housework and sewing. They, too, were dear to the author, who lauds their accomplishments. His son Jacob probably survived the attack and was not eulogized.

The family unit of the Rokeah was thus close-knit and small, consisting of only five souls: father, mother, two daughters, and a son. It also comprised two generations; there is no indication that grandparents were part of the household. Had a member of a third generation been present, some reference to his or her fate would have been made. There is no reason to doubt that at least one grandparent was still alive; the Rokeah was probably thirty to thirty-six years old at the time of the attack, and his wife somewhat younger. As for the individual family members, each of them was skilled and educated. There also appears to have been some correspondence between the size of the family and the patent emotional links binding family members together. In short, the family of the Rokeah appears best characterized as a two-generation, affective, and self-sustaining nuclear family unit, and one in which women as well as men played economic and even intellectual roles. The Rokeah's family also seems to have represented a Jewish norm.

The structure of the Rokeah's family was especially typical. It differed little from that of families whose members perished during the First

4. Stow, 1987.

Crusade massacres in 1096. The names of these martyrs were recorded for posterity on memorial lists deliberately arranged by family units.[5] The Hebrew chronicles of the First Crusade, in particular that of Solomon ben Samson, also stress that the martyrs died as families. Indeed, hoping for safety, the Jews of Mainz entered the keep of the local bishop *en bloc*, not in panic but a full day prior to the attack. When the attack came, it is doubtful that families found themselves divided, with some members within and others outside the keep. The names on the memorial lists accordingly represent entire family units. More than 120 such families appear on the list from Mainz, a large majority of the city's Jewish inhabitants. This, of course, is insufficient information to allow what specialists call family reconstruction (over generations), but it does make possible reconstruction for one particular moment in time.

Specifically, the entries on the Mainz martyr list may be broken down into 168 distinct units, 122 of which represent families, and 46 of which represent unmarried individuals, or solitaries. The latter were probably students, domestics, or orphans not yet ready for marriage. Nearly all Jews eventually married. Unlike Christians, Jews had no way of resolving the problem of unmarriageable sons and daughters through oblation and religious vocation. Marriage was also encouraged by Jewish inheritance laws and practices, which assigned equal portions of the estate to all males, except the first son, who received a double share, and 10 percent to daughters, in the form of a marriage portion, or dowry,

The number of children in the Mainz families was small. Only 26 families, or about 20 percent of the total, had 3 or more children. Forty-one families had 2 children, 34 had 1 child, and 20 had none. All together, the Jews of Mainz had 216 children, for an average of 1.77 per family (or 2.02 children if only the families with children are counted). Considering medieval medical technology, none of these figures, including that for fertility, is unreasonable. Nearly identical figures can also be established for the Jewish families of Worms and Cologne, as well as for other German cities, where pogroms occurred and new martyr lists were compiled in the years 1241 and 1298. Tables 9.1–9.4 offer details.[6]

The conclusions drawn from the Jewish martyr lists are confirmed by the Crusade chronicle of Solomon bar Samson. Here, too, only 20 percent of the families had more than two children. This is significant.

5. Salfeld, 1898: 10–12.
6. Stow, 1987: 1090,1091,1093.

Table 9.1. Families in Mainz.

Number of children	Number of families	Percent of families	Total children	Percent of children
0	20	16.39	0	—
1	34	27.87	34	15.74
2	42	34.43	84	38.88
3	11	8.66	32	14.69
4	5	4.33	21	9.78
5	5	4.33	21	9.78
6	3	2.16	16	7.34
≥3	1	.82	≥3	1.85
≥4	1	.82	≥4	1.85
Total	122	99.81	216	99.91

Source: Stow, 1987: 1090.

Table 9.2. Comparision of families in Mainz, Worms, and Cologne.

Number of children	Mainz		Worms and Cologne	
	Observed	Expected	Observed	Expected
0	20	21.96	22	20.00
1	34	33.90	31	30.96
2	16	16.20	15	15.17
3	4	2.13	0	1.94
4	2	2.61	≥3	2.38
≥5	3	2.13	1	1.94
Total observed	79	—	72	—
Number of observations ≥2	43	—	44	—
Total	122	—	116	—

Source: Stow, 1987: 1090.

Studies of non-Jewish families in both the medieval and early modern periods have shown that the more settled, aristocratic, or monied a family, the more likely it was to have a larger number of children and a more complex family structure.[7] The martyrs in Solomon bar Samson's chronicle, many of whom had been living in the city of Mainz for as long as two hundred years, came from precisely such well-entrenched families. These families should have been the largest in the community. Their small

7. Stow, 1987: 1089, and n. 20.

Table 9.3. Combined Mainz, Worms, Cologne families.

Number of children	Number of families	Percent of families
0	42	17.7
1	65	27.3
2	92	38.8
3	12	5.0
4	15	6.3
5	12	5.0
Total	238	99.6

	Mainz	Worms	Cologne	Total
Number of families	122	96	20	238
Number of children	216	164	23	403
Number of adults	198	152	35	385
Average number of children	1.77	1.74	1.15	1.69
Median	2	2	1.5	
Average family size	3.39	3.29	2.9	3.31

Source: Stow, 1987: 1091.

size confirms the accuracy of the martyr lists. The equality of family size throughout the community, with 80 percent of all families having two or fewer children irrespective of their social standing, is also evidence that the Jewish society of the Rhineland was a homogeneous one.

Unfortunately, the absence of Christian documentation makes it impossible to compare the sizes of Jewish and Christian urban families in the eleventh century. On the other hand, the size of Jewish Rhineland families nearly matches that ascertained for Florentine families in 1427 or for the families of tradesmen in the early modern period.[8] Also noteworthy is the fact that the martyr lists for Frankfurt am Main from 1241, and for numerous other German cities from 1298, show only a slight upward moderation in Jewish family size. At the end of the thirteenth century, the overall European population had reached the bursting point. Jews, perhaps, were consciously regulating births. Contemporary discussions about the permissibility of the *mokh,* a cervical sponge or cap used to prevent pregnancies,[9] suggest this possibility.

Jews must have been conscious of their small family size. Even a casual glance at their Jewish neighbors would have revealed that well over half

8. Herlihy and Klapisch-Zuber, 1985.
9. Feldman, 1974: 161–162.

Table 9.4. German cities, 1241 and 1298.[a]

Number of children	Frankfurt am Main		Nuremberg		Würzburg		Bamberg		Neumarkt		Forchheim	
	Number of families	Percentage of families	Number of families	Percentage of families	Number of families	Percentage of families	Number of families	Percentage of families	Number of families	Percentage of families	Number of families	Percentage of families
0	8	23.5	37	21.6	26	16.4	5	16.1	2	13.3	9	37.5
1	9	26.5	50	29.2	49	31.0	12	38.7	5	33.3	5	20.8
2	5	14.7	27	38.9	35	22.2	11	35.5	3	20.0	5	20.8
3	4	11.8	22	12.8	21	13.3	2	6.5	4	26.7	5	20.8
4	4	11.8	16	9.4	17	10.8	—	—	1	6.7	—	—
5	2	5.9	16	9.4	3	1.9	—	—	—	—	—	—
6	1	2.9	2	1.2	6	3.7	—	—	—	—	—	—
7	1	2.9	1	0.6	1	0.7	—	—	—	—	—	—
Total	34		171		158		30		15		24	
Adults	57		297		281		45		24		43	
Children	60		343		321		40		27		30	
Average number of children	1.77		2.0		2.03		1.33		1.8		1.25	
Average family size	3.40		3.75		3.81		2.83		3.4		3.04	

a. Total families = 432; total adults = 802; total children = 791; average children per family = 1.83; average family size = 3.69.
Source: Stow, 1987: 1093.

of all families contained no more than four persons. Moreover, following the lead of the Crusade chroniclers, who spoke of fathers slaughtering wives and children—and of the authors of the martyr lists, who grouped victims almost exclusively according to conjugal units—Jews surely considered the standard family to be two-generational. They also must have viewed the primary family relationships as those between husband and wife and parent and child, just as did the Rokeah. Some evidence even suggests that Jews looked askance at families or households with members from a third generation. The number of these larger families, whether joint (multigenerational) or extended (many nuclear units linked by formal or institutionalized bonds), was in any case limited. Of 122 family units on the Mainz martyr list, only 15 met these criteria. So weak was the drive to create extended family structures that Rhineland Jews eschewed marriage with cousins as a normal practice—even though, unlike Christians, Jews could marry first cousins and nieces, and even though, among the Jews of the Middle East, first-cousin marriages were the norm.[10]

Jews, of course, did attach significance to units other than nuclear ones. The Rokeah himself was a descendant of one of the illustrious Kalonymides, and he made a great point of recording the names of prominent (male) ancestors who, for over four hundred years, had carried forward the chain of scholarly traditions on which his learning and piety were based. Ahimaaz ben Paltiel, too, memorialized three centuries of illustrious forebears, including significant women. Yet despite the importance of such leading families, true houses or clans did not emerge (at least not in the north, although they did in Spain). They would have been superfluous. Their traditional function of preserving property and honor had become obsolete. Jews (again with the exception of those in Spain) did not own large tracts of land, nor did they belong to nobilities of blood. As for political power, even within rabbinic families themselves, that primarily was a function of superior learning. Attempts to increase power through marital unions intentionally pairing learning with wealth were a very late development.

Family Law and Practice

Jewish family law and legal interpretation reinforced the conjugal family's standing by defending the rights of individual family members, especially

10. Goitein, 1974: 25–35.

wives. Monogamy was the strict rule from no later than the eleventh century. Divorce was permitted, which disadvantaged women, since they could not legally initiate proceedings. But women could "demand" (if not always receive) a divorce, even on the grounds that they "loathed" their husbands. No husband could divorce his wife without her consent. Nor was he permitted to beat her, a rule that surely was imperfectly observed. Husbands could not absent themselves from their wives for more than eighteen months at a time. This was significant in a community largely composed of commercial travelers. Men were also warned not to leave home for a journey immediately after a quarrel, before the "peace of the home" had been restored. Men could not easily extricate themselves from a match once they had consented to it. Numerous rules prevented breaking a betrothal. On the other hand, should it be discovered that the woman had been cajoled into giving her consent, the community was obligated to have the betrothal annulled.[11] Texts showing the application of this most unusual rule have survived from later thirteenth-century Spain and sixteenth-century Italy; it was no doubt applied earlier in the Rhineland, too.[12]

Women possessed property. In theory, married woman could not own property outright;[13] in fact, they did. Women also had a normally accepted right to a dowry amounting to 10 percent of their father's estate. Husbands could be held accountable for the ways in which they invested the dowry's principal; it was not theirs to use at will. It also had to be returned in the event of a divorce. A widow had the option of collecting the full value of the dowry, together with an additional sum promised at the time of the wedding contract, or of taking an oath of relinquishment (mohel), receiving a quittance, and gaining direct control over some share of her husband's estate before any other claims on it were made. This property became effectively the widow's own. It did not automatically revert to the husband's family at her death and might be willed to heirs of the widow's choosing. A fourteenth-century Florentine widow, by contrast, could control her dowry only if she agreed to remain in her late husband's home.[14]

Jewish women were sufficiently involved in business affairs that it was decided to circumvent the Talmud's original ruling and allow them to appear in court on their own behalf. Perhaps earlier in the Middle Ages,

11. Stow, 1987: 1098–1102.
12. Stow, 1986a: 63–65.
13. Morell, 1982: 189–210.
14. Klapisch-Zuber, 1985a.

some of these appearances would have been related to commerce. Later on, most would have been related to loans, since, like the wife of the Rokeah, many Jewish women were lenders. Numerous records of the number and size of the loans they made, as well as of the interest they collected, have survived as a result of thirteenth-century royal French *enquêtes*.[15] With few exceptions, such as in thirteenth-century southern France, these Jewish women lenders appear not to have had contemporary Christian counterparts. In northern Europe, the multitude of economic activities in which non-Jewish women engaged seems to have included finance beginning only in the later fourteenth century.[16] Whether their economic skills strengthened the hand of Jewish women both before and after marriage must remain speculative. But if so, that hand was certainly not weakened by the obvious fact that if women were lending, they were also reading, writing, and keeping books.[17]

What women saw as their due was not, however, always given, and sometimes they had to petition the courts. These petitions were often successful, as shown by the records of litigations preserved in the responsa literature of the eleventh and twelfth centuries. One lady, who had been married as an eleven-and-a-half-year-old minor (which seems to have been a rare occurrence) and whose husband had compromised in accepting less than the standard 10-percent dowry, upon reaching maturity went to court to claim the difference—and apparently got it. In another case, a man tried to disinherit the children of his second wife in favor of those of a deceased first wife, claiming that the business activities of the second made her financially independent, with means sufficient to provide for her offspring. The second wife rejected this claim, and the court agreed. In a third instance, a thrice-divorced woman initiated a suit to collect more of her dowry than her husband felt she was legally entitled to, given her presumed infertility.[18]

Jewish women frequently headed families. Women comprised 22.6 percent of all family heads on the martyr list from Mainz, a percentage nearly identical to the 21.4 percent of female heads of families in Pistoia in 1428.[19] This headship was permanent. Jewish women family heads normally were not replaced by their sons, even after the latter reached maturity and married.

15. Jordan, 1978: 39–56.
16. Nicholas, 1985: 84–87; see also Reyerson, 1985: 67,73–74.
17. See Marcus, I., 1986: 36.
18. Stow, 1987: 1100–1102.
19. Herlihy, 1967: 249.

The relatively strong position of Jewish women—it goes without saying that comparisons with today's expectations are futile—indirectly enhanced the centrality, as well as the self-sufficiency, of the conjugal family unit. This centrality was enhanced even further by the enunciated ideal that husbands, wives, and children should cultivate strong emotional bonds. Emotional well-being was to begin in infancy. The fourteenth-century Spanish guide to religious practice, the *Zedah la-derekh,* building on Rhenish precedents, advises mothers to sing to their babies in order to promote their children's happiness and contentment. Older children, too, merited affection. In the chronicle of Ahimaaz, Shefatiah "greatly cherished" his marriageable daughter. And certain texts in *Sefer Hasidim* suggest that the tender feelings of the Rokeah for his children were not unusual. A sense of tenderness is portrayed in the Crusade chronicles, which were composed in no small part to reenact for succeeding generations the severe emotional trauma suffered by Jews sacrificing their spouses and other relatives, but especially their children. There are also passages in the writings of Rashi and other commentators reflecting on the expectations sons had of motherly love and their eventual transference to a wife. To wit: "So long as a man's mother is alive, he is attached to her [literally, 'bound up with her']; when she dies, he takes [physical and emotional] solace from his wife."[20]

Nowhere is the desirability of emotional bonds uniting Jewish spouses more visible than in discussions of sexuality. These define not only the limits of acceptable sexual behavior but also the role of sexuality in generating proper affective relationships. Jewish writers—the same scholars and rabbis who set other communal standards—viewed sexuality in a very positive light. When appropriately expressed within the framework of marriage, sexual activity required no apologies, transferences of meanings, or obligatory links with procreation. This view recurs in texts from talmudic times, through the sixteenth-century manual of halachic behavior the *Shulhan 'Arukh,* and beyond. Decisions by Italian Jewish arbiters in 1540, for example, instruct feuding spouses, especially husbands, to love their wives as befits a husband and to unite with them in sexual union. Accordingly, stress was placed on the achievement of sexual balance and mutuality, not the prevention of sin and the avoidance of the promptings of the Devil. As summed up pointedly by Maimonides in the twelfth century and repeated by others: "A man should not be like a cock with his wife, . . . but should make his cohabitation into an act of

20. Rashi, Genesis, 24:67.

mutual joy." Building on concepts like this, the thirteenth-century Italian Isaiah of Trani—and, apparently, the twelfth-century Isaac of Dampierre—cleverly permitted the use of the *mokh* to prevent pregnancy, if the intent of the partners was not to prevent conception but to enjoy sexual activity or preserve a wife's beauty.[21]

The need on the part of both men and women for sexual release was unconditionally accepted. Husbands were obligated to fulfill the *mizvah* ("religious obligation") of *'onah,* the timely—normally, weekly— gratification of their wives' sexual needs. Sexual indulgence was also considered necessary to keep men's minds from wandering during study. Jewish views on sexuality contrasted with the negativity, or at best the ambivalence, expressed by Christian clerics. Egbert of Shonau, for example, cautioned that "sexual activity for purposes expressly not related to procreation is a major sin, which may be nullified only by the salutary effects of marriage."[22] Jewish attitudes stand out even more sharply against Gratian's urgings of a "minimal frequency" in marital intercourse, or his argument that nothing is filthier than the "excessive love of one's wife." Admittedly, Christian pastoral ideals often differed sharply from the opinions and practices of the laity. This did not stop Jews from being perplexed. Reacting to clerical celibacy, one Jewish polemicist derisively said that priests and nuns must burn up in their unconsummated desires.[23]

With such attitudes toward sexuality, it is doubtful that Christian pastors, no matter how positively they spoke of conjugal understanding,[24] would have viewed sexual intimacy as an act of care and respect. The late twelfth-century Abraham ben David of Posquieres in southern France did just that, declaring that the test for deciding on the propriety of specific forms of coital embrace was mutual consent: if a husband forces himself upon his wife, it is sinful. Rather, "he must act with her knowledge, endearing himself to her until she is willing." Abraham ben David's attitude was typical. What concerned him was uncontrolled sexuality. A properly channeled sexual drive received every encouragement—to the point, in fact, of prescribing a proper diet to stimulate virility or the avoidance of vegetables that create bad breath and interfere with sexual pleasure. What mattered were the intentions and attitudes expressed by spouses to each other *during* the act of intercourse. As put by the mystical

21. Stow, 1987: 1102–1107.
22. Leclerq, 1980: 21.
23. Berger, 1969: 69.
24. Herlihy, 1983: 127.

Zohar—whose authors argued that human actions should emulate those of the divine, heavenly realms—a man must "speak sweetly to his wife, after he has received her consent, . . . so that their will shall be one, with no force involved." He must "attract her through love and unite [physically] with her," as it is written (in Genesis 2:24) that "man must leave his father and mother and cling to his wife." "With his kisses there will be a union of his soul with hers." On the other hand, physical union in the absence of appropriate feelings produced anxiety. To cite Abraham ben David: "Sexuality unaccompanied by the proper intentions becomes an evil rather than a good and a blessing, a sin rather than a source of reward." Similarly, Rashi warns against having sexual relations with a wife who has become hateful; for if a man hates his wife and thinks of another, the coitus is not fulfilled, and it is no better than fornication and prostitution.[25]

Jewish views on sexuality thus encouraged individuals to enter into a partnership based on intense emotional transactions within the framework of marriage. Carried on in this way, sexual activity promoted what Jacob ben Asher in the *Tur,* his great summarizing code of the fourteenth century, described as the central purpose of marriage, saying: "Whoever lives without a wife lives without well-being, blessing, home, Torah, a protective wall, and indeed without peace."

This marital ideal, within the context of an affectively and economically self-sufficient conjugal family unit, was one that Christian society could not easily adopt. Christian society contained nobles and peasants, whose marital practices were designed to meet needs that Jews did not have, such as those associated with the ownership of land or group-intensive labor. There were also differences of structure, law, and behavioral expectations. Nearly all Jews eventually married; many Christians took clerical vows. Jews were free to divorce; Christians were not. Furthermore, Jews married within the limits of consanguinity forbidden by the Christian Church. The majority of Jewish marriages were, by Catholic standards, incestuous. Beginning in the eleventh century, the clergy had sought to halt such unions among Christians by insisting that marriage be sacralized and controlled by the Church.[26] In this context, the "incestuous" Jewish unions, against which clerics were powerless to act,

25. Abraham ben David, 1964: 122–123; Tishby, 1961: 2:635; Cohen, J., 1992: passim; idem, 1989a: 203,218.
26. Duby, 1978.

must have bred dissatisfaction. Worse, clerics observed rabbis encouraging behavior which they considered wholly repugnant—for example, second and sometimes third marriages for both widows and widowers.[27]

Perhaps not unexpectedly, therefore, Christian preachers criticized Jewish sexual behavior, real and imagined. William of Tournai said that Jews took second wives while their first ones were pregnant, in order to provide for sexual release.[28] Guibert de Nogent associated Jews with lewd sexual perversity. More fundamentally, Jewish thinkers linked sexuality with holiness; the Franciscan Bernardino da Siena, in the fifteenth century, viewed sexuality as defilement, condemning couples who sought comfort in sexual embrace and warning that it distanced them from God and religious devotion. Before copulation, husband and wife should pray and take communion, to avoid "disorder" and to save their marriage from falling into the Devil's hands.[29] Bernardino also accused the overwhelming number of Christian marriages of being of the Devil, because, he said, couples were experimenting with methods of controlling fertility and hence limiting the number of souls that would be born and baptismally saved. Numerous rabbis, in contrast to Bernardino, condoned the contraceptive *mokh*.

What remained was for preachers like Bernardino to attack the Jewish ideal of the self-sufficient and effectively self-contained conjugal family unit. Bernardino surely appreciated the constant potential for a rupture between such a family and the one he advocated, wholly submissive to pastoral guidance.[30] Such a family was also at permanent odds with that other clerical ideal, a "spiritual family" consisting of the Church and its body of faithful.[31] Did not Pope Urban II tell the assembled nobles at Clermont in 1095 to put aside their concerns for "children, parents, and wives" and to enroll in the crusading army, for only there would they gain the eternal life? The rupture that Bernardino feared may, moreover, have actually occurred. In terms of its behavior as a self-contained and increasingly autonomous unit, the Christian conjugal family (especially as it existed in fourteenth- and fifteenth-century Italy) seemed more and more to be like that of the Jews. Nevertheless, this growing similarity was something about which Bernardino chose not to comment. To impugn

27. Stampfer, 1988: 85–114; Chavarria, 1988: 679–723.
28. D'Alvray, 1980: 100.
29. Bernardino da Siena, 1958: sermons 19,20,21.
30. Herlihy, 1970: 88–101.
31. Brentano, 1974: 171–210; Herlihy, 1985: 122–123; cf. Goody, 1983.

the very family ideals that leading Italian merchant families held so dear[32] would perhaps have driven away his most needed allies. It was more productive to attack, as he in fact did, the Jews' obvious "crimes": their lending practices and the Talmud's supposed blasphemies. Such attacks bore heavy fruit.

Preachers like Bernardino may not have been the only Christians for whom the Jewish family was problematic. Considering the volatility of the life-style and the behavior of the marginals and pilgrims who attacked the Jews of the Rhineland in 1096, there is every reason to believe that they, too, may have been threatened by the Jews' social stability, at whose core the Jewish family stood. In which case, the distinctive Jewish family, especially in terms of its relationship to the other institutions of Jewish society, had become a source of enormous friction. Its very existence added a social dimension to the Jewish image that was as dangerous as the religious one embodied in the charge of deicide.

32. See Klapisch-Zuber, 1985: 68–93; Becker, 1968: 1:40–41,192,226–227.

10 Economics

Nothing medieval Jews did created more friction than their economic activities. Fifteenth-century Franciscans even believed that these activities—especially the lending of money at interest—mortally threatened society. In maintaining this belief, they were joined throughout the Middle Ages by various Christian moralists. But no one was more convinced of lending's supposed dangers or spoke out more vociferously than the Franciscans. In particular, Bernardino da Siena, Bernardino da Busti, and Bernardino da Feltre launched a virulent campaign against "the raging abyss of usury and the raging perfidy and stiff-necked implacability of the Jews, the usurpers of Christian substance and the suckers of Christian blood."[1]

This campaign lasted the duration of the fifteenth century, with preaching so incendiary that the pope intervened to prevent violence from erupting. Nevertheless, the immediate effects were mixed. Lending might be summarily halted, to be just as quickly resumed when passions ebbed, or it might be partially or wholly replaced by publicly funded associations called the *Monti di Pietà,* organized to grant interest-free loans.[2] But expulsions of Jewish lenders, which the Franciscans called for, were rare. And the *Monti* themselves often became profit-making, interest-collecting institutions. More than one of them survives today as a respectable Italian banking house (or, as is the case at Rome, as a summer cold-storage vault for winter furs). The real success of the Franciscans—and of others of their ilk throughout Latin Europe—was a long-range ideological one. The specter of the Jewish moneylender has haunted generations of non-Jews.

1. Esposito, 1988: 103.
2. Poliakov, 1977: 146–159.

Karl Marx wrote that Jewish "finance capital" was at the root of all social disequilibria.[3]

Even recently, it has been maintained[4] that the Franciscans, as skilled economists,[5] were combating the further impoverishment of the already marginally poor; they were not persecuting the Jews. What perturbed the Franciscans was a crux that has aroused indignation since the time of Aristotle: money—a seemingly passive object in contrast to, say, cloth, which may actively be transformed into a rich tapestry—almost mysteriously increases in value by virtue of one party's letting a second party enjoy its use for a prescribed period of time. It was, some medieval Christians said, as if lenders were selling time itself, a commodity (if it may be called that) which was assumed to belong to God alone.[6] Indeed, everybody acknowledged that in principle to take interest was wrong. And every Western religious tradition forbade—and technically still forbids—its members to take interest on loans made to a member of the same faith. In the Christian tradition an interest-bearing loan to even a foreigner may be justified canonically only as an act of war.[7] Christian moralists lambasted all who lent money at interest, whom they labeled usurers. For these moralists, "usury"—a term that today means lending at exorbitant interest—meant any openly charged interest whatsoever.

Yet no lending was considered more disturbing than that carried on by Jews. Lending was perceived as a Jewish act; lenders themselves were considered (even legally) to be Jews. Edward I scornfully labeled English lenders "Judaizers" (although this did not prevent him, and other rulers as well, from tolerating and financially benefiting from their activities), and in Bruges (Flanders), Italian lenders were as socially segregated as were Jews.[8] The tone was set by Bernard of Clairvaux, who in the twelfth century called Christian lenders "wretched Judaizers" and "baptized Jews." In the early thirteenth century, the leading Parisian theologian Peter the Chanter testily stigmatized Christians who lent by saying, "These are *our* Jews." He may as well have called them "renegades."[9]

3. Marx, 1959: 37–38.

4. Meneghin, 1974; Muzzarelli, 1983; cf. Segre, 1978; Toaff, 1989: 238; Boesch, 1983.

5. Gilchrist, 1969: 66.

6. Nelson, 1969: 3–28; Noonan, 1957: 11–20,21–37; Baldwin, 1958; idem, 1970: 270–273; Le Goff, 1980: 29.

7. Nelson, 1969: 46.

8. De Roover, 1948: 152; Prestwich, 1972: 178–180,204–210.

9. Migne, 1844: 182:567; Baldwin, 1970: 298–300.

This hostility and the identity of lending, Jews, and Judaism is no mystery. Lending at interest was by definition an act of war; insolvent debtors who forfeited their property were victims; and the supposed Jewish victimization of credulous Christian borrowers rang of that purported Jewish seductiveness against which preachers like John Chrysostom, Agobard of Lyons, and Ratherius of Verona had protested since the very early Middle Ages. Thus, Peter the Venerable of Cluny, at the time of the First Crusade, called the profits of lending outright theft, and he was especially incensed when the "thieves" were Jews. Jewish lending, Peter believed, did more than allegedly victimize Christians; it also unjustly inverted what he saw as society's proper order. It made Christians look like inferiors, or, to paraphrase Pope Gregory the Great, it allowed Jews seemingly to trample on the body of Christ by trampling on its (individual Christian) members; its pursuit appeared to violate the conditions set by the canons and laws guaranteeing the security of only law-abiding Jews.

These arguments were repeated by fifteenth-century Franciscans.[10] They were also amplified. "Money," said Bernardino da Siena, "is the vital warmth of a town . . . When blood and warmth leave . . . it is a sign of death. The danger is incomparably more imminent when wealth . . . accumulates in the hands of the Jews . . . for every Jew is the deadly enemy of the Christians."[11] Christian society, accordingly, had to save itself from a wretched death; it had to expel the Jews. Using similar metaphors, Bernardino da Busti took up this idea again in 1496, this time in reaction to what da Busti called the Talmud's poisonous doctrines.[12] The matter of Jewish lending had ominously been integrated into a broader Jewish iconography; the issue, for the Franciscans, was not an economic one alone. The charge that the Jews had life-draining capacities in fact echoes Bishop Ildefonse of Toledo, who, in the seventh century, called Jews rebels and criminals, a gangrenous limb that ought to be lopped off.[13] In turn, this Franciscan iconography was graphically portrayed by the fifteenth-century painter Paolo Uccello.

Uccello's six-part painting "The Profanation of the Host," which now graces the ducal palace at Urbino, depicts a host-desecration libel and the death at the stake of its alleged perpetrators, including a young Jewish

10. Segre, 1978.
11. Poliakov, 1977: 142.
12. See Merchavia, 1972.
13. Blumenkranz, 1963: 120.

girl and boy. The story, of French origin, opens in a Jewish pawnshop: a penniless Christian woman client is offered her pledge in return for securing a host, Christ transubstantiated. This host the Jewish pawnbroker then fries in a pan, a torture of Christ that makes a thinly veiled analogy to the draining of Christian blood worked daily through the evils of lending. The punishment of the pawnbroker's wife and children alongside him reveals that the villain is, by extension, any Jew, old, young, man, woman, or child. The traditional Jewish religious enemy had become synonymous, interchangeable, with the new economic one, both of whom equally threatened Christian salvation.

But this was Paolo Uccello's perception,[14] not the historical fact, which must now be sought out. What were the real terms of Jewish medieval economic behavior, and what has made these terms prone to being mythically transformed into both secular and religious iconographies since the time of Paolo Uccello (and even previously), down to that of Marlowe's base Jew of Malta, Shakespeare's more human Shylock, and, for that matter, modern Nazi caricatures? And why as late as the 1980s was it said that medieval Jewish family life revolved primarily around the issues of loans and banking?[15] On the other hand, it must not be said that medievals always viewed Jewish economic activities hostilely or considered them acts of war.[16] Just as the Duke of Milan ignored Bernardino da Busti's call to expel the Jews, so—along with many other Italian rulers—did he also choose to ignore the Franciscan arguments about lending, preferring instead to follow the example of the pope himself, for whom Jewish lending, despite its "sinfulness," was considered necessary enough to be sustained in the papal domains for hundreds of years.[17]

The Origins and Practice of Jewish Lending

It is frequently assumed that Jews began lending at interest because legislation against their owning land drove them away from that primary medieval occupation, farming. This is not true: ownership was usually legal, and up until the end of the Middle Ages, Jews throughout Europe owned land,[18] as is confirmed by charters, cases in court, laws, and,

14. Francastel, 1952; Grayzel, 1989: 196–199.
15. Muzzarelli, 1983: 71; Toaff, 1989: 290,295–299.
16. Shatzmiller, 1990: 104–122 and 43–70; cf. Stow, 1981.
17. Poliakov, 1977: 71–82,211–218; Toaff, 1988: 118.
18. Kisch, 1949: 116,209–210.

somewhat ironically, by the insistence of Church officials that Jews pay tithes on lands acquired from Christians. On the other hand, except in Spain and Sicily, where a landed Jewish nobility and possibly common Jewish farming persisted through the fifteenth century, the parcels Jews owned were usually small ones, suitable for houses in cities and for vineyards outside city walls. Larger holdings, acquired through the default of lenders, were normally sold. The last certain knowledge of Jews owning estates comes from the letters of Pope Stephen IV in the late eighth century. There was no realistic basis for the claim made by such later medieval worthies as Louis IX, Edward I, Thomas Aquinas, and John Pecham that Jews could easily desist from lending and seek their livelihood through labor—including, presumably, agricultural labor.[19] At the most, theirs was a delusion, akin to that so vividly entertained in the fifteenth century by the Alsatian abbot Geiler of Kaiserberg: "Are the Jews, then, better than Christians, that they will not work with their hands? Are they not subject to the decree of God—in the sweat of thy brow shalt thou earn thy bread? Making money by usury is not working; it is flaying others while themselves remaining idle."[20]

Apart from their obvious inability to acquire and retain land by engaging in feudal warfare, or to defend the land which they already possessed against "overt and covert assault" (as the twelfth-century philosopher Peter Abelard[21] phrased it), what most directly prevented Jewish landowners from working the soil was competition for cheap labor. Here Christians were clearly advantaged. For nothing stood in the way of their dominating peasant workers; even Roman law tied peasants (colonii) to the soil. But the canons—reinforced by ecclesiastics' urgings to lay rulers over the course of four centuries—prohibited Jews from lawfully retaining in their employ, or under their roofs, Christian domestics, serfs, and slaves.[22] Pope Gregory IX in the thirteenth century may have still objected to Jewish ownership of Christian slaves, but by then their numbers had been enormously reduced. Constant pressure had persuaded Jews to keep Christians in their close employ only when doing so was unavoidable. Retaining a sufficient number of servants and serfs to manage land, especially an estate, had become impossible. The prohibition against Jews' owning Christian slaves also created obstacles to Jews acquiring

19. Baron, 1952: 11:29–31.
20. Janssen, 1881: 2:77.
21. Boureau, 1986: 31.
22. Lotter, 1989: 35–36,48–49.

abandoned children and exploiting their labor, a common practice among early medieval Italian farmers.[23] Other restrictive measures, once again thwarting competition, lessened the Jewish role in crafts, especially in southern Europe, where artisanry had once been almost a Jewish monopoly. The closed guilds which dominated the crafts in the later Middle Ages never dreamed of admitting Jews. Christian suggestions, including that of Louis IX, that artisanry replace Jewish lending were no more realistic than were those promoting Jewish farming.

The Jews might have prospered in labor-unintensive viticulture, as in fact some did, including Rashi and Rabbenu Tam. Indeed, campaigns spearheaded once again by the Franciscans to stop the sale of Jewish wine to Christians were mostly ineffective. The argument that one should not reward the Jews by buying their wine, since, for religious reasons, Jews refrained from consuming wine produced by gentiles, fell mostly on deaf ears.[24] Opposition did not completely exclude Jews from artisanry either, especially dyeing and goldsmithing. Jewish artisans in these and in other crafts, as well as Jewish vintners, were to be found in the south of France and were still flourishing in Palermo, Sicily, and parts of Spain in the late fifteenth century. Roman Jews were often tailors and wholesale purveyors of foodstuffs; Jewish armorers were known in Prague.[25] Yet most Jews turned their backs on these occupations. Large numbers of Jews had never engaged in them, much less in farming. They had preferred first commerce and, afterward, lending; so many Jews began their medieval sojourn as urban or traveling merchants. In this profession, the profits were potentially great—despite the risks—and the competition was often minimal. Competition was particularly slight in the early Middle Ages, when Christians were still deterred from commercial endeavor by the lingering stigma that ancient Roman society had attached to it.[26]

But the Jews lost their competitive advantage in the European commercial and monetary reawakening of the tenth and eleventh centuries, which was fueled by the revival of urban centers. In these centers, noble disdain of commerce was irrelevant. The activities of indigenous Christian merchants soon pushed Jews to the sidelines. Jewish trade did not completely cease. As late as the thirteenth century, *taqqanot* ("ordinances") warned husbands against effectively deserting their wives by

23. Boswell, 1988: 201–222.
24. Toaff, 1989: 95.
25. Baron, 1952: 11:58; Ashtor, 1979: 233–236.
26. Lopez, 1971: 8.

embarking on overly long commercial voyages. In the following two centuries, many German Jews migrated to Italy expressly to engage in trade. Jewish international traders, and adventurers, were likewise active in southern Europe until the end of the Middle Ages. Indeed, the early modern period saw a recrudescence of Jewish trade on a significant scale, first in Turkey, then in Italy, and finally in northern Europe.[27] Yet by the High Middle Ages, most Jews seem to have abandoned commerce in favor of exploiting the capital acquired through their previously successful trading. The European commercial resurgence required funding, and Jews were among those who could provide it, which they did through lending, especially to individuals of the lower and middle social ranks. Crusaders, too, however paradoxically, were constantly in need of borrowed funds. When Jews settled for the first time in England, in the wake of the Norman Conquest of 1066, they did so expressly to lend. The remarks by Ephraim of Bonn about the Second Crusade indicate that Jewish lending was already well established. Its expansion was not the fruit of a mere half-century's duration.

The Jews' incentives to lend were more than commercial ones. Lending as an occupation perfectly suited the Jewish ideal. To lend was profitable, but not time consuming. Jewish lenders had the repose for scholarship and communal leadership. Jewish lenders also included women, whose loans were normally small. And this points to another advantage of lending. It could be practiced by anyone with a modicum of free funds. Royal inquiries in mid-thirteenth-century France reveal large numbers of very small loans made by women to other women, presumably to be used in purchasing staples, and perhaps for modest luxuries. At the other extreme, a few Jewish lenders were great magnates.[28] Late medieval Spanish grandees were the financiers of the Castilian and Aragonese crowns. Aaron of Lincoln was among the wealthiest men in England at the close of the twelfth century, and the da Pisa family of Tuscany in the fifteenth and sixteenth centuries developed a far-flung banking network with many employees and elaborate family connections to ensure the family's survival in the event one banking branch should fail. Toward the end of the Middle Ages, the single rich banker, or group of rich bankers, with numerous employees—often housed together with the banker under one roof—was typical of Jewish lending in both German and Italian

27. Israel, 1985: 35–70; Schwarzfuchs, 1989a: passim.
28. Jordan, 1978; Stacey, 1987: 201–204.

cities.[29] In Italy, the banker or bankers had a contract *(condotta)* stipulating the length of time they were *required* to spend in the city, the amount of capital they would bring to start up a bank, and the rates of interest they would charge on private loans to individuals and on public ones to the communal government. Jewish bankers had the satisfaction of knowing that the city needed them as much as they needed it. This mutual need did much to weaken the force of the fifteenth-century Franciscan arguments.[30]

Most loans made by these bankers were against pledges. Pledges ranged from small household items to large estates, and often they were the source of problems. Stolen pledges were hard to identify. How were unsuspecting Jewish lenders who accepted such pledges to be indemnified, or were they to be indemnified at all? The law in almost all countries, including the *ius commune*, said that they were to receive compensation. Christian lenders did not receive compensation, even when their loans were legal ones that bore no openly charged interest. This arbitrarily preferential treatment for Jews aroused much ire. No less problematic were pledges in the form of grain, cattle, and other comestibles. How were the complexities of pasturage, storage, and eventual transportation to be resolved? And was it desirable for Jews to be the purveyors of food to Christians, especially since Jews with their exacting dietary laws would never accept the reverse? But the most difficult pledges were landed ones. How was the Jew to dispose of them and, more ticklishly, to whom? No less entangling were items given in pledge that had been taken from a church or those stained with blood.[31] The canon law forbade Jews to accept the former for obvious reasons of ecclesiastical honor; common sense warned against the latter. Jewish lenders, however, sometimes lacked that desirable quality.

Yet for all these potential snares, pledges were preferable to contractual loans. Pledges were value in the lender's hands. Contracts might be arbitrarily and summarily canceled, as happened in 1146 at the order of Louis VII. Contracts could also be registered by royal officials. In England, an entire Exchequer of the Jews was established to perform this task and to oversee all matters related to Jewish lending; the starrs (a term deriving from the Hebrew word *shtar,* meaning "contract") them-

29. Toch, 1980; Luzzati, 1985: 218–219.
30. See Boesch, 1983.
31. Poliakov, 1977: 87–92; Baron, 1952: 10:181–191.

selves were stored in local and regional royally supervised *archae* ("chests"). The French kings, too, required that Jewish loans be written down. Such registration gave the king leverage over individual lenders and over the Jews as a whole. It also made taxing Jews dreadfully simple. Alternatively, kings inventoried Jewish wealth, contracts, and pledges by means of inquests that were invariably terrifying ordeals.[32] No less daunting was the fact that since 1223 the French king had made treaties with his principal counts restraining both lending and the Jews' personal freedom of movement: the Jews of one count who fled to the county of another were to be seized and extradited "like [fugitive] slaves" *(tanquam servi)*.[33]

Friction

The Jews thus had reason to be wary of lending, no matter how readily they engaged in it, and no matter how advantageous or profitable they considered it to be. They also had halachic reservations. In the eleventh century, Joseph Tov Elem spoke sharply against those who mocked the Torah, saying: "If Moses had known that [lending] was profitable, his Torah would *not* have prohibited it."[34] In fact, the halachah forbade Jews to lend money at interest even to gentiles. Jewish scholars were thus left in a quandary. Lending to Christians was an economic necessity. If Jews take interest from Christians, explained Rabbi Isaac of Dampierre in the twelfth century, they do so from fear of going hungry, not by right.[35]

Such pragmatic justifications did not allow Jews so readily to ignore the halachah prohibiting them from charging interest to one another. Lending between Jews at interest still unleashed torrents of censure in the early sixteenth century—for example, from the Italian Yehiel Nissim da Pisa, himself a member of a distinguished banking clan.[36] Yet if Jews had not had access to Jewish loans, as would have resulted from observing the prohibition against mutual borrowing, they presumably would have lost innumerable opportunities to supply desirous Christians with capital. For loans between two Jews must commonly have occurred during the everyday practice of one bank's borrowing from another in order to

32. Nahon, 1969.
33. Langmuir, 1960.
34. Soloveitchik, 1972: 228.
35. Katz, 1961: 30, citing *tosafot* on Babylonian Talmud, Baba Mezia 70b, Avoda Zara, 15a.
36. Rosenthal, 1962: passim.

maintain liquidity and meet clients' demands. The ingenious solution to this crux—perhaps first proposed, if cautiously, by Rashi himself—was to mediate between Jewish lenders and borrowers by employing a gentile straw man. For some, however, this solution was too clever; rabbinic authorities, particularly in thirteenth- and fourteenth-century Germany, protested resorting to such a transparent halachic evasion.[37] A similar problem, that of Jews' creating business partnerships with gentiles, exercised rabbinic scholars in the eastern Geonic world. The methods subtly devised for making possible such partnerships contributed to the development of commercial documentary forms that eventually entered European practice.[38]

Negative attitudes toward lending and the fear that it might lead to exploitation were thus not a Christian monopoly. Nor were these attitudes and fears the product of economic ignorance. Medievals well understood such subjects as liquidity, balance of trade, the comparative value of currencies, and the intricacies of devaluation. They also possessed some knowledge of funding debts by borrowing.[39] Yet the subject of interest—or usury, as it was always called—was governed by unique rules. For medievals, interest by its nature was repugnant, especially when it was contractually undisguised, openly charged, and could not be described as legitimate profit or as the just fruits of real added value. The problem of the Jews in this scheme was that all the interest they took was openly charged. Moreover, often it was possible to draw a direct connection between loans, Jewish interest, and the misfortunes of Christian borrowers—in particular, those resulting from the forfeiture of land.

Forfeitures caused by default to Jews occurred everywhere, as detailed lists, particularly for England and for Perpignan in the Pyrenees, attest.[40] In England, the problem was so acute that it figured in the Magna Carta, the Great Charter of liberties King John granted to his barons in 1215. The barons insisted that minors, before reaching maturity, should not have to repay the debts contracted by their late fathers, since such massive obligations, together with payments on the large death duties they owed the king, would quickly bankrupt them and cause them to forfeit their lands.[41] The barons were no doubt equally disturbed about what followed forfeitures, since Jews did not retain the lands they acquired.

37. Soloveitchik, 1972: 229–231.
38. Udovitch, 1970.
39. Miskimin, 1963: 12–14.
40. Richardson, 1960: 76,229–231; Emery, 1977: 76,84–93.
41. See Holt, 1965.

Unable, among other things, to take the confessional oaths of fealty or homage that bound together feudal lords and vassals, Jews sold forfeited lands, often to royal favorites, but also to greater and wealthier lords. In the later thirteenth century, the queen mother especially profited from these transfers. In a variation on this theme, royal favorites acquired lands by buying risky loans from the Jews at a discount before the borrower defaulted. The Jews thus became an instrument of royal and baronial manipulation.[42] Nevertheless, bankrupt barons considered the Jews themselves to be as responsible as the king for their misfortunes. At York in 1190, violence against Jewish lenders was tempered neither by declarations that the Jews' property belonged to the king, "as though [the Jews] were royal chattels," nor by the obvious conclusion that the king, rather than the Jews, was their ultimate creditor.

Other Christians, too, were perturbed by Jewish lending. The indigent mother who had to borrow small sums from Jewish women in order to make ends meet exposed her want not only before the Jew, but also before her young children, who often accompanied her to the Jewish lender's home. The result was impotent rage on both her part and that of her children, for whom the Jew appeared to be the initiator of their mother's shame.[43] Large numbers of farmers must have felt similarly exposed and defenseless. Without Jewish loans, they could neither buy seed for planting in the spring nor "tide themselves over" until the unpredictable harvest came in. The blame, of course, lay with the predicament itself, which grew more severe as money (after the eleventh century) again came into common circulation and became the principal means of European commercial exchange. The fact that Jewish merchants had the money which farmers, and others, needed to cope with the new economic conditions could only arouse envy—and provoke demands for some miraculous relief—as farmers hoped somehow to escape the borrower's "money-cycle,"[44] their dependence on the seasons, or the misfortunes caused by an untimely death.

Yet numerous Frenchmen, who in the thirteenth century had clamored for such relief through the ouster of Jewish lenders, found themselves wishing, in the fourteenth century, that these same Jews, now expelled, might be allowed to return. The clandestine Christian lenders who had all too readily replaced the ousted Jews were charging interest at higher

42. See Wood, 1989: 401.
43. Jordan, 1978: 52.
44. Murray, 1987: 67–71; Ginzburg, 1989: 25.

rates.[45] One wonders if, like these fourteenth-century Frenchmen, others, especially kings and rulers, ever appreciated the virtues of the readily available and reasonably priced Jewish loan. For although the authorities benefited from lending, they were at best highly ambivalent about it. The toleration of lending was the toleration of sin. More than one ruler, attentive to ecclesiastical denunciations, queried Church officials as to whether he or she should halt Jewish lending and forgo the benefits of Jewish taxes, since the monies that the Jews paid were the profits of "usury." Yet even had the most famous of these questioners, the Duchess of Brabant, *not* been consoled by Saint Thomas Aquinas himself—who told her she could accept these taxes—she, like so many other rulers, would probably have continued to support Jewish financial activity.[46] For beyond the profits they made through Jewish taxes, rulers used Jewish money to ensure short-term financial liquidity. The large sums needed to finance long-term expenses, which took considerable time to raise, kings negotiated with Italian Christian bankers. Jews, who with rare exceptions did not control such huge capital sums, could be relied upon for the immediate cash needed to pay and feed armies until taxes were collected. In the short run, therefore, Jews and Jewish lending were a powerful asset. In the long run, the value of this asset was doubtful. Rulers must have seen dependence on Jews for cash flow and liquidity as a blot on their public honor. It exposed their fiscal weakness, much as it embarrassed the borrowing housewife and the farmer. This was a situation that could not be allowed to continue indefinitely.

The Role of the Church

Similar attitudes should have prevailed in Italy, especially in the small and medium-sized centers such as Cesena and Siena, where Jews (whose settlement in very restricted numbers dates only from the later thirteenth century) provided not only liquidity but also loans for longer-range needs. In 1456, the Sienese told the pope that "the city of Siena could ill govern itself without [Jewish] loans, because of the wars it has had to wage for many years. [Hence, the city or] its authorized citizens should be able to contract loans without prejudice to their souls."[47] Some Italian Jews appear to have become large-scale financiers, replacing the Lombard and

45. Baron, 1952: 9:44; Schwarzfuchs, 1967; and see Spufford, 1988: 344–348.
46. D'Entreves, 1959: 84–95.
47. Boesch, 1983: 207; Bonazzoli, 1990: 59–67, esp. 62.

Tuscan Christian bankers who had recently transferred their lucrative enterprises to large Italian cities and to the north. Regrettably, a systematic study confirming this possibility by quantifying the number and size of Jewish loans to the communes has yet to be made.[48] Yet regardless of the size of Jewish loans, one is struck by the openness with which the communes requested the pope to license Jewish lending. Italian communal authorities appear to have been much less concerned about the moral and psychological implications of lending than were their northern counterparts. Substantive public efforts in Italy to contain Jewish lending did not in fact begin until the later fifteenth century.[49]

The temptation is great to ascribe this acceptance of lending to an Italian conviviality[50] that was expressed in business, daily life, and even intimate relations. Nevertheless, Italians also erupted into violence—for example, during the Trent blood libel, in 1475, and during the sack, in 1471, of the house of the banker Yehiel of Pisa. In 1556, the Udinese town council exultantly exploited potential anti-Jewish violence and petitioned the town's Venetian overlords to send the Jews packing.[51] The initial openness of the communes to Jewish lending was not, then, a result of positive feelings about the Jews themselves. Instead, it hinged on the unlikely combination of need and the ecclesiastical establishment's discerning support. There was also the matter of self-interest. More than one Christian invested goodly sums with Jews, thereby financing—for a healthy return—Jewish lending operations.[52] Jewish lending obviously had advantages for these Christians.

The medieval Church first seriously confronted the problem of interest in the mid-twelfth century, at the time of Europe's commercial revolution. The Church was concerned primarily with usury itself, not with the Jewish or Christian identity of its practitioners. Accordingly, all the canons dealing with usury, including that imputed to Jews, are gathered together in the title (chapter) *De usuris* of Gregory IX's normative *Decretals* of 1234. The first of these canons to deal directly with the Jews, *Post miserabilem* (issued in 1198), does not prohibit Jews from taking interest. Rather, it grants Crusaders (and them alone) a moratorium.

48. See Bonfil, 1990: 58–64.
49. Pullan, 1971: 431–621.
50. E.g., Muzzarelli, 1983: 24–25.
51. Milano, 1963: 199,202,204; Stow, 1988a; now see Esposito and Quaglioni, 1990.
52. Pullan, 1971: 533–534; Poliakov, 1977: 63–64.

Payments on loans they took would not fall due until their return from the Holy Land, nor would interest accrue in the interim. This stipulation was repeated seventeen years later in the canon *Ad liberandam*—a product of the Fourth Lateran Council—whose full text deals chiefly with launching a new Crusade. Both of these canons were far less demanding than the *Quantum praedecessores*—the original bull issued in 1145 to regulate *Christian* lending to Crusaders—which declared a moratorium on repayment of the principal and required lenders to free Crusaders from their oaths to pay interest. Any interest already paid was to be remitted. *Post miserabilem* and *Ad liberandam* insisted that Jews, too, remit such interest. But upon the Crusaders' return, that interest was to be repaid, along with the additional interest accruing after their return. The fundamental canonical legislation concerning Jews and interest thus seems to have privileged Jewish over Christian lenders. Moreover, a third canon, *Quanto amplius,* which concerns *all* Christian borrowers, is even more permissive, stipulating in calculatedly inelegant phrasing that Jews were to accept "no immoderate usury" *(non immoderatas usuras)*. Within limits, Jews were apparently to be permitted that which to Christians was completely forbidden—namely, the collection of at least a reasonable rate of interest.[53] The Church seems indirectly to have been aiding Jewish economic endeavor.

This does not mean that the Church, as embodied by its papal head, was doing such things as exploiting Jewish bankers to help itself achieve financial control over its Italian domains, which might explain why the popes guaranteed and cultivated Jewish lending in Italy through the end of the Middle Ages.[54] The Jews' civil dependence on the papacy in its Italian domains[55] may have tempted the popes to support profitable Jewish lending, just as the Jews' civil dependence on them tempted secular rulers elsewhere, including the most pious. Nonetheless, in the papal domains, and as a general rule, what most determined papal policies toward Jewish lending was the frequently reiterated canonical principle that the Jews' traditional rights must be preserved. The popes seem also to have intuited that it was preferable to limit sin by dominating and regulating lending, rather than by waging an unwinnable war. It was this intuition, as well as an awareness that credit was a necessity—as the

---

53. Stow, 1981; see also McLaughlin, 1939: 81–147; idem, 1940: 1–22.
54. Toaff, 1983: 1:191; idem, 1986: 2:99–117.
55. Thomas Aquinas, 1947: II, IIae, 10, 10.

Sienese so aptly put it—that led the popes to seek a middle course of licensing and controlling Jewish lending, which they abandoned only in 1682.[56]

The interest that ecclesiastical authorities permitted Jewish lenders to collect under the heading of *non immoderatas usuras* was normally 20 percent. This was the same rate that Italian Christian lenders, about the year 1200, were charging for commercial loans secured by landed collateral. Jewish and Italian rates were also alike in being much higher (rates of as much as 43.3 percent were not unknown) on unsecured loans made to risky borrowers, such as nobles and princes. In the Renaissance, rates were set at 24 percent against pledges, but were then lowered to 18 percent. The Jews' privilege of charging these rates is attested to by the records of Church courts, such as those in medieval Perpignan, and by papal letters which berate authorities, both secular and ecclesiastical, for violating written contracts that specified moderate interest alone. Meir ben Simeon, in his *Milhemet Mitzvah,* stated outright that the pope permitted a rate of 20 percent, and so too, in 1270, did the German bishop Otto of Minden, referring specifically to the edict of the Fourth Lateran Council.[57] This limit was carefully monitored. As willingly as the popes supported "not immoderate interest," so they condemned exorbitant rates and vehemently demanded that offending Jews be punished for unfairly manipulating "Christian hospitality."[58]

In fact, the popes were perched on the horns of a dilemma. Canon law formally could sanction no interest whatsoever, not even 1 percent. Dominican and Augustinian opponents thus censured the fifteenth-century Franciscan protagonists of the *Monti di Pietà* for deciding to cover operational expenses by charging interest rates of up to 5 percent. A similar theoretical consistency was voiced by the noted fifteenth-century jurisconsult Alexander de Nevo,[59] who ignored centuries of practice and said that the blanket prohibition against interest must also be applied to Jewish lenders. De Nevo also rejected the fiction *(dissimulatio)* devised by other jurisconsults prohibiting the pope from openly sanctioning interest but allowing him to refrain from punishing those Jews who accepted it. This fiction, or one like it, had been used for dealing with

56. Stow, 1992b; cf. Baron, 1952: 14:36–37; Cooperman, 1987.
57. Spufford, 1988: 261; Stow, 1981: 165.
58. Grayzel, 1966: nos. 39,58,60,70,115,117; Simonsohn, 1990: vol. 1.
59. Poliakov, 1977: 29–35.

Christian lending since 1235.[60] At that time, Pope Gregory IX had suspended the clauses of *Quantum praedecessores* canceling interest due, which were preventing Crusaders from receiving sorely needed financing. Without the expectation of a reasonable profit, lenders were refusing to open their purses.

Strict constructionism, however, had originated in the thirteenth century, not the fifteenth, for the most part among academic canonists who taught and wrote in a university atmosphere. Their objection to a positive formulation about interest reflects a commitment to principles no less staunch than that of the thirteenth- and fourteenth-century Jewish halachists who rejected the artificiality of the gentile straw man. Among the strict constructionists there were also religious purists who feared Jewish "contamination" and who believed that Jewish usury threatened social stability. Odo of Sully, about 1200, thus demanded that all trade with Jews cease, for it invariably resulted in interest-bearing contracts. In 1213, Robert of Courson said that should interest be wholly forbidden, "thus would be removed all usurers, all factious men and all robbers; thus would charity flourish and the fabric of the churches again be builded; and thus would all be brought back again to its pristine state."[61] In this same utopian spirit, in 1285, the Franciscan archbishop of Canterbury, John Pecham, protested to King Edward I. Why, Pecham wanted to know, had the king not enforced his statute of 1275 that forbade Jews to lend; for only by so doing could he prevent his subjects from falling headlong into the "abyss of usury."[62] The line is clearly a direct one from Pecham and Courson to the Franciscans and the other radicals of the fifteenth century.

Yet Pecham did not call for the Jews' expulsion; hesitantly, he accepted their presence in Christian society. A formal link between lending and expulsion was made only in 1451, when, at the Synod of Bamberg, the cardinal legate and canonist Nicholas of Cusa propounded that only those Jews who did *not* lend ought to be tolerated.[63] The pope, Nicholas V, quickly condemned his legate's stance, just as two hundred fifty years earlier Innocent III had restrained the radical preaching of Robert of Courson.[64] In defending the Jews and moderate interest, these two popes

60. De Susannis, 1558: pt. 1, chap. 11; Gilchrist, 1969: 64.
61. Mundy, 1973: 175.
62. Grayzel, 1989: 295.
63. Stern, 1893: 52–54, no. 47.
64. Baldwin, 1970: 297.

may have been considering not only canonical propriety but also the example set by Abbot Suger in the twelfth century. The revenues Suger derived from taxing Jewish lenders living on his estates had played an important role in constructing the first Gothic chapel at St. Denis; and subsequently Suger's example had been followed by numerous other monasteries and religious foundations.[65] An increasing number of churchmen were realizing that Jewish lending might directly benefit the fabric of the Church. Interest taken under careful ecclesiastical supervision might, accordingly, be a good work.

The Unexpected Stand of Thirteenth-Century Rulers

Edward I of England did not share this belief. His response to John Pecham's demand was not a rebuff but the lament that "he [the king] did not know what to do." Indeed, Edward was no less disturbed by lending than was the archbishop, and his prohibition of lending in 1275 in fact culminated a policy begun in 1269. But Edward was not the first king to oppose Jewish lending. In 1146, Louis VII of France had applied to the Jews the restrictions of *Quantum praedecessores,* and in 1206, Louis' son, Philip II, put a ceiling on the interest rates Jews might charge, anticipating, as it were, by nine years *Quanto amplius,* with its stipulation of *non immoderatas usuras.* Philip had already called in Jewish loans during his temporary expulsion of the Jews from Ile-de-France in 1182. In 1223, Louis VIII ordered that no new interest-bearing loans be contracted and that no additional interest accrue on loans already outstanding. Louis IX went further. In 1230, he announced that even the principal would be forfeit on loans thereafter contracted, noting pointedly—in the words of ecclesiastical purists—that usury meant "anything beyond the principal." When loans continued to be made, Louis responded with confiscations, inquests, partial remissions of principal, and even a limited expulsion in 1254. Monies that fell into his hands were all applied to projected Crusades or sent to relieve the Roman emperor at Constantinople. As for the Jews themselves, Louis repeatedly demanded that they live solely by labor or trade. Other contemporary rulers followed Louis IX's lead—for example, James I of Aragon, who intermittently canceled outstanding interest, and Alphonse of Poitiers, Louis IX's brother, who

65. Grabois, 1969.

convoked Dominican inquisitors to hear complaints about Jewish usurious excesses.[66]

In the words of Meir ben Simeon, the kings were increasingly exceeding the demands of the papal Church. In a letter he "would have liked to send to [the king]," Meir excoriated Louis IX, charging him with paving the way for his counts to fleece their captive Jews and confiscate their possessions. Jews were going hungry, for they had no source of livelihood. They had lost the principal on their loans and the interest as well. Why, Meir asked, had the king surpassed the demands of the pope by improperly annulling the oaths to repay that lenders had taken? The pope, Meir trenchantly noted, would have never taken such a step. By his actions, the king had violated the pacts his fathers had made with the Jews (actually, Louis IX's methods of dealing with Jewish lending had first been tried by Philip Augustus a half-century earlier); he had violated the law itself. How could it be, Meir therefore asked the archbishop of Narbonne, William de la Brou, that he had adopted the king rather than the pope as his guide in the matter of lending? Had the king replaced the pope as William's spiritual mentor? For at Louis IX's instance, William at the Council of Béziers in 1255 had approved an edict ordering Jews "to desist from usury, blasphemy, and magic."[67]

Yet why did the kings, who for so long had reaped the fruits of Jewish lending, now take the lead in quashing it? And why, for that matter, did they also begin opposing Christian lending, from which they had profited no less? In part, they were motivated by clerical urgings, but their own piety weighed no less. Louis IX viewed as a holy obligation the extirpation of lending, for whose ills he held himself personally responsible. To his councillors, who told him that "without lending, his people would not survive, nor would the land be tilled, and [that the already damned] Jewish lenders were preferable to . . . Christian ones," Louis said: "I leave Christian lenders . . . to the prelates; the Jews . . . are in servitude to me . . . Either they cease their usuries or they leave my lands."[68] They must stop "infecting my land with their poison." The zeal of Louis IX—Saint Louis, whose reign has been likened to an unending Crusade,[69] including his two actual crusading ventures of 1248 and 1270—is not surprising.

66. Stow, 1981: 174–178; Baron, 1952: 11:143.
67. Meir ben Simeon, 78v,33v.
68. Grayzel, 1966: 46.
69. See Jordan, 1979.

But similar feelings were expressed by Edward I, a king whose priorities are normally judged to have been political, economic, and military.[70] To explain the expulsion from England in 1290, Edward said that he had acted to uproot the "heinous offense" of usury and the "abasement of our people," "to guarantee the honor of God and the public utility of the Kingdom."[71] And, of course, the appointed steward for performing this political and pious task—whether it was to protect the English "public utility" or, as the French put it, the "mystical body politic"—was the king. For were not kings, at this time, also claiming as their own some of the spiritual initiatives which the popes—since Gregory VII in 1073—had viewed as papal monopolies?

Such a view of kingship and of its obligations made it imperative for the kings to confront lending's allegedly corrupting and devastating consequences. From the time of Philip II Augustus, kings were convinced, however falsely, that loans, and not bad harvests or slack demand, made "little" people suffer; and thus, in a rare show of royal "charity," Philip, in 1219, proscribed loans to artisans and peasant farmers.[72] Kings were more troubled by the effects on the lower and upper nobility of land transfers resulting from default. Any direct monetary benefits or rewards to favorites obtained through these transfers were outweighed by the animosities they generated—such as at York in 1190, and during the English baronial revolts of 1215, and of 1264 to 1266—contributing to the outbreak of civil war and the temporary disenfranchisement of the English king. These animosities reached the boiling point again in 1290, just before the English expulsion. In France, Louis IX worried over the effects of lending's being outlawed solely in the royal domain, and, accordingly, he ordered applied throughout the realm the mutual extradition treaties he had made with his barons concerning the return of fleeing Jews. Without those treaties and with the king alone opposing lending, the counts, at obvious royal expense, would have resettled fleeing Jews and fostered Jewish lending activities.

When the issue was lending, the line separating the spiritual and practical aspects of statecraft was blurred. Lending at interest was a spiritual sin; the punishment for allowing it was civil unrest, the "abasement of the people," and the sullying of the "public utility." Lending exposed the king's own dependence, and its excesses were blamed on him,

70. Watt, 1988.
71. Rigg, 1902: xli.
72. Jordan, 1989: 82–83.

not only because he profited from it but because the Jews were, by the king's claim, his "chattel," his "serfs," exclusively subject to direct royal control. Good governance, therefore, dictated that kings had best turn their backs on lending. Knowing that his prohibition on lending of 1275 had failed dismally, in 1287 Edward I rejected out of hand proposals to revise closely supervised Jewish loans at 43.3 percent.[73] By that time, furthermore, the Jewish capital that Edward, and especially his father, Henry III, had so profitably taxed was nearly depleted, and the Jews were no longer a source of financial liquidity. The cycle of royal dependence on the Jews for that liquidity was broken. Edward was free to guide himself by what he considered the joint spiritual and practical needs of his rule, to respond as he truly *desired* to John Pecham's petition of 1285.

But a scenario such as this one was possible only in England and to some extent in France. No other medieval kingdoms or governmental units were so politically unified in the thirteenth century (irrespective of subsequent grave crises) or so civilly self-aware. In divided Germany, lending and the emotions it evoked generated endless conflicts, sometimes worse in their savagery than the regulated brutality of expulsions. To the east, the era of Jewish lending was only beginning; its leading theme would be royal and ducal financial exploitation. The charters awarded by Duke Frederick II of Austria in 1244 and by King Boleslav of Poland twenty years later both view the Jews as exclusively revenue-producing instruments. Reading these charters, it is easy to see why certain late nineteenth-century historians theorized that the Jews were economic pioneers and the vanguard of capitalism.[74] The truth is far less pretentious. The Jews simply provided liquidity in those places where others *would* not. It was no accident that their entrance into the towns of central and north-central Italy occurred at just that moment when Lombard and Tuscan lenders were moving north or into the cities in search of larger and more profitable investments. The Jews' tenure in these towns, moreover, was in principle assured only so long as they were liquidity's sole—or at least its prime—purveyors and in some cases also the main source of long-term communal loans.

However, in the long run, these new Italian communities did not quickly disappear. For beyond their economic desirability, their continuity was also fostered by a combination of uniquely Italian factors—

73. Rigg, 1902: liv–lxi.
74. Kisch, 1944; and see Sombart, 1962: passim.

namely, a stable ecclesiastical policy, a political leadership that followed the papal lead with regard to lending, and a civil status rooted in Roman law, its successor the *ius commune,* and a sense of civic commitment and realism that foreshadowed Renaissance humanism and its more balanced concepts of statecraft. Such foundations obviated political theologies like that of the northern European "mystical body politic," which perceived the Jew in terms that were ever more mythical than real. Let us now look at the implications of these two opposing portraits, that of the north and that of the south.

11 Instability and Decline

The Mythical Jewish Protagonist

Jewish life in medieval Europe was never wholly peaceable. The late sixth-century narratives of Gregory of Tours suggest that Jews were always subject to Christian volatility. That volatility increased as the Middle Ages advanced. Violence became regional rather than local. The pogroms of 1298 that became known as the Rindfleisch massacres, possibly after their leader (sometimes thought to have been a butcher), progressed episodically throughout nearly the whole of Bavaria, in at least forty-four separate communities, an area far greater than the limited segment of the Rhine valley where the massacres of 1096 occurred. The Jewish Memory Books record at least 3,400 martyrs, far more than during the First Crusade. This enormous increase in victims and in geographic diffusion has prompted the opinion that the Rindfleisch massacres were a turning point with regard to Jewry's *physical* security.[1] Subsequent massacres, such as that of 1320 in southern France, that of 1336–1338, again in Germany, and those of 1348, accompanying the first outbreak of the Black Death, took place over even broader areas. That of 1391, in Spain, encompassed the entire Iberian peninsula. Furthermore, the accelerant of these massacres was a more explosively defined one than the nebulous transfer of frustrations from real causes to the mythical Jewish enemy that had inflamed the crusading pilgrims of 1096. The Rindfleish massacres, and afterward those of "Armleder," in 1336–1338, were set off by a libel claiming that Jews had desecrated the host. In 1321 and again in 1348, Jews were accused of poisoning

1. Lotter, 1988a.

wells—an accusation possibly believed[2] even by the king of France and by Pope John XXII.

Christian society was growing universally ill at ease with the Jewish presence, a dissatisfaction that it was occasionally prepared to express in violence. During the fourteenth century, on the then-justified pretext that such protections were needed, Jewish neighborhoods in Germany were gradually enclosed by walls. Bishop Rudiger of Speyer, the first to use this pretext, in 1084, must have been thinking of limited flare-ups, to which in fact all new merchant communities (which also lived within walls) were subject. The fourteenth-century wall builders feared wanton destruction. Such walls would certainly have helped forestall the Spanish massacre of 1391, which lasted for months, left almost no Jewish community untouched, and was carried out by members of nearly every social class.

Nevertheless, Jewish life was not an unmitigated "Vale of Tears," as the sixteenth-century Jewish historian Joseph ha-Cohen named his chronicle. Nor may Jewish history be divided according to *shemadot* ("massacres"), as Joseph ha-Cohen's near-contemporary Salomon ibn Verga did, somewhat facetiously, in his *Shevet Yehudah*. Much of the time, Jews and Christians enjoyed a modus vivendi that sometimes bordered on sociability. As late as the 1280s, when Jews in England literally feared for their lives, Christians still attended Jewish feasts and wedding celebrations. The Franciscans at the monastery of Assisi, even in the fifteenth century, bought Jewish-made wine and were also known to consume it at Jewish tables, despite canonical regulations. Elsewhere, Jews and Christians launched joint business ventures.[3] Why, therefore, was this modus vivendi so often, and so violently, disrupted?

The root of the problem was the inability of the Jew to be integrated into the "Christian civic community," or polity—a concept that had existed since the time of Justinian's late Roman Christian Empire, was revived in the ninth century under the name of a reformed Christian society by Agobard of Lyons, was repeated by dozens of legists even up to early modern times, and was still being invoked in the late eighteenth century, by (for example) the reformer C. W. Dohm,[4] who favored expanding the Jews' privileges but considered politically unacceptable their holding public office and exercising power over Christians.[5] The concept of a Christian polity played a notable role in the libels of ritual murder

2. Ginzburg, 1989: 21; see also Given, 1989.
3. Toaff, 1989: 200,215; Baron, 1952: 11:183–188.
4. Dohm, 1957: 65–66.
5. See also Goode, 1981: passim.

that, in the fourteenth and fifteenth centuries, proliferated in several imperial cities. The charge that Jews had murdered a Christian child, either to reenact the crucifixion of Jesus or to use Christian blood in Jewish ritual, was followed by trial, torture, and frequently (although not invariably) judicial murder. These calumnies were repeated as late as the early twentieth century in czarist Russia and although condemned by emperors, popes, and even hostile converts to Christianity,[6] in imperial cities, in particular, much of the galvanized citizenry, including the patriciate, believed what it heard. Others, principally patricians and lawyers, exploited the libel and the subsequent trial to test the claims of a faltering German emperor that he alone could try and punish Jews. At the same time, it appears that concerted action against the Jews following a libel was seen as an act of civil defense in which unrestrained zeal for Christian purity was identified with civic fulfillment and with the goals of Christian reform.[7] The Christian polity was being articulated in a mode that even Agobard would have called radical.

Yet why might violence, judicial murder, or other repressive measures such as restrictive legislation, fines, and expulsions be necessary to protect the Christian polity? And why did that protection become synonymous with maintaining civic purity and effecting Christian reform? The explanation lies partly in the early medieval transposition to a societal level of Paul's unresolvable theological confrontation between "unbelieving Jews" and "believing Christians." Through this transposition, society itself, and no longer individual religious consciousness, became the arena for spiritual confrontation. The conflict between Christian and Jew, as well as Paul's apocalyptic resolution of it—which foresaw either mass conversion (surrender) or mass expulsion (defeat and punishment)—was now mythologized into a cosmic struggle between Christian citizens and tolerated Jewish residents. The polity in which this struggle took place was variously pictured. For the Visigoths, whose actions may be said to have anticipated Agobard's ideas, it was a ritually designated but always intrinsically earthly one. For the crusading army that took Jerusalem in 1099, the earthly was confounded with the spiritual and the mystical. For Rindfleish, and for others involved in the 1298 slaughter, the this-worldly and other-worldly were equally present. It was as the Christian pilgrim pursuing his way to God, bearing a cross before him, that Rindfleish appeared before the walls of Uffenheim, called upon its people

6. See Langmuir, 1990a: 263–271,307–310.
7. Hsia, 1988: 36.

to admit his pillaging band, and warned that only the godless would dare protect the Jews. Uniquely, "the citizens of Regensburg (represented by its Council) refused to kill and destroy the Jews without legal proceedings, in their desire to *honor the city*."[8]

What made the confrontational depiction of the Jew so seductive was its fictitiousness. This was a competition with only one active competitor, the Christian, who alone set the rules and named the game. The Jew, from the time of Paul in Romans, was a passive player, whose game was portrayed and interpreted within the Christian's confrontational perspective, perhaps most vividly in the case of Jewish loans. The Jew could be made to personify Christian deficiency, as well as the entirety of Christian society's failings and flaws. The more these failings proliferated, especially toward the later Middle Ages when internal dissidence was matched in intensity by famine, disease, and economic failures, the stronger became the sense of competition and the more the Jews' supposedly competitive behavior was tropologically and symbolically portrayed.

It has been suggested that as early as the eleventh and twelfth centuries, court-employed clerics consciously began to create a satanic Jewish image and to initiate Jewish persecutions, impelled by their unfounded anxiety that the Jews—who were in fact too absorbed in the Talmud to devote themselves to mastering Latin—might compete for dearly won bureaucratic posts.[9] In truth, so explicitly satanic an image of the Jewish opponent did not mature until the later thirteenth and fourteenth centuries and especially the fifteenth century, when Christians began openly to profess that men could literally become demonic and not merely temporarily demonically possessed.[10] Nevertheless, in the interim, the Jew was steadily depersonified and reduced to set mythical roles—for example, Robert Courson's description of the Jewish lender as the apocalyptic impediment to social perfection and Guibert de Nogent's fantasies of the Jew as agent of sexual perversion, destroyer of monkish chastity, and fomentor of incest. Agobard, in the ninth century, was already drawing comparisons between the Jew and the Antichrist. And Peter of Blois, in the twelfth century,[11] associated the Jewish Messiah with the Antichrist and spoke figuratively of the Jew "changing himself into monstrous shapes." By the later thirteenth century, Judaism itself would be called

8. Lotter, 1988a: 413.
9. Moore, 1987: 80–88; 1988.
10. Ladner, 1967: 254.
11. Baron, 1952: 11:132.

the "religion of Satan," no longer that of the Torah of Moses. Jews, as people, were mocked, despised, and attributed with the negative qualities of owls and monkeys. On another plane, women's putatively haughty and stubborn behavior, disguised by a mask of humility, was sometimes denounced as a replica of that of the Jews.[12]

The Jew had become the perennial opposite, the contrary, the inverse. In the words of Agobard of Lyons, the Jew was an *impedimentum* to social unity—a *moqesh* ("snare"), as a Hebrew text later phrased it.[13] The Jew was injustice incarnate, the negation of that which medievals considered a divine virtue; he was executed, accordingly, by being hanged upside down.[14] Moreover, had not the Jew, as some claimed, allegedly discarded the basis of his own justice, the Torah of Moses, and, in its place, espoused the Talmud's perverse rabbinic *deleria*? It is no wonder, then, that from the early Middle Ages, heresy was (sometimes) identified with Judaism. By the same logic—although Jews themselves were rarely if ever accused of witchcraft—witches were sometimes said to initiate their careers by desecrating the host,[15] and they were occasionally punished by having to wear a Jew's cap.[16] The socially pernicious was thus systematically linked to Judaism. In the medieval pecking order, the Jew's rung was only slightly higher than that of a dog—if at all.[17] Acts against Jews—committed not in an effort to find scapegoats on whom to deflect guilt, but in the full and ingenuous belief that Jews were truly guilty as charged—were thus invested with the power potentially to purify, to blot out real enemies, and ultimately to herald personal and group salvation.

The good Christian shunned the Jew. When the Italian bishop of Ventimiglia, who defended the Jews against a blood libel in 1475, was charged with being a bad Christian, his biographer refuted the charge by noting "that he [the bishop] never shared the Jews' table."[18] Indeed, food touched by Jews was considered throughout the southern European tier, and sometimes in the north, as being polluted.[19] In the marketplace, in these regions, the Jew used a stick to indicate his purchases. To eat with

12. Trachtenberg, 1943: 46–52; Delumeau, 1978: 319–320; and see Baron, 1952: 133–138; also Langmuir, 1990a: 207.

13. Gilboa, 1964: 11–12.

14. Cohen, E. 1989: 411.

15. Ladner, 1967: 254.

16. Baron, 1952: 11:139; Russell, 1980: 167–168.

17. Cohen, E., 1989: 411.

18. Battista de'Giudici, 1987: 55.

19. See Kriegel, 1976.

a Jew was to pollute oneself in the most literal sense. He who refrained from sitting at a Jew's table was surely a person of good faith. These were, of course, castelike distinctions. Discriminating about what and with whom one eats often betokens a search for, or a reaffirmation of, caste identity—in the case of the medieval Christian, the identity of the True Israel and the exclusive rights to that caste name.[20]

If the sharing of food could create such anxieties, the mixing of blood was all the more disturbing. A Jew's blood, wrote Thomas of Cantimpre in the thirteenth century, is impure.[21] To have sexual relations with a Jew, where blood might be mixed, was, in the words of Caesar of Heisterbach, "super harlotry," the equivalent of denying Christ.[22] It was also "bestiality," for which at least one fourteenth-century French judge said that the guilty ought to be burned at the stake, since "for a Christian to have sexual relations with a Jewish woman is to have sexual relations with a dog."[23] In Calatayud (Spain), the town's leaders sought to restrict the Jews' place of residence, "lest these faithless dirty people infect [sexually] the purity of Christians."[24] And in 1306, Duke Robert of Calabria considered expelling the remaining Jews in his kingdom for indulging in illicit sexual relations—relations that in this case were considered especially pernicious, since they may have been with former Jews (in fact the majority of southern Italian Jewry) who just a decade earlier, under circumstances that have yet to be explained, had been forced to convert.[25]

Blood was the source of enormous perplexity for medievals. Its presence, especially at awkward moments, denoted unresolved conflict. If, as the Dominicans argued in opposition to the Franciscans, it was true that Mary did not menstruate, then how could Jesus have been generated with the true human nature—his body and blood—which the wine and the wafer of the Eucharist were said to reconstitute?[26] Yet the Eucharistic host was often visualized not only as Jesus incarnate but also as a child, and sometimes as Isaac, the perfect sacrifice. Held aloft by the priest, its very sight could spark adorational fervor, especially on the simplest popular level: "Stoupe downe, thou fellowe afore, that I may see my

20. Douglas, 1971: 64–65.
21. Baron, 1952: 11:153.
22. Baron, 1952: 11:80.
23. Cohen, E., 1989: 411.
24. Baron, 1952: 11:90.
25. Starr, 1946; Cohen, J., 1982: 84–89.
26. See Wood, 1981.

maker," one "rude" bumpkin is reported to have said to a man standing in front of him in church. "Heave it a littel hyer," said another to the priest.[27] To verify this image, people craved reassurance; and that which most satisfied them seems to have come from the "testimonies" and, even more, the "impieties" of the Jews. Whether through actual accusations, beginning in the thirteenth century, through fables that often found their way into miracle plays, or through artistic representations, the Jew was said to verify the actuality of transubstantiation—that is, of the Real Presence of Jesus—by stabbing the host and making it bleed. On occasion, Jews also gave proof that the host had been transformed into a child. Upon seeing that child, one Jew reportedly converted. Another Jew, in a verse homily composed around 1400, saw something else as well. The child into which the host had been transformed was then devoured by the officiating priest and his congregants.

Rarely do such repressed fantasies surface even orally, let alone in writing. Normally, like so many other psychological deviations, they are denied by their inventors and transferred onto the "other." In medieval terms, one avoided judging oneself by judging one's fellows, a *iudicium alienum*.[28] With respect to the Jews, this is precisely what happened. It was, therefore, not the Christian but the Jew who was said to molest or cannibalize the host; just as putatively it was not the Christian but the Jew who consumed the body and blood of the eucharistically fantasized child Isaac, the sacrificial, atoning lamb (that is, the blood of Jesus who is "sacrificed" during the Mass).

Similar transferals of anxiety fueled the charge that Jews "crucified" young boys[29] (again, surrogates for Jesus) and sometimes ritually used their blood. No one—as has cogently been argued in connection with the case of William of Norwich (the first alleged victim of such an act, in 1144)—would have wanted to admit his need for a crucifixional reenactment in order to "create" a personal intercessor before God, who specially protected the founders and perpetuators of his cult.[30] Cannibalistic anxieties may have been at work here, too. A Florentine miniature depicting the alleged murder, in 1475, of Simon of Trent shows Simon crucified; another representation, a German bridge decoration, portrays Simon slaughtered and bled dry of his blood like a butchered pig (much

27. Sinanoglou, 1973: 493,498.
28. Ladner, 1967: 255.
29. Langmuir, 1977.
30. Langmuir, 1984.

in the same way that Bernardino da Siena stigmatized Jewish lending as bleeding dry the vital wealth of towns and just as Hugh of Lincoln—supposedly murdered in 1253—was said to have been "stuck like a pig").[31] But the crucifixional depiction appears as the lower half of a carving whose upper half portrays the *Judensau,* the Jew-pig, suckling her Jewish offspring; Jews were said literally to give birth to pigs.[32] They were also pigs themselves, certainly their equals. Was not the "stone of Saint Paul," mined in the grotto of Saint Paul on Malta, said to afford protection from poison, rabies, and incantations to all "baptized creatures" and "animals," but not to dogs, Jews, and pigs?[33] Yet Christian folklore also attributes to pigs the qualities of children, and in certain southern European dialects one of the pig's vertebrae is named after Jesus.[34] Simon of Trent is thus at once child, pig, the Jew's offspring, and the crucified Christ about to be consumed. His imputed murder would have been as cannibalistic in intent as it would have been deicidal.

Some Christians did not cavil about making such cannibalistic accusations openly. Gregory X's rebuttal, in 1272, of ritual murder charges makes this absolutely clear: "It is," said the pope, "totally false (as some Christians have asserted) that Jews secretly . . . kill Christian boys and sacrifice these boys' hearts and their blood. For the Jews' law expressly . . . prohibits them from sacrificing or *consuming* [human] blood. Jews may not even drink or eat the blood of [kosher] animals having a cloven hoof."[35] The Jew of the ritual-murder libel, therefore, was not a real but a mythical one whose imputed nature was wholly unrelated to that of his real-life counterpart, for whom "the blood [is forbidden], since it is life" (Dt. 12:23). Rather, this mythical Jew incarnated an inverse Christian ideal—as, in fact, Paul had no less mythically described him at Christianity's inception; or perhaps more precisely, he incarnated some of that ideal's more troublesome aspects.

What, then, could have been more logical than to make Jews into the locus of all aberrant behavior, of all alien activities, and of alienation itself? By the later Middle Ages, the Jew whom persons at all social levels envisioned was a mirror image. He reflected—by embodying them—per-

31. Langmuir, 1990: 238.
32. Fabre-Vassas, 1984: 68–69; Trachtenberg, 1943: 8; Baron, 1952: 11:137; Shachar, 1974: 36, plate 33.
33. Toaff, 1989: 152.
34. Fabre-Vassas, 1984: 71.
35. Grayzel, 1989: 116–120.

sonal inadequacies and society's irremediable flaws; he represented the failure to achieve that which medievals themselves called "harmony from dissonance,"[36] whether on the intellectual plane, the political plane, or the everyday plane of physical existence. It only remained, therefore, to reenact the crucifixion, via the ritual-murder libel, and then mythically to repair the social fabric by publicly—indeed, civically—punishing that (ancient) event's *as yet* unpunished perpetrator, the Jew.

Moreover, it has been observed[37] that the more the perception of imperfection alienated medieval people from themselves and from society, the more violently they acted out their sense of alienation; for medievals were *viatores,* pilgrims, seeking the road to God's kingdom. On earth, that kingdom was manifest as the "Christian polity," a polity, indeed, which—thanks to the increasingly popular Corpus Christi civic processions—was being ever more likened to the body of Christ; and a polity which equally had to be redeemed from imputed Jewish violence, just as the Jews' supposedly repeated assaults on Christ's very person had to be avenged. Potentially, therefore, all medievals might behave toward Jews as did the crusading pilgrim, Emicho of Leiningen, Rindfleisch, and the masses who attacked the Jews during every wave of the Black Death, in 1348, 1360, 1369, and 1375. Consciously, these pilgrims were taking vengeance on the Jews, whom they believed had poisoned the wells and disseminated the plague. But such widespread and repeated violence indicates that on an unverbalized level, their goal must have also been the chimerical one of restoring to perfection a society bogged down in uncertainty and chronic despair.[38] No one seems to have been exempt from this pursuit. Even kings confounded reality and myth. Henry III of England executed Jews charged with ritual murder, and Philip IV of France executed those accused of desecrating the host.

Such a universal tendency to act out in moments of fear, weakness, and socially threatening stress was not one on which medievals possessed a monopoly. Such medieval behavior recalls the recent psychiatric argument made with respect to Nazi medical atrocities, that "human beings kill in order to assert their own life power."[39] But did not nineteenth- and twentieth-century Germans also mythify the Jews, accusing them—in what has been labeled Germany's "cultural despair"—of destroying sac-

36. Lourie, 1986: 201–202; Kuttner, 1960; see also Langmuir, 1987.
37. Ladner, 1967: 255.
38. Carpentier, 1971.
39. Lifton, 1986: 467.

rosanct cultural and national values?[40] How different was this, one would like to know, from the attitude of the fifteenth-century Italian Franciscans, who associated "the impurity of the Jew with the impurity of urban society"?[41]

And yet it must be recalled that, for the most part, rage directed at medieval Jews was checked, and those who would have acted out their fantasies were stopped. To this end, sophisticated rituals were also developed, simultaneously providing outlets for pent up feelings and reaffirming ideals that excessively permissive behavior had called into question. Especially revealing was the Eastertime stoning of Jewish homes in fifteenth-century Umbria, in response to annual Franciscan calls for Christians to expiate their sins.[42] This stoning was fully anticipated; and before it began, Jews safely closed themselves behind shutters and bolted doors. No one was hurt, nor was any such harm intended. This continued to be the case even in twentieth-century Poland, where the Eastertime stoning was still annually reenacted. By throwing the stones, Christians were theatrically striking out against and punishing the menacing Jew. The prodigal Christian sons guilty of fraternization were also expiating their sins. Equilibrium was restored, and the normal balance between conviviality and anxiety was free to resume until the next Easter season approached. When, in 1510, one Jew dared to hurl a stone back, he was considered a menace; he had denied the annual ritual its therapeutic function.

Protest, too, was ritualized, as in the stonings common at Italian funerals.[43] The burial in potentially sacred Christian ground of the carnal Jewish corpse, with its unsaved soul, might disturb the perfection of the End of Days. Some, at least formal, protest had to be made. The early medieval, southern French "colaphization"—in which, once again at Eastertime, a select Jew was publicly, and sometimes roughly, slapped—may also have been a rite of protest, as well as one designed to restore social calm. Ritualized, but rarely intensive, proselytizing among Jews that was fitfully carried on throughout the Middle Ages may have performed a similar function. In moments of heightened millennial expectation, this proselytism might take on a more intensive aspect.[44] At the same

40. Stern, 1965: passim.
41. Hughes, 1986: 19.
42. Toaff, 1989: 224–225.
43. Toaff, 1989: 67–68.
44. Stow, 1977: 262–277; Berger, 1986.

time, it has been said that even such conversionary episodes were "substantially rites of consolidation and stability that restrained violence, fixed it in codified and dramatized forms, and contained its extremes."[45]

It may have been more than violence that these rituals postponed. They may have also postponed the inevitable—namely, the wholesale banishment of the Jews from the lands of western Europe. For although by sometime in the thirteenth century the Jew's mythified image had made his continued presence in medieval society no longer viable, the end was was not swift. The kings of France dallied with expulsion as early as 1182. They did not take permanent steps until 1306, which even then were followed by partial reprieves. To provoke a permanent expulsion, something special was needed, and that was what the patricians of the Friulan city of Udine pointed to in 1556, when they petitioned their Venetian overlords to expel the city's Jews. According to the almost gleeful statements of these patricians, the mob violence threatened by vagabonds (who at the height of a plague had planned to attack these Jews, and who themselves were summarily hanged) provided an *occasione per scacciare gli ebrei*—literally, "a perfect occasion to chase out the Jews."[46] Expulsions, like violence, took place only under necessary and sufficient conditions. Opportunity was as important as motive.

During the hundred or so years before their expulsion from England and France, as well as prior to the later expulsions from the cities and regions of Germany, therefore, the Jews of Latin Europe may have lived in a state of existential ambivalence, and a will to expel them may have existed. But opportunity had yet to knock. As one writer succinctly remarked: "They reside in their own fatherlands, but as if they were non-citizens; they take part in all things as if they were citizens and suffer all things as if they were strangers; every foreign country is a fatherland to them and every fatherland is to them a foreign country."[47] Ironically, the anonymous early Christian author of the Epistle to Diognetus wrote these words to describe the terrestrial lot of Christians, not of Jews. In the intervening millennium since they were written, however, matters had come full circle. It was now the Jews, not the Christians, who were the "non-citizens" and the "strangers." In such a state of limbo, it was possible to carry on and "to take part," as the Jews in fact did. But like

45. Foa, 1988: 159–160.
46. Stow, 1988a; Pullan, 1971: 526.
47. Ladner, 1967: 236.

all states of indecision, this limbo could only temporarily endure. Indeed, it was ultimately the very combination of being at once "strangers" (perhaps best understood as "mythicized opponents") and "non-citizens" (in the sense that the Jews were coming ever more to live by a unique legal and constitutional code marginalizing them from the Christian polity) that provided the necessary and sufficient conditions for ending Jewish tenure in all of western Europe. Only a final spark, like that at Udine in 1556, was required to make expulsion a fact.

This was not the case with regard to the papally headed Church. In papal terms, and in those of the canon law as well, the Jews were neither "strangers" nor "non-citizens." In the all-encompassing ecclesiastical structure, the Jews had a permanent place. Church teachings directly militated toward neither attack nor expulsion. Acts such as the libels of ritual murder spread by the thirteenth-century clergy at Lincoln Cathedral and the fifteenth-century Italian Franciscans were notable exceptions to the rule.[48] How advantageous this situation was must now be considered.

The High Medieval Church

The Persistence of Traditional Behavior

The Church did not ameliorate medieval Jewry's lot. Its well-known[49] restrictive legislation increasingly isolated the Jews, as persons, from the surrounding society. Certain members of the clergy, especially Dominican and Franciscan mendicant friars, condemned Jewish actions and Judaism itself, and many of them undertook lengthy campaigns that justly may be called anti-Jewish.[50] Nevertheless, in the long run, ecclesiastical behavior was potentially stabilizing, as none other than medieval Jewish writers themselves repeatedly said. In their estimation, the Church was consistent, with respect to its priorities and within its own frame of reference, which consisted of Christian salvation, the promotion of the Church's spiritual and worldly institutional ends, and the Jews' ultimately Christian soteriological role. In each case, the Jews' continued presence in Christian society was judged necessary, if only for them to personify the

---

48. Langmuir, 1972; Milano, 1963: 204; and see Grayzel, 1989: 235–236.
49. See, e.g., Chazan, 1980; Ben-Sasson, 1976; Parkes, 1938; Grayzel, 1966.
50. Cohen, J., 1982; idem, 1986a; idem, 1989.

absence of belief and its punitive effects.[51] The desire to retain the Jews in order to achieve these ends (as stated by Paul in Romans) was balanced by a fear of "contamination" (as stated by Paul in Galatians). But the tension was resolved by invoking the idea of contingency: Jewish acts—including the very observance of Jewish rites—were permitted so long as, at least indirectly, they benefited Christianity. This idea governed the policies of Gregory I and moderated the wrath (and possibly the designs) of John Chrysostom and Agobard of Lyons. Eventually, the idea was verbalized by Alexander II, whose letters to Spain in 1063 indicated that Jews were to be protected, accepted into Christian society, and guaranteed their rights, since they acquiesced to Christian rule. This formulation was reaffirmed by churchmen throughout the Middle Ages and into the early modern period.[52] In about 1140, it was incorporated into Gratian's *Decretum* (the *Concord of Discordant Canons*) as the canon *Dispar nimirum est* (causa 23, questio 8, canon 1).

It has been said that "what is remarkable in the Middle Ages is not that the [ecclesiastical] doctrine on the Jews was emphasized, but that it underwent so little change."[53] Indeed, the principles for dealing with Jews elaborated in the early Christian centuries were not abandoned even in the thirteenth century when the Church set out to eradicate heretical deviance, nor were they jettisoned by a conscious shift toward a policy of Jewish containment. During the course of that century there were innovations, but these, more than anything else, drew the implications of long-standing policies and heightened their definition. The papal doctrine that permitted Jews to collect "not immoderate usury" is a bellwether of thirteenth-century ecclesiastical intentions. The ecclesiastical hierarchy would take no steps to prohibit Jews from lending, so long as that lending conformed to theological and legal exigency. This yardstick also applied to encounters between the Jews and the papal Inquisition, and even during the mid-century struggle over the Talmud. In 1266, Pope Clement IV pointedly warned the Talmud's Spanish opponents that their actions must not "violate those privileges which the Apostolic See has conferred upon the Jews."[54]

The canons on which nearly all subsequent Jewry policies would be based already existed by about the early eleventh century. And most had

51. Thomas Aquinas, 1947: IIa, IIae, quest. 10.
52. Stow, 1988: 58,61.
53. Langmuir, 1963: 235.
54. Grayzel, 1989: 92–93.

been collected, first, in the influential *Decretum* (about 1012) of Burchard of Worms, and then, about 1094, in the works of Ivo of Chartres.[55] Twelfth- and thirteenth-century canonists editorially perfected and elaborated Burchard's and Ivo's work. But, especially with respect to the Jews, neither they nor the theologians who heavily relied on them altered goals and strategies. In fact, they emphasized the rootedness of Jews in Christian society—for example, by enhancing the rights of Jewish parents over their children.[56] They also went beyond Alexander II's *Dispar nimirum est* and incorporated into Church law the canon *Sicut iudaeis non,* which unambiguously defined the Jews' right to live peacefully and securely among Christians. Moreover, Jews and Judaism were not identified with heresy. Rather, Jews were uniquely "Jews," a distinction that Honorius III explicitly reaffirmed in 1225.[57]

This legal, theological, and strategic consistency is well illustrated by radical behavior, which included spates of venom, attacks on Jewish institutions, and efforts to launch a sustained missionary campaign, but which did not extend to calling openly for extreme measures, such as expulsion. Even late in the fifteenth century, when these measures were finally advocated, they were tellingly justified by saying that Jews had irremediably violated the canons and the law.[58] In the thirteenth century, Dominicans such as Raymundus Martinus still clung to the traditional Pauline formulation reserving the Jews' mass conversion for the End of Days. Martinus acquiesced to the Jews' presence in Christian society, despite his conviction that contemporary, talmudic Judaism was a demonic invention and that its observance diverted the Jews from following what he called their authentic, biblical (by which he meant christologically oriented) faith. "The Jews," he said, "are like the pomegranate tree, which is spiny and emits a foul odor, but eventually produces sweet fruit."[59]

Ecclesiastics who overstepped bounds, as papal Inquisitors sometimes did, were restrained by the popes themselves. The Jews, said the popes, were to live in a state of Perpetual Servitude *(Perpetua servitudo),* a term first enunciated in the bull *Etsi iudaeos,* issued in 1205 by an angry Pope Innocent III. "While the Jews are mercifully admitted into our intimacy,"

55. See Gilchrist, 1988.
56. Pakter, 1974: 306.
57. Grayzel, 1966: 173.
58. Stow, 1988: 55–56.
59. Raymundus Martinus, 1687: pt. 3, chap. 10, pars. 21–23.

the pope said, "they threaten us with . . . retribution."[60] Specifically, he had just learned that at Eastertime, Jews were forcing Christian wet nurses to spill their milk into the "latrine." The canons, to begin with, forbade Jews to employ these nurses. But the violation was now compounded, since these nurses had just received the Eucharist, as medievals did just this once during the year.[61] The Church was also specially arguing at this time that the wine of the Eucharist was literally transformed into Christ's blood. It was this claim that must have perturbed the Jews. Medievals believed that mother's milk was a derivative of blood. Should Jewish children suckle the milk of these communicant Christian nurses, would they not via this milk become unwitting participants in what Judaism considered to be an idolatrous ritual? From the Jews' point of view, it was better to let their infants go hungry. Innocent III disagreed. The Jews' were snubbing Christianity's most holy sacrament and taunting the resiliency of the Christian social order. They were forgetting that their status was "wholly diverse" from that of the Saracens—as Alexander II had said in 1063—only because they had accepted their merited "subservience." Accordingly, said Innocent III, at both the beginning and the end of *Etsi iudaeos,* the Jews must realize that their "guilt has consigned them to Perpetual Servitude," and their actions must exemplify this state.

As a term and a name, Perpetual Servitude was new; its conceptual infrastructure was not.[62] Its purpose was to designate a mode of behavior realized through the Jews' thoroughgoing adherence to canonical regulations. Its invocation was intended to remind both Jews and Christians of this behavior, and so restore, when necessary, a ruptured social equilibrium. Quite purposefully, Innocent III created the term by combining Alexander II's dictum that the Jews "are ever prepared to be subservient" *(servire)* with Paul's polemical image—used by Innocent III himself—that the Jews were the sons of the slave Hagar whereas Christians were sons of the free woman Sarah. Yet as canonists often stressed, the submission that Perpetual Servitude signified was not that of real, legal bondage; the great Hostiensis called Jews *cives* (roughly, "citizens").[63] Nor was Perpetual Servitude a device invented in order to claim direct papal political suzerainty over all Jews.[64] Perpetual Servitude, as Innocent applied the

60. Grayzel, 1966: 114.
61. Sinanoglou, 1973: 498.
62. Gilchrist, 1988: 10–11.
63. Pakter, 1874: 306; De Susannis, 1588: pt. 2, chap. 6.
64. Baron, 1972.

term in *Etsi iudaeos,* thus did not excuse draconian measures. Rather, it justified the demand that Jews instantly dismiss their Christian wet nurses. Appreciating this, a perspicacious eighteenth-century canonist, Lucio Ferraris, argued that *Etsi iudaeos* exemplified Christian society's willingness to accept Jews into its midst; for was not its sole remedy for (putatively) egregious Jewish behavior the restoration of traditional canonical order, and nothing worse?

It goes without saying that in current terms, the Jews' acquiescence to this order was a euphemism for humiliation. But that is a moralistic judgment, not a historical one. Historically and in his own terms, Innocent III, by enunciating doctrines such as that of Perpetual Servitude, was more firmly anchoring his spiritual authority and that of the Church by a process of summary and consolidation. All thirteenth-century popes shared this goal. These intensive papal labors of summation reached a climax at the ecumenical Fourth Lateran Council of 1215, over which Innocent III presided, and whose decrees sought to further papal power by anticipating a new Crusade, prescribing ways to maintain mendicant Franciscan and Dominican orthodoxy, and initiating measures to combat heresy.[65] The council's decrees concerning Jews were also intended to strengthen the papal hand by renewing, and granting papal sanction and ecumenical force to (that is, making universally binding), hitherto locally issued edicts which for centuries had been flouted, often with official, secular connivance.

However, the decrees concerning Jews promulgated at the Fourth Lateran Council—as well as those issued at the Third Lateran, summoned in 1179 by Alexander III—were almost all previously well known. The most important are found in the canonical collections of Burchard of Worms and Ivo of Chartres, and many of Burchard's canons reappeared, verbatim, in at least thirty-four additional collections. Gratian's mid-twelfth-century *Decretum* contains more than fifty canons regulating the Jews in matters of social segregation, testimony against Christians, behavior during Easter week, the possession of Christian slaves, the holding of public office, the number of synagogues to be erected, and the reception of converts to Christianity.[66] These same themes were reiterated at the Lateran councils. The Third Lateran Council forbade Jews to maintain Christian servants in their homes, including wet nurses, and declared

---

65. Alberigo, 1962: 241–243; Jedin, 1960: 77–81.
66. Stow, 1977: 304–315.

Christian testimony against Jews always acceptable, "since it was correct that Jews be subservient to Christians." The Fourth Lateran ordered Jews not to appear in public during Easter week, and denounced Jews holding public office, as well as the Christians who appointed them.[67]

The labor these conciliar decrees initiated was completed by the Jewry canons of the *Decretals*—the unprecedented, and comprehensive, official papal collection of ecumenical canon law issued in 1234 by Pope Gregory IX (following a fifty-year-long compilatory process). The *Decretals* streamlined to about thirty the approximately fifty canons concerning Jews found in earlier collections, closed old loopholes, and sometimes stiffened penalties.[68] These restrictions made the limits clear. The precise terms they set for taking interest, for example, were found by Jewish commentators to be much preferable to the capriciousness of the French barons, whose manhandling of Jewish lenders in 1233 provoked a papal condemnation.[69]

Lending, however, was one sphere in which the Fourth Lateran Council did innovate—yet its usury legislation concerned Christians as much as it did Jews. Christians were forced to cancel all interest owed them by Crusaders; Jews were told *when* interest from Crusaders might be collected. A second novelty was the attempt to make Jews pay "tithes" on land that Christians may once have owned, although, for this innovation, there are certain early medieval precedents.[70] A third novelty, the question of having Jews litigate with clerics in ecclesiastical rather than secular courts, was a problem of the thirteenth century in particular, once again for both Christians and Jews. A fourth innovation, which has made the Fourth Lateran Council appear to have drastically shifted the Church's position concerning the Jews, was the imposition on them of the requirement to wear distinguishing clothing.

The "Badge"

The concept of special Jewish dress was not itself a new one. Quite likely, it was borrowed from the ubiquitous and centuries-old Islamic practice of making Jews wear honey-colored turbans or sashes. It is also becoming increasingly clear that Innocent III was not rationalizing when he said

67. Grayzel, 1966: 278,306–313.
68. Pakter, 1974: 120.
69. Grayzel, 1966: 200.
70. Grayzel, 1966: 36; Grayzel, 1989: 284–286.

that without special clothing "it sometimes happens that by mistake Christians have intercourse with Jewish or Saracen women, and Jews or Saracens with Christian women . . . [which is] a grave sin."[71] Sexual contact between Christians and non-Christians—whether Jews or Muslims—was a reality, and one that had long been a thorn in the ecclesiastical side.

Yet Innocent III's language was vague. He spoke of "habits," not the intrinsically discriminating round badge or rectangular patch that within a few years of 1215 was selectively being adopted. Nothing suggests that either Innocent or his successors intended to confer upon the "habit" an inherently pejorative cast. In 1250, Innocent IV did complain that "undeserved reverence" was being accorded Jews who wore typically round clerical capes.[72] But it was only centuries later that writers began to compare the Jews' "sign"—their yellow hat (then in vogue) or even women's earrings[73]—to the dress of prostitutes and to call it a mark of dishonor.[74] The meaning of the original decree of 1215 was reemphasized in 1233 by Gregory IX, who stated that "it was decreed in the General [Fourth Lateran] Council . . . that the Jews everywhere must be made distinguishable from Christians . . . in their clothing, lest there result a wicked mingling . . . of Jews with Christian women," and of Christians with Jewish women. Innocent IV said nearly the same thing in 1250. And so, for that matter, did Franciscan preachers in the fifteenth century.[75]

The Jews' special "habit," therefore, originated as—and remained—an executive measure effected to promote a traditional goal. Innocent III's grounding of its necessity in the biblical command that Jews must place fringes on their clothing also suggests a traditional concern, to demonstrate that the "habit" did not violate the Jews' "good customs," which popes had repeatedly sworn to protect. Nevertheless, the urgency with which both popes and numerous councils repeatedly referred to Jewish dress—altogether twenty-nine times in forty years—suggests that the habit was inexorably acquiring an added significance. It was one, moreover, that greatly appealed to secular rulers—so much so, in fact, that even while they questioned or rejected other ecclesiastical legal demands, they took the lead in transforming the vague habit of the 1215 decree

71. Grayzel, 1966: 309; Brundage, 1988: 30; Kriegel, 1979: 50; Boureau, 1986: 29.
72. Grayzel, 1966: 281.
73. Hughes, 1986: 24–26.
74. De Susannis, 1588: pt. 1, chap. 4.
75. Grayzel, 1966: 206–207,272,283; Toaff, 1989: 219.

into a sharply defined rectangular or round "badge." Thus, in 1222 the Church council of Oxford called for "woolen patches," and in 1227 that of Narbonne required a round sign. But through the agency of the papal legate Guala, the young Henry III of England had already made such a demand in 1218, and in 1221 Frederick II ordered the Jews of Sicily to wear a blue patch. In 1228, James I of Aragon ordered his Jews to wear a "sign." Only in the Empire was there a delay. Jews living there had signs, or a distinctive pointed hat, imposed upon them only about 1270. Therefore, although this was never stated in so many words, the badge was coming visibly to signify the Jews' inferior status, tangibly confirming their social marginality.[76] The other medieval group that was forced to wear special clothing was the lepers.[77]

Yet by visually indicating the Jews' status, the badge, somewhat para-doxically, may have lessened anxieties and fostered a modus vivendi. Very likely, both clerical and lay communities adopted the badge so rapidly because what they saw, they might better know; what they knew, they might less fear; and what they less feared, they might more securely live with and successfully control. In the thirteenth century, such control was an urgent desideratum. Dissatisfied laymen had mythically inflated the dimensions of "Jewish misconduct," uneasy clerics (and sometimes the popes) doubted that Jews' willingly submitted to Christian dominion, and clerical radicals were again arguing that Jewish actions contaminated the societas fidei. They claimed that to protect and stabilize this society, greater heed—embodied by such as the badge—must be given to Galatians' segregationist warnings.[78]

This urge to visibly segregate the Jews reflects the thirteenth-century Church's broader predicament. Despite the apparently enormous power and prestige the institutionalized, papally directed Church had achieved, the perennial goal of reforming and of perfecting society in the Augustin-ian mode was becoming ever more elusive. The thirteenth century marked the apogee of papal power. Nevertheless, that power was constantly being challenged by outbreaks of heresy, the failure of the Crusading ideal, and the unrestrained taxation of the clergy by the kings of England and France, who were also trying clerics in royal courts rather than exclu-sively in ecclesiastical ones. There was also dissension within orthodox

76. Grayzel, 1966: 60–70.
77. Ginzburg, 1989: 11.
78. Stow, 1984: 34; see Cohen, J., 1989: passim.

clerical ranks. At Paris, the seculars (meaning roughly the nonmonastic clergy) and the regulars (ordained monks, but especially mendicants) virtually went to war with each other—ostensibly over the distribution of professorial chairs but in fact over the question of whether the regulars would displace the seculars as lay Christianity's spiritual guides. In addition, there were signs that some Parisian theologians were still preferring the Sacred Biblical Page and its direct interpretation over papal interpretative authority,[79] a challenge which never ceased and eventually boiled over into Luther's so-called heretical, antipapal schism of 1517.

At the moment of its greatest achievements, therefore, medieval Christianity experienced enormous disillusionment. However close it had come, it would never realize in full the reformers' centuries-old ideal of a unified and obedient *corpus mysticum ecclesiae*. Some radicals blamed this failure on what they perceived to be the Church's corrupt, even demonic leadership. The Spiritual Franciscans, heirs in part to the visions of the late twelfth-century Calabrian abbot Joachim of Flore, constructed a topsy-turvy apocalyptic world view in which the popes were villains and they themselves angelic heroes.[80] Such millenarianism encompassed the Jews. Joachim of Flore anticipated their mass conversion,[81] fantasizing—as a way out of despair—an impending utopian world order.[82] A similar vision underlies Robert of Courson's belief that an end to usury, especially Jewish usury, would restore society to its "pristine state."

But visions like these spring from a wish-fulfilling logic. By forcing the Jews into total submission—especially that *visibly* imposed by the "badge"—Christians could pretend that the order which was universally unrealizable could be microcosmically achieved. The Jews' submission might even be illusorily mistaken for dominance over the whole. To such highly seductive fantasies, even popes fell victim, although never completely before the sixteenth century. In the thirteenth century, papal susceptibility and reactions to illusion were limited. As individuals, or even as ecclesiastical officers, the popes were not immune from sentiments felt by other clergy. The Jews' flouting of ecclesiastical rules—for example, their Eastertime (mis)treatment of Christian wet nurses—was surely perceived not only as offensive to "Christian order" but also as symbolic

79. Morrison, 1969; and see William of St. Amour, 1632.
80. Benz, 1934: passim.
81. Frugoni, 1957: 3.
82. Freud, 1946: 73–88.

of that order's imperfection. This realization was surely responsible for much of the rhetoric and determination that give contemporary papal policies their special stridency. The *Proemia* ("introductions") to papal letters bristle with such terms as Jewish "contumely" and "contempt." Gregory IX said that "if what is said [about the Jews is correct, then] no punishment would be sufficiently . . . worthy of their crime."[83] Nicholas IV wrote that the Jews "corrupt our faith and daily foment apostasy."[84] In this spirit, the popes, too, no doubt invested the badge and habit with a broad social meaning.

But rhetoric, anger, and discriminatory beliefs imply neither political nor legal violence, nor do they mandate programmatic change. Whatever additional meaning the popes attributed to the habit, they did not allow Innocent III's original intentions to be obscured. In some regions of their own papal states (for example, Umbria), they refrained from implementing the demand for special Jewish dress until they were given specific reason for doing so by Franciscan complaints that Jews and Christians were engaging in illicit sexual relations. And that was in the fifteenth century.[85] Even in the matter of the badge or habit, therefore, papal policy toward the Jews maintained a consistent posture. It is no wonder, then, that however greatly he was infuriated by the Jews' treatment of Christian nurses, Innocent III called for correction, not reprisals, and that he reacted with the same prescription upon learning that Jews were allegedly making light of both Christianity and the Eucharist by selling to Christians unkosher portions of meat and, perhaps worse, quantities of wine, some of which found its way into the Communion chalice.[86] Innocent's successors responded similarly to even greater (putative) Jewish provocations.

The Attack on the Talmud and on Rabbinic Texts

About 1236, the convert Nicholas Donin composed and sent to Pope Gregory IX a tract listing thirty-five charges against the Talmud, in whose aggadic sections, especially, Donin claimed to have found evidence of blasphemy, the malediction of non-Jews, the attribution to God of human

83. Grayzel, 1966: 240–241.
84. Grayzel, 1989: 175.
85. Toaff, 1989: 213.
86. Grayzel, 1966: 127.

emotions, and the attribution to the Jews of the ability to modify divine precepts. The Talmud also was said to view Jesus as the son of a whore.[87] Were Donin correct, the Jews could be accused not only of violating the canons but also of false Jewish observance for having "set aside the Old Law received from Moses and of adopting another in its place."[88] The Dominican Raymundus Martinus would later say that contemporary talmudic Judaism was a perverse set of false practices given to the Jews by the demonlike Bentalamion;[89] he supported these charges with ample citations from midrashic literature, citations that apparently he did not invent.[90] These charges were also especially dangerous, since they raised the specter that Jews were no longer fulfilling their traditional role of being witnesses to Christian truth.

The claim that rabbinic literature had perverted biblical Judaism or that it contained negative statements about Christianity was not new. As early as about 135, Justin Martyr had accused Jews of falsifying the biblical text. The uncomplimentary story of Jesus' origins in the *Toledoth yeshu* was known from the time of Agobard of Lyons. In the early twelfth century, the convert Peter Alfonsi attacked several talmudic passages. But like those who followed him, Alfonsi neglected to indicate that originally the bulk of these passages were directed against pagans, and that he had misrepresented them by stripping them of their specific aggadic context,[91] which was a simple task, since the Talmud is an amalgam of diverse legal and midrashic comments made over hundreds of years. And out of context, any one of them could be attributed with untrue meanings. Alfonsi's remarks were taken up about forty years later by the Cluniac abbot Peter the Venerable. His charges had no effect, for the simple reason that Christians themselves had as yet no direct talmudic access.

In the thirteenth century, matters changed. Christian study of Hebrew, Aramaic, and the Bible, as well as of Rashi's commentaries, formed a natural gateway to the Talmud itself. Just as the Jews' first, biblical canon was said to foreshadow Christianity and demonstrate its truth, so ought their second, talmudic one to perform the same function. Christian exegetes found what they sought. But they could not ignore what had been said in the past. The upshot was the *Pugio fidei* ("Dagger of Faith"), a

---

87. See Rosenthal, J., 1956.
88. Grayzel, 1989: 98.
89. Bonfil, 1971; cf. Cohen, J., 1982: 131–153; Chazan, 1989.
90. Merchavia, 1988: 203–207; Leiberman, 1939.
91. Merchavia, 1973: 93–127.

work produced about 1278, probably by Raymundus Martinus, who was aided by other like-minded Dominican Hebraists.[92] Divided into three sections, this massive, essentially polemical work first validates Christianity on the basis of ancient pagan philosophy, then condemns contemporary Judaism by attacking one body of midrashim, and concludes by reaffirming Christianity through exploiting another. The condemned midrashim are vilified as false rabbinic concoctions; the true ones—often drawn from obscure and sometimes no longer extant midrashic collections—are honored as those miraculously left unexpunged.

Looking backward from the *Pugio fidei,* it is possible to understand why the Spanish Dominican school that produced it called, a decade earlier, for the Talmud to be not destroyed but censored. The Talmud's blasphemous texts were to be erased, its Christological ones exploited, with (it was hoped) conversionary results parallel to those the mendicants sought through missions to the newly accessible territories of eastern Asia and through the establishment of schools for the study of oriental languages, including Hebrew. What saved the Jews was that these missions, as well as the challenge to the Talmud itself, were pursued only fitfully. Obligatory royal preaching licenses were sought in Spain sporadically— in 1242, in the 1260s, in the later 1270s, and in 1296. Similar inconsistency prevailed throughout England, where no preaching license was issued before 1280, and throughout France, where the Dominican convert Pablo Christiani first preached in 1269. The Dominican Christological exploitation of the Talmud thus may be ascribed to apologetic as much as to missionary needs.[93]

But that exploitation threatened the Jews. At a grandiose inquest held before the king at Barcelona in 1263, Pablo Christiani debated midrashic texts with Rabbi Moses ben Nahman (Nahmanides).[94] So well equipped was this convert, that the otherwise illustrious rabbinic scholar was forced to hide behind an innovative distinction that he himself may have personally rejected.[95] The Talmud, Nahmanides said, is binding upon the Jews; the midrashic literature—which he called a wholly separate category from that of the Talmud—does not bind them at all. The Dominicans were furious at these tactics, as well as at other blasphemous

92. Raymundus Martinus, 1687; see Cohen, J., 1986a: 612.

93. See Baer, 1961: 1:155–156,168; Cohen, J., 1982: 82–84; Berger, 1986; Stacey, 1989; Jordan, 1989: 161; Browe, 1942: 17–21.

94. Cohen, J., 1982: 108–122.

95. Fox, 1989.

statements that Nahmanides was reported to have made subsequently in a pamphlet claiming victory. In 1266, they enlisted papal help to have the rabbi punished. They did so again, a few months later, to have the Talmud confiscated and censored. That help was qualified. In a letter admonishing King James I of Aragon to punish the rabbi (who, in fact, was forced to flee to the Land of Israel), the pope stipulated that the king must not "violate those privileges which the Apostolic See has [otherwise] conferred upon the Jews." Even in the face of purported blasphemy, tradition and law were to be preserved without exception.

Papal stipulations about adherence to the law were also significant in France. Gregory IX initially responded to Donin's accusations by ordering a confiscation of Jewish books. At a subsequent investigation, most likely a quasi-Inquisitorial proceeding in 1242 (in the presence of royalty), the Tosafist Rabbi Yehiel of Paris failed to "prove" the Talmud's innocence. Found blasphemous, twenty-four cartloads of the work were publicly burned. In 1244 a similar incident occurred.[96] Yet it appears that in 1247 a Jewish delegation sent to Innocent IV was able to prevent a third conflagration. Like Clement IV after him, Innocent stipulated that the Jews enjoyed certain unimpeachable privileges, one of which was to retain the books necessary for interpreting their religion.[97]

In his response to the Jewish delegation, however, Innocent IV called for a new investigation under the aegis of his Parisian legate, the cardinal bishop of Tusculum, Eudes of Chateauroux, who was also chancellor of the University of Paris. And Eudes confiscated and once again condemned the rabbinic texts. Yet no records, papal or otherwise, confirm that a new burning took place; although it is possible that in 1248 or 1249 a burning was ordered by King Louis IX.[98] Innocent IV himself remained silent. Nor were there any further papal pronouncements on the Talmud before 1258, when Alexander IV demanded that books be confiscated in Burgundy, Anjou, and Provence. What ensued is unknown, but Alexander may have been responding to a continuing initiative of the king; in 1255, at the provincial church council of Béziers, the Talmud had been burned at Louis IX's behest.[99] Other royally sponsored sequestrations of books, perhaps with the aid of Inquisitors, seem to have taken place in 1269, 1283, and 1299. Indeed, if credence is to be given to Jewish reports,

96. Pakter, 1974: 30–31.
97. Grayzel, 1966: 275; Baer, 1961: 1:158–159.
98. Grayzel, 1966: 32; Urbach, 1955: 374–378; Yerushalmi, 1970: 350.
99. Grayzel, 1989: 64–65; Grayzel, 1966: 336–337.

which indicate that talmudic literature in France was becoming difficult to obtain, then the kings seem to have been primarily responsible.[100] Inquisitors, however, not the king, initiated the attack on rabbinic works at Paris and in the south of France in 1310 and 1319.[101]

In 1321, the initiative reverted to the pope. At the order of the Avignonese John XXII, the sole medieval pope who expelled Jews from his own domains (which John did that very year, albeit temporarily, for reasons unexplained), the Talmud was again burned in southern France.[102] In the sixty-three years between Alexander IV and John XXII, the popes had referred to the Talmud only twice. Furthermore, when in 1286 Honorius IV denounced the Talmud as the "poisonous diet" the Jews fed their sons,[103] he may have been responding to a request by the Franciscan archbishop of Canterbury John Pecham,[104] perhaps even mechanically repeating the archbishop's precise formulations. This may explain why in the end no action seems to have been taken.[105] The second reference to the Talmud was in 1267, when Clement IV appointed a panel of talmudic censors; yet, like Innocent IV before him, Clement directed that books free from blasphemies or errors be returned. No doubt taking advantage of this directive, Jews assiduously, and successfully, petitioned James I of Aragon to dilute the impact of this order. Indeed, with the exception of the verbal attacks of Martinus' *Pugio fidei,* the Talmud was left in relative peace until 1412, at which time the Spanish "antipope" Benedict XIII again prescribed burning. But even he reconsidered shortly afterward and reverted to the idea of censorship.[106] To find a renewed example of papal Talmud burning, we must move forward to 1553. In that year, by order of Julius III, the Talmud was burned in several Italian cities, most notably Rome.[107]

In retrospect, the papal attacks on the Talmud appear episodic and cautious, whether in the thirteenth century or later. Gregory IX's first letter concerning the Talmud states: "*If* what is said about the Jews . . . is true, no punishment would be sufficiently great." Gregory was not

100. See Urbach, 1955: 378.
101. Grayzel, 1966: 341–344; Grayzel, 1989: 316–319,317–320; Yerushalmi, 1970: 326–327,351.
102. Ginzburg, 1989: 20.
103. Grayzel, 1989: 157.
104. Cohen, J., 1982: 80.
105. Grayzel, 1989: 160–162,160, n. 3.
106. Baer, 1961: 2:224–230; Baron, 1952: 9:67–69.
107. Stow, 1972.

being merely rhetorical. His use of the conditional embodied the kind of reservation and hesitancy that would recur again and again in such missives. The caustic *Nimis in partibus* of 1286 still uses the phrasing "It is said"; and Innocent IV's call, in 1247, for a new investigation followed by only three years his first order to have the Talmud burned. In the fourteenth century, this papal caution even made its way into letters inserted into Bernard Gui's Inquisitor's manual, which directed that innocent books be separated from offensive ones and "restored to the [Jews] . . . as is *just*."[108] Such caution can be ascribed neither to ignorance—although it is true that no pope ever demonstrated first-hand knowledge of rabbinic literature—nor to forgetfulness. If individual papal memories, like individual pontificates, were short, those of the papal chancellery and of its professional clerks were long. Innocent IV, Honorius IV, and John XXII assuredly knew, or were given to know, that they were reissuing a preexisting order. Did not Innocent IV, the canonist, in his *Apparatus* (commentary) to Gregory IX's *Decretals*—completed about 1245—admit that both Gregory IX and Innocent IV had justly ordered the blasphemous Talmud burned?[109] Nonetheless, actual papal orders to confiscate or investigate rabbinic literature, prior to that of John XXII, never recalled a precedent. The popes were surely being hesitant.

This impression is reinforced by the events surrounding Gregory IX's initial confiscatory order. That order was sent to archbishops throughout France, as well as specifically to the bishop of Paris, and to the Parisian heads of the Dominican and Franciscan orders. Multiple copies were also addressed to the kings of England, France, Aragon, Navarre, Castile, Leon, and Portugal. But every one of these letters was "mailed" via Paris; the "mailman" was none other than Nicholas Donin; and, most important, it was only at Paris that results followed.[110] It has not gone unnoticed that the Talmud affair—perhaps instigated by Nicholas Donin—was quickly transformed into a Parisian clerical initiative, as was also the 1248 talmudic condemnation orchestrated by Eudes of Chateauroux.[111] Such initiatives surely gave Gregory IX and his successors reason for concern. For the popes may have considered the Talmud suspect, but they also accepted their obligations. As put in 1247 by Innocent IV, who was

108. Grayzel, 1966: 343.
109. Pakter, 1974: 31.
110. Baron, 1952: 9:67.
111. Merchavia, 1973: 349–360, esp. 356; Stow, 1976: 144.

rethinking his actions of 1244, the pope must "harm no one unjustly . . . [He is] in justice bound to exact what is just, and to render to each his due." Consequently, he had to weigh the Jews' claims. For they claimed that "without the . . . Talmud, they cannot understand . . . their statutes and laws," which the Church had agreed to tolerate. The question of the Talmud thus presented the popes with a potential conflict of interest. As again put by Innocent IV, "Like the animals which John saw in the apocalypse, which were covered with eyes both front and rear, so the Supreme Pontiff, many-eyed, looks all about him, debtor alike of wise and foolish."[112]

Pope Innocent may also have been alert to a potential challenge to the papacy. For Paris, Innocent knew, had long been the home of those protagonists who preferred scriptural to papal interpretative authority. To be sure, papal authority had prevailed, as witnessed by the over-whelming number of papally authored canons in the *Decretals* of Gregory IX. Nevertheless, the attack on the Talmud may have allowed this seemingly resolved conflict to be reopened. Just as the Talmud was said by its Parisian opponents perversely to have supplanted the Bible as the Jews' source of religious authority, so might the same be said of the papal canons.

Such thinking might have emanated from the Abbacy of St. Victor, the seat of Hebraically based Biblical study. One signer of Eudes of Chateauroux's 1248 condemnation was the abbot of St. Victor himself. Twenty-seven of the remaining forty signatories—including all of the signing canon lawyers—were (secular clerical) masters at the University of Paris, a second seat of dissent.[113] These masters' support for unshakable scriptural authority was crucial in sparking their aforementioned dispute with the mendicants, which simmered during the 1240s and boiled over into unrestrained polemic during the 1250s. The seculars' spokesman, William of St. Amour, charged that the mendicants had "introduced certain superstitious novelties *not* within the tradition of the Church . . . *contrary* to divine Scripture."[114]

Of course, neither the secular masters nor anybody else would have openly charged the pope, or his canons, with violating scriptural tenets. But questions of the pope's exceeding his authority or of his possible

112. Grayzel, 1966: 275.
113. Merchavia, 1973: 452,356–360; cf. Cohen, J., 1982: 73–74; idem, 1986a: 609–610.
114. Cited in Cohen, J., 1982: 258; and cf. Pakter, 1974: 28–30.

theological errors, including heretical ones, did lie behind the still tentative thirteenth-century voices calling for the Church to be ruled by a hierarchically constituted council, rather than by the pope alone.[115] The rapid adoption by the Parisian masters of Nicholas Donin's charge of talmudic (antibiblical) innovations and their signatures on Eudes' condemnation may thus have been intended to signal the pope that, like the Jews, he could not place himself above Scripture. Innocent IV responded to this with silence. It should also be noted that in the fight between the Parisian secular and regular clergy, the pope took the mendicant side. William of St. Amour was declared a heretic.[116]

Ironically, therefore, the Talmud's fate may be a measure of how capably the thirteenth-century popes withstood challenges to their legal and institutional primacy. By 1267, the papacy seems even to have adopted a new strategy. By responding to the Dominican initiative and ordering the Talmud censored[117] rather than burned (as members of both mendicant orders had at first advocated), the question of legal origins or authority became much less problematic. For were not the Dominicans touting two talmudic-rabbinic traditions, one of which they said was false whereas the other was Christological and true, despite post-biblical origins of both? And these developments were not necessarily unrelated. Innocent IV's original order of 1247 to return certain Hebrew books may have provided the stimulus prompting the Dominicans first to weigh the Talmud's possible Christological verities. The conduit linking the pope to the friars would, of course, have been Raymond of Penaforte, the Dominican General, who both edited Gregory IX's *Decretals* and dominated events in Spain.[118] Moreover, in condemning the Talmud in 1258, did not Alexander IV mention only its alleged blasphemies? Likewise, accusations of blasphemy were the only ones that John XXII launched against rabbinic literature in 1320 and 1321. Along with a generic reference to "errors" against Christian belief, blasphemy was also the single accusation raised by the formulaic letters of confiscation found in Bernard Gui's Inquisitor's manual, as well as in Gui's discussion of Jewish prayers and biblical glosses. The charge that the Talmud was an "other law," first made in 1239 by Gregory IX and curiously repeated one last time in 1267 by Clement IV—despite (or perhaps because of) his decision to impose

115. Tierney, 1964: 124–125.
116. Dawson, 1978; Douie, 1954.
117. Grayzel, 1989: 99; Stow, 1972.
118. Cf. Cohen, J., 1986a: 608.

censorship—was no longer heard.[119] Almost without exception, the question of false, extrascriptural traditions was being astutely swept aside.

The Friars and the Inquisition

On the subject of Jewish books, Inquisitors, on the whole, appear willingly to have followed the papal lead. This was as it should have been, since Inquistors were directly appointed by the popes to staff the Papal Inquisition, a special court founded in the 1230s to deal with Christian heresy. Many of the Inquisitors were also Dominicans. Any books they returned were likely to have been those they hoped to manipulate Christologically. Moreover, the Dominicans proved to be remarkably constant, as opposed to the unpredictable Franciscans, who often exceeded their Inquisitorial mandates.[120] The Dominican theologian Albertus Magnus did sign Eudes of Chateauroux's condemnation of the Talmud, but he was only one of eleven mendicants who did so. On the other hand, the Franciscan Alexander of Hales apparently agreed with Innocent IV: only blasphemous Jewish books were to be burned. Alexander was writing in the context of a fuller discussion that perfectly encapsulates thirteenth-century papal attitudes toward the Jews.[121] Jewish "contempt," he said, was to be severely restrained; nevertheless, the Jews' traditional theological role had not been superseded. Their rites remained licit, and their relationship to Christians was to be viewed as being far *different* from that of the pagans who controlled the Holy Land. No one should object to Jews living peacefully in Christian society.

The same conclusion was reached in 1274 by the former Dominican General Humbert of Romans. In the agenda for debate at the Second Ecumenical Council of Lyons, prepared at the express directive of Pope Gregory X, Humbert deliberately paraphrased Alexander II and said: "The Jews, vanquished by knowledge and stripped of power, plot [literally, 'know'] nothing against the Christian people, nor are they capable of any such action." Christians, Humbert added, suffered Jews to reside among them because the latter would eventually be saved (he meant "converted"); because the prophets had warned against killing them—

119. Grayzel, 1966: 343; Bernard Gui, 1927: 12–19; Yerushalmi, 1970: 351–352; cf. Cohen, J., 1982: 92–93.

120. Francis, 1880: 10–11; see also Jedin, 1960: 100–101, and 96–99.

121. Alexander of Hales, 1925: 3:729; Chazan, 1980: 43–51 (trans.); cf. Cohen, J., 1986a: 608.

lest Christians forget (the Jews' negative example); but, most important, because "it was cruel [arbitrarily to exercise sovereign power and] to butcher one's subjects."[122] In this spirit, the Dominican Inquisitor Arnold Dejean promised in 1295 never detrimentally to modify the privileges of Pamiers' Jewry.[123] The Jews were, more than anything else, the Christians' pliant subjects. They were *fideles* of the Roman Church Militant, said the fourteenth-century lawyer Baldus de Ubaldis.[124] Clerical discussions of "toleration," in terms of whether Jews were or were not to be expelled, thus took place as scholastic, academic exercises, until Bernardino da Busti changed the tone of discourse in the 1490s. Thomas Aquinas, the greatest medieval theologian, did not discuss expulsion at all.

Though Aquinas denounced Jewish blasphemy (and even suggested that the Jews knew they were crucifying not only Jesus but God), his fundamental—and chronologically his last—discussion of Jews (in his *Summa Theologica*) treats them as an indispensable strand in the seamless scholastic fabric of society and its ideals.[125] The Jews' role is that of the inverse mirror-image. If it is natural to believe, says Aquinas, then unbelief is contrary to nature. Belief resides in one's intellect; unbelief is the product of the intellect (inappropriately) moved by the will. The unbeliever is separated from God. The Jews and their fate, Aquinas continues, illustrate these theological verities; Jewish life in Christian society must be regulated accordingly. Hence, Jews are not heretics, nor are they to be treated as such, for their sins are certainly much less grave. Yet unbelief does lead Jews to sin, especially through false textual interpretations. Christians therefore must be on their guard lest through these interpretations, as well as through their other activities, Jews corrupt the faithful. Only those expertly trained should confront Jews in debate. Likewise, all contacts with Jews are to be restricted and supervised. This is so even if Jews, as Jews, are outside the body of the faithful and may not be restrained through spiritual punishments like excommunication. On the other hand, Jews may enjoy no dominion over the faithful, whether spiritual or temporal; in particular, they may not hire Christian domestics. At the most, Jews may hire Christian day laborers to work outside the home. Jews may observe their rites, for in this way human government

122. Grayzel, 1989: 127–130.
123. Palès-Gobilliard, 1977: 98.
124. Grayzel, 1966: 343; Stow, 1984: 20 (citing Baldus).
125. Thomas Aquinas, 1947: IIa, IIae, quests. 10–12.

imitates that of God by allowing "certain evils" that portend the good—in this instance, the testimony Jewish rites provide to the Christian truth which, of old, they foreshadowed. By the same token, no one may force Jews to embrace the faith; although, should Jews be baptized, they may be compelled to constancy. Jewish children, too, may not be converted against their parents' will. To do so would be to invite apostasy; more important, it would be to defy natural justice, which even the Church may not do.

Aquinas' concise presentation reflects the policies of the papal *Decretals*. Accordingly, for him, as well as for most others, the justice to be meted out to the Jews was synonymous with the theological and canonical principles embodied in the *Summa* and the decretal collections, not with equality. To burn allegedly blasphemous Jewish books or to force Jews to wear a badge was no less just than to denounce accusations of ritual murder. In the same vein, the order given to the Inquisition by the first Franciscan pope, Nicholas IV, instructing it to proceed against apostates, Judaizers, and those who aided them, does not contradict the letter also sent by Nicholas, in 1290, to the Roman clergy, berating it for unjustly fining and otherwise oppressing that city's Jews.[126]

A similarly double-edged sense of justice informs three other letters Nicholas sent, warning Inquisitors against prejudicing cases (including those against Jews) by unwarrantedly changing venues.[127] The popes had authorized specific Inquisitorial prosecutions of Jews, but, as more than one dozen sometimes angry and deprecating letters delivered to Inquisitors confirm, the latters' intemperance would not be tolerated. Inquisitorial excess certainly existed. It is visible in the procedures detailed in Inquisitors' manuals,[128] as well in the complaints Jews lodged with popes and kings. Regrettably, the extant records of actual Inquisitional proceedings against Jews, especially north of the Pyrenees, are woefully limited; there are few hard facts that support confirmation or denial. Despite several papally initiated Inquisitorial proceedings in southern France,[129] only three transcripts of Inquisitorial trials held there in the early fourteenth century involving Jews have survived.[130]

Against which Jews, and why, did the Inquisition proceed? The bull

---

126. Grayzel, 1977.
127. Grayzel, 1989: 179–186.
128. Yerushalmi, 1970: 343–350.
129. See Simonsohn, 1990: 1:408–413.
130. Palès-Gobilliard, 1977: 101.

Turbato corde, issued in 1267, resurrected laws of the late ancient The-odosian and Justinianic Codes and specified that the Inquisition might prosecute "Christians . . . who have defected to Judaism" and Jews who had induced the former into taking this step. A reissue of *Turbato corde* in 1274 by Gregory IX noted that these defectors were sometimes "born Christians." Ostensibly, therefore, with respect to Jewish individuals, the Inquisition was given only one area of competence, the prosecution of apostates and their accomplices, which had been its putatively exclusive domain since its founding.[131]

What complicated the issue was the origin of these apostates. Some were backsliding voluntary converts, who, according to Church doctrine, were "fair game." Others were forced converts, victims of sporadic outbreaks of violence, often known to us principally through papal denunciations. In 1247, for example, Innocent IV condemned the forcible conversion of Jewish children in Valreas (Provence) following a ritual-murder accusation originated by two Franciscans and supported by the town's secular lord. Similar incidents, this time resulting from Crusaders' excesses, occurred in 1236 and 1290.[132] Though isolated, these incidents, along with missionary successes, created a notable body of converts, of whom many, if not the majority, desired to revert to Judaism. But fearing that such a step might instigate Inquisitorial prosecution, they acted with restraint, limiting themselves to "Judaizing" half-measures, a process that has justly been named "pre-Marranism."[133] The children of these con-verts found themselves in an awkward predicament. Often, they had been born following their parents' forcible conversion and so had been bap-tized at birth. Far worse than a forced convert's defection, their reversion to Judaism was an act of unmitigated apostasy. When Gregory X spoke of "born Christian" defectors, he was surely referring to them. Yet was it truly proper to prosecute such unwilling Christians? And what of their forcibly converted parents? Was not forced baptism illegal?

In fact, as early as 633, the Fourth Toledan Council had decreed that compulsion was illegal only prior to baptism; after baptism, the honor of the Church had to be preserved at all costs. This decree became a staple of subsequent canonical collections. However, because it contradicted the Jews' other rights, the decree's adoption into an authorized papal decretal collection was postponed until 1298; it remained for thirteenth-century

131. See Given, 1989.
132. Grayzel, 1966: 262–267, also 226; see also Jordan, 1989: 150.
133. Kriegel, 1978a.

popes and legists to harmonize the rights of the Jews with those of the Church, which was accomplished by Innocent III's brilliant distinction between absolute force and conditional force. The former was a vehement refusal to accept baptism even under physical duress.[134] A later refinement limited to only three months the period in which such "absolutely" forced converts were allowed to abjure. It goes without saying that few persons ever qualified under these requirements or, perhaps more precisely, ever lived to qualify. Those who silently assented, hoping subsequently to revert to Judaism, were trapped by the doctrine of conditional force. Their baptism was valid; so said Jacques Fournier—bishop, Inquisitor of Pamiers, and future Benedict XII. Fournier made this point while presiding at the trial of a certain Baruch, one of many Jews who had been coercively baptized in 1320 during the so-called Shepherds' Crusade. Yet Fournier took seriously the distinction between absolute and conditional force. During the trial, he repeatedly asked Baruch whether he had verbally expressed his negative will. Baruch had not; canonically, he was obligated to remain a Christian.[135] Nevertheless, Fournier seems to have given Baruch a mild sentence, perhaps because Baruch sagely asked the bishop for a series of lessons in Christian doctrine (these lessons have been incorporated into the trial record).

Fournier's leniency was not unique. Some of those charged by the Inquisition were wholly acquitted.[136] Still, not every case was so straightforward as that of Baruch. Much depended on a particular Inquisitor's sense of justice, or on his ferocity. Bernard Gui seems to have taken more delight in drawing and quartering the Franciscan heretic Fra Dolcino of Novara, in 1307,[137] than he did three years later in exercising the newly found Inquisitorial power to burn Jewish books.

Yet Inquisitorial zeal sometimes led to special severity with Jews. Prosecutions might be deliberately aimed at entrapment—or worse, such as when Inquisitors changed venues at will. There were also technical loopholes. The number of people who had been forcibly baptized, for example, was apparently so large that it was easy to accuse any Jew who had dealings with them of proselytizing. One such accusation, in 1315, was exploited in order to confiscate (albeit incompletely, thanks to royal intervention) the entire wealth of Majorca's Jews. Five years later, a

134. Grayzel, 1966: 100–103.
135. Grayzel, 1958: 114; see also Albert, 1974; Yerushalmi, 1970: 330.
136. Palès-Gobilliard, 1977: 102–103; Shatzmiller, 1973: 332.
137. Mundy, 1973: 553–555.

similar accusation forced many Jews of Tarragona into exile, while those remaining paid a stiff fine.[138] There was substance behind Martin IV's warning, in 1281, that Inquisitors ought neither to force Jews into confessing nor to prosecute any of them who may unwittingly have had social contact (familiaritas) with a convert.[139] It was in such an atmosphere that in 1354 a Jewish synod at Barcelona insisted that the pope publicly restate the limits of Inquisitorial juridical competence over Jews.[140]

Inquisitors sometimes prosecuted Jews without first requesting royal consent. In 1323, James II of Aragon complained that by circumventing his authority, the Inquisitor Bernardus de Podio Certosa had "caused the king's Jewish communities to be destroyed without reason."[141] Of course, not every ecclesiastical tribunal that tried Jews was an Inquisitorial one, nor were the Jews' always charged with offenses related to apostasy. Sometimes Church courts sought to prosecute Jews for brawling with a cleric or for refusing to pay the tithes the Church said Jews owed. In doing so, that courts often aroused the choler of secular rulers, who were furious that their claim to exclusive jurisdictional rights over Jews was being infringed.[142]

Certain Inquisitional initiatives did, however, gain royal assent, as, for instance, the fourteenth-century campaign against Jewish books in southern France[143] (although, paradoxically, some of the books may have been confiscated from Christian hands, into which they had fallen after the Jews' expulsion from France in 1306). By this time, Inquisitional initiatives had also veered off onto a new and threatening tack. Bernard Gui was claiming the right to expurgate Jewish books of prayer. The Inquisition was exceeding the limits of Turbato corde's mandate, as well as those previously established for dealing with Jewish books. Applying a concept first asserted by Innocent IV,[144] that the Church might directly judge Jewish religious error, the Inquisition apparently intended to supervise the whole of Jewish religious practice, which, in fact, it abusively did. The petition made in 1354 by Barcelonan Jewry accordingly requested

138. Baer, 1961: 2:10–14.
139. Grayzel 1989: 22,149.
140. Finkelstein, 1972: 330–331; Grayzel, 1989: 21.
141. Baer, 1961: 12.
142. Friedberg, 1965; see Grayzel, 1989: 19–20.
143. Yerushalmi, 1970: 352.
144. Kedar, 1979; Pakter, 1974: 30.

the pope to direct the Inquisition to prosecute Jews not for espousing beliefs consonant with Judaism but only for rejecting beliefs "common to all religions, such as denying God or saying that God in Heaven did not give the Torah."[145] Jewish apprehensiveness in this regard was not lessened by the conversionary sermons Inquisitors sometimes delivered.[146]

It was not apprehension but sheer terror that Inquisitors in southern Italy aroused in the early 1290s, when, in league with Charles II of Anjou, they forced more than half of that region's Jews to convert, the others fleeing to Sicily or the Italian north. These events have been linked to riots following a blood libel inspired by mendicant Inquisitors[147] and to Charles II's purported ultimatum—recorded in a chronicle of 1304—that the Jews convert or perish.[148] Most likely, the full story will never be known.[149] Yet there seems to be no question that in these events Charles II played a central role. His support for Inquisitorial coercion was unheralded. And his example was not followed until 1497, when King Manuel of Portugal—without an Inquisition to aid him—had all the Jews of his realm forcibly baptized. Even in Spain, in 1492, Ferdinand and Isabella eschewed force and expelled the Jews who refused to convert. Qualitatively, nevertheless, Charles's actions were not unique. The willingness of other contemporary secular rulers to license forced preaching and to order Jewish books indiscriminately confiscated and burned violated the Jews' "good customs" and abrogated the Jews' traditional rights no less seriously than had Charles's complicity with the Inquisition.

This behavior differed sharply from that of the popes. With regard to Inquisitional activities, the popes remained faithful to *their* concept of Jewish due legal process. In 1299, Boniface VIII even extended to Jews the right—normally forbidden in Inquisitorial proceedings to persons of influence—to know their accusers.[150] Likewise, Martin IV's improbable defense of Jews who unwittingly had social contact with converts[151] was accompanied by a threat that false accusers would suffer the same penalty that they had plotted for innocent Jews.[152] Concern for legality also

145. Finkelstein, 1972: 331.
146. Grayzel, 1989: 141.
147. Roth, 1946: 100.
148. Milano, 1963: 103.
149. Starr, 1946; Cohen, J., 1982: 85–88.
150. Grayzel, 1989: 204–206.
151. Grayzel, 1989: 149,141, nn. 1,2.
152. Grayzel, 1989: 44, n. 132.

explains the unusual phrasing of the bull *Vineam sorec,* issued in 1278 by Nicholas III to promote missionary sermons.[153]

Churchmen, including the pope, were slow to act when it came to encouraging missions to the Jews. They were also ambivalent, lamenting Jewish stubbornness but fearing conversion en masse, lest the Second Coming still not ensue. Church doctrine—which from Paul's day had explicitly linked the two events—would quite literally have been put to the lie.[154] Only in the late sixteenth century did the popes flirt with a mass conversionary policy, and still there were ambivalences.[155] Matters in the thirteenth century were no different. Unlike kings, the popes even scrupled at forcing Jews to attend missionary sermons. Despite his professed joy at a 1245 edict of James I of Aragon, which renounced the standard (yet papally censured) royal practice of confiscating converts' property, Innocent IV said nothing about the edict's second paragraph, which ordered royal officials to compel Jews to hear missionary sermons. Privately, Innocent may have approved; publicly, he felt obligated to remain silent, and did.[156] No doubt Nicholas III shared these sentiments.

It was his great desire, Nicholas said in the introduction to *Vineam sorec*—a bull that was sent to Dominicans and Franciscans in Lombardy, Sicily, Austria, and perhaps other places as well—to "enlighten" the Jews. In this spirit, preaching friars were to be trained and sent forth to expound the Gospel message. Yet *Vineam sorec* lacked teeth. Should the Jews prove stubborn and refuse to hear the preachers, Nicholas weakly concluded, he should be informed, "so that he might . . . consider some remedy." Nicholas had come to the edge of the cliff, so to speak, but balked at jumping. Jews could be prodded to attend missionary sermons, but not truly compelled. This was a doctrine that, until 1584, the popes would consistently honor.[157] Even in the early fifteenth century, Benedict XIII, whose conversionary devotion far surpassed that of any of his predecessors, went no further than calling for a Christian boycott against reluctant Jews. Nicholas III himself effectively reaffirmed his hesitations in *Vineam sorec* only three years after its issuance, reprimanding Franciscan friars at Pamplona in 1281 because their unwanted sermons were

153. Grayzel, 1989: 142.
154. Foa, 1988: 155–160.
155. Stow, 1992.
156. Grayzel, 1966: 254–257.
157. Simonsohn, 1990: 3:no. 1295.

unjustly disturbing Jewish communal prayers.[158] As arabesque—and lop-sided—as this course of action appears, it represented justice for the Jews. There were real, almost tangible limits, limina not to be crossed, borders that were clearly defined. Indeed, the bull and eventual canon *Sicut iudaeis non* had made these distinctions as early as the year 1119.

Equilibrium and Myth

Sicut iudaeis non was the basic text delimiting and stabilizing Jewish status. It was no accident that the order Nicholas III dispatched to Pamplona, curbing Franciscan sermons, was incorporated into a reissuance of just this text. A reissuance of *Sicut iudaeis* was also the setting for Martin IV's warning about slanderously accusing Jews before the Inquisition, as well as for Gregory IX's condemnation in 1272 of the charge that Jews used Christian blood in their rituals.[159] *Sicut iudaeis* was again reissued at Lyons in 1274, perhaps to confirm Humbert of Romans' proposition that Jews were to bow before Christian rule. What ensured the canon's efficacy was its contractual nature; indeed, its formulas are derived from the *tuitio* charters issued by emperors Louis the Pious and Henry IV to guarantee the rights, both general and specific, of Jews who offered "fidelity"—that is, service—in return for protection. In *Sicut iudaeis* that "fidelity" meant submission to the papally ruled Christian social order; it also meant the acceptance of canon law and of its controls. Only in return for the Jews' submission could their religious practices and "good customs" be safeguarded. To emphasize this mutuality, Gregory the Great prefaced the text's contractual formulas by paraphrasing the Theodosian Code: "Just as the Jews should not have license to do in their synagogues more than the law permits, so should they suffer no limitations on that which they are allowed."[160]

A reissuance of *Sicut iudaeis* ratified fundamental legal and constitutional doctrines; accordingly, from the time of Innocent III, the text was known as the *Constitutio pro iudaeis,* the "Jews' Charter of Rights" and also of their obligations. The rights in question went beyond those the text itself specified, embracing all the privileges canon law conceded the

158. Grayzel, 1989: 141.
159. Grayzel, 1989: 116–120.
160. Codex Theodosianus, 1954: bk. 16, title 8, law 18; Grayzel, 1966: 92; Stow, 1984: 16; see Grayzel, 1962.

Jews. For this reason, the leading fifteenth-century canonist Panormitanus said that the prescriptions of *Sicut iudaeis* defined the limits of the Jews' Perpetual Servitude. Putatively, *Sicut iudaeis* required no repetition at all, for it had been incorporated into Gregory IX's permanently binding *Decretals*.[161] But constant violations, Inquisitorial excesses, and even massacres had made repromulgation a necessity.

Repromulgations were especially requested by the Jews themselves; they knew that even their harshest detractors recognized *Sicut iudaeis*' validity. Eudes of Chateauroux, for example, did not consider his condemnation of the Talmud in 1248 incompatible with his signing copies of *Sicut iudaeis* reissued by Alexander IV, in 1255, and by Urban IV, in 1262.[162] It was in this context that the anonymous chronicler of the apocryphal events of the year 1007 placed full faith in the ability of an itinerant papal legate to halt a royal massacre by publicly reiterating *Sicut iudaeis*' principles. Jews relied so heavily on *Sicut iudaeis*—so confident were they of papal consistency with its terms—that they may have even forged copies of its text. It has been suggested (albeit hesitantly) that the versions attributed to Nicholas III and Martin IV, prohibiting forced sermons and denouncing false Inquisitorial accusations, were indeed forged.[163] Yet on several occasions, especially after 1267, *Sicut iudaeis* was reissued along with a renewal of *Turbato corde*, a conjunction that has raised some doubts as to whether the spirit of the latter had not vanquished that of the former.[164] In fact, the papal goal remained, as always, to achieve an equilibrium like the one signified when Panormitanus juxtaposed *Sicut iudaeis* and the doctrine of *Perpetua servitudo*.

Nevertheless, such equilibria fare better in theory than in practice. For example, Clement IV apparently accepted Thomas Aquinas' arguments about Jewish rights in natural law and ordered that a recently but dubiously baptized seven-year-old girl be returned to her Jewish father, who "was being tormented by fatherly emotions." Yet Clement also said that when the child came of age, she was to be restored to the Church, since the sign of baptism was indelible.[165] Was the Jewish father expected to raise his daughter as a Christian? So it appears. What is more, later popes seem to have accepted Clement's decision as setting precedent.

161. Panormitanus, 1559: on *Decretals*, bk. 5, title 6, canon 9.
162. Grayzel, 1989: 56,71.
163. Grayzel, 1989: 141, n. 2.
164. Grayzel, 1977.
165. Grayzel, 1989: 113–115.

More than two hundred years later, in 1496, Pope Alexander VI rendered an identical verdict under almost identical circumstances.[166] The two popes, one assumes, must have thought that they were doing equal justice to the father and to the Church. In fact, they were subordinating the "natural" rights of the Jewish fathers to the "divine" ones of the Church. The stakes were now also extremely high. In the sixth century, the Jews of Palermo had suffered only material loss when Gregory the Great decided that they were to receive monetary compensation for communal buildings that had been confiscated and consecrated as churches—since to deconsecrate them was unthinkably offensive to Christianity. In the thirteenth century, the Jews' losses in similar cases of conflicting priorities were often those of fatherly "emotional torment," as Clement IV himself put it.

The rules thus remained unchanged; their application was becoming ever more detrimental to Jewish well-being. New modes of enforcement had also been instituted. In order to see their Jewry canons enforced, the popes at one time had depended exclusively on aid from secular rulers, or, wherever possible, had threatened uncooperative Christians with excommunication. But in 1245, in his scholarly *Apparatus* to the *Decretals,* Innocent IV argued that the pope "may judge the Jews."[167] This claim had grown out of originally theoretical, academic discussions of whether papal power embraced nonbelievers as well as Christians. Once applied in practice, its potential effects were enormously dangerous—more so, in fact, than those any specific executive act could have produced. For what the popes really were claiming, as Innocent IV explicitly said, was the right to "judge the Jews if they act contrarily to their law in issues of morality, . . . and if they fall into heresy with respect to their own law." That is, the popes were claiming the authority to define Judaism's permissible limits. In so doing, they were seriously weakening *Sicut iudaeis'* guarantees, especially those pertaining to free Jewish religious practice. Nobody had so imperiled Judaism since the Theodosian Code had warned that the Jews' religious privileges would be abrogated should their rites offend Christianity. The Talmud, as Innocent IV himself admitted, was the first victim of this new jurisdictional claim. But even more harmfully—as seen in Bernard Gui's expurgation of Hebrew prayer books and in the Jews' Barcelona appeal of 1354—this claim exposed

166. Toaff, 1989: 194–195.
167. Kedar, 1979.

Jews and Judaism to direct Inquisitorial scrutiny, even when apostasy or its abetment was not at issue.

Yet by finding ever more direct ways to assert its authority over the Jews, by defining ever more sharply the lines of permissible Jewish behavior, and by succeeding in having canon law more consistently observed, the thirteenth-century papacy was also neutralizing potentially inflammatory accusations and, possibly, violent behavior—including its own. And it was doing so exactly as both Augustine and Gregory the Great had in the past, by reaffirming the traditional Pauline myth. Judaism, and Jews, were to be protected because their negative evaluation created for them a niche in the Christian cosmic structure. In this spirit, papal bulls couched concessions in expressions of papal graciousness to the otherwise stubborn and ungrateful Jews and tempered warnings against alleged excess in deliberately harsh rhetoric, yet not the inflammatory Agobardian rhetoric that spoke of danger to the Christian polity—a form of expression which mendicants, especially Franciscans, were beginning to resuscitate and expand. Consciously or not, by reasserting the Pauline myth, the thirteenth-century popes were combating newer and more threatening attitudes.

The popes took this stance for the benefit not of the Jews but of the Church.[168] Aquinas, in his balanced social structure, required that the Pauline Jewish myth be maintained to exemplify for Christians the fruits of the absence of faith. And the popes agreed with Aquinas. It was therefore beneficial to the Church that the Talmud not be indiscriminately burned, that Jews not be forced to attend missionary sermons, that entire communities not be charged with abetting heresy, and that ritual-murder libels, especially those accusing the Jews of ritually using Christian blood, be denounced. This papal position was also espoused by the majority in the organized Church. In the records of more than twenty-five local Church councils held in the second half of the thirteenth century, there is not one reference to the Talmud, the Inquisition, or forced sermons. On the contrary, papal Jewry policy as expressed in the canons of the *Decretals* was time and again overwhelmingly approved.[169]

The Jews themselves keenly observed this papal and conciliar conduct. However much they surely resented it, they also recognized its virtues. As Meir ben Simeon of Narbonne said in the letter "he would have liked to send the king" (Louis IX), the popes "[do] not forbid us our reli-

168. Stow, 1986b.
169. Grayzel, 1989: 235.

gion."[170] For the anonymous chronicler of the apocryphal events of the year 1007, the popes exercise *memshelet reshut* ("lawful authority"); kings represent *memshelet zadon* ("unlawful rule"). The pope guarantees Jewish safety in a Christianly dominated world; the king desires "one people"—perhaps an allusion to the "wicked" Antiochus Epiphanes, who (in the First Book of Maccabees, 1:10 and 1:41) is said to have issued a "decree . . . [that] his subjects were all to become one people and abandon their own laws and religion." It was thus possible to interpret papal Jewry policy by applying to it traditional Jewish exegetical categories. And thus (the 1007 chronicler seems to have been saying) that policy might also be made palatable, and manipulated, by appealing to the pope in moments of need. Yet even this perspicacious chronicler spoke only in hints. For papal aid was contingent on the Jews' first becoming wards of a papal guardian. And that, our author admitted, entailed accepting the papal claim—precisely as enunciated by Innocent IV—to define normative Judaism.

The price of Jewish safety was thus enormous. As canonically defined, Jewish due legal process[171] required the Jews to cede their honor. It forced them to remain passive while their papal guarantors called them a "miserable people" and to concede that "to this day, the dispersed Jews do not want to understand, as well as they might, that sufficient humaneness is accorded them when they are permitted to dwell among the faithful without burdensome disgrace."[172] Is it any wonder that some Jews, like Natan Officiel, the mid-thirteenth-century author of the *Debate of Rabbi Yehiel of Paris*, confronted the pope with a good deal of ambivalence? At the beginning of the "debate," the queen of France tells Yehiel that the pope has ordered the Talmud burned. Toward its close, the pope is proclaimed a sure protector.[173]

Natan may also have doubted the efficacy of papal Jewry policy. At one extreme, he saw Christians who—despite papal warnings—would and did attack the Jews. At the other, he saw the inconsistent kings. Medieval Christian secular (and sometimes ecclesiastical) rulers were far from being material susceptible to molding by the papal hand. Often they simply did not enforce the canons, especially those regarding the Jews' Christian servants, wet nurses, Easter week limitations, and the pledging of possibly stolen or even ecclesiastical items; exemptions from wearing

170. Meir ben Simeon, 71v, and cf. 65r,68r,70v,226v.
171. Watt, 1965.
172. Grayzel, 1989: 97–102.
173. Greenbaum, 1873: 12; Stow, 1984: 42.

the "badge" were at times offered for sale. Jealous for their jurisdictional rights—irrespective of their usual sympathy for Inquistorial aims—kings also decreed that the Inquisition could summon before it only those Jews whose prosecution had previously been royally approved. On the other hand, jealousy to preserve judicial primacy did not prevent kings from authorizing forced sermons, from exceeding canonical demands regarding lending at interest, from allowing the Inquisition to expand its mandated scope, and even from believing libels of ritual murder and desecration of the host.[174]

Kings and other secular rulers also had the final say. In the words of his hero Jacob ben Yequtiel, the 1007 chronicler argued to the Jews' assailants, "You do not have the governance over the Jews [in spiritual matters] . . . that belongs to the pope"; to the pope himself Jacob said, "The Jews live under your jurisdiction." But in fact, as Thomas Aquinas had stipulated, "the Jews were bondsmen of princes by civil bondage."[175] Kings, therefore, might—and did—limit at will the extent of papal Jewish rule, tolerating it only when it suited their royal interests. These interests, moreover—contrary to what is sometimes thought[176]—were not necessarily congruent with what today would be called secular, political ones but often transcended,[177] or at least enveloped them in a spiritual cloak. Did not Edward I justify his expulsion in 1290 by saying that Jewish lending activities were endangering the commonwealth's well-being, possibly inveighing, in the same breath, against the dangers of apostasy? Kings were being ever more attracted to the myth of Galatians, which prescribed that the son of Hagar be dismissed.

This process occurred, furthermore, at a moment of unheralded papal inconsistency vis-à-vis the Jews. At the end of the thirteenth century, the popes remained strangely silent when Jews were expelled from England and France. In the fourteenth and fifteenth centuries, they unpredictably revoked privileges and exemptions, burned the Talmud, and once temporarily expelled Jews from their domains. This was in contrast to their frequently allowing Jews to serve Christians—including themselves—as physicians, to move about without wearing a "badge," and even to sell Christians the unkosher quarters of slaughtered animals. This chapter in

174. Stow, 1984: 38; Roth, 1964: 77–78.
175. Stow, 1984: 36; cf. Chazan, 1987a: 730; Thomas Aquinas, 1947: IIa, IIae, quest. 12.
176. See Chazan, 1980: 318.
177. Jordan, 1989: 252.

papal-Jewish relations has yet to be properly examined; we note only that it unfolded in a period of extreme papal disorientation, including a schism that produced not two but three simultaneous papal reigns.[178] Yet even at this time, the theoretical continuity of papal policies did not become wholly unstuck. In 1422, Martin V reprimanded overzealous Franciscan preachers. Their emotionally charged sermons, he said, were inciting riots and causing damage to Jewish life and property. These sermons were also driving away from the faith Jews who, led by kindness, might otherwise convert. A year earlier, Martin had threatened to excommunicate anyone who forcibly baptized Jewish children against their parents' will.[179] Similar warnings were made as late as the first half of the sixteenth century.

But perhaps the best testimony to the continuity of papal Jewry policy, revealing also the policy's complexity and its inner contradictions, is provided by the example of the militant antipope Benedict XIII. In 1415, in the bull *Etsi doctoris,* Benedict attacked the Talmud, called for missionary sermons, proposed obligatory Jewish residential districts, demanded that Jews always wear the "badge," and decried Jewish communal self-rule, all for conversionary ends. Nevertheless, mindful of the canons, Benedict set firm limits. "Jews," he said—in an obvious paraphrase of *Sicut iudaeis*—"are never to be burdened beyond the limits of the present constitution, . . . to be molested, to be offended in their persons, or to have their goods seized . . . [Rather, they are to be treated] humanely and with clemency . . . For the troubled spirit is believed to offer a sacrifice acceptable to God on the altar of the heart when that sacrifice is offered voluntarily, not through coercion."[180] Unfortunately, the absence of coercion, as the popes sometimes defined it, left the Jews with little room to maneuver safely.

The King's Jews

Civil and Constitutional Status

The situation under the kings was often worse. Jews, as Thomas Aquinas said, were indeed the "bondsmen of princes" *(servi regis).* They were also

178. See Renouard, 1970.
179. Stern, 1893: nos. 22–36.
180. Stow, 1977: 288.

servi camerae nostrae ("serfs of the royal chamber"), *sicut nostrum proprium catallum* ("our effective property"), those who were to be treated *tanquam servi* ("like serfs"), or simply *judaei nostri* ("our Jews"). According to Meir ben Simeon of Narbonne, these terms were to be taken at face value. The Jews, he said, were the *'avadim* ("slaves") of the king (Louis IX of France). The understanding of kings and the Jews' other rulers seems to have been far less literal. In their eyes, the Jews were civilly "Jews"[181]—unique, set apart, and living under a law all their own, *ius singulare*.[182] In theory, this status bound Jews and rulers together, potentially guaranteeing the former's physical security.[183] The Jews' *ius singulare,* in particular, may have originated in the failure of the various so-called Landpeaces, instituted in the Empire from 1103, to protect Jews and other defenseless persons, such as women and priests.[184] Nevertheless, the reality was that (by no later than the age of Philip Augustus of France, 1180–1223) the Jews had become wholly dependent, for their rights, their privileges, and their governance, on royal or baronial dictates.

This dependency exacted from the Jews a high price. In particular, the freedom of movement that had once been so central a feature of their charters of privilege had been canceled. Jews were bound to their lords even more firmly than were serfs, who, if they fled, could gain their freedom after an absence of a year and a day. Jews, at least those of France, were always subject to being returned. They were also subject to *captiones* ("takings") of their outstanding credits, which were often accompanied by bodily arrests and the payment of heavy ransoms.[185]

Medieval kings, however, knew that actions such as these had to be justified. "The Ruler," said Lucas da Pena in the fourteenth century, "should personify the idea of justice."[186] Vassals fully agreed. Kings who tried to circumvent the law, like John Lackland of England (Philip Augustus' contemporary), found the continuity of their rule threatened. The Jews' dependence on kings, or on major barons, had to be based on law. Indeed, kings had to explain the Jews' very presence in Christian territories from a civil (nonreligious) and constitutional point of view.

181. Langmuir, 1981: 33.
182. Kisch, 1949: 150–153.
183. Baron, 1952: 11:7; see also Langmuir, 1981: 37.
184. Kisch, 1949: 132–138.
185. Jordan, 1989: 133, also 29,145.
186. Ullmann, 1946: 39.

This they did—or at least tried to do—by adopting terms like *servi camerae nostrae* or *judaei nostri*.

In a certain sense, the relationship between the Jews and their rulers indicated by these terms was already anticipated in the charters of privilege—such as those granted by Louis the Pious and Henry IV—which stated that Jews were being taken into their rulers' *tuitio,* or protection. This *tuitio* originated as a personal grant bestowed upon individuals who independently were considered "permanent residents" of the realm and who enjoyed a fully defined legal and constitutional status. By the time of emperor Henry IV (1090), however, *tuitio* was being given to Jewish communities as integral wholes, and no longer to individuals. The old basis for a collective Jewish status, the Roman law, had fallen into disuse; the *tuitio* offered by charters of privilege had taken its place and now became the primary justification for allowing the Jews to reside in a specific place. The Jews were neither denizens nor strangers, but people who had privileges *because* they were specially protected by direct royal patronage.

This definition—implying a passage by the Jews to a virtual yet imperfect feudal status—was no less obviously vague and defective to medievals than it is today. In 1157, the emperor Frederick I (Frederick Barbarossa) tried to remedy the situation. Ratifying the charter first given in 1090 by Henry IV, he said that the Jews were protected because *ad cameram nostram attineant* (or *pertineant*)—that is, because "they 'pertain' to our chamber."[187] It is doubtful that by "pertain" Frederick meant literally "to belong,"[188] but he did mean "subordinated," an idea to which other rulers also subscribed. For instance, about 1200, English kings altered the Jews' previous legal freedoms by obligating the Jews (as, incidentally, English serfs were likewise obligated) to seek justice only before the court of their immediate lord—namely, that of the king.[189] Charters containing similar stipulations were granted by monarchs as diverse as Richard I of England in 1189; "Edward the Confessor" earlier in the twelfth century, Sancho VI of Navarre to the Jews of Tudela in 1170, Alfonso II of Aragon to the Jews of Teruel in 1176, his grandson James I to those of Valencia in 1239, Duke Frederick II Hapsburg of Austria in 1244, and King Boleslav of Poland in 1264.[190] However, the

187. Aronius, 1902: nos. 280,171.
188. Chazan, 1980: 64.
189. Stacey, 1992.
190. Beinart, 1967; Parkes, 1938: 391–404; Chazan, 1980: 60–93.

truly essential concept in these charters concerns not subordination itself but to whom, or what, the Jews were to be subordinated. Frederick I's introduction of the word *camera* next to *pertineant* makes precisely this point.

The *camera* was the king's chamber and his treasury. But in the twelfth century it also denoted the permanence of the crown and the kingdom, their continuity above and beyond the actual span of a specific king's or duke's personal domain and governance. By saying that the Jews "pertain to the *camera*," Frederick was indicating that they were to receive rights and privileges because they were an integral part of the ongoing kingdom. Such a status, directly linking all citizens to the mythical, abstract body of the sovereign state, may be normal in the twentieth century, but in the twelfth century only the Jews found their status so defined and justified. Frederick Barbarossa's terminology thus bestowed upon the Jews a constitutional status that was not only unique but also a wholly artificial invention.

It is this artificiality which explains the introduction of references to subordination, and even to possession or servitude, found in English, French, and Spanish charters. Why, a contemporary might have asked, was the king giving Jews such rights as he did? Because, answers the (charter) text, the Jew is the king's *servus,* his *catallum,* his *res propriae.* And in the relatively strong kingdoms of France, England, and even parts of Spain, this blatantly hollow excuse could be, and was, accepted. For in those regions the Jews were truly dependents of the king or—at his will—of a particular baron, noble, or church prelate. The nobility had to accept that by proffering at least some justification, the king was conceding, however weakly, the necessity of respecting due legal process. In the Empire, things were different. Control over imperial Jews was anything but tightly held, and the claim to its possession had to be particularly well grounded. Consequently, Frederick I resorted to the ingenious phrase "pertain to our chamber."

Eight decades later, in 1234, Frederick II—a truly embattled ruler—emended his grandfather Barbarossa's formulation. The Jews, Frederick said (probably borrowing from usages like *tanquam servi*),[191] were given imperial protection not simply because they pertained to the *camera* but because they were its *servi*. Specifically, they were *servi . . . nostrae camerae speciales*—or, as the expression is familiarly rendered, "chamber serfs," living in a state of chamber serfdom.

191. Langmuir, 1981: 27–29; cf. Kisch, 1949: 145–153.

Contemporaries, justly dubious about Frederick II's innovation, re-sorted to locating its origins in myth. A late thirteenth-century legal compilation, the *Schwabenspiegel*, stated that when Titus conquered Jerusalem, he enumerated the Jews' laws and privileges and made them serfs of the Roman imperial chamber; later, in gratitude to Josephus Flavius, who had cured his seriously ailing son, Vespasian is said to have lightened the Jews' burdens of servitude.[192] In the event, chamber serfdom was a contrivance of the High Middle Ages invented when it became obvious that imperial control over the Jews could not directly be claimed (let alone realized). The acuteness of this problem in the Empire accounts for the term "chamber serfdom" itself; the predicament underlying the term's invention was really a universal one. Even with regard to other contemporary kingdoms, where terms such as "serf" appear principally to legitimate a recognized royal claim, one must ask what other civil or constitutional framework could have incorporated the Jews by that time. They were not foreigners, who held only specific and temporary charter rights; nor, despite their physical residence in towns, could they have been classed as townsmen, who were increasingly being related to their larger civic body on the basis of incipient public (rather than the old, and now waning, personal) law. Moreover, Jews did not acquire rights—especially those of citizens or citizenship—through Roman law, at least not in the Empire (where that law was once again brought to bear on Jewish status only in the early modern period). In the High Middle Ages, a Jewish status based on Roman law was possible only in Italy and, partially, in southern France, prior to the Capetian conquest of 1226. Paradoxically, Jews were not real serfs either, just as they could not legally be dubbed knights or ennobled. Nor did the concept of Perpetual Servitude, or even the usage of ecclesiastical theorists, who called the Jews "members" of the Church Militant, impinge on their civil status. The one solution was to invent a status; the result was to leave the Jews isolated and exposed.

The Effects of Constitutional Singularity

The major threat Jews faced was royal arbitrariness. If ecclesiastical Perpetual Servitude was molded by consistently applied precepts, the Jews' civil status was affected by erratic fiat or idealistic willfulness. Admittedly, in affairs of justice, especially criminal ones, Jews might appear in regular royal courts and plead their cases according to common

192. Aronius, 1902: 328, no. 771.

law, as in England they often did.[193] German legal collections, too, as well as court practice, show Jews being treated on a par with Christians, at least until 1286.[194] Kings may also have entertained and uniformly applied[195] some theoretical concept of Jewish justice, but its underpinnings were far from clear. Philip III of France had judges restore confiscated, nonusurious property to its Jewish owners. However, disregarding ecclesiastical flexibility, Philip permanently sequestrated everything connected to lending, whether principal or interest. Barons in southern France were also unexpectedly prohibited from supporting Jewish lending, as they had in the decades immediately succeeding the Capetian conquest. It was such behavior that evoked Meir ben Simeon's charge that the Jews' were the king's 'avadim.[196]

As a civilly unique body of persons, subject to almost exclusive royal control, the Jews could be indiscriminately exploited to attain royal ends—in particular, financial ones. The captio, or seizure of debts, became a regularly used device in both France and England. The French kings, to be sure, considered it a means to halt Jewish lending. The credits Jews relinquished were often put to pious uses, especially to financing the Crusades. But in the process, the king also raised huge windfall revenues, which, in the early thirteenth century, sometimes amounted to as much as 10 percent of annual royal income.[197] The English kings were perhaps more venal, as witnessed by the huge Bristol tallage of 1210 and the subsequent highly organized captio and taxation of 1239–1242.[198]

Kings also used their authority over Jews to widen powers over major vassals. At first glance, the treaties of nonretention made between the French kings and their barons (mandating the return of Jews fleeing from one region to another) appear to have apportioned royal power. In fact, this apportionment was more apparent than real; no French king could have dictated regulations about Jews to the quasi-independent Count of Champagne. The latter's entrance into a covenant with the king concerning the Jews was itself a royal advance, for the count had at least vaguely acknowledged that the right to initiate legislation pertaining to Jews was exclusively the king's. Justly, therefore, these covenants and treaties are

193. Langmuir, 1963: 203–204.
194. Lotter, 1988: 86–87.
195. Jordan, 1989: 151–152.
196. Stow, 1988d.
197. Jordan, 1989: 66–69,95–104.
198. Stacey, 1987.

today recognized as being among the first attempts at kingdomwide French legislation.[199] Indeed, the treaty drafted at Melun in 1230 unified all the major barons of the kingdom in a common legal observance. At Melun, moreover, Louis IX particularly exploited the situation, at the expense of even the Count of Champagne. The previous treaty between king and barons, made in 1223 by Louis VIII, had been a negotiated one. The treaty of Melun was imposed, by royal order.[200] A royal order, too—that of Rudolph I of Hapsburg, issued in 1286—attempted to apply the principles of Melun to the Empire. However, the right to restrict Jewish movement was not shared with imperial barons but reserved in theory for Rudolph alone, a fact that indicates imperial weakness.

Royal exclusivity vis-à-vis Jews was a potentially powerful weapon. In 1239, Frederick II locked horns with Gregory IX over the feudal income and taxes produced by Jews living in the shadow of the southern Italian abbacy of Monte Cassino. Frederick—whose rule was often more effective in large stretches of Italy than it was in his German domains—demanded these revenues for himself; the Jews, he said, were part and parcel of his imperial *camera*. His ploy went unchallenged. Mentioning neither ecclesiastical sovereignty nor the possible implications of Perpetual Servitude,[201] the pope countered only by censuring the attempt to change established custom, which assigned to the abbacy's monks all income derived from the Jews.

Through their civil status, Jews thus were victimized. It was principally the Jews who suffered when, in the Magna Carta of 1215, John Lackland granted minor heirs a moratorium on the interest they owed to Jewish creditors. Jews were exposed to risk once again, between 1269 and 1271, when complaints about the effects of insolvency on Christian borrowers finally convinced Edward I to prohibit Jewish lenders from further enjoying the benefits and security of landed collateral. The Jews, one might say, were made to function like a pressure valve. Their royal lord "opened and bled" them when his exploitation of the nobility became excessive. The mandated end to English lending, in 1275, also fulfilled the royal political obligation to respond to the needs of subjects, both high and low. But it was their own wounds, too, that kings assuaged at Jewish expense. The eventual wholesale suppression of lending in both England

199. Langmuir, 1960: 231.
200. Jordan, 1989: 133.
201. Grayzel, 1966: 192–193.

and France served the formal, as well as the sincere, interests of the kings' personal piety, even though, if truth be told, the principal from residual Jewish loans was still being collected by royal officials long after the expulsions of 1290 and 1306.

Worse than victimization was the fact of the Jew's "civil isolation." While others were slowly being amalgamated into the kingdom through common legal and ultimately constitutional bonds, the Jew was being pushed out. Moreover, was not the medieval civil polity also a Christian one, a *corpus reipublicae mysticum*, a holy entity? The Jew's civil isolation thus paralleled and was eventually identified with his religious one. And like the mythical Jew, the real one was fated eventually to disappear.

It is this merger of the Jews' spiritual and civil identities that the anonymous author of the tale of 1007 seems to have been emphasizing. In contrast to the pope (he wrote), the king was prepared—should the Jews refuse to convert—to revoke his protection and violently persecute them for motives that were unquestionably those of faith; for the king and those who attacked the Jews in his name intended "to make the Jews desert their Torah." But the Jews' steadfast adherence to Judaism, together with their troublesome legal status, was also a civil "impediment"—the very term used four hundred years earlier by Agobard of Lyons—standing in the way of the royal will to create "one people." The chronicle of 1007 was also not a wholly literary invention. In the thirteenth century, Louis IX was exploiting the Jews' dependence and civil vulnerability to espouse what has insightfully been called a policy of conversion induced through preaching and impoverishment.[202] Alternatively, Louis more than once flirted with expulsion. His grandson Philip IV (Philip the Fair)—following English and French royal and comitial precedents—did much more than flirt. The Jews were "his Jews"; the decision to retain or expel them was his alone to make.

202. Jordan, 1989: 154,180.

12 Expulsion

The story of the Jews' final decades in the kingdoms of Europe—England, France,[1] numerous imperial cities,[2] and eventually Spain and parts of southern Italy[3]—is a sorry tale of exorbitant taxation, arrests, false charges, libels, executions, and spoliation. Economic activity became less and less productive. Institutional and, above all, intellectual creativity effectively ceased. What is known in specific of this period derives almost without exception—at least for northern Europe—from records such as those pertaining to *captiones* or royal arrests on charges of clipping coins. The precise and difficult course of the expulsions themselves must be learned from brief passages in Christian chronicles or Jewish poetic laments. The number of those expelled, possibly no more than five thousand in England, fifty thousand in Italy, and a hundred thousand in France and Spain, cannot be determined. Except for Spain, the decrees of the major expulsions have not survived in full.

Jews were expelled from England in 1290 and from France in 1306. In both countries, there had been numerous local and regional expulsions after the 1250s. Eventually, Jews were expelled from much of the Empire, although not before the end of the fifteenth century. They were expelled from Spain and Spanish-ruled Sicily in 1492, from the Kingdom of Naples (ruled by a collateral Aragonese branch) in 1510, and from various segments of the Italian north toward the end of the sixteenth century. By about 1550, western Europe contained very few openly professing Jews (crypto-Jews, the so-called Marranos in the Netherlands and on the Iberian peninsula, formed a class unto themselves).[4]

1. Jordan, 1989; Stacey, 1992; idem, 1990; and see idem, 1993.
2. Hsia, 1988; Haverkamp, 1981; Baron, 1952: vols. 9 and 11.
3. Kriegel, 1977; idem, 1978b; Gampel, 1989; Milano, 1963.
4. Israel, 1985: 5–35.

Explaining why the Jews were expelled, especially from England and France, is extremely difficult. For example, there is very little evidence, if any, linking expulsion to specifically ecclesiastical initiatives.[5] Nor is it easy to ascribe it to royal economic wants.[6] At the time of their expulsion, tallaging (taxing) and fines had everywhere massively diminished the Jews' financial base.[7] The number and value of their now illegal, yet still outstanding loans had also been severely reduced. They had very little money left to despoil. In England, the expulsion may have netted Edward I no more than nine or ten thousand pounds.[8] In France, a tallage (tax) of 1295, whose results were equal to twelve times the regular annual Jewish tax, brought French Jews near to financial ruin.[9] Admittedly, the expulsion of 1306 brought King Philip the Fair a windfall in property and chattels, as well as in uncollected debts, that was about five times what he had collected in 1295. And popular belief held that the departing Jews had hidden away vast, untapped treasures. Yet even if Philip the Fair needed an especially large sum to finance his wars, as well as perhaps to offset the effects of his recent devaluation of French money,[10] prudence would have dictated that he not reverse traditional policies. Since the time of Louis IX, monarchs had collected much more from the Jews in carefully spaced installments.

A once and for all spoliation suggests an awareness that Louis IX's programs—notwithstanding their conversionary bent—were no longer viable. The kingdom as it had come to be in the later thirteenth century lacked the means to hold onto the Jews. The medieval kingdom was maturing; it was mobilizing itself politically. And one means of mobilization was to achieve consensus and solidarity by exploiting existing antipathies to the Jews, and even by expelling them.[11] Yet this was not only a manipulative process; it was one that kings themselves effectively participated in.[12] Together with their subjects, medieval kings were pledging their fidelity to the kingdom, not as a modern nation[13] but as the

5. Roth, 1964: 68–90; Singer, 1964.
6. Chazan, 1980: 318.
7. Richardson, 1960; Elman, 1936.
8. Roth, 1964: 88; Richardson, 1960: 230.
9. Jordan, 1989: 198–213.
10. Schwarzfuchs, 1967.
11. Jordan, 1989: 255.
12. Kriegel, 1978.
13. Baron, 1952: 11:192–283.

corpus reipublicae mysticum, the "holy kingdom with its holy people." These were terms that originated as propagandistic slogans,[14] but they had struck firm roots; their verity was widely accepted, even by their royal promoters.

The Nature of the Medieval Kingdom

By the end of the thirteenth century, the secular kingdom had become a sanctified entity in people's minds. As contemporary texts affirm, the kingdom had replaced the Church as the *communis patria* (literally, "common fatherland," but perhaps a term best left untranslated); knights were prepared to die for it—*pro patria mori*—in battle.[15] Kings, notably Louis IX, but others, too, struggled to reform the kingdom's political and even its financial institutions in terms of Christian ideals; Louis' special goal was to purify the land and prepare the way for a Crusade.[16] Membership in such a body was obviously limited. Those who would deform or corrupt it were not welcome. John of Paris, around 1302, thus spoke of the kingdom and of its people as a body composed of a head and many members.[17] John was particularly concerned with the role of the pope. Were the pope, he said, to make himself into the kingdom's second political head, the body politic would be disfigured. By implication, that body's members, too, ought to be formed correctly. Artificial though the metaphor may be, it was one that gained prominence at the time of the Jews' expulsion, and, as such, it may have contributed indirectly to hastening the event. For in the "Christian polity," was not the Jew considered to be a misshapen appendage[18] which handicapped the entire body?

No one was more consciously committed to realizing these metaphoric visions of the kingdom than were the thirteenth-century kings. At that time, such a commitment made good political sense. In the medieval world, the sacred and the profane had to be coordinated as though they were one.[19] Thus, Frederick II's unremitting struggle with the papacy

14. Spiegel, 1977.
15. Kantorowciz, 1957: 232–249.
16. Wood, 1989: 398.
17. John of Paris, 1971: 133,135–136,182–183,192–196.
18. See Langmuir, 1960: 225,232,239–244.
19. Watt, 1988.

about control of his Italian domains did not prevent him from voraciously extirpating heresy and supporting the Inquisition. Right belief was a fundamental political desideratum. Edward I concurred, responding evasively, but also dutifully, in 1285, to a petition in favor of Inquisitional judges made by the Franciscan archbishop of Canterbury, John Pecham.[20] Philip III, too, encouraged the Inquisition, even if he, like Edward, was concerned that it not usurp royal jurisdictional prerogatives. This commitment to defend the faith and to uphold piety was no formal one. Edward's father, Henry III, so tarried at every chapel and wayside shrine—on the route to negotiate feudal agreements with Louis IX—that even Saint Louis saw fit to order chapels down the road closed, lest Henry never arrive at all. Louis IX dressed and behaved like a monk. Frederick, Edward, and Louis all spent years on Crusades. Louis made the Crusade into the telos of his rule.[21]

Admittedly, the piety of certain kings, especially Edward I of England, is arguable.[22] But irrespective of their personal bents, there is no question that medieval monarchs attributed spiritual dimensions to their rule. In their minds, they presided over a body politic, whose continuity was symbolized by the king's crown and also by his "two bodies": the physical one, which perished at his death, and the political one, which symbolically lived forever, just as did the kingdom itself. Hence the cry, "The king is dead—long live the king!" Herein lie the seeds of a concept that matured only in early modern times: that of the sovereign state,[23] the fictional and undying corporate body in which all moderns live and to which, knowingly or not, they attribute spiritual qualities.[24] The kingdom as a corporation was an idea already known in the thirteenth century, thanks to the renewed study of Roman law. Kings drew on this idea and viewed themselves as that corporation's guardian. The kingdom was their ward, a minor (as legally all corporations are) for whose physical and spiritual welfare, the *utilitas communis* ("public utility"),[25] they, the kings, were responsible.[26]

20. Grayzel, 1989: 297.
21. Jordan, 1979: passim.
22. Richardson, 1960: 226; Prestwich, 1985; Stacey, 1989; see also Langmuir, 1979: on Bachrach, 1977.
23. Kantorowicz, 1957: 271–272.
24. See Berger, P., 1969.
25. Kantorowicz, 1957: 163; Powicke, 1962: 523.
26. Post, 1964; Ullmann, 1965.

Res quasi sacrae and the Expulsion of the English Jews

In dealing with the Jews, kings could not divorce themselves from any of these images, all the more because these images were regularly expressed through such reworked theological idioms as *communis patria, corpus mysticum,* and, most notably, *res quasi sacrae* ("quasi-holy things"), the term used by the thirteenth-century English jurist Bracton to refer to "things pertaining to the king's peace and jurisdiction."[27] Was it not, then, a foregone conclusion that in their ward's best interests, kings would have to restrain their Jews—that perennial threat to the integrity of the *utilitas communis*—by assiduously applying canon law, by prohibiting lending, or by forcing Jews to convert? But might kings not also abuse their power as guardians by monopolizing the Jews, as the barons often complained? Such a monopoly could have been theoretically sustained. Jewish serfdom and the king's claim to exclusive Jewish jurisdiction, medieval legists might have argued, derived from the Roman legal maxim that the king is freed from or above the law *(rex legibus solutus est)*. Alternatively, it might be said that the king was forbidden to alienate or renounce that which belonged to the crown or fisc (that is, to the *camera*—in this case, its *servi*, or the English equivalent thereof). Yet in the long run, kings understood, or were made to understand, that regardless of theoretical underpinnings—which thirteenth-century jurists did invoke in sundry cases brought against the English crown[28]—artificial advantages such as the ones they derived from the Jews and their unique status could not perpetually endure. Even as guardians, kings realized, they too had to live under the rule of law; for, by common opinion, kings, like their subjects, were "the debtors of justice."[29] This realization and its implications guaranteed the Jews' eventual expulsion. Indeed, in England, the Jews were expelled during what might be called a protracted constitutional crisis.

This crisis[30] occurred on ecclesiastical, baronial, and knightly fronts. The ecclesiastical crisis—actually part of a constant struggle between crown and church for what the latter called "ecclesiastical liberties" (meaning the right to run its own house)—began in 1285. Archbishop

27. Kantorowicz, 1957: 168.
28. Kantorowicz, 1957: 163–164.
29. Kantorowicz, 1957: 163.
30. See esp. Stacey, 1992; idem, 1990; see also Miller, 1987.

John Pecham petitioned Edward I and protested, among other things, royal interference in trials of apostates to Judaism and the continuing malice of Jewish usurers. Pecham also demanded that the king "reconfirm the charters." On these Jewish issues, Pecham would receive no definitive royal answer until 1290. The charters he referred to were the Magna Carta, first issued by John Lackland in 1215 to resolve a civil war, and the subsequent Forest Charter of 1217. During the course of the century, and especially during the baronial revolt in the late 1250s and 1260s, these charters became a rallying point. English kings were forced to reconfirm them in 1217, 1225, 1237, 1253, and (what is important for our story) in 1297 and 1300.[31]

The intent of the charters was to make the king observe the law. As far back as the reign of Henry II, in the twelfth century, the barons had watched the king enhance his powers by enforcing statutes.[32] It was only a matter of time before the barons started demanding of the king that he, too, accept legal constraints. Accordingly, the Magna Carta stipulated consent as a prerequisite to extraordinary taxation, set limits on royal interference in clerical elections, reaffirmed the liberties of the Church, and, most important, mandated the observance of due legal process. The king had at least agreed[33] to place himself under the law.

In practice, kings were forever circumventing these restrictions. To prosecute wars, including the Crusades, they raised revenues, with or without baronial consent. They also curbed ecclesiastical liberties that would have put clerics and Church courts beyond their judicial control. Such actions provoked harsh responses. Profligate spending, coupled with frequent demands for new monies, led, in 1258, to Henry III's temporary cession of his rule to a baronial council. In 1296, Edward I clashed with the pope, Boniface VIII, on the issue of taxing the clergy,[34] who normally "were brought into the fold to be shorn."[35] Eventually, Edward won. He bested the laity, too, never fully accepting the principle of consensual taxation until the Charter Confirmation of 1297.[36] Nevertheless, on the subject of consent, the barons had made headway. Kings had even grown accustomed to summoning Great Councils, or parliaments, in order to

31. Lunt, 1957: 146.
32. Stacey, 1987a: 4–9.
33. Lunt, 1957: 139; see also Stacey, 1991.
34. Lunt, 1957: 204.
35. Powicke, 1962: 523.
36. Lunt, 1957: 201.

gain this consent. The only other way to raise funds was through emergency levies, which were theoretically exempt from the rule of consent yet which could be imposed only on such pretexts as the need to pay a royal ransom. There were also the Jews, a royal chattel, whom the kings could, and did, tax at will. Hence the debilitating Jewish taxation of the 1240s to 1260s, which brought the Jews to financial ruin. Indirectly, however, these taxes ruined Christians, too. And thus in part was generated the eventual constitutional crisis.

Every time the Jews were taxed, they raised the necessary funds by either selling overdue bonds of indebtedness to the highest bidder (at discounted rates) or by handing over these bonds for immediate repayment to the king's special court of the Jewish Exchequer.[37] In either case, the original Christian borrower was bankrupted, whether directly, through his insolvency, or indirectly, when the Christian purchasers of his overdue bonds, or the kings, confiscated the land pledged as collateral. Such bankrupted Christian borrowers must have seen themselves as doubly wronged: the "devastation of [Jewish] usury" had not only destroyed their material wealth but had also made them rather than the Jews into the real payers of the Jews' tallage. Worse, this was a tallage to which these borrowers (usually Christian knights) had not consented. Indeed, to be taxed at royal will was the mark of the Jewish royal serf, not of freemen such as they were. By tallaging the Jews, therefore, the kings must have appeared to be inverting the social order. What is more, clauses in the Magna Carta forbade dispossessions when debts owed to Jews by minors fell into royal hands.[38] These clauses were often violated, and this is precisely what must have been happening here.

Dispossessions were also favored by the kings. For dispossessions, by ensuring a rotation of scarce landed resources, allowed royal power to entrench itself.[39] Such redistributions were also achieved by the discounted sales of Jewish bonds.[40] These sales not only led to the redistribution of land but also reduced the estates of great barons and magnates, the very nobles who had pretensions of making the kings share royal power with them. As a result of the brisk trade in discounted Jewish bonds, major barons often lost choice manors (previously held by now insolvent vassal-tenants) to royal favorites, or to the queen or her mother,

37. Richardson, 1960: 153–154,168–170; Stacey, 1990.
38. Stacey, 1987a: 9.
39. Wood, 1989: 402.
40. Richardson, 1960: 71–76,111–117; Stacey, 1990.

or even to a monastery. Such purchasers were normally beyond a baron's feudal control or even his ability to demand rents and services. A prime baronial demand during the revolt of 1258 was that Henry III correct the damage caused by these sales.[41] The issue appeared again among the complaints that led to the prohibition of Jewish lending against landed collateral in 1269, and was a reason for the mandated end to Jewish lending in 1275. Yet the practice never stopped, no matter how the volume of Jewish lending was reduced; instances even occurred during the years following the expulsion.

The kings again used the Jews to their own advantage with respect to the Magna Carta's guarantee, "To no one will we sell, to no one will we deny or delay right or justice,"[42] a clause that was understood as enabling freemen to plead their cases before whatever court they chose. For the kings, by-passing this guarantee, were permitting no one to contest Jewish loans except before royal justices, specifically those of the Jewish Exchequer. In effect, freemen were being reduced to a legal par with the royal Jews, who always had to approach the king's bench.

But the English kings were sensitive to the popular mood.[43] They knew that their legal manipulations, the effects of bankruptcies and land transfers, and, in particular, Jewish lending itself were threatening political stability, for all three were perceived to be gnawing away at the social order.[44] Moreover, as Jewish funds dwindled and lending, after 1275, became a clandestine practice, the cost of credit soared. The result was a vicious circle; insolvencies and dispossessions became more probable, and rage potentially increased—directed, of course, at the culpable Jewish lender. Furthermore, anyone might succumb to debt, and, accordingly, anxieties must have become universal, no matter how out of proportion they were to the real volume of Jewish loans.

These anxieties had to be calmed. Consequently, it was imperative that the royal guardians of the "public utility"—the phrase Edward I so frequently invoked to rally baronial support—bring lending to a halt. Edward I's decision, in 1287, not to revive Jewish lending was thus inescapable. The hope for royal profit was by then too slight; the social and political price was potentially too high. Most of all, the constitutional order established by the Magna Carta (whose insistence on lawful behav-

41. Stubbs, 1900: 377; see also Baron, 1952: 11:205.
42. Stacey, 1987a: 6.
43. Langmuir, 1960: 242.
44. Langmuir, 1960: 216–219,242.

ior essentially favored the king perhaps even more than the barons) was jeopardized. The barons might again revolt, or, more simply, the barons and the commons might withhold a much needed tax. The fact that, in all of this, non-Jewish lenders were, at least for the time being, passed over in silence only testifies to the mythical dimensions that both the Jews and their lending had attained.

In weighing his actions, the king also had to consider the clergy. John Pecham had complained in 1285 about usury. Within the scope of canon law, which obliquely consented to "no immoderate interest," that complaint could be circumvented. But Pecham's complaint about apostasy could not be. Apostasy in a medieval kingdom was unthinkable; and, in the later thirteenth century, apostasy to Judaism was not a spurious issue. The pious Henry III had made great efforts to convert the Jews. He had opened a *domus conversorum* ("home for converts") and forced monasteries to feed and shelter converts, much as had his contemporary Louis IX. Like other royal contemporaries, including James I of Aragon, Louis and Henry believed that missionizing was a kingly obligation. So, too, did Henry's son, Edward I. From 1280, Edward forced Jews to attend missionary sermons. Probably, Edward was responding to the bull *Vineam sorec* and to Archbishop Pecham's urgings. But he was responding willingly. Canonically speaking, forced sermons were illegal. Edward could have flatly rejected any entreaties about sermons.

However, Edward's sermons had little practical effect. It was Henry III who was more successful. From the 1240s to the 1260s, about three hundred of England's five thousand Jews converted. Yet these converts, including the notables Elias L'Eveske and Isaac of Norwich, appear to have been persuaded less by reason than by the threat of capital punishment or by Henry's financial soakings.[45] The potential for such converts to apostatize was extremely great. And apostatize they did, as indicated by Pecham's complaint of 1285, which was echoed the following year in the bull that Pecham solicited from Pope Honorius IV, *Nimis in partibus*. Edward I also agreed readily that it was his duty to intervene (once, of course, the matter of judicial prerogatives had been settled).[46] To make matters worse, a Dominican, Robert of Reading, had converted to Judaism in 1274. Others, perhaps, might follow his example. During the 1280s, English official circles may well have viewed apostasy with great

45. Stacey, 1989: 13.
46. Grayzel, 1989: 295; Baron, 1952: 11:205.

concern.[47] The claim that in ordering the Jews expelled, Edward singled out apostasy—along with usury—as a fundamental reason for expulsion must be weighed seriously.[48] Clearly there were spiritual as well as civil dimensions to Edward's conception of the "public utility."[49] Moreover, one would be hard pressed to see where these two dimensions might be separated and made distinct. Religiosity, social perceptions, and political aims had become intertwined, much as they had in Visigothic Spain. Accordingly, it was Edward's binding obligation to counter the threat which the "Jewish impediment" was posing to England's "common weal."

But measures taken toward this end had so far resolved nothing. Instead, they had brought into even sharper relief the conflict of royal, baronial, and knightly interests, which on a day-to-day basis overshadowed possibly common goals. The very *Statutum de Judaesimo* of 1275, which forbade future lending, was structured as a standard charter of *tuitio* (in the tradition of charters issued by Louis the Pious, Henry IV, and Frederick II). Only the legal and civil status of the Jews was still being regulated by this device, a fact that emphasized both its artificiality and the special relationship between the Jews and the king. The basic crux was thus left unresolved. Indeed, even with lending outlawed, the Jew remained outside the normal system of law, and his master, the king, above it. By exploiting his Jewish serfs, the king could continue unjustly to enhance his prerogatives at baronial or knightly expense.[50] This situation might also have continued indefinitely. Even the most "constitutional ruler," as some medieval kings have been called,[51] is loath to alienate his prerogatives. Moreover, Bracton had said that to do so was illegal.[52]

The Final Act

An opportunity to resolve these issues presented itself in 1290. As would happen three hundred year later at Udine, the English, in 1290, were presented with an *occasione* for expelling the Jews. It was, moreover,

47. Stacey, 1989, 1992.
48. Hyams, 1974: 270; Logan, 1973: 214.
49. Powicke, 527.
50. See *Statutes of the Realm*, 1810: 1:220–221.
51. Strayer, 1971.
52. Kantorowicz, 1957: 168.

truly an occasion. The idea to act so radically and decisively was not one that had slowly matured. Just thirty days before the actual expulsion, Edward had sealed the royally supervised Jewish loan chests, anticipating a tallage that would have taken months or even years to collect, notwithstanding the Jews' woefully depleted funds. Yet this tallage was only part of a larger picture. In 1290, Edward desperately needed revenues. His recent diplomatic initiatives against the French in Gascony had put him heavily in debt.[53] So desperate was Edward, that already in May 1290 he had convoked a parliament and asked the assembled barons, knights, and prelates to approve a subsidy (tax). But the parliament was in a fiesty mood. Before it granted a subsidy, questions had to be discussed and royal concessions made. These discussions produced the idea of the expulsion. With the aid, in particular, of two recent studies,[54] let us look at how this idea came about.

The barons at the 1290 parliament were especially exercised by the question of franchises. These were special baronial privileges which, for years prior to 1290, Edward had been trying to undermine, since they visibly limited his administrative powers. A particularly valued franchise allowed barons, in lieu of royal officials, to execute royal commands on baronial estates. And in 1279, a parliamentary trial had ended with the verdict that barons were entitled to exercise any franchises they held by "immemorial tenure." The king countered by having his royal attorneys appeal—in royal courts—every baronial claim to immemorial tenure made between 1285 and 1290. The barons now insisted that these royal appeals be halted. On May 21, Edward responded. He issued the statute *Quo warranto* which concedes the immemorial tenure of franchises certifiably granted before 1189.[55] Ostensibly, this statute does not concern Jews; in fact, it may have sealed their fate.

A second issue raised at the 1290 parliament concerned Jews directly. On July 8, only ten days before the expulsion, Edward issued the statute *Quia emptores*, again in reply to baronial complaints. Had the statute mentioned Jews explicitly, it would have been superfluous. Its purpose was to allow tenants of lords to alienate (sell) their holdings freely, yet also to ensure that such a transfer did not prejudice feudal privileges—in other words, to allow sales, but not to deprive lords of their traditional

53. Stacey, 1992; cf. Harris, 1975: 3–48, esp. 41.
54. Stacey, 1992; idem, 1990.
55. Stacey, 1992.

rights and income. A new holder would have to become the lord's tenant, just as had been the person who transferred or sold the land—regardless of whether this new holder were the queen or even a monastery. Before *Quia emptores,* these privileged purchasers escaped the bonds of the feudal chain. With respect to Jews in particular, *Quia emptores* meant that the sale of their bonds of indebtedness would no longer result in the piecemeal dismemberment of baronial and knightly estates.[56]

But the barons remained correctly suspicious. Indeed, immediately after the parliament, Edward reneged on enforcing the statute. Moreover, in the not infrequent event that land legally fell to the king, the statute—or any other control, for that matter—would have been meaningless. The king of England, who held lordship *(dominium)* over the entire country, could be nobody's tenant. Would it not then be preferable to attack the problem frontally, or at least that part of it involving Jews, whose indirect role in land transfers through bond sales was still a palpable one? The anxious barons, furthermore, had probably inflated in their minds that role's true dimensions. As for the method of attack, had not Edward I himself already shown the way?

Following the example of other regional French lords, Edward—as lord of vast French estates—had, in 1289, expelled the Jews of Gascony. Nobody has satisfactorily explained these regional expulsions. The motives may have been quick financial gain, the desire to escape the justice of the French king expressed through claims over a local baron's Jews, or simply the exercise of the option to act decisively, which was more readily available to a local noble than to a king. There was also a momentum to these expulsions, which in fact had also occurred in English towns and boroughs.[57] Besides, by the later thirteenth century, the Jews' mythical image, against the background of imputed events, had rendered their presence wholly undesirable in every region. In 1290, there was no reason why the English barons and knights in parliament should not ask the king to expel all English Jews.[58]

Edward must have liked the proposal; or perhaps, sensing the broad base of the discontent, it was one he made himself. He may also have initiated the subsequent step, although so, too, could the knights of the shires, many of whom—even more than the barons—still owed Jews

56. Stacey, 1992.
57. Roth, 1964: 81–83; Richardson, 1960: 225–226.
58. See Jordan, 1989: 181–183.

money. That the two sides reached an agreement is certain. In return for expelling the Jews, the knights and commons would grant the king a large immediate subsidy.[59] The king would take possession of the Jews' bonds and then allow the knights to repay gradually these so-called *debita iudaeorum*, minus the interest (as was the practice, and, for that matter, precisely as the Magna Carta dictated). Since Edward alone held the records of Jewish loans, and since only he could have known how lopsided the agreement was (the subsidy brought him 115,000 pounds, as opposed to the approximately 10,000 pounds in outstanding Jewish loans), he had every reason to accept it. Yet even had the knights been aware of the agreement's lopsidedness, they may still have acted as they did, out of fear and anxiety. It was better to pay insurance now, despite the high premium, than to face a later disaster.

Still, Edward may have been most persuaded to expel the Jews by something even more powerful than his immediate windfall—no matter how much in the short range he needed the money—and that persuading factor was the statute *Quo warranto*. Like *Quia emptores*, this statute was not enforced. Yet more important to the king than whether he managed to circumvent the statute was baronial consent to its implications. In accepting *Quo warranto*, the barons had admitted that, as a whole, franchises belonged to the past. Franchised baronial courts, in particular, were frozen into the outmoded feudal matrices of 1189 and their modernization was blocked. From now on, the only court that could keep pace with current needs was that of the king, the *curia regis*, which would soon achieve a monopoly, or at least a near monopoly, on justice and its dispensation.[60] But if that was so, then the king no longer needed to exploit his "chattel," the Jew, as a means to enhance his judicial prerogatives. Rather than depending on the wholly superseded Carolingian *tuitio* (as it was applied to the Jews) in order to bring Christian debtors and others into the royal courts, the king could henceforth dominate justice by relying on the developing English common law.

Thus, whatever the Jews' role in the slow process (since the end of the twelfth century) toward royal control over justice, that role was now played out. *Quo warranto*—by itself, in conjunction with *Quia emptores*, and followed by a baronial subsidy—made this fact absolutely clear. Moreover, since the concept of "Jewish chattel," like that of *servi cam-*

59. Stacey, 1990.
60. Munro and Strayer, 1942: 429–430.

erae, was purely a lawyers' construction, to expel the Jews was fully legal. By ridding himself of his now unwanted Jewish chattel, Edward I was not illegally diminishing the real substance of the *res quasi sacrae* embodied by the royal prerogative. Indeed, he may have even been enhancing it, trading—as he effectively did—the fictitious substance of his Jewish chattel for the real one of expanded royal justice. Rather than impeding the Jews' expulsion—as did the canons and the *ius commune* in Italy— legal theory in England may actually have encouraged it.

This logic may also explain why the English clergy, as well as the pope in Rome, did not object to the expulsion's canonical impropiety. To do so would have been politically pointless. At the same time, the English clergy's silence may really have been one of tacit approval. For did not the English prelates at the 1290 parliament vote for what appears to have been a large subsidy?[61] Nevertheless, their motives remain unclear. As late as 1286, at the synod of Exeter, the diocesan bishops made no reference to John Pecham's protests of 1285, nor did they recall the demands of the recent bull *Nimis in partibus,* concerning apostates, the Talmud, and conversionary sermons. No record of a clerical call for expulsion exists.[62] With the exception of some of its radical members such as John Pecham, therefore—and even Pecham respected canonical limits—the English prelates, until virtually the eve of the expulsion, appear to have held fast to traditional ecclesiastical postures. *Quia emptores* may have changed their minds. For however personally English bishops and abbots viewed the Jews, however faithful they were to canonical propriety, and however seriously they took the charges of apostasy and other Jewish malfeasance, they, like the king, had also benefited from the Jews through transactions such as the purchase of bonds and the acquisition of rent-free land. *Quia emptores* threatened to bring all this to an end. Had the statute become operative, even churchmen would have become baronial tenants. Yet such a situation would also have liberated prelates from weighing the church's material glory against that of its spirit. In turn, they might choose to ignore traditional doctrines about a necessary Jewish presence and allow themselves to be enveloped by the mounting calls for expulsion. Regrettably, we will never know whether this is what really happened.

But it is certain that the prelates did not openly object to the expulsion. In fact, said the chronicler Pierre de Langtoft, "there is nobody who

---

61. Grayzel, 1989: 294–297.
62. Grayzel, 1989: 257–258.

opposes it."[63] In which case, it appears that for an instant, the expulsion truly did create "one people"—or at least the illusion of it. The superficial unity of purpose achieved on July 18, 1290 (the day the edict of expulsion was issued), quickly faded. So completely did Edward I renege on his statutes that in 1297 he was compelled anew to reconfirm the charters. In the fourteenth century, friction between king and barons once more led to violence. Yet the edict of expulsion was never revoked. As befitted the *res quasi sacrae* of the now "much wider political nation,"[64] political and social conflict had been resolved by a Pauline solution. The mythical Jew—this time the son of the slave Hagar—had once and for all been driven out.

France, Spain, and the Empire

England at the end of the thirteenth century was distinguished by a certain cohesiveness. For example, there was universal acceptance of a common law, of a unified royal rule (despite the fact that individual kings and their programs were sometimes hotly, even violently, challenged), and of the need for baronial consultation and participation, which eventually gave birth to the idea that sovereignty belonged to the "king *in* parliament." These commonly held perceptions of governance may have helped ensure the expulsion's finality. None of them had been compatible with the Jew's special laws, status, and observances. By contrast, in the much less cohesive entity of France, the expulsion—although first decreed by Philip IV in 1306—became final only under Charles VI in 1394. The expulsion of 1306 was also from royal lands alone. Those barons who held a small percentage of French lands free from (or, strictly speaking, outside) the royal dominion had either expelled their Jews previously or were not going to expel them at all. Jews would not be wholly ejected from southeastern France until 1501;[65] they were never permanently expelled from the papal territories around Avignon, near Marseilles. As for the Jews dismissed in 1306 from royal France, they were recalled by Louis X in 1315, dismissed anew by Philip VI in 1322, and recalled a second time by John II in 1359, even though these recalls were far from complete, especially the second one, which encompassed only a limited number of Jewish bankers. Such a checkered pattern suggests that in

63. Baron, 1952: 11:210; see also Langmuir, 1960: passim.
64. Stacey, 1992: 21 (typescript).
65. Iancu, 1981.

France, neither a well-grounded cohesiveness nor a royal-baronial consensus but primarily a royal initiative determined the course of events. Indeed, was not one motive for expelling the Jews to rally popular support for royal political goals?[66]

But unilaterality, manipulativeness, and even inconsistency must not be mistaken for cynical exploitation. In a kingdom so heavily dependent, as was France, on the concept of a unifying sacred ruler[67] and on the vision of itself and of its people as constituting an unblemished *corpus mysticum,* propaganda was destined eventually to be accepted as fact; at which point, the kingdom's leader—who perhaps took these political metaphors more seriously than anyone else—would consider himself obligated to eradicate perennially dangerous sources of opposition and deviance. And this the French kings did, eliminating first the Cathar heretics and then the Jews. At the same time, the catalyst that pushed the French king to act, given his latitude for personal maneuver, could have been less than a constitutional crisis. Even libels of ritual murder seem to have been sufficient, as was the case in 1182, when Philip Augustus temporarily expelled the Jews.[68] The memory of a purported Jewish eucharistic desecration about 1290 may have bolstered Philip the Fair's decision to expel the Jews in 1306.[69] The expulsion of 1322 has been attributed to Louis X's supposed belief that Jews had made league with lepers and others in order to poison French wells.[70]

More substantially, the French kings may have felt that the Jews' continued presence allowed barons or even foreign rulers to interfere in what the kings believed to be exclusively royal jurisdictional concerns.[71] Baronial meddling was in fact partly responsible for the failure of the royal program intended to stop usury and promote conversion, a failure that weighed enormously on the royal spiritual and political conscience. Not unconnected were disputes with the popes and the papal Inquisition, such as Philip the Fair's objection to the Inquisition's judging apostates and their Jewish accomplices without first securing royal permission.[72] The French kings may also have needed to distract attention from unsa-

66. Kriegel, 1978; see also Menache, 1983; Kohn, 1988.
67. Grabois, 1984.
68. Jordan, 1989: 18–19.
69. Jordan, 1989: 191.
70. Ginzburg, 1989: 20.
71. Saperstein, 1986.
72. Stow, 1984: 40–41.

vory maneuvers such as the currency devaluation of 1306. Still, no single one of these motifs may alone be considered responsible for the expulsion. Indeed, because of the very personal nature of the initiative, the events leading to the French expulsion have eluded precise identification.[73]

The French kings and princes were also unpredictable. Charles of Anjou, the nephew of Louis IX, expelled the Jews of Maine and Anjou in 1289, because, he alleged, they practiced perfidious usury, seduced Christians to become Jews, and wantonly had sexual relations with Christian women.[74] Charles also seems to have been the principal antagonist behind the massive forced conversion of southern Italy in the early 1290s. Yet in 1306, Charles—or his son Robert, who may have just then come to power—also accepted into his Provençal domains Jews fleeing from the Kingdom of France.[75] Such inconsistency may partially explain why the king recalled the Jews in 1315 and 1359. Nevertheless, the process to a final expulsion was inexorable. As occurred in England, a continued Jewish presence came to be viewed ever more negatively.[76] Accordingly, on three separate occasions, at an—almost certainly unplanned—moment, the Jews of France were expelled.

In 1492, a similar process took place on the Iberian peninsula. Against the backdrop of the truly self-conscious (if far from unified) contemporary Spanish society,[77] Ferdinand of Aragon and Queen Isabella of Castile decided that there could be no further postponement in resolving a problem which had been a burning issue ever since riots in 1391 had resulted in massive forced conversions throughout Spain—namely, that of Jews living alongside *converso* new Christians. The problem was exacerbated following the Tortosa disputation in 1413 and 1414, when thousands more Jews "voluntarily" converted.[78] And internal Jewish weaknesses never allowed matters to stabilize. The efforts of the Jewish communities to restructure and build strong defenses failed, in part because so many Jews, including notable ones, had converted, in part because old social problems, many related to interfamily rivalries, re-

73. Jordan, 1989: 199–202,255–259.
74. Jordan, 1989: 182.
75. Jordan, 1989: 181–182,230.
76. Jordan, 1989: 257–258.
77. Braudel, 1972: 802–826.
78. See Baer, 1961: 2:95–243; Stow, 1977: 278–289; Yerushalmi, 1971: 1–50; Cohen, G., 1966: 182; Netanyahu, 1967: 235–245.

mained as intractable as ever. The greatly reduced numbers and communities of Spanish Jews were also weakened by a skewed social structure. A few privileged, oligarchical grandees stood at the top; a large base of generally poor artisans was fixed below. Spanish Jewry was suffering from its own failings.[79]

However, Spanish Jewry was ruined by neither its social weakness nor the skepticism that purportedly was so rife among its upper classes.[80] The final Spanish Jewish crisis was generated from without. The conversionary pressure, perhaps ebbing temporarily toward the mid-fifteenth century, never wholly ceased. The number of *conversos* constantly swelled, and the often justified Christian doubt that the *conversos* were loyal to their new faith accordingly grew. Matters then worsened when the Spanish national Inquisition (founded in 1478) failed to rid the country of allegedly heretical *conversos* and punish their Jewish abettors. During the fifteenth century, mendicant friars added to the predicament by accusing the Jews of host desecration and ritual murder. But the Jews' presence in Spain was exceedingly well rooted. The Spanish monarchs long hesitated to consider solving the *converso* question by any means so radical as expulsion. Even purported Inquisitorial plots[81] left them unmoved.

Marvelously, the approximately 100,000 Spanish Jews who never converted seem to have continued their daily and personal routines without interruption, albeit in difficult social and economic straits. This reality is confirmed by notarial documents from Navarre, a small enclave that formally remained outside Spain until 1498, but otherwise differed little in its manners and mentalities from the rest of the Iberian peninsula.[82] In other regions, especially Castile, even Jewish autonomous powers remained intact through the 1480s. Only beginning in this decade were the Jews denied these and other communal powers and were experiments tried such as restricting Jewish areas of residence or expelling Jews from specific localities and regions. Still, even in the first months of 1492, Ferdinand and Isabella were not yet contemplating a change of course.[83]

The actual decision to expel the Jews was made at the last minute. Seizing his *occasione*—namely, the conquest of Granada and the expulsion of the Moors in 1492—the Chief Inquisitor, Thomas Torquemada,

79. Baer, 1961: 244–323; Suarez-Fernandez, 1983: 250–283.
80. Baer, 1961: passim; Gutwirth, 1989a.
81. Baer, 1961: 324–423; see also Beinart, 1981a; Kamen, 1985; Edwards, 1984.
82. Gampel, 1989: 22–86.
83. Suarez-Fernandez, 1983: 282.

convinced the monarchs that a continued Jewish presence in Spain was no longer viable.[84] In the words of the decree of expulsion, Ferdinand and Isabella were now persuaded that the Jews were causing irremediable "damage to the realm," because they were contaminating the purity of the *conversos'* faith. Accordingly, the Jews had to go; for "to remedy . . . this great opprobrium and offense to the Christian religion . . . [necessitates] eliminating its principal cause."[85] Religiosity and politics had become indissolubly one.

That oneness, however, was a prescription for mass exodus, not violence, at least not that of a direct or organized kind. Most Spanish Jews were able to arrive safely in Italy, the Ottoman Empire, and especially Portugal, although in 1497 the ones in Portugal were all forcibly converted. In the Empire—possibly because of its enormous political and social instability—opportunities to purify the Christian polity more often than not produced mayhem. Jews were slaughtered in the Rindfleisch massacres in 1298, in the Armleder massacres in 1336–1338, and most especially in forty-seven distinct episodes during the first two years of the Black Death after 1348. By 1350, all the great Jewish communities of the German south and west had been destroyed. Some of these communities were later revived, but only on a selective and limited basis. By the mid-fifteenth century, the once great medieval community of Frankfurt numbered no more than seventeen families. The charters now granted these communities were of specifically limited duration. They also soon proved to be worthless.

Beginning in the early fifteenth century, Jews were expelled from one urban center after another. In the second half of the century, a series of libels led to riots and to the "legal" execution of hundreds of Jews by burning. Jews also suffered "takings" and financial spoliations, as they had in Capetian France. These seizures provided the emperor not only with money but also with a way to reassert authority in cities that had otherwise become virtually independent. The Jews owed him taxes, the emperor claimed, since they were still his *servi camerae*. The cities sometimes agreed, with the result that the Jews were doubly taxed, first by the emperor and then by the cities themselves. Alternatively, the seizure was carried out by territorial princes and ecclesiastical lords to whom the emperor had transferred imperial rights, including that of chamber serf-

84. Kriegel, 1978b; cf. Haliczer, 1973; Kamen, 1988.
85. Baer, 1936: 404–408.

dom, as imperial power itself slackened and became increasingly decentralized.

Still, decentralization often postponed expulsion. Individual local rulers, rather than the emperor, decided when expulsion had become unavoidable. In the case of independent towns, Jews were able to resist until (as occurred in Speyer in 1435 and Regensburg in 1519) they became pawns in internal conflicts, usually between ruling oligarchies and those contesting their power.[86] The Protestant Reformation and the teachings of Martin Luther heightened these problems.[87] Believing that the Jews were partly responsible for the supposedly Judaizing sect of the Sabbatarians, Luther attacked "the Jews' lies" and intervened to urge expulsions at princely courts. As it turned out, he was unsuccessful. During the latter part of the sixteenth century, rulers calculatingly invited Jews to resettle the German cities, which they did in ever growing numbers. Luther's view was also challenged. Landgrave Philip of Hesse, querying the leading Protestant theologian Martin Bucer, asked whether Luther's teachings did not violate the soteriological doctrines of Paul.[88]

To what extent more abstract factors played a role in all of these conflicts, expulsions, and violent episodes, we may only speculate. The later thirteenth century marked the height of medieval growth; during the fourteenth century, Europe suffered "disease, social upheaval, political instability, and a general malaise and unhappiness."[89] It was a time of economic dislocation, monetary shortage, and, above all, famine. Between 1315 and 1322 people starved by the thousands. Only the decimations of the Black Death at mid-century eliminated the problem. In response, "the men of the fourteenth century resorted to all sorts of desperate expedients as a way of finding a solution to their troubles, whose ultimate root was much more mysterious to them than the economic collapse of our century to us. They betrayed, deposed, and murdered kings; they engaged in savage wars against each other; they tried to summon divine assistance through mystical experiences or by joining heretical cults; they burned witches. But nothing seemed to help."[90]

---

86. Baron, 1952: 11:271–280; Voltmer, 1981; Maimon, 1981; Haverkamp, 1981; Littman, 1928.
87. Oberman, 1984; Stow, 1977: 234–248; Luther, 1971; idem, 1971a; idem, 1971b.
88. Israel, 1985: 10–13,38–45; STOW, 1977: 238–239.
89. Cantor, 1963: 577.
90. Cantor, 1963: 578.

What of the immediately preceding decades? The end of the thirteenth century, when the Jews were expelled, was not a period of enormous upheaval. And yet, matters had already taken a turn for the worse. In the 1290s, there were scattered bouts of famine. Productive arable land was becoming scarcer, grain dearer, the cost of seed and of the credit to purchase it higher; less grain and meat per capita were arriving in the markets.[91] Disastrous climatic conditions reduced output even further. Old manorial relationships between lord and tenant, and between lord and serf, too, were changing, especially through the conversion of service obligations into financial ones. These "feudal" shifts were paralleled by those in towns and cities, where growing stratification was distinguishing rich "bourgeois" from craftsmen, laborers, and the chronically unemployed. The rich had developed an appetite for rural estates. These they often purchased from insolvent nobles; and then, as new bourgeois landowners, they were allowed to move out of town and escape urban tax rates, to the detriment of the entire urban population.[92] Exacerbating all these changes was an overexpanded population, the ultimate cause of the early fourteenth-century famines.[93] Yet in the later thirteenth century, people did not understand the relationship between demographic growth and the supply of food. They were primarily aware that daily life, whether in the cities or on rural estates, was becoming ever more difficult and that they and their children were sometimes forced to go hungry.

In this perplexing atmosphere, charges against the Jews were bound to acquire additional force. Frustration and confusion were imperceptibly transferred from the unfathomable and attached to that which people believed they understood. The store of other components constituting the mythical Jewish image was thus increased by the addition of social and demographic ones. Together, they all militated toward the growth throughout Christian society, at the end of the thirteenth century, of "a profound desire that [the Jews] would just go away for good."[94] The Jews had become *personae non gratae*, a thoroughly unacceptable minority in a now wholly alien world. The result was expulsion or, in those places where Jews still resided after 1300, sporadic violent attacks: the massacres in the Empire between 1298 and 1348, the assaults during the southern French Shepherd's Crusade of 1320, and the riots of 1391

91. Mundy, 1973: 151,173.
92. Mundy, 1973: 250.
93. Herlihy, 1967: 104–120; Gottfried, 1985: 5:3–9.
94. Jordan, 1989: 258.

throughout the Iberian peninsula—all accompanied by forced and voluntary baptisms. Jewish life throughout western and central Europe was steadily retreating; its center was moving eastward and to the south.

The East, Italy, and the End of an Era

The fourteenth and fifteenth centuries in fact witnessed new beginnings. Major Jewish communities arose in Poland and in what eventually became Austria and Hungary. Numerically these communities remained small until the turn of the sixteenth century. Polish Jewry, in 1500, numbered only about 30,000. However, by the end of the century, this number had increased more than fivefold;[95] it was then that the so-called Golden Age of Polish Jews began.

In many ways, the story of these eastern Jewries continued that observed in the west. The charter of 1244 issued by Frederick Duke of Austria is a modified *tuitio* text that differs from predecessors primarily because of its emphasis. As Rudiger in 1084 settled Jews in Speyer to enhance the town's commercial prospects, Frederick now settled them in Austria specifically to lend; so, too, in 1264, did Boleslav of Poland. In both places, the Jews were also made dependent on their rulers for rights and privileges, meaning that from its beginnings, eastern European Jewry was a civilly distinct body, limited by the same liabilities and negative image that had characterized the Jewries of the west.[96]

Within the Jewish communities, too, there was continuity. Poland's first Jewish settlers may have included members of the Hasidei Ashkenaz.[97] Western communal institutions were also transplanted. In Poland, in the seventeenth and eighteenth centuries, the Ashkenazic board of *Sheva tovei ha'ir* ("the seven selectmen") developed into a potent, nationwide jurisdictional and governing force, the famous Council of Four Lands. What did not survive in eastern Europe was the homogeneous nature of the early Ashkenazic communities. Homogeneity steadily yielded to an oligarchic social structure, typified by alliances between wealth and learning and by a semipatriarchal family structure.[98]

New communities also arose in the center and north of Italy. Jews, often from Rome and its environs, settled in small to middle-sized towns

95. Israel, 1985: 26–31.
96. Weinryb, 1973: 33–40.
97. Ta Shema, 1988a.
98. Katz, 1971: 199–209; Ben-Sasson, 1959: 186.

in Tuscany, the Marche, and Emilia-Romagna, principally to engage in lending. In the later fourteenth and fifteenth centuries, Jewish merchants and lenders migrated to the Veneto from the Empire; Jews from Provence entered northwestern Piedmont and Savoy. These Jews were attracted by commercial opportunities as much as they had needed to escape a difficult social and political situation. Perhaps more significant than the rise of these new Italian centers was the survival of older ones. Those in the central Papal States even expanded. The Jewries in southern Calabria and Apulia, weakened by the mass conversions of the 1290s, revived. Sicilian Jews under Aragonese rule formed a case apart. Economically diverse, although mostly poor, approximately fifty thousand of them were expelled in 1492, as were Jews elsewhere in the south between 1510 and 1541.[99]

The bulk of Italian Jewry was saved from this fate by the *ius commune* (Italian Roman common law). Once Jews were admitted into an Italian town (Venice, Genoa, and scores of other places constantly refused to do so), this law ensured that their right of residence was, for once, theoretically upheld. It also worked as a brake against endless Franciscan denunciations.[100] Jews did suffer canonical discrimination, and sometimes civic authorities required them to wear distinguishing signs or clothing.[101] Yet with the notable exception of the murder accusation of 1475 at Trent (and some sporadic local outbursts), Italian Jews were immune from the libels and repeated violence of the Empire and from the kind of conversionary pressures that were applied in fourteenth- and fifteenth-century Spain. Thus, in Italy, Jewish existence ought to have continued uninterruptedly; but it did not.

In part, Italian Jewry's troubles were caused by ecclesiastical radicals. Around 1494, for example, the Franciscan Bernardino de Busti called (unsuccessfully) for the Jews of Milan to be expelled, since their blasphemies were irreversibly endangering the city's social integrity. To make his point, Bernardino appealed not to myths but to Roman law, which, he said, the Jews had once too often violated.[102] Such arguments underlie the claim of the jurist Marquardus de Susannis, who, when in 1556 the Jews were expelled from his own northeastern Italian city of Udine, said that this had been done "by the best law" *(optimo iure)*; in fact, he could

99. Shulvass, 1973: 1–11.
100. Poliakov, 1977: 142.
101. Hughes, 1986.
102. Stow, 1988: 55–59; see also Simoncelli, 1988.

cite no one law in particular. It was this very expulsion which stimulated Marquardus' cousin Pagano, an Udinese city councillor, to write that its events provided the longed-for *occasione scacciare gli ebrei* ("opportunity to chase out the Jews"). It appears that private attitudes toward Jews in the European south were turning public policy in the same direction that it had taken in the north.

But this Udinese expulsion—as well as the others like it which occurred in the second half of the sixteenth century in various northeastern Italian towns and in the Spanish-ruled Duchy of Milan[103]—was not the turning point for Italian Jews. Nor was the expulsion from the small towns and villages of the Papal State, which was decreed in 1569 by Pius V, reversed in 1585 by Sixtus V, and again renewed in 1593 by Clement VIII—only to be canceled de facto almost immediately afterward.[104] The justifications for expulsion proffered by Pius V and Clement VIII—that the Jews nefariously practiced usury, seduced Christian women, received stolen goods, and dealt in magical incantations—did not mean that the popes had wholly abandoned the past. Rather, an irrevocable change in the tenor of Italian Jewish life was signaled by the decision, in 1569, of the former Chief Inquisitor Ghislieri—now Pope Pius V—*to exempt* from the expulsion the Jews of Rome, Ancona, and the papal French possessions in and around Avignon. In 1593, Clement VIII followed Pius V's lead, even allowing expellees to enter Rome and Ancona. The willingness of the popes to accept the arguments and rationales of Franciscans such as Bernardino da Busti was, therefore, limited. Their essential concern was not to be rid of the Jews but to gather as many of them as possible within the walled neighborhoods where Jews had been required to live since July 1555. The papal expulsions thus propelled the Jews not from society but *into* the ghetto.

Indeed, the papally instituted ghettos were not born of a "profound desire" to eliminate a supposed Jewish danger. That (as Ferdinand and Isabella had correctly observed in 1492) could be accomplished only by a general expulsion; partial expulsions or segregation in designated areas of Jewish residence—which were fitfully tried in Spain, as well as at Frankfurt am Main in 1462—were ineffective. Moreover, the papally instituted ghetto was not a compromise between idealism and pragmatism, like the agreement made to permit a permanent Jewish settlement

103. Sonne, 1954: 183–220; see also Simonsohn, 1982.
104. Stow, 1977: 34–35; 1991.

at Venice in 1516 (the word "ghetto" actually derives from the location in Venice where the Jews were forced to dwell).[105] Rather, the papal ghetto was an entirely new institution whose purpose was to integrate the Jews into society by way of their conversion.

In the edict of 1555 establishing the Roman ghetto, Paul IV made his aims perfectly clear. He was, he said, taking this step because Christian society tolerated the Jews "for the very reason [*ad hoc ut*] . . . that they make all haste to arrive at the true light of the Catholic faith."[106] This was a novel formulation. In the past, papal letters had either restricted Jews in order to "restrain their insults" or justified toleration on the grounds of "Christian charity." Paul IV now dropped all reference to charity and linked toleration to restriction and to the hope for the Jews' imminent conversion. Paul IV and his successors also pursued this conversion with unheralded vigor. They burned the Talmud, enlarged the house for converts (whose founding in 1543 had anticipated the actual beginnings of the new papal policy), burdened Jews with unbearable taxes to break their will, and violated canonical limits by forcing Jews to attend conversionary sermons. Most of all, these popes insisted on the ghetto. The ghetto was to anchor a program of rigorous canonical regulation. Its existence was to provide what in 1513, in a long discourse on the Jews' conversion, two Camaldulese monks called the "salutary pious lashes" *(piis verberibus)* needed to predispose the Jews to accept Christian truth.[107]

That the discipline of pious lashes might foster the Jews' conversion was not a new idea. It had been discussed as early as the thirteenth century by Alexander of Hales (possibly basing his argument on a text in Gratian's *Decretum*); touted in the fourteenth century by the Spanish convert Abner of Burgos; and even briefly applied in the early fifteenth century by the Spanish antipope Benedict XIII.[108] The sixteenth-century popes, in committing themselves irrevocably to a program of pious lashes, were thus finally realizing a long-standing ideal. Yet in doing so, the popes were also being quite up to date. The notion that a highly supervised, disciplined ghetto life might make the Jews change their ways went hand in hand with the novel sixteenth-century social theory that criminal incarceration and the enforced regimen of life in a "workhouse"

105. Pullan, 1971: 510–538; Ravid, 1987.
106. Stow, 1977: 292–298; Prosperi, 1989: 174–175.
107. Giustiniani, 1773, cols. 631, 717–719; Stow, 1977: 217–220 (trans.).
108. Stow, 1977: 278–289.

could personally reform and socially reintegrate criminals and indigents.[109]

The originality of the ghetto's integrative purpose cannot be overstressed. In the past, radical measures such as segregation or absolute expulsion had often followed a conversionary policy's failure; they had not heralded its inception, as in the Papal State. The systematic pursuit of conversion by the popes was itself revolutionary. Paul IV found its justification in the portentous events of his day. The Protestant schism, the advances of the Turks on European soil, and the air of thorough reform within the Catholic Church convinced this fanatical, octogenarian former Chief Inquisitor that the End of Days was near. But if this was true, then, as Saint Paul had said, the moment for the Jews "to enter" had arrived. Their mass conversion had to be precipitated, even if doing so necessitated resorting to what other contemporaries called "predisposing force." As Paul IV wrote to his sister Maria, he was obligated to "do the violence" that would hasten the advent of the End of Days.[110] At the same time, that "violence" had its limits. Following the precepts of Saint Paul (in Romans), as indeed Paul IV did, the Jews were to be retained, not expelled; absorbed, rather than excluded.

Paul IV's followers ratified his break with the past. However little they may have been apocalyptically motivated and however much they may have wavered about pursuing large-scale conversion, they all realized that old solutions no longer worked. The medieval equilibrium—open toleration of the Jews in exchange for their accepting an inferior status (which the medieval popes had, for so many centuries, considered to be a social and religious imperative)—was now permanently upset. Paul IV's policies were thus sustained. Indeed, in 1589, in order to relieve severe overcrowding in the Roman ghetto, Sixtus V enlarged its area rather than allowing select Jews to live outside. The ghetto was to be all-inclusive, as well as enduring. Enduring, too, was the doctrine of pious lashes. As late as 1668, an anonymous cleric of the papal chancellery argued that Jewish banking in the Papal States should at last be brought to a halt, since "true Christian piety does not indulge the Jews in usurious matters. Rather it strictly restrains them from becoming wealthy; not, of course, to coerce them into becoming Christians, but to remove any obstacle in their way. As Gratian has said: 'If the sons of the freewoman are to be provoked

109. Yutte, 1981: 49–52; Stow, 1986: 185–186.
110. Stow, 1977: 269–273.

by the *tribulations of the lash* to doing good,' how much the more are *servi* and the sons of the handmaiden to be aroused to convert through laborious want."[111]

Ideas like these gradually took hold in the other Italian cities and states where Jews still dwelled. Within one hundred years of 1555, the ghetto was instituted throughout Italy's center and north.[112] And even without its founder's original zeal, the ghetto remained unique. Unlike expulsions, with their finality, the ghetto separated the Jews only temporarily from society, isolating them physically and psychologically—especially at night, when the ghetto gates were locked—but always reminding them that the duration of their isolation was theirs alone to decide. Whether they wanted to leave the ghettos in the Papal State or those in the secularly ruled Italian duchies, Jews might always convert, as hundreds in fact did, and so reenter society. Medieval Jews had never been forced to make so stark a *social* choice.

The Italian ghetto was thus a limbo, and as such it endured until the revolutionary ideas that the Napoleonic invasion of 1797 imported into Italy forced its demise. The modern, secular concept of citizenship and of the contractual, nonconfessional state simply could not tolerate the ghetto as an institution. The ghettos of the Papal State, however, and especially that of Rome, continued to exist until 1870 (with only a brief interruption between 1798 and 1800); the fact that the Papal State was neither wholly theological nor wholly secular in nature ensured the status quo. Conversionary pressures accordingly continued, and each year ten Roman Jews on average converted.[113] But the mass conversion Paul IV dreamed of never materialized. For the Jews of Rome, as well as those of Ancona, the ghetto became "our *ghet*" (a pun on the Hebrew for "bill of divorce"). And so "divorced," they retreated into their own Holy Community *(kehillah kedoshah)*, established mechanisms of self-defense, and, with little fear of being compromised, borrowed at will—although ever less frequently—from the culture outside.[114]

Yet what occurred in Rome and in the other Italian ghettos has an overarching significance, beyond what it reveals about the Jews' determination or the failure of papal policy. With the institution of the ghettos,

111. *JTS,* fol. 95, citing Gratian, C. 23, q. 5, c. 33, gloss, and C. 23, q. 6, c. 4; Stow, 1992b.

112. Simonsohn, 1960; Roth, 1946: 320–328.

113. Milano, 1970.

114. Stow, 1992.

the Jews of early modern Italy were time and again forced to confront an existential dilemma: there was no longer any way for them, as Jews, to continue living within society;[115] at the same time, they were constantly being challenged to give up their Judaism and to enter society anew. But this dilemma of being forced to choose between ghetto insularity and social integration was one also faced by Jews in countries other than Italy. The question of choosing, in whole or in part, between isolation and integration has been and in some ways continues to be one of modern— no longer medieval—Jewish history's central problems. How paradoxical it is that the Jews were first made to confront this choice by, of all people, the Counter-Reformation popes!

This paradox, of course, predetermined the result. The self-abnegating, conversionary terms in which the option of social integration was first framed by Paul IV made it wholly unacceptable. The Jews of the ghettos preferred insularity. Only later, when modern secular states began offering somewhat more advantageous terms, did western Jews begin to weigh the alternative. However, even these Jews remained cautious. Were they being asked to embrace an entirely new doctrine, or what was, in fact, Pauline theology in secular dress? It was impossible to know how much one's Jewish identity could be retained. For that matter, Jews could never be certain that once they had opted for integration, they would be fully received. All too often, they were not—as the course of modern Jewish history has revealed time and again.

115. See Bonfil, 1992.

Bibliography

Abraham ben David of Posquierres. 1964. *Sefer ba'alei ha-nefesh*, ed. J. Kafah (Jerusalem).

Adelman, H. 1987. "From Zion Shall Go Forth the Law: On the 500th Anniversary of the Birth of Joseph Karo," *Jewish Book Annual* 45: 143–157.

Adler, M., ed. and trans. 1907. *Sefer massa'ot shel R. Binyamin* (London).

Aescoly, A. Z. 1956. *Jewish Messianic Movements* (in Hebrew; Jerusalem).

Agus, Irving. 1952. "Democracy in the Communities of the Early Middle Ages," *Jewish Quarterly Review* 43: 165.

—— 1965. *Urban Civilization in Pre-Crusade Europe* (New York).

—— 1969. *The Heroic Ages of Franco-German Jewry* (New York).

Alberigo, J., ed. 1962. *Conciliorum Oecumenicorum Decreta* (Basel).

Albert, Bat Sheva. 1974. *The Case of Baruch* (in Hebrew; Ramat Gan).

—— 1990. "Isidore of Seville: His Attitude toward Judaism and His Impact on Early Medieval Canon Law," *Jewish Quarterly Review* 80: 207–220.

Alexander of Hales. 1925. *Summa Theologica* (Quaracchi).

Allport, Gordon. 1958. *The Nature of Prejudice* (New York).

Ankori, Zevi. 1959. *Karaites in Byzantium* (New York).

Archivio Storico Capitolino. Sezione III, Notai Ebrei (Rome), Fascicle 9, Book 12.

Aronius, J. 1902. *Regesten zur Geschichte der Juden in Frankischen und Deutschen Reiche* (Berlin).

Ashtor, Eliyahu. 1979. "Palermitan Jewry in the Fifteenth Century," *Hebrew Union College Annual* 50: 219–253.

—— 1980. "Gli ebrei nel commercio Mediterraneo nell'alto medioevo," *Gli Ebrei nell'Alto Medioevo,* Centro Italiano di Studi sull'Alto Medievo (Spoleto).

Assaf, Simha. 1925. *Meqorot le-toledoth ha-hinukh be-Yisrael,* 4 vols. (Tel Aviv), "Huqe ha-Torah."

—— 1942. *Tequfat Ha-Geonim* (Jerusalem).

Augustinus Aurelius. 1950. *City of God,* trans. M. Dods (New York).

—— 1965. "Adversus Judaeos," *Fathers of the Church* (Washington, D.C.) 27: 391–416.

Avi Yonah, Michael. 1976. *The Jews of Palestine: A Political History from the Bar Kokhba War to the Arab Conquest* (Oxford).

Avneri, Zvi. 1960. "Going to Gentile Courts" (in Hebrew), *Zion* 25: 57–61.

Bachrach, Bernard. 1973. "A Reassessment of Visigothic Jewish Policy," *American Historical Review* 78: 11–54.

———— 1977. *Early Medieval Jewish Policy in Western Europe* (Minneapolis).

———— 1984. "Enforcement of the *Forma Fidelitatis*: The Techniques Used by Fulk Nerra, Count of the Angevins (978–1040)," *Speculum* 59: 796–820.

Baer, F. Y. 1936. *Die Juden im Christlichen Spanien* (Berlin).

———— 1961. *A History of the Jews in Christian Spain,* trans. L. Schoffman, 2 vols. (Philadelphia).

———— 1961a. "Israel, the Christian Church and the Roman Empire," *Scripta Hierosolymitana* 7: 79–150.

———— 1985a. "Hamegammah ha-datit-ha-hevratit shel 'Sefer Hasidim,'" *Studies in the History of the Jewish People* (Jerusalem) 2: 175–224.

———— 1985b. "Ha-yesodot ve-ha-hathalot shel 'irgun ha-kehillah ha-yehudit be-yemei ha-beinayim," *Studies in the History of the Jewish People* (Jerusalem) 2: 60–100.

———— 1985c. "Sefer Yossipon ha-'Ivri," *Studies in the History of the Jewish People* (Jerusalem) 2: 101–27.

Baldwin, John. 1958. "The Concept of the Just Price: Theory and Economic Reality," *Journal of Economic History* 18: 418–434.

———— 1970. *Masters, Princes, and Merchants: The Social Views of Peter the Chanter and His Circle,* 2 vols. (Princeton).

———— and C. W. Hollister. 1978. "The Rise of Administrative Kingship: Henry I and Philip Augustus," *American Historical Review* 83: 867–895.

Baron, S. W. 1948. *The Jewish Community,* 3 vols. (New York).

———— 1952. *A Social and Religious History of the Jews* (Philadelphia), vol. 11.

———— 1972. "Plenitude of Apostolic Powers and Medieval Jewish Serfdom," in *Ancient and Medieval Jewish History,* ed. A. Hertzberg and L. Feldman (New Brunswick).

Barraclough, Geoffrey. 1961. *The Making of Medieval Germany,* 911–1250 (Oxford).

Battista De' Giudici. 1987. Apologia Iudaeorum, ed. and trans. Diego Quaglioni (Rome).

Bazak, J. 1968. *Beyond the Senses* (in Hebrew; Tel Aviv).

Becker, Marvin. 1968. *Florence in Transition,* 2 vols. (Baltimore).

———— 1981. *Medieval Italy: Constraints and Creativity* (Baltimore).

Beinart, Haim. 1967. *Kitve zekhuyot kellaliot* (typescript; Jerusalem).

———— 1971. "Hispanic Jewish Society," in *Jewish Society through the Ages,* ed. H. H. Ben-Sasson (New York).

———— 1981. *Atlas Karta Le-Toledoth 'Am Yisrael be-Yeme Ha-Beinayim* (Jerusalem).

———— 1981a. *Conversos on Trial: The Inquisition in Ciudad Real,* trans. Yael Giladi (Jerusalem).

Ben-Sasson, H. H. 1959. *Hagut ve-Hanhaggah* (Jerusalem).

———— 1960. "Musagim u-misi'ut be-historiah yehudit be-shalhei yemei ha-beinaiyim," *Tarbiz* 29: 297–312.

———— 1971. "The 'Northern' European Community and Its Ideals," in *Jewish Society through the Ages,* ed. H. H. Ben-Sasson (New York).

———— 1976. *A History of the Jewish People* (Cambridge, Mass.).

Ben-Sasson, Menahem. 1989. "The Structure, Goals, and Content of the Story of Nathan Ha-Babli," in *Culture and Society in Medieval Jewry*, ed. R. Bonfil, J. Hacker, and M. Ben-Sasson (Jerusalem).

Benson, Robert. 1968. *The Bishop Elect* (Princeton).

Benton, J. F. 1970. *Self and Society in Medieval France* (New York).

Benz, Ernst. 1934. *Ecclesia Spiritualis* (Stuttgart).

Berger, David, 1969. *The Jewish Christian Debate in the High Middle Ages* (Philadelphia).

———— 1972. "The Attitude of St. Bernard of Clairvaux toward the Jews," *Proceedings of the American Academy of Jewish Research* 40: 89–108.

———— 1986. "Mission to the Jews and Jewish-Christian Contacts in the Polemical Literature of the High Middle Ages," *American Historical Review* 91: 576–591.

Berger, Peter. 1969. *The Sacred Canopy* (New York).

Berkner, Lutz K. 1973. "Recent Research on the History of the Family in Western Europe," *Journal of Marriage and the Family* 35: 395–405.

Berliner, Abraham. 1969. "Le-toledoth perushei Rashi," in *Selected Writings Translated from German to Hebrew* (Jerusalem).

Bernard Gui. 1927. *Manuel de l'Inquisiteur*, ed. G. Mollat 2 vols. (Paris).

Bernardino da Siena. 1958. *Le Prediche Volgari*, ed. Ciro Cannarozzi (Florence).

Bloch, Marc. 1941. "The Rise of Dependent Cultivation and Seignorial Institutions," in *Cambridge Economic History*, ed. M. M. Postan (Cambridge), vol. 1.

Blumenkranz, Bernhard. 1946. *Die Judenpredigt Augustins* (Basel).

———— 1955. "Deux compilations canoniques de Florus de Lyon et l'action antijuive d'Agobard," *Revue Historique de Droit Français et Etranger* 33: 227–254, 560–582.

———— 1960. *Juifs et chrétiens dans le monde occidental, 430–1096* (Paris).

———— 1963. Les auteurs chrétiens latins du Moyen Age sur les juifs et le judaïsme (Paris).

———— 1963a. "La conversion au judaïsme d'André, archevêque de Bari," *Journal of Jewish Studies* 14: 33–36.

———— 1966. "Germany, 843–1096," in *The Dark Ages*, ed. C. Roth (Tel Aviv).

Boesch, Sofia. 1983. "Il comune di Siena e il prestito ebraico nei secoli XIV e XV," *Aspetti e problemi della presenza ebraica nell'Italia centro-settentrionale* (Rome).

Bonaventura, Saint. 1953. *The Mind's Road to God*, trans. G. Boas (New York).

Bonazzoli, Viviana. 1990. *Il prestito ebraico nelle economie cittadine delle Marche fra '200 e '400* (Ancona).

Bonfil, Robert. 1971. "The Nature of Judaism in Raymundus Martini's Pugio Fidei," *Tarbiz* 40: 360–375.

———— 1987. "Bein 'Erez Yisrael le-vein Bavel," *Shalem* 5: 1–30.

———— 1989. "Myth, Rhetoric, History? A Study in the Chronicle of *Ahima'az*" (in Hebrew), in *Culture and Society in Medieval Jewry*, ed. M. Ben-Sasson, R. Bonfil, and J. Hacker (Jerusalem).

———— 1990. *Rabbis and Jewish Communities in Renaissance Italy*, trans. J. Chipman (Oxford).

———— 1990a. "Jewish Lenders in Italy during the Renaissance: An Economic Force?" *Pa'amim* 41: 58–64.

—— 1992. *The Jews in Renaissance Italy* (Berkeley).

Boswell, John E. 1988. *The Kindness of Strangers* (New York).

Boureau, Alain. 1986. "L'inceste de Judas: Essai sur la genèse de la haine antisémite au XIIe siècle," *Nouvelle Revue de Psychanalyse* 33 (*L'amour de la haine*): 25–41.

Bowman, Steven. 1985. *History of the Jews in Byzantium, 1204–1453* (Tuscaloosa, Alabama).

Braudel, Fernand. 1972. The Mediterranean and the Mediterranean World in the Age of Philip II, trans. Sian Reynolds (London).

Brentano, Robert. 1974. *Rome before Avignon* (New York).

Bressolles, Mgr. 1949. *Saint Agobard, évêque de Lyon, 760–840* (Paris).

Breuer, Mordecai. 1976. The Rabbinate in Ashkenaz during the Middle Ages (in Hebrew; Jerusalem).

Browe, Petrus. 1942. *Die Judenmission im Mittelalter und die Paepste* (Rome).

Brown, Peter. 1972. *Religion and Society in the Age of Saint Augustine* (New York).

—— 1982. *Society and the Holy in Late Antiquity* (London).

Brundage, James. 1988. "Intermarriage between Christians and Jews in Medieval Canon Law," *Jewish History* 3, no. 1: 25–41.

Bullarium Franciscanum. 1898. Ed. Conrad Eubel (Quaracchi), vol. 5.

Cantor, Norman F. 1963. *Medieval History* (New York).

Caro, Georg. 1964. *Sozial- und Wirtschaftsgeschichte der Juden*, 2 vols. (Hildesheim; orig. pub. 1920–1924).

Carpenter, D. E. 1986. *Alfonso X and the Jews: An Edition of and Commentary on* Siete Partidas 7:24, "De los judios" (Berkeley).

Carpentier, Elizabeth. 1971. "The Plague as a Recurrent Phenomenon," in *Black Death: A Turning Point in History?*, ed. William Bowsky (New York).

Chavarria, Elisa. 1988. "Ideologia e comportamenti familiari nei predicatori italiani tra cinque e settecento: Tematiche e modelli," *Rivista Storica Italiana* 100: 679–723.

Chazan, Robert. 1968. "The Blois Incident: A Study in Jewish Intercommunal Organization," *Proceedings of the American Academy for Jewish Research* 36: 13–31.

—— 1970. "The Persecution of 992," *Revue des Etudes Juives* 129: 217–221.

—— 1970a. "The Bray Incident of 1192: 'Realpolitik' and Folk Slander," *Proceedings of the American Academy for Jewish Research* 38/39: 11–18.

—— 1972. "1007–1012: Initial Crisis for Northern European Jewry," *Proceedings of the American Academy for Jewish Research* 38/39: 101–117.

—— 1973. *Medieval Jewry in Northern France: A Political and Social History* (Baltimore).

—— 1980. *Church, State, and Jew in the Middle Ages* (New York).

—— 1987. *European Jewry and the First Crusade* (Berkeley).

—— 1987a. "Review of K. Stow, *The '1007 Anonymous' and Papal Sovereignty*," *Speculum* 62: 728–731.

—— 1989. Daggers of Faith: Thirteenth-Century Christian Missionizing and Jewish Response (Berkeley).

Chodorow, Stanley. 1972. *Christian Political Theory and Church Politics in the Mid-Twelfth Century* (Berkeley).

Codex Theodosianus. 1954. *Theodosiani libri XVI*, ed. Theodor Mommsen and P. Meyer (Berlin).

Cohen, Ester. 1989. "Symbols of Culpability and the Universal Language of Justice: The Ritual of Public Executions in late Medieval Europe," *History of European Ideas* 11: 407–417.

Cohen, Gerson D. 1960. "The Story of the Four Captives," *Proceedings of the American Academy for Jewish Research* 29: 55–131.

————— 1966. "B. Netanyahu's *The Marranos of Spain*," *Jewish Social Studies* 29: 178–184.

————— 1967. "Esau as Symbol," in *Jewish Medieval and Renaissance Studies*, ed. A. Altman (Cambridge, Mass.).

————— 1968. *The "Sefer ha-qabbalah," by Abraham ibn Daud* (Philadelphia).

————— 1968a. Lectures on Medieval Jewish History, Columbia University. Unpublished.

Cohen, Jeremy. 1982. *The Friars and the Jews* (Ithaca, N.Y.).

————— 1983. "The Jews as the Killers of Christ in the Latin Tradition, from St. Augustine to the Friars," *Traditio* 39: 1–27.

————— 1986. "Robert Chazan's 'Medieval Anti-Semitism': A Note on the Impact of Theology," in *History and Hate: The Dimensions of Antisemitism*, ed. D. Berger (Philadelphia).

————— 1986a. "Scholarship and Intolerance in the Medieval Academy: The Study and Evaluation of Judaism in European Christendom," *American Historical Review* 91: 592–613.

————— 1987. "The Mentality of the Medieval Jewish Apostate: Peter Alfonsi, Hermann of Cologne, and Pablo Christiani," in *Jewish Apostasy in the Modern World*, ed. Todd Endelman (New York).

————— 1989. "Recent Historiography on the Medieval Church and the Decline of European Jewry," in *Popes, Teachers, and Canon Law in the Middle Ages*, ed. J. R. Sweeney and Stanley Chodorow (Ithaca, N.Y.).

————— 1989a. *Be Fertile and Increase, Fill the Earth and Master It* (Ithaca, N.Y.).

————— 1992. "Rationales for Conjugal Sex in RaAvaD's *Ba'alei HaNefesh*," *Jewish History* 6: 1–2.

Cohen, Mark R. 1980. *Jewish Self-Government in Medieval Egypt* (Princeton).

Colafemmina, Cesare. 1980. "Insediamenti e condizioni degli ebrei nell'Italia meridionale e insulare," *Gli Ebrei nell'Alto Medioevo*, Centro Italiano di Studi sull'Alto Medievo (Spoleto).

Colorni, Vittore. 1945. *Legge ebraica e leggi locali* (Milan).

————— 1980. "Gli ebrei nei territori italiani a nord di Roma dal 568 agli inizi dal secolo XIII," *Gli Ebrei nell'Alto Medioevo*, Centro Italiano di Studi sull'Alto Medievo (Spoleto).

Cooperman, Bernard. 1987. "Venetian Policy towards Levantine Jews and Its Broader Italian Context," in *Gli Ebrei di Venezia*, ed. G. Cozzi (Milano).

Corpus Iuris Civilis. 1906. Ed. Paul Kreuger and Theodor Mommsen, 3 vols. (Berlin).

Dalvray, A., and M. Tausche. 1980. "Marriage Sermons in *Ad Status* Collections of the Central Middle Ages," *Archives d'Histoire Doctrinale et Littéraire du Moyen Age* 47: 71–119.

Dan, Joseph. 1966. "The Beginnings of Jewish Mysticism in Europe," in *The Dark Ages*, ed. C. Roth (Tel Aviv).

————— 1968. *The Esoteric Theology of Ashkenazi Hasidism* (in Hebrew; Jerusalem).

——— 1971. "Demonological Stories in the Writings of R. Yehuda Hehasid" (in Hebrew), *Tarbiz* 30: 273–289.

——— 1974. *The Hebrew Story in the Middle Ages* (in Hebrew; Jerusalem).

——— 1982. "The Emergence of Mystical Prayer," in *Studies in Jewish Mysticism*, ed. J. Dan and F. Talmage (New York).

Davies, W. D. 1960. *Paul and Rabbinic Judaism: Some Rabbinic Aspects in Pauline Theology* (London).

Dawson, D. 1978. "William of St. Amour and the Apostolic Tradition," *Medieval Studies* 40: 223–238.

De Lange, N. 1976. *Origen and the Jews* (Cambridge).

Delaurière, Eusèbe de, et al., eds. 1723. *Ordonnances des roys de la troisième race*, 22 vols. (Paris), vol. 1.

Delumeau, Jean. 1978. *La peur en Occident* (Paris).

D'Entreves, A. P. 1959. *Aquinas: Selected Political Writings* (Oxford).

De Roover, Raymond. 1948. *Money, Banking, and Credit in Medieval Bruges* (Cambridge, Mass.).

De Susannis, Marquardus. 1558. *De Iudaeis et Aliis Infidelibus* (Venice).

Dietrich, Claude. 1991. "Gregor von Tours und die Juden: Die Zwangsbekehrungen von Clermont," *Historisches Jahrbuch* 111: 137–147.

Dobson, R. B. 1974. *The Jews of Medieval York and the Massacre of March 1190* (York).

Dohm, W. C. 1957. Concerning the Amelioration of the Civil Status of the Jews, trans. Helen Lederer (Cincinnati).

Douglas, Mary. 1972. "Deciphering a Meal," *Daedalus* 101: 61–82.

Douie, Decima. 1954. *The Conflict between the Seculars and the Mendicants at the University of Paris in the Thirteenth Century* (London).

Duby, Georges. 1978. *Medieval Marriage* (Baltimore).

——— 1983. *The Knight, the Lady, and the Priest*, trans. B. Bray (New York).

Dunlop, D. M. 1967. *The History of the Jewish Khazars* (New York).

Edwards, John. 1984. "Jewish Testimony to the Spanish Inquisition: Teruel 1484–7," *Revue des Etudes Juives* 143: 333–350.

Ehrhardt, A. R. 1959. "Constantine, Rome, and the Rabbis," *Bulletin of the John Rylands Library* 42: 288–312.

Elfenbein, Israel. 1943. *Teshuvot Rashi* (New York).

Elman, Peter. 1936. "The Economic Causes of the Expulsion of the Jews in 1290," *Economic History Review* 7: 145–154.

Emery, R. W. 1977. "Le prêt d'argent juif en Languedoc et Roussillon," in *Juifs et judaïsme de Languedoc, XIIIe siècle–debut XIVe siècle*, ed. M. H. Vicaire and B. Blumenkranz (Toulouse).

Encyclopaedia Judaica. 1971. (Jerusalem.)

Ennen, Edith. 1972. *Die europäische Stadt des Mittelalters* (Göttingen).

Esposito, Anna. 1983. "Gli ebrei a Roma nella seconda metà del '400, attraverso i protocolli del notaio Giovanni Anselmo Amati," in *Aspetti e problemi della presenza ebraica nell'Italia centro-settentrionale*, ed. S. Boesch (Rome).

——— 1988. "Prestito ebraico e monti di pietà nei territori pontifici nel tardo quattrocento: Il caso di Rieti," in *Credito e sviluppo economico in Italia dal medio evo all'età contemporanea*, Società Italiana degli Storici dell'Economia (Verona).

—— and D. Quaglioni. 1990. *Processi contro gli ebrei di Trento, 1475–1478* (Padua).

Eusebius Pamphili. 1965. Ecclesiastical History, trans. R. J. Deferrari, in *Fathers of the Church* (Washington, D.C.).

Evergates, Theodore. 1983. "Ban, Banalité," *Dictionary of the Middle Ages* (New York) 2: 69.

Fabre-Vassas, Claudine. 1984. "Autour du Cochon," in *Identité alimentaire et altérité culturelle: Colloque d'Ethnologie de Neuchâtel* (Neuchâtel).

Fasoli, Gina. 1974. *Scritti di storia medievale*, ed. F. Bocchi et al. (Bologna).

Feldman, D. M. 1974. *Marital Relations, Birth Control and Abortion in Jewish Law* (New York).

Ferrari Dalle Spade, G. 1956. *Scritti giuridici* (Milano), vol. 3.

Finkelstein, Louis. 1972. *Jewish Self-Government in the Middle Ages* (Westport, Conn.; orig. pub. 1924).

Flandrin, J. L. 1976. *Families in Former Times: Kinship, Household and Sexuality,* trans. R. Southern (Cambridge).

Fleischer, Ezra. 1975. *Hebrew Liturgical Poetry in the Middle Ages* (Jerusalem).

Flusser, David. 1953. "Mehaber Sefer Yossipon, Demuto u-tequfato," *Zion* 18: 109–126.

—— 1960. "The Jewish Origins of Christianity" (in Hebrew), in *Sefer Yovel Baer* (Jerusalem), *Zion* 50 (1985): 75–98.

—— 1979. *Sefer Yossipon,* 2 vols. (Jerusalem).

Foa, Anna. 1980. *La stregoneria in Europa* (Turin).

—— 1988. "Il gioco del proselimitismo: Politica della conversioni e controllo della violenza nella Roma del Cinquecento," in *Ebrei e Cristiani nell'Italia medievale e moderna: Conversioni, scambi, contrasti,* ed. M. Luzzati (Rome).

Fox, Marvin. 1989. "Nahmanides on the Status of Aggadot: Perspectives on the Disputation at Barcelona, 1263," *Journal of Jewish Studies* 40: 95–109.

Francastel, Pierre. 1952. "Un mystère parisien illustré par Uccello: Le miracle de l'hostie d'Urbino," *Revue Archéologique,* 180–191.

France, J. 1989. *Rodolfi Glabri Historiarum Libri Quinque* (Oxford).

Francis of Assisi. 1880. *Opuscoli del Serafico Patriarca S. Francesco d'Assisi* (Florence).

Frank, Moshe. 1935. "Toward a History of the Kahal in Ashkenaz" (in Hebrew) *Zion* 1: 337ff.

Freud, Anna. 1946. *The Ego and the Mechanisms of Defense* (New York).

Friedberg, Emil. 1965. *De Finium inter Ecclesiam et Civitatem Regundorum Judicio* (Leipzig; orig. pub. 1861).

Friedman, Yvonne. 1978. "An Anatomy of Anti-Semitism: Peter the Venerable's Letter to Louis VII, King of France," in *Bar Ilan Studies in History,* ed. P. Artzi (Ramat Gan).

Frugoni, Arsenio, ed. 1957. *Adversus Judaeos di Gioacchino di Fiore* (Rome).

Funkenstein, Amos. 1986. "The Image of the Ruler in Medieval Jewish Political Thought," in "Congress: Jewish Societies in Transformation," unpublished (Jerusalem).

Gager, John. 1983. *The Origins of Antisemitism* (Oxford).

Gampel, Benjamin. 1989. *The Last Jews on Iberian Soil* (Berkeley).

Ganshof, François. 1941. "Medieval Agrarian Society in Its Prime," in *Cambridge Economic History*, ed. M. M. Postan (Cambridge), vol. 1.

Gil, Moshe. 1983. *'Eres Yisrael ba-Tequfah ha-Muslimit ha-Rishonah*, 634–1099 (Tel Aviv).

Gilboa, Akiva, ed. and trans. 1964. Agobardi Lugdunensis Archiepiscopi: Epistolae contra Iudaeos (Latin text with Hebrew trans.; Jerusalem).

Gilchrist, John. 1969. *The Church and Economic Activity in the Middle Ages* (London).

———— 1988. "The Perception of Jews in the Canon Law in the Period of the First Two Crusades," *Jewish History* 3, no. 1: 9–25.

———— 1988a. "Review of Jonathan Riley-Smith, *The First Crusade and the Idea of Crusading*," *Speculum* 63: 714.

Ginzburg, Carlo. 1989. *Storia notturna* (Turin).

Giustiniani, P., and P. Quirini. 1773. *Libellus ad Leonem Decem*, ed. J. B. Mittarelli and A. Costadoni, *Annales Camuldulenses* (Venice) 9: 612–719.

Given, James. 1989. "The Inquisitors of Languedoc and the Medieval Technology of Power," *American Historical Review* 94: 302–336.

Glick, T. F. 1979. *Islamic and Christian Spain in the Early Middle Ages* (Princeton).

Goitein, S. D. 1953. "Obadyah, a Norman Proselyte," *Journal of Jewish Studies* 4: 74–84.

———— 1964. *Jews and Arabs* (New York).

———— 1967. *A Mediterranean Society*, vol. 1: *Economic Foundations* (Berkeley).

———— 1971. *A Mediterranean Society*, vol. 2: *The Community* (Berkeley).

———— 1974. "The Jewish Family in the Days of Maimonides," *Conservative Judaism* 29: 25–35.

———— 1978. *A Mediterranean Society*, vol. 3: *The Family* (Berkeley).

Golb, Norman. 1965. "Obadiah the Proselyte: Scribe of a Unique Twelfth-Century Hebrew Manuscript Containing Lombardic Neumes," *Journal of Religion* 45: 153–156.

———— 1965a. "Notes on the Conversion of European Christians to Judaism in the Eleventh Century," *Journal of Jewish Studies* 16: 69–74.

———— 1985. *Les juifs de Rouen au Moyen Age* (Rouen).

Goode, William. 1981. *Die rechtliche Stellung der Juden in den Schriften deutschen Juristen des 16 und 17 Jahrhunderts* (Singmaringen).

Goodenough, E. R., and A. T. Kraabel. 1968. "Paul and the Hellenization of Christianity," in Essays in Memory of Erwin Ramsdell Goodenough, ed. J. Neusner (Leiden).

Goody, Jack. 1983. *The Development of the Family and Marriage in Europe* (Cambridge).

Gottfried, R. S. 1985. "Famine," *Dictionary of the Middle Ages* (New York) 5: 3–9.

Grabois, Aryeh. 1966. "Le souvenir et la légende de Charlemagne dans les textes hébraïques médiévaux," *Le Moyen Age* 72: 5–41.

———— 1969. "L'abbaye de Saint Denis et les juifs sous l'abbatiat de Suger," *Annales ESC* 24: 1187–1195.

———— 1975. "The *Hebraica Veritas* and Jewish-Christian Intellectual Relations in the Twelfth Century," *Speculum* 50: 613–635.

——— 1983. "Mi-Nesi'ut la-hanhagat ha-parnasim: ha-temurot ba-mishtar shel kehillat Narbonnah ba-me'ah ha-yod-gimmel," in *Ummah Ve-Toledothehah*, ed. M. Stern, Part 1 (Jerusalem).

——— 1984. "La royauté sacrée au XIIe siècle: Manifestation de propagande royale," in *Idéologie et propagande en France*, ed. M. Yardeni (Paris).

Graetz, Heinrich. 1939. *A History of the Jews*, 6 vols. (Philadelphia).

Grayzel, Solomon. 1958. "The Confessions of a Medieval Convert," *Historia Judaica* 17: 89–120.

——— 1962. "The Papal Bull 'Sicut Iudaeis,'" in *Studies and Essays in Honor of A. A. Neuman*, ed. M. Ben-Horin (Leiden).

——— 1966. *The Church and the Jews in the Thirteenth Century*, vol. 1. (New York; orig. pub. 1933).

——— 1977. "Popes, Jews, and Inquisition, from 'Sicut' to 'Turbato corde,'" in *Essays on the Occasion of the Seventieth Anniversary of the Dropsie University*, ed. A. Katsch and L. Nemoy (Philadelphia).

——— 1989. *The Church and the Jews in the Thirteenth Century, vol. 2: 1254–1314*, ed., arranged, and annotated by K. R. Stow (New York).

Greenbaum, Shmuel, ed. 1873. *Vikuah R. Yehiel* (Thorn, Poland).

Gregory of Tours. 1927. *History of the Franks*, trans. O. M. Dalton (Oxford).

Grossman, Avraham. 1975. "The Attitude of the Early Scholars of Ashkenaz towards the Authority of the 'Kahal'" (in Hebrew), *Annual of the Institute for Research in Jewish Law* 2: 175–199.

——— 1980. "Family Lineage and Its Place in Early Ashkenazic Jewish Society" (in Hebrew), in *Studies in the History of Jewish Society Presented to Professor Jacob Katz on his Seventy-Fifth Birthday*, ed. I. Etkes and Y. Salmon (Jerusalem).

——— 1981. *The Early Sages of Ashkenaz* (in Hebrew; Jerusalem).

——— 1983. "The Origins and Essence of the Custom of 'Stopping the Service,'" *Milet* 1: 199–220.

——— 1985. "From Father to Son: The Inheritance of Spiritual Leadership in the Jewish Communities of the Early Middle Ages" (in Hebrew), *Zion* 50: 189–220.

——— 1988. "The Historical Background to the Ordinances on Family Affairs Attributed to Rabbenu Gershom Me'or ha-Golah (The Light of the Exile)," in *Jewish History: Essays in Honour of Chimen Abramsky*, ed. A. Rapoport-Albert and S. Zipperstein (London).

——— 1988a. "The Relationship between the Social Structure and Spiritual Activity of Jewish Communities in the Geonic Period" (in Hebrew), *Zion* 53: 259–272.

——— 1989. Lecture delivered at Bar Ilan University, unpublished (Ramat Gan).

Grundmann, Herbert. 1971. *Religiöse Bewegungen im Mittelalter* (Darmstadt).

Guibert of Nogent. 1970. *Self and Society in Medieval France*, ed. J. F. Benton (New York).

——— 1981. *De Vita Sua*, ed. E. R. Labande (Paris).

Gurevich, Aron. 1988. *Medieval Popular Culture: Problems of Belief and Perception*, trans. J. M. Bak and P. A. Hollingsworth (Cambridge).

Gutwirth, Eliezer. 1989. "Duran on Ahitophel," *Jewish History* 4, no. 1: 59–74.

——— 1989a. "Abraham Seneor: Social Tensions and the Court Jews," *Michael* 11: 169–229.

Haberman, A. M. 1971. *Sefer Gezerot 'Ashkenaz ve-Zarfat* (Jerusalem).

Hadas, Moses. 1959. *Hellenistic Culture: Fusion and Diffusion* (New York).

Hakohen, Joseph. 1895. *'Emeq ha-bakha'*, ed. M. Letteris (Cracow).

Haliczer, Stephen. 1973. "The Castilian Urban Patriciate and the Jewish Expulsion of 1480–92," *American Historical Review* 78: 35–62.

Harkavy, A. 1903. "Hadishim gam yeshanim," in *Sefer Yovel le-Avraham Berliner*, ed. A. Freimann (Berlin), 34–40 ("Megillat benai Netira").

Harris, G. L. 1975. *King, Parliament, and Public Finance in Medieval England to 1369* (Oxford).

Harris, Monford. 1959. "The Concept of Love in Sepher Hassidim," *Jewish Quarterly Review* 50: 13–44.

Haverkamp, Alfred. 1981. "Die Judenverfolgungen zur Zeit des Schwarzen Todes im Gesellschaftsgefüge deutscher Städte," in *Zur Geschichte der Juden im Deutschland des späten Mittelalters und der frühen Neuzeit* (Stuttgart).

Heilperin, Hermann. 1963. *Rashi and the Christian Scholars* (Pittsburgh).

Hendrix, S. H. 1976. "In Quest of the *Vera Ecclesia*: The Crises of Late Medieval Ecclesiology," *Viator* 7: 347–378.

Herlihy, David. 1967. *Medieval and Renaissance Pistoia: The Social History of an Italian Town* (New Haven).

—— 1970. "The Tuscan Town in the Quattrocento: A Demographic Profile," *Medievalia et Humanistica* (n.s.) 1: 81–110.

—— 1983. "The Making of the Medieval Family: Symmetry, Structure, and Sentiment," *Journal of Family History* 8: 116–130.

—— 1985. *Medieval Households* (Cambridge).

Herlihy, David, and Christiane Klapisch-Zuber. 1985. *Tuscans and Their Families* (New Haven).

Holt, J. C. 1965. *Magna Carta* (Cambridge).

Hominer, Hayim. 1978. *Josiphen* (Jerusalem).

Horowitz, Elliott. 1986. "The Way We Were," *Jewish History* 1, no. 1: 75–90.

Hsia, Ronnie Po-Chia. 1988. *The Myth of Ritual Murder* (New Haven).

Hughes, Diane Owen. 1986. "Distinguishing Signs: Ear-Rings, Jews and Franciscan Rhetoric in the Italian Renaissance City," *Past and Present* 112: 3–59.

Hyams, P. R. 1974. "The Jewish Minority in Medieval England," *Journal of Jewish Studies* 25: 270–293.

Iancu, Daniele. 1981. *Les juifs en Provence, 1475–1501* (Aix-en-Provence).

Idel, Moshe. 1983. "Cabala," Dictionary of the Middle Ages (New York) 3: 1–3.

Isaac of Vienna. 1862. "*Hilkhot Shabbat*," 84: 3; *Or Zaru'a* (Zhitomer, Russia).

Israel, Jonathan. 1985. *European Jewry in the Age of Mercantilism, 1550–1750* (Oxford).

Janssen, Johannes. 1881. Allgemeine Zustande des deutschen Volkes (Freiburg).

Jedin, Hubert. 1960. *Ecumenical Councils in the Catholic Church: An Historical Survey* (New York).

John of Paris. 1971. *On Royal and Papal Power*, trans. and introd. J. Watt (Toronto).

Jordan, William C. 1978. "Jews on Top: Women and the Availability of Consumption Loans in Northern France in the Mid-Thirteenth Century," *Journal of Jewish Studies* 29: 39–56.

—— 1979. *Louis IX and the Challenge of the Crusade* (Princeton).

—— 1989. *The French Monarchy and the Jews: From Philip Augustus to the Last Capetians* (Philadelphia).

Joseph Kimhi. 1972. *The Book of the Covenant,* trans. F. Talmage (Toronto).

JTS. Jewish Theological Seminary, microfilm, 9486, fol. 6 (New York).

Juster, Jean. 1976. *The Legal Condition of the Jews under the Visigothic Kings,* trans. A. M. Rabello (Jerusalem).

Justin Martyr. 1965. *Dialogue with Trypho,* trans. T. B. Falls in *Fathers of the Church,* vol. 6 (Washington, D.C.).

Kamen, Henry. 1985. *Inquisition and Society in the Sixteenth and Seventeenth Centuries* (London).

—— 1988. "The Mediterranean and the Expulsion of Spanish Jews in 1492," *Past and Present* 119: 30–55.

Kanarfogel, E. 1984. "Attitudes toward Childhood in Medieval Jewish Society," in *Approaches to Judaism in Medieval Times,* ed. D. Blumenthal, vol. 2 (Chico, Calif.).

Kantorowicz, E. H. 1957. *The King's Two Bodies* (Princeton).

Kantorowicz, Herman. 1964. "Notes on the Development of the Gloss to the Justinian and Canon Law," in *The Study of the Bible in the Middle Ages,* ed. Beryl Smalley (Notre Dame, Ind.).

Katz, Jacob. 1958. "Even Though a Sinner, He is Still of Israel" (in Hebrew), *Tarbiz* 27: 203–227.

—— 1961. *Exclusiveness and Tolerance: Studies in Jewish-Gentile Relations in Medieval and Modern Times* (New York).

—— 1971. *Tradition and Crisis* (New York).

—— 1979. "Rabbinical Authority and Authorization in the Middle Ages," *Studies in Medieval Jewish History and Literature,* ed. I. Twersky (Cambridge, Mass.).

Kedar, B. Z. 1979. "Canon Law and the Burning of the Talmud," *Bulletin of Medieval Canon Law* 9: 79–82.

King, M. H. 1985. "Hagiography, Western European," *Dictionary of the Middle Ages* (New York) 6: 64–71.

Kisch, Guido. 1944. "The Jew's Function in the Medieval Evolution of Economic Life," *Historia Judaica* 6: 1–12.

—— 1949. *The Jews in Medieval Germany: A Study of Their Legal and Social Status* (New York).

Klapisch-Zuber, Christiane. 1985. "Kin, Friends, and Neighbors: The Urban Territory of a Merchant Family in 1400," in *Women, Family, and Ritual in Renaissance Italy,* trans. Lydia Cochrane (Chicago).

—— 1985a. "The Cruel Mother," in *Women, Family, and Ritual in Renaissance Italy,* trans. Lydia Cochrane (Chicago).

Klar, Benjamin. 1974. *The Scroll of Ahimaaz* (in Hebrew; Jerusalem).

Kohn, Roger. 1984. "Royal Power and Rabbinical Authority in Fourteenth-Century France," in *Approaches to Judaism in Medieval Times,* ed. D. Blumenthal, vol. 2 (Chico, Calif.).

—— 1988. *Les juifs de la France du nord dans la seconde moitié du XIVe siècle* (Louvain).

Kohut, Alexander. 1878. *Aruch Completum,* 8 vols. (Vienna).

Krey, A. C. 1921. *The First Crusade: The Account of Eye-Witnesses and Participants* (Princeton).

Kriegel, Maurice. 1976. "Un trait de psychologie sociale dans les pays Mediterranéens du Bas Moyen Age: Le juif comme intouchable," *Annales ESC* 31: 326–330.

―――― 1977. "La communauté juive dans les états de la couronne d'Aragon sous Ferdinand le Catholique et son expulsion," diss., University of Paris (Paris).

―――― 1978. "Mobilisation politique et modernisation organique: Les expulsions de juifs au Bas Moyen Age," *Archives de Sciences Sociales des Religions* 46: 5–20.

―――― 1978a. "Prémarranisme et Inquisition dans la Provence des XIIIe et XIVe siècles," *Provence Historique* 29: 313–323.

―――― 1978b. "La prise d'une decision: L'expulsion des juifs d'Espagne en 1492," *Revue Historique* 260: 49–90.

―――― 1979. *Les juifs à la fin du Moyen Age dans l'Europe méditerranéenne* (Paris).

―――― 1989. "A Note on the Doctrine of the Just Price in *Sefer Hasidim*" (in Hebrew), in *Studies in Jewish Thought,* ed. S. H. Wilensky and M. Idel (Jerusalem).

Kuhnel, Bianca. 1978. *From the Earthly to the Heavenly Jerusalem* (Freiburg).

Kuttner, Stephen. 1960. *Harmony from Dissonance* (Latrobe, Pa.).

―――― and G. Fransen, eds. 1969. *Summa "Elegantius in Iure Divino" seu Coloniensis* (New York).

Ladner, Gerhard. 1967. "Homo Viator: Medieval Ideas on Alienation and Order," *Speculum* 42: 233–259.

―――― 1967a. *The Idea of Reform* (New York).

Langmuir, Gavin. 1960. "Judaei Nostri," *Traditio* 16: 203–239.

―――― 1963. "The Jews and the Archives of Angevin England," *Traditio* 19: 183–244.

―――― 1972. "The Knight's Tale of Young Hugh of Lincoln," *Speculum* 47: 459–482.

―――― 1977. "L'absence d'accusation de meurtre rituel à l'ouest du Rhône," in *Juifs et judaïsme de Languedoc,* ed. B. Blumenkranz and M. H. Vicaire (Toulouse).

―――― 1979. "Review of B. Bachrach, *Early Medieval Jewish Policy,*" *Speculum* 54: 104.

―――― 1980. "From Ambrose of Milan to Emicho of Leiningen," *Gli Ebrei nell'Alto Medioevo,* Centro Italiano di Studi sull'Alto Medievo (Spoleto).

―――― 1981. "*Tanquam Servi:* The Change in Jewish Status in French Law about 1200," in *Les juifs dans l'histoire de France,* ed. Miriam Yardeni (Leiden).

―――― 1984. "Thomas of Monmouth, Detector of Ritual Murder," *Speculum* 59: 820–847.

―――― 1987. "Toward a Definition of Antisemitism," in *The Persisting Question,* ed. H. Fein (New York).

―――― 1990. *History, Religion, and Antisemitism* (Berkeley).

―――― 1990a. *Toward a Definition of Antisemitism* (Berkeley).

Leclercq, Jean. 1980. *Le mariage vu par les moines au XIIe siècle* (Paris).

Le Goff, Jacques. 1980. *Time, Work, and Culture in the Middle Ages,* trans. A. Goldhammer (Chicago).

―――― 1988. *Medieval Civilization, 400–1500,* trans. J. Barrow (Oxford).

Leiberman, Saul. 1939. Shkiin (Jerusalem).

Leibeschutz, Hans. 1959. "The Crusading Movement and Its Bearing on the Christian Attitude Towards Jewry," *Journal of Jewish Studies* 10: 97–111.

Le Roy Ladurie, E. 1973. "L'aiguillette," in *Le territoire de l'historien* (Paris).

Levi, Israel. 1914. "L'apocalypse de Zorobabel et le roi de Perse Siroes," *Revue des Etudes Juives* 68: 129–160; 70: 108–121; 71: 57–65.

———— 1899. "La lutte entre Isaie, fils d'Abba Mari, et Yohanan, fils de Matatia, pour le rabbinat de France," *Revue des Etudes Juives* 39: 85–94.

Levin, B. M. 1972. *'Iggeret Rav Sherira Gaon* (Jerusalem).

Levy, Hans. 1968. *'Olamot nifgashim* (Jerusalem).

Levy, M. J., Jr. 1965. *Aspects of the Analysis of Family Structure*, ed. A. J. Coale (Princeton).

Lewicki, Thadeus. 1980. "Les commerçants juifs dans l'Orient islamique non méditerranéen au IX–XI siècles," *Gli Ebrei nell'Alto Medioevo*, Centro Italiano di Studi sull'Alto Medievo (Spoleto).

Liber, Maurice. 1970. *Rashi* (in Hebrew), trans. A. Szold (New York; orig. pub. 1906).

Lifton, R. J. 1986. *The Nazi Doctors* (New York).

Linder, Amnon. 1985. "Jerusalem as a Focus of Confrontation between Judaism and Christianity," in *Vision and Conflict in the Holy Land,* ed. R. I. Cohen (Jerusalem).

———— 1987. *The Jews in Roman Imperial Legislation* (Detroit).

———— 1988. *The Jews in the Legal Sources of the Early Middle Ages* (typescript; forthcoming, Israel Academy of Sciences, Jerusalem).

———— 1990. "The Liturgy of the Liberation of Jerusalem," *Medieval Studies* 59: 110–131.

Littmann, Ellen. 1928. "Studien zur Wiederaufnahme der Juden durch die deutschen Städte nach dem Schwarzen Tod," *Monatsschrift für die Geschichte des Wissenschaft des Judenthums* 72: 576–600.

Loevinson, E. 1932. "La concession de banques de prêts aux juifs par les papes," *Revue des Etudes Juives* 92: 1–30; 93: 27–52, 157–178; 94: 57–72, 167–183; 95: 23–43.

Logan, F. D. 1973. "Thirteen London Jews and Conversion to Christianity: Problems of Apostasy in the 1280s," *Historical Research* 45: 214–229.

Lopez, R. S., and J. Raymond. 1955. *Medieval Trade in the Mediterranean World* (New York).

———— 1962. *The Birth of Europe* (London).

———— 1971. *The Commercial Revolution of the Middle Ages, 950–1350* (Englewood Cliffs, N.J.).

———— 1982. "Fulfillment and Diversion in the Eight Crusades," in Outremer, ed. B. Z. Kedar et al. (Jerusalem).

Lotter, Friedrich. 1987. "Zur Ausbildung eines Kirchlichen Judenrechts bei Burchard von Worms und Ivo von Chartres," *Antisemitismus und Jüdische Geschichte: Studien zu Ehren von Herbert A. Strauss,* ed. R. Erb and M. Schmidt (Berlin).

———— 1988. "Hostienfrevelvorwurf und Blutwunderfälschung bei den Judenverfolgungen von 1298 ('Rintfleisch') und 1336–1338 ('Armleder')," in

Fälschungen im Mittelalter: Fingierte Briefe, Frömmigkeit und Fälschung, Realienfälschungen, Monumenta Gerrmaniae Historica, Schriften, vol. 33, II (Hanover).

—— 1988a. "Die Judenverfolgung des 'König Rintfleisch' in Franken um 1298," *Zeitschrift für Historische Forschung* 15: 385–422.

—— 1989. "The Scope and Effectiveness of Imperial Jewry Law in the High Middle Ages," *Jewish History* 4, no. 1: 31–59.

Lourie, Elena. 1986. "A Plot which Failed," *Mediterranean Historical Review* 1: 187–220.

Lunt, W. E. 1957. *History of England* (New York).

Luther, Martin. 1971. "Against the Sabbatarians," trans. M. H. Bertram, in *Luther's Works* (Philadelphia), vol. 47.

—— 1971a. "Concerning the Jews and Their Lies," trans. M. H. Bertram, in *Luther's Works* (Philadelphia), vol. 45.

—— 1971b. "That Jesus Christ Was Born a Jew," trans. W. I. Brandt, in *Luther's Works* (Philadelphia), vol. 47.

Luzzati, Michele. 1985. *La casa dell'Ebreo* (Pisa).

—— 1989. "Le ricerche prosopografiche sulle famiglie ebraiche italiane (secoli XIV–XVI)," in *La storia degli ebrei nell'Italia medievale: Tra filologia e metodologia,* ed. M. G. Muzzarelli and G. Todeschini (Bologna).

Macdonald, R. A. 1985. "Law and Politics: Alfonso's Program of Political Reform," in *The Worlds of Alfonso the Learned and James the Conqueror: Intellect and Force in the Middle Ages,* ed. R. I. Burns (Princeton).

Maimon, Arye. 1981. "Der Judenvertreibungsversuch Albrechts II von Mainz und sein Misserfolg," in *Zur Geschichte der Juden im Deutschland des späten Mittelalters und der frühen Neuzeit,* ed. A. Haverkamp (Stuttgart).

Makdisi, George. 1974. "The Scholastic Method in Medieval Education," *Speculum* 49: 640–662.

Mann, Jacob, 1931. *Texts and Studies,* 2 vols. (Cincinnati).

Marcus, Ivan G. 1976. "The Jews in Western Europe, Fourth to Sixteenth Century," *Bibliographical Essays in Medieval Jewish Studies,* ed. L. Berman et al. (New York).

—— 1981. *Piety and Society: The Jewish Pietists of Medieval Germany* (Leiden).

—— 1982. "From Politics to Martyrdom: Shifting Paradigms in the Hebrew Narratives of the 1096 Crusade Riots," *Prooftexts* 2, no. 1: 40–52.

—— 1986. "Mothers, Martyrs, and Moneylenders: Some Jewish Women in Medieval Europe," *Conservative Judaism* 38, no. 3: 34–45.

—— 1986a. "The Devotional Ideals of Ashkenazic Pietism," in *Jewish Spirituality,* ed. A. Green (New York).

—— 1986b. "Hierarchies, Religious Boundaries and Jewish Spirituality in Medieval Germany," *Jewish History* 1, no. 2: 7–26.

—— 1989. "Review of Robert Chazan, *European Jewry and the First Crusade,*" *Speculum* 64: 685–688.

Marcus, J. R. 1965. *The Jew in the Medieval World* (New York).

Marcus, Joseph. 1934. "Studies in the Chronicle of Ahimaaz," *Proceedings of the American Academy for Jewish Research* 5: 85–93.

Marrou, H. 1957. *Saint Augustine and His Influence Through the Ages,* trans. E. Hill (New York).

Martène, E., and U. Durand. 1717. *Thesaurus novus anecdotorum* (Paris), vol. 4.

Marx, Karl. 1959. *A World without Jews,* ed. D. Runes (New York).

McLaughlin, M. 1974. "Survivors and Surrogates," in *The History of Childhood,* ed. Lloyd de Mause (New York).

McLaughlin, T. P. 1939. "The Teachings of the Canonists on Usury (XII, XIII, XIV Centuries)," *Medieval Studies* 1: 81–147; 2: 1–22.

Meeks, W. A., and R. L. Wilkens 1978. *Jews and Christians in Antioch in the First Four Centuries of the Common Era* (Missoula, Mont.).

Meir ben Simeon. *Milhemet Mizvah,* ms. Parma, 2749 (Parma).

Melamed, Abraham. 1986. "The Perception of Jewish History in Italian Jewish Thought of the Sixteenth and Seventeenth Centuries: A Re-examination," in *Italia Judaica II* (Rome).

Menache, Sophia. 1983. "Vers une conscience nationale: Mythe et symbolisme au début de la Guerre de Cent Ans," *Le Moyen Age* 89: 85–97.

––––––– 1987. "The King, the Church, and the Jews: Some Considerations on the Expulsions from England and France," *Journal of Medieval History* 13: 223–236.

Meneghin, V. 1974. *Bernardino da Feltre e i Monti di Pietà* (Vicenza).

Merchavia, C. M. 1972. "La polemica di Bernardino di Busti contro gli ebrei ed il Talmud," *Michael* 1: 223–250, Hebrew numbering.

––––––– 1973. *The Church versus Talmudic and Midrashic Literature* (Jerusalem).

––––––– 1988. "*Pugio Fidei:* An Index of Citations," in *Exile and Diaspora,* ed. A. Grossman, J. Kaplan, and A. Mirsky (Jerusalem).

Migne, J. P. 1844. *Patrologia: Cursus Completus Series Latina* (Paris).

Mihaly, Eugene. 1964. "A Rabbinic Defense of the Election of Israel," *Hebrew Union College Annual* 35: 103ff.

Milano, Attilio. 1935. "I capitoli di Daniele da Pisa e la comunità di Roma," *La Rassegna Mensile di Israel* 10: 324–338, 409–426.

––––––– 1963. *Storia degli ebrei in Italia* (Turin).

––––––– 1964. *Il ghetto di Roma* (Roma).

––––––– 1970. "Battesimi di ebrei a Roma dal Cinquecento all'Ottocento," in *Scritti in memoria di Enzo Sereni,* ed. A. Milano, S. Nachon, and D. Carpi (Jerusalem).

Miller, Deborah Jo. 1987. "The Expulsion of the Jews from England," undergraduate paper, Yale College (New Haven).

Mintz, Alan. 1964. *Hurban: Responses to Catastrophe in Hebrew Literature* (New York).

Miskimin, Harry. 1963. *Money, Prices, and Foreign Exchange in Fourteenth-Century France* (New Haven).

––––––– 1969. *The Economy of Early Renaissance Europe* (Englewood Cliffs, N.J.).

Monod, B. 1903. "Juifs, sorciers, et hérétiques au Moyen Age, d'après les mémoires d'un moine du XIe siècle," *Revue des Etudes Juives* 46: 237ff.

Moore, Robert I. 1987. *The Formation of a Persecuting Society* (Oxford).

––––––– 1988. "Power and Culture: The Making of Antisemitism in the Twelfth-Century West," lecture given at conference entitled "The Parting of the Ways" (York, England).

Mordekhai ben Hillel. 1911. *Mordekhai* (Vilna; Vilna edition of the Babylonian Talmud).

Morell, Shmuel. 1971. "The Constitutional Limits of Communal Government in Rabbinic Law," *Jewish Social Studies* 33: 87–119.

—— 1982. "An Equal or a Ward: How Independent Is a Married Woman According to Rabbinic Law?" *Jewish Social Studies* 44: 189–210.

Morris, Nathan. 1977. *A History of Jewish Education*, 3 vols. (in Hebrew; Jerusalem).

Morrison, K. F. 1964. *The Two Kingdoms* (Princeton).

—— 1969. *Tradition and Authority in the Western Church, 300–1140* (Princeton).

Moses ben Nahman (pseud.). 1963. "'Iggeret ha-qodesh," in Kitvei ha-Ramban, ed. C. Chavel (Jerusalem), vol. 2.

Mueller, Joel. 1881. *Teshuvot hakhmei Zarfat ve-Lotair* (Vienna).

Mundy, John. 1973. *Europe in the High Middle Ages* (New York).

Munro, Dana, and Joseph Strayer. 1942. *The Middle Ages, 395–1500* (New York).

Murray, Alex. 1987. Reason and Society in the Middle Ages (Oxford).

Muzzarelli, M. G. 1983. *Ebrei e città d'Italia in età di transizione: Il caso di Cesena dal XIV al XVI secolo* (Bologna).

Nahon, Gerard. 1969. "Le crédit et les juifs dans la France du XIIIe siècle," *Annales ESC* 24: 1121–1148.

Nelson, Benjamin. 1969. *The Idea of Usury* (Chicago).

Nemoy, Leon. 1952. *Karaite Anthology* (New Haven).

Netanyahu, B. 1967. *The Marranos of Spain* (New York).

Neubauer, Adolph. 1895. *Medieval Jewish Chronicles,* vol. 2: "Seder Tana'im ve-Amora'im" and "Report of Nathan the Babylonian" (Oxford).

Nicholas, David. 1985. *The Domestic Life of a Medieval City: Women, Children and the Family in Fourteenth-Century Ghent* (Lincoln, Nebr.).

Noonan, John. 1957. *The Scholastic Analysis of Usury* (Cambridge, Mass.).

Oberman, Heiko. 1984. *The Roots of Antisemitism in the Age of Renaissance and Reformation,* trans. J. I. Porter (Philadelphia).

Origen. 1965. *Contra Celsum,* trans. H. Chadwick (Cambridge).

Pacaut, Marcel. 1964. *Louis VII et son royaume* (Paris).

Pakter, Walter. 1974. "*De His Qui Foris Sunt:* The Teachings of the Medieval Canon and Civil Lawyers Concerning the Jews," diss., Johns Hopkins University (Baltimore).

Palès-Gobilliard, A. 1977. "L'Inquisition et les juifs: Le cas de Jacques Fournier," *Juifs et judaïsme de Languedoc,* ed. B. Blumenkranz et M. H. Vicaire (Toulouse).

Panormitanus (Nicholas de Tudeschi). 1559. *Lectura super Libros V Decretalium* (n.p.).

Parkes, James. 1934. *The Conflict of the Church and the Synagogue* (London).

—— 1938. *The Jew in the Medieval Community* (London).

Poliakov, Leon. 1977. *Jewish Bankers and the Holy See, from the Thirteenth to the Seventeenth Century,* trans. M. Kochan (London).

Post, Gaines. 1953. "Two Notes on Medieval Nationalism," *Traditio* 9: 281–320.

—— 1964. *Studies in Medieval Legal Thought: Public Law and the State, 1100–1322* (Princeton).

Powicke, Maurice. 1982. The Thirteenth Century, 1216–1307 (Oxford).

Prestwich, Michael. 1972. War, Politics, and Finance under Edward I (London).

———— 1985. "The Piety of Edward I," in *England in the Thirteenth Century,* ed. W. H. Ormrod (Harlaxton, England).

Prosperi, Adriano. 1989. "La chiesa e gli ebrei nell'Italia del '500," in *Ebraismo e antiebraismo: Immagine e pregiudizio* (Florence).

Pullan, Brian. 1971. *Rich and Poor in Renaissance Venice* (Cambridge, Mass.).

Quaglioni, Diego. 1983. "*Inter Iudaeos et Christianos commertia sunt permissa:* 'Questione ebraica' e usura in Baldo degli Ubaldi (c. 1327–1400)," in *Aspetti e problemi della presenza ebraica nell'Italia centro-settentrionale,* ed. S. Boesch (Rome).

Rabello, A. M. 1983. *The Jews in Visigothic Spain in the Light of the Legislation* (in Hebrew) (Jerusalem).

Rashi. *Babylonian Talmud, Ketuboth,* 62b, *Lel Oneg.*

Ravid, Benjamin. 1983. "Republica nifredet mikol shilton 'aher," in *Thought and Action,* ed. A. Greenbaum and A. Ivry (Tel Aviv).

———— 1987. "The Religious, Economic, and Social Background and Context of the Establishment of the Ghetti of Venice," in *Gli ebrei e Venezia,* ed. G. Cozzi (Milan).

Raymundus Martinus, 1687. *Pugio Fidei adversus Mauros et Judaeos,* ed. J. B. Carpzov (Leipzig; photo reprint Farnsborough, England, 1967).

Reisenberg, Peter. 1958. *The Medieval Town* (Princeton).

Renouard, Yves. 1970. *The Avignon Papacy,* 1305-1403, trans. D. Bethell (London).

Reuther, R. R. 1974. Faith and Fratricide (New York).

Reyerson, K. 1985. *Business, Banking and Finance in Medieval Montpellier* (Toronto).

Richardson, H. G. 1960. *The English Jewry under Angevin Kings* (London).

Rigg, J. M. 1902. *Select Pleas, Starrs, and Other Records from the Rolls of the Exchequer of the Jews,* A.D. 1220-1284 (London).

Riley-Smith, Jonathan. 1982. "The First Crusade and St. Peter," in *Outremer,* ed. B. Z. Keder et al. (Jerusalem).

———— 1984. "The First Crusade and the Persecution of the Jews," *Studies in Church History* 21: 51–72.

———— 1986. *The First Crusade and the Idea of Crusading* (Philadelphia).

Roberti Monachi. 1963. "Speech of Pope Urban II at the Council of Clermont, 1095," in *The Medieval World,* ed. N. Cantor (New York).

Rokeah, David. 1971. "The Jews and Their Law in the Pagan Christian Polemic in the Roman Empire" (in Hebrew), *Tarbiz* 40: 462–471.

Rosenthal, G. S. 1962. *Banking and Finance among Jews in Renaissance Italy* (New York).

Rosenthal, Judah. 1956. "The Talmud on Trial," *Jewish Quarterly Review* 47: 58–76, 145–169.

Roth, Cecil. 1946. *The History of the Jews of Italy* (Philadelphia).

———— 1964. *A History of the Jews in England,* 3rd ed. (Oxford).

———— 1966. "Italy," in *The Dark Ages,* ed. C. Roth (Tel Aviv).

Rubin, A. 1965. "The Concept of Repentence among the Hasidey Ashkenaz," *Journal of Jewish Studies* 16: 161–176.

Russell, Jeffrey. 1980. *A History of Witchcraft, Sorcerers, Heretics, and Pagans* (London).

Salfeld, Sigmund. 1898. *Das Martyrologium des Nürnberger Memorbuches* (Berlin).

Saltman, Abraham. 1988. "Hermann's *Opusculum de Conversione Sua:* Truth or Fiction?" *Revue des Etudes Juives* 147: 31–56.

Samuel ben Meir. 1969. *Perush 'al ha-Torah,* ed. A. Bromberg (Jerusalem).

Saperstein, Marc. 1986. "The Conflict over the Rashba's Herem on Philosophical Study: A Political Perspective," *Jewish History* 1, no. 2: 27–38.

———— 1989. *Jewish Preaching, 1200–1800* (New Haven).

Sayles, G. O. 1975. The King's Parliament of England (London).

Schaefer, Peter. 1989. "The Ideal of Piety of the Ashkenazi Hasidim," *Jewish History* 4, no. 2: 9–23.

Scharf, Andrew. 1971. *Byzantine Jewry* (New York).

Scherer, J. E. 1901. *Die Rechtsverhältnisse der Juden in den deutsch-österreichischen Ländern* (Leipzig).

Schiffmann, Sara. 1930/1931. "Die Urkunden für die Juden von Speyer 1090 und Worms 1157," "Heinrichs IV Verhalten zu den Juden zur Zeit des Ersten Kreuzzuges," "Die deutschen Bischöfe und die Juden zur Zeit des Ersten Kreuzzuges," *Zeitschrift für die Geschichte der Juden im Deutschland* 2: 28ff.; 3: 39ff.; 3: 233ff.

Scholem, Gershom. 1938. *Major Trends in Jewish Mysticism* (New York).

———— 1969. *The Kabbalah and Its Symbolism* (New York).

———— 1974. *Kabbalah* (New York).

Schwarzfuchs, Simon. 1966. "France and Germany under the Carolingians," in *The Dark Ages,* ed. C. Roth (Tel Aviv).

———— 1966a. "France under the Early Capets," in *The Dark Ages,* ed. C. Roth (Tel Aviv).

———— 1967. "The Expulsion of the Jews from France (1306)," 75th Anniversary Volume of the Jewish Quarterly Review (Philadelphia).

———— 1986. *Kahal: La communauté juive de l'Europe médiévale* (Paris).

———— 1989. "The Place of the Crusades in Jewish History" (in Hebrew), in *Culture and Society in Medieval Jewry,* ed. R. Bonfil et al. (Jerusalem).

———— and A. Toaff, eds. 1989a. *The Mediterranean and the Jews: Banking, Finance, and International Trade, XVI–XVIII Centuries* (Ramat Gan).

Segre, Renata. 1978. "Bernardino da Feltre, i monti di pietà e i banchi ebraici," *Rivista Storica Italiana* 90: 818–833.

Seiferth, W. S. 1970. *Synagogue and Church in the Middle Ages* (New York).

Septimus, Bernard. 1982. *Hispano-Jewish Culture in Transition* (Cambridge, Mass.).

Sergi, Giuseppe. 1990. "Le istituzioni dimenticate: Il medioevo," *Quaderni Storici* 74: 405–420.

Sermoneta, G. 1965. "La dottrina dell'intelletto e la fede filosofica di Jehuda Romano," *Studi Medievali* 3, no. 4: 1–76.

———— 1976. "Considerazioni frammentarie sul giudeo-italiano," *Italia* 1: 1–29; 2: 62–106.

Sestan, Ernesto. 1977. "La città comunale italiana dei secoli XI–XIII nelle sue note caratteristiche rispetto al movimento comunale europeo," in *Forme di potere e struttura sociale in Italia nel medioevo,* ed. G. Rossetti (Bologna).

Shabbetai Donnolo. 1968. *Sefer Hakhmoni,* in *Sefer Yezirah* (Jerusalem), 123–148.

Shachar, Isaiah. 1974. *The Judensau* (London).

Shatzmiller, Joseph. 1973. "L'Inquisition et les juifs de Provence au XIIIe siècle," *Provence Historique* 23: 327–338.

——— 1987. "La famille juive au Moyen Age," *Provence Historique* 37: 489–600.

——— 1990. *Shylock Reconsidered: Jews, Moneylending, and Medieval Society* (Berkeley).

Shilo, Samuel. 1974. *Dina De-malkhuta Dina: The Law of the Land Is the Law* (in Hebrew; Jerusalem).

Shirman, Haim. 1951. "Samuel Hannagid: The Man, the Soldier, the Politician," *Jewish Social Studies* 13: 99–227.

——— 1979. *Studies in the History of Hebrew Poetry and Drama* (Jerusalem).

Shulvass, M. A. 1973. *The Jews in the World of the Renaissance,* trans. E. Kose (Leiden).

Simon, Marcel. 1962. "La polémique antijuive de S. Jean Chrysostome et le mouvement judaïsant d'Antioche," in Simon, *Recherches d'Histoire Judéo-Chrétienne* (Paris).

——— 1964. "Verus Israel," in Simon, *Etude: sur les relations entre chrétiens et juifs dans l'Empire Romain* (Paris).

Simoncelli, P. 1988. "Inquisizione romana e riforma in Italia," *Rivista Storica Italiana* 100: 5–125.

Simonsohn, Shelomo. 1960. "Ha-Ghetto be-'Italiah u-mishtaro," in *Y. F. Baer Jubilee Volume* (Jerusalem).

——— 1977. *History of the Jews in the Duchy of Mantua* (Jerusalem).

——— 1982. *The Jews in the Duchy of Milan,* 4 vols. (Jerusalem).

——— 1990. *The Apostolic See and the Jews,* 4 vols. to date (Toronto).

Sinanoglou, L. 1973. "The Christ Child as Sacrifice," *Speculum* 43: 491–509.

Singer, Sholom. 1964. "The Expulsion of the Jews from England in 1290," *Jewish Quarterly Review* 55: 117–136.

Sirat, Collette. 1975. *Jewish Philosophical Thought in the Middle Ages* (in Hebrew; Jerusalem).

Smalley, Beryl. 1964. *The Study of the Bible in the Middle Ages* (Notre Dame, Ind.).

Smith, Morton. 1967. "The Reason for the Persecution of Paul and the Obscurity of Acts," in *Studies in Mysticism and Religion Presented to Gershom C. Scholem,* ed. E. Urbach, Z. Werblowsky, and H. Wirszubski (Jerusalem).

Soloveitchik, Haym. 1972. "Pawnbroking: A Study in *Ribbit* and of the Halakhah in Exile," *Proceedings of the American Academy of Jewish Research* 38/39: 203–268.

——— 1976. "Three Themes in *Sefer Hasidim,*" *AJS Review* 1: 311–357.

——— 1987. "Religious Law and Change: The Medieval Ashkenazic Example," *AJS Review* 12: 205–223.

Sombart, Werner. 1962. *The Jews and Modern Capitalism,* ed. B. Hoselitz (New York).

Sonne, Isaiah. 1954. *Mi-Pavolo ha-Revi'i 'ad Pius ha-Hamishi* (Jerusalem).

Southern, R. W. 1963. *The Making of the Middle Ages* (New Haven).

Spiegel, Gabrielle. 1977. "Defense of the Realm: Evolution of a Capetian Propaganda Slogan," *Journal of Medieval History* 3: 115–133.

Spiegel, Shalom. 1969. *The Last Trial,* trans. J. Goldin (New York).

Spufford, Peter. 1988. *Money and Its Use in Medieval Europe* (Cambridge).

Stacey, Robert. 1987. "Royal Taxation and the Social Stucture of the Medieval Anglo-Jewry: The Tallages of 1239–1242," *Hebrew Union College Annual* 56: 175–249.

——— 1987a. *Politics, Policy and Finance under Henry III, 1216–45* (Oxford).

——— 1988. "1240–1260: A Watershed in Anglo-Jewish Relations?" *Historical Research* 61: 135–150.

——— 1989. "The Conversion of Jews to Christianity in Thirteenth-Century England," paper presented to the Delaware Valley Medieval Association (Wilmington).

——— 1990. "The Expulsion of 1290: Economics, Sociology, Politics," unpublished paper (Ithaca, N.Y.).

——— 1991. "Crusades, Crusaders, and the Baronial *Gravamina* of 1263–1264," *Thirteenth-Century England III*, ed. P. R. Coss and S. D. Lloyd (Woodbridge, England).

——— 1992. "Thirteenth-Century Anglo-Jewry and the Problem of the Expulsion," in *The Expulsion of the Jews from England in 1290 and Its Aftermath*, ed. Yosef Kaplan and David Katz (Jerusalem).

——— 1993. The Jews in England, forthcoming (Oxford).

Stampfer, Shaul. 1988. "Remarriage among Jews and Christians in Nineteenth-Century Eastern Europe," *Jewish History* 3, no. 2: 85–114.

Starr, Joshua. 1946. "The Mass Conversion of Jews in Southern Italy, 1290–1293," *Speculum* 21: 203–211.

Statutes of the Realm, 1259–1713. 1810. (London).

Steinschneider, Moritz. 1893. Die hebräischen Übersetzungen des Mittelalters und die Juden als Dolmetscher (Berlin).

Stern, Fritz. 1965. *The Politics of Cultural Despair* (New York).

Stern, Moritz, and Adolph Neubauer. 1892. *Hebräische Berichte über die Judenverfolgungen während der Kreuzzüge* (Berlin).

——— 1893. *Urkundliche Beiträge über die Stellung der Päpste zu den Juden* (Kiel).

Stern, Selma. 1965. *Yosel of Rosheim*, trans. G. Hirschler (Philadelphia).

Stillman, Norman. 1970. "East-West Relations in the Islamic Mediterranean in the Early Eleventh Century," diss., University of Pennsylvania (Philadelphia).

——— 1979. *The Jews in Arab Lands* (Philadelphia).

Stobbe, Otto. 1968. *Die Juden in Deutschland während des Mittelalters in politischer, sozialer, and rechtlicher Beziehung* (Amsterdam; orig. pub. 1923).

Stock, Brian. 1983. *The Implications of Literacy* (Princeton).

Stow, K. R. 1972. "The Burning of the Talmud in 1553, in the Light of Sixteenth-Century Catholic Attitudes toward the Talmud," *Bibliothèque d'Humanisme et Renaissance* 34: 435–459.

——— 1974. "Agobard of Lyons and the Medieval Concept of the Jew," *Conservative Judaism* 29: 58–65.

——— 1976. "The Church and the Jews: From St. Paul to Paul IV," in *Bibliographical Essays in Medieval Jewish Studies*, ed. L. Berman et al. (New York).

——— 1976a. "Conversion, Christian Hebraism and Hebrew Prayer in the Sixteenth Century," *Hebrew Union College Annual* 47: 217–236.

—— 1977. *Catholic Thought and Papal Jewry Policy, 1555–1593* (New York).

—— 1978. "Il mito del giudaismo nell'antico cristianesimo," Rassegna Mensile di Israel 44: 512–517.

—— 1981. "Papal and Royal Attitudes toward Jewish Lending in the Thirteenth Century," *AJS Review* 6: 161–184.

—— 1981a. "Jewish Approaches to the Papacy and the Papal Doctrine of Jewish Protection, 1050–1150" (in Hebrew), *Studies in the History of the Jewish People and the Land of Israel* 5: 75–90.

—— 1982. *Taxation, Community and State: The Jews and the Fiscal Foundations of the Early Modern Papal State*, in *Päpste und Papsttum*, vol. 19, ed. G. Denzler (Stuttgart).

—— 1984. *The "1007 Anonymous" and Papal Sovereignty: Jewish Perceptions of the Papacy and Papal Policy in the High Middle Ages* (Cincinnati).

—— 1986. "Delitto e castigo nello stato della chiesa: Gli ebrei nelle carceri romane dal 1572 al 1659," in Italia Judaica II (Rome).

—— and S. D. Stow. 1986a. "Donne ebree a Roma nell'età del ghetto: Affetto, dipendenza, autonomia," *Rassegna Mensile di Israel* 52: 63–116.

—— 1986b. "Jews and the Catholic Church," *Dictionary of the Middle Ages* (New York) 7: 75–79.

—— 1986c. "Jews in Western Europe, 900–1500," *Dictionary of the Middle Ages* (New York) 7: 86–94.

—— 1987. "The Jewish Family in the Rhineland: Form and Function," *American Historical Review* 92: 1085–1110.

—— 1987a. "The Church and Neutral History: The Attitude of the Church to the Jews in the Light of Modern Historiography," in *Studies in Historiography* (in Hebrew), ed. M. Zimmerman et al. (Jerusalem).

—— 1987b. "The Medieval Jewish Community Was Not a Corporation," in *Priesthood and Kingship*, ed. Y. Gafni and G. Motzkin (in Hebrew; Jerusalem).

—— 1987c. "Jacob of Venice and the Jewish Settlement in Venice in the Thirteenth Century," in *Community and Culture*, ed. N. Waldman (Philadelphia).

—— 1988. "Expulsion Italian Style: The Case of Lucio Ferraris," *Jewish History* 3, no. 1: 55–64.

—— 1988a. "The Jew as Alien and the Diffusion of Restrictions: An Expulsion Text from Udine, 1556," in *The Jews in Italy*, ed. Haim Beinart (Jerusalem).

—— 1988b. "Life and Society in the Roman Community in the Sixteenth Century" (in Hebrew), *Pa'amim* 37: 55–66.

—— 1988c. "Hatred of the Jew or Love of the Church: The Policy of the Medieval Papacy toward the Jews," in *Antisemitism through the Ages*, ed. S. Almog (New York).

—— 1988d. "Servi Camerae Nostrae," *Dictionary of the Middle Ages* (New York) 11: 209–211.

—— 1989. "La storiografia del ghetto romano: Problemi metodologici," in *La storia degli ebrei nell'Italia medievale: Tra filologia e metodologia*, ed. M. G. Muzzarelli and G. Todeschini (Bologna).

—— 1992. "The Papacy and the Jews, Catholic Reformation and Beyond," in *Frank Talmage Memorial Volume*, ed. B. Walfish, *Jewish History* 6, nos. 1–2.

—— 1992a. "A Tale of Uncertainties: Converts in the Roman Ghetto," in *Festschrift Shelomo Simonsohn*, ed. D. Carpi (Tel Aviv).

—— 1992b. "The Good of the Church, the Good of the State: The Church and Jewish Money," *Economics and Religion*, ed. M. Ben-Sasson (in Hebrew; Jerusalem).

Stow, Sandra Debenedetti. 1983. "Hararah, pizza nel XIV secolo," *Archivio Glottologico Italiano* 68: 80–81.

—— 1986. "Judaeo-Italiano," *Dictionary of the Middle Ages* (New York) 7: 175–176.

—— 1990. *La chiarificazione in volgare delle "espressioni difficili" ricorrenti nel Mišnèh Toràh di Mosè Maimonide: Glossario inedito del XIV secolo* (Rome).

Strayer, Joseph. 1971. "Philip the Fair: A Constitutional King," in *Medieval Statecraft and the Perspectives of History* (Princeton).

Stroll, Mary. 1987. *The Jewish Pope* (Leiden).

Stubbs, William. 1900. *Select Charters Illustrative of English Constitutional History* (Oxford).

Suarez-Fernandez, Luis. 1983. *Les juifs espagnols au Moyen Age,* trans. R. Israel-Amsaleg (Paris).

Synan, E. M. 1965. *The Popes and the Jews in the Middle Ages* (New York).

Tabacco, Giovanni. 1977. "Lo sviluppo del banno signorile e delle comunità rurali," in *Forme di potere e struttura sociale in Italia nel medioevo,* ed. G. Rossetti (Bologna).

Talmage, Frank. 1986. Personal communication.

Ta Shema, Israel. 1977. "Misvat talmud torah ke-ba'ayah hevratit-datit be-*Sefer Hasidim*," *Sefer Bar Ilan* 14/15: 20–41.

—— 1988. "On the History of Polish Jewry in the 12th–13th Centuries," *Zion* 53: 347–370.

—— 1988a. "Ashkenazi Jewry in the Eleventh Century: Life and Literature," in *Ashkenaz: The German Jewish Heritage*, ed. G. Hirschler (New York).

Tellenbach, Gerd. 1970. *Church, State, and Christian Society at the Time of the Investiture Contest,* trans. R. F. Bennett (Oxford).

Tertullian. 1971. *Adversus Iudaeos,* trans. U. Thelwall, in *Ante-Nicene Library* (Grand Rapids, Mich.).

Thomas Aquinas. 1947. *Summa Theologica* (New York).

Thompson, E. A. 1966. *The Visigoths in the Time of Ulfila* (Oxford).

Tierney, Brian. 1964. *The Crisis of Church and State* (Englewood Cliffs, N.J.).

Tishby, Isaiah. 1961. *Mishnat ha-Zohar,* 2 vols. (Jerusalem).

Toaff, Ariel. 1983. "Gli ebrei romani e il commercio del denaro nelle comuni dell'Italia centrale alla fine del duecento," in *Italia Judaica I* (Rome).

—— 1984. *Il ghetto di Roma nel cinquecento: Conflitti etnici e problemi socioeconomici* (Ramat Gan).

—— 1986. "Il commercio del denaro e le comunità ebraiche 'di confine' tra cinquecento e seicento," *Italia Judaica II* (Roma).

—— 1988. "Jewish Banking in Central Italy, Thirteenth through Fifteenth Centuries" (in Hebrew), in *Jews in Italy*, ed. H. Beinart (Jerusalem).

—— 1989. *Il vino e la carne* (Bologna).

Toch, Michael. 1980. "The Jewish Community of Nuremberg in the Year 1489: Social and Demographic Structure" (in Hebrew), *Zion* 45: 60–72.

Todeschini, G. 1990. "Familles juives et chrétiennes en Italie à la fin du Moyen Age: Deux modèles de développement économique," *Annales ESC* 45: 787–818.

Trachtenberg, Joshua. 1943. *The Devil and the Jews* (New Haven).

Turner, Victor. 1978. *Image and Pilgrimage in Christian Culture* (Oxford).

Twersky, Isadore. 1957. "Review of E. E. Urbach, *Ba'alei ha-Tosafot*" (in Hebrew), *Tarbiz* 26: 215–227.

Udovitch, Abraham. 1970. "Theory and Practice of Islamic Law: Some Evidence from the Geniza," *Studia Islamica* 32: 289–303.

Ullmann, Walter. 1946. *The Medieval Idea of Law: Lucas da Penna* (London).

—— 1962. *The Growth of Papal Government in the Middle Ages* (London).

—— 1965. "Juristic Obstacles to the Emergence of the Concept of the State in the Middle Ages," in *The Church and the Law in the Earlier Middle Ages* (London).

Urbach, E. E. 1955. *Ba'alei ha-Tosafot* (Jerusalem).

Voltmer, Ernst. 1981. "Zur Geschichte der Juden im spätmittelalterlichen Speyer: Die Judengemeinde im Spannungsfeld zwischen König, Bischof und Stadt," in *Zur Geschichte der Juden im Deutschland des späten Mittelalters und der frühen Neuzeit,* ed. A. Haverkamp (Stuttgart).

Walsh, W. H. 1958. *Philosophy of History* (New York).

Watt, J. A. 1965. "The Term 'Plenitudo Potestatis' in Hostiensis," in *Proceedings of the Second International Congress of Medieval Canon Law,* ed. S. Kuttner (Vatican City).

—— 1988. "The English Episcopate, the State and the Jews: The Evidence of the Thirteenth-Century Conciliar Decrees," in *Thirteenth-Century England II,* ed. P. R. Coss and S. D. Lloyd (Newcastle upon Tyne).

Weinryb, Bernard. 1973. *The Jews of Poland* (Philadelphia).

Werblowsky, R. H. Zvi. 1978. *Joseph Karo, Lawyer and Mystic* (London).

Werner, Eric. 1959. *The Sacred Bridge* (New York).

Westreich, Elimelech. 1988. "Polygamy and Compulsory Divorce of the Wife in the Decisions of the Rabbis of Ashkenaz in the Eleventh and Twelfth Centuries" (in Hebrew), *Bar Ilan Law Studies* 6: 118–164.

Wilks, Michael. 1963. *Sovereignty in the Later Middle Ages* (Cambridge).

William of St. Amour. 1632. *De Periculis Novissimorum Temporum,* in *Opera Omnia* (Constance).

Wirszubski, Haim. 1975. *Three Studies in Christian Kabbala* (in Hebrew; Jerusalem).

—— 1977. *A Christian Kabbalist Reads the Law* (in Hebrew; Jerusalem).

Wistinetzki, Jehuda. 1924. *Das Buch der Frommen* (Frankfurt am Main).

Wood, Charles. 1981. "The Doctor's Dilemma: Sin, Salvation, and the Menstrual Cycle in Medieval Thought," *Speculum* 56: 711–727.

—— 1989. "The Return of Medieval Politics," *American Historical Review* 94: 391–404.

Yassif, Eli. 1984. "'Iyyunim ba-'amanut ha-sippur be-megillat 'ahimaaz," *Mehkarim Yerushalayyim be-sifruth 'ivrit* 4: 18–42.

Yerushalmi, Y. H. 1970. "The Inquisition and the Jews of France in the Time of Bernard Gui," *Harvard Theological Review* 63: 317–376.

—— 1971 *From Spanish Court to Italian Ghetto* (New York).

—— 1976. *The Lisbon Massacre of 1506* (Cincinnati).

Yutte, Robert. 1981. "Poor Relief and Social Discipline in Sixteenth-Century Europe," *European Studies Review* 11: 25–52.

Yuval, Yisrael. 1983. "An Appeal against the Proliferation of Divorce in Fifteenth-Century Germany" (in Hebrew), *Zion* 48: 177–216.

—— 1989. *Hakhamim be-Doram* (Jerusalem).

Zedeqiah ben Abraham. 1987. *Shibbolei ha-Leqet* (Jerusalem).

Zimmels, H. 1966. "Science," in *The Dark Ages,* ed. C. Roth (Tel Aviv).

Zimmer, Erich. 1965. *The Inner Organization of the Fifteenth-Century Jewish Communities in Germany* (New York).

—— 1978. *Jewish Synods in Germany during the Late Middle Ages* (New York).

Zinberg, Israel. 1972. *A History of Jewish Literature,* trans. B. Martin (Cleveland).

Zuckerman, Arthur. 1972. *A Jewish Princedom in Feudal France, 768–900* (New York).

Index